Bud‹

Building a Britain of economic strength and social justice

Economic and Fiscal Strategy Report and Financial Statement and Budget Report

April 2003

Return to an Order of the House of Commons dated 9 April 2003

Copy of Economic and Fiscal Strategy Report and Financial Statement and Budget Report – April 2003 as laid before the House of Commons by the Chancellor of the Exchequer when opening the Budget.

Ruth Kelly
Her Majesty's Treasury
9 April 2003

Ordered by the House of Commons to be printed 9 April 2003

HC 500   LONDON: The Stationery Office   £45.00

HM Treasury contacts

For enquiries about the Treasury and its work, contact HM Treasury Public Enquiry Unit:

Public Enquiry Unit
HM Treasury
1 Horse Guards Road
London
SW1A 2HQ

Tel: 020 7270 4558

Fax: 020 7270 4574

E-mail: public.enquiries@hm-treasury.gov.uk

This document can be accessed from the Treasury's Internet site at:

www.hm-treasury.gov.uk

This and other government documents can be found on the Internet at:

www.official-documents.co.uk

The Economic and Fiscal Strategy Report and the Financial Statement and Budget Report contain the Government's assessment of the medium-term economic and budgetary position. They set out the Government's tax and spending plans, including those for public investment, in the context of its overall approach to social, economic and environmental objectives. After approval for the purposes of Section 5 of the European Communities (Amendment) Act 1993, these reports will form the basis of submissions to the European Commission under Article 99 (ex Article 103) and Article 104 (ex Article 104c) of the Treaty establishing the European Community.

CONTENTS

OVERVIEW

The Government's objective is to deliver high and stable levels of growth and employment, with opportunity and rising living standards for all – a Britain of economic strength and social justice. Against a backdrop of global uncertainty, Budget 2003 describes how the Government is seeking to meet the long-term challenges of globalisation, achieving both flexibility and fairness together.

Budget 2003, *Building a Britain of economic strength and social justice*, presents updated assessments and forecasts of the economy and the public finances, reports on how the Government's policies are helping to deliver its long-term goals and describes the further steps that the Government is now taking to advance its goals. The Budget:

- demonstrates that the economy is on course to maintain stability and that the Government is on track to meet its fiscal rules over the economic cycle, while meeting its international and public spending commitments;

- sets out new proposals to promote greater flexibility in the housing market and to streamline and simplify the planning regime;

- strengthens the drivers of enterprise and productivity, improving flexibility with further support to reduce regulatory burdens, simplify tax, boost research and development and improve access to finance for small businesses;

- takes further steps to increase flexibility in the labour market, with additional measures to raise workforce skills, new support to help people master change, and reforms to spread employment opportunity to disadvantaged groups;

- introduces a new Child Trust Fund to strengthen the saving habit of future generations, and provides further support for pensioners;

- advances fairness within the tax system, to ensure that businesses and individuals contribute fairly to the public services from which they benefit; and

- describes a range of further action to protect and enhance the environment, including through more sustainable waste management.

BUILDING ECONOMIC STRENGTH AND SOCIAL JUSTICE

1.1   The Government's objective is to deliver high and stable levels of growth and employment, with opportunity and rising living standards for all – a Britain of economic strength and social justice.

1.2   Globalisation has brought new opportunities for individuals, businesses and countries to develop and prosper, but it has also brought new risks. In the modern global economy, the challenge for governments is to devise ever more effective ways of achieving high and stable levels of growth and employment, with policies for stability, employment and fairness matched with greater flexibility in labour, product and capital markets. New technologies, global competition and evolving demands for skills require businesses and individuals to adapt quickly to change so that growth and prosperity can be maintained. Flexible and dynamic markets are a precondition for economic strength and for securing fairness and social justice.

1.3   Just as the long-term forces of globalisation create significant challenges for policy-makers, so recent international developments demonstrate the need for vigilance. Weakened global growth and protracted uncertainty highlight the risks of global markets and pose threats to the prosperity and living standards of many. Events leading up to hostilities in Iraq have heightened economic uncertainty, dented confidence and brought further volatility to financial markets, posing new and immediate challenges to the delivery of high and stable levels of growth and employment around the world.

1.4   Over the past six years, the Government has recognised the importance of increasing productivity and flexibility in the UK economy:

- in labour markets, through investment in skills, additional help with jobsearch, and increased work incentives from tax credits, to equip people to adapt to change and deliver employment opportunity for all;

- in product markets, with reforms to strengthen the competition regime and to boost enterprise and innovation to ensure that firms can seize the opportunities created by change and technological improvements; and

- in capital markets, with reforms to modernise financial regulation and improve the financing options for investment and new businesses.

1.5   Budget 2003 builds on these reforms to meet the long-term challenges of globalisation and ensure that the UK is well placed to take advantage of opportunities as the global recovery takes hold. The Budget sets out the next steps in the Government's programme of economic reform to build a stronger, more enterprising economy based on dynamic and flexible markets and underpinned by fairness and social justice. It describes how, through this programme of reform, the Government will advance its long-term goals of:

- maintaining economic stability, ensuring that the fiscal rules are met and that inflation remains low;

- raising the sustainable rate of productivity growth through reforms to enhance the flexibility of product and capital markets and to promote enterprise, innovation and skills;

- sustaining a higher proportion of people in work than ever before on the basis of a flexible labour market that adjusts rapidly to changing conditions and delivers employment opportunity for all;

- creating a fairer, more inclusive society with opportunity and security for all, eradicating child poverty and tackling pensioner poverty;

- establishing world class public services to underpin a flexible and high productivity economy, through investment and reform; and

- tackling the global challenges of poverty and climate change through steps to achieve the Millennium Development Goals and to deliver the UK's commitments under the Kyoto Protocol.

MAINTAINING MACROECONOMIC STABILITY

1.6   The Government's macroeconomic goal is to maintain economic stability, ensuring that the fiscal rules are met and that inflation remains low. Chapter 2 describes how the Government is working to achieve this goal and summarises prospects for the UK economy and the public finances, full details of which are set out in Chapters B and C of the *Financial Statement and Budget Report* (FSBR).

The policy **1.7**   The Government's macroeconomic policy framework is based on the principles of
framework transparency, responsibility and accountability, and is designed to ensure lasting economic stability so that businesses, individuals and the Government may plan effectively for the long term. The Bank of England has operational independence to meet the Government's symmetrical inflation target, while fiscal policy is underpinned by two strict fiscal rules which ensure sound public finances over the medium term. The fiscal rules underpin the Government's public spending framework which ensures that public resources are used productively and delivers a sharper focus on the quality of outcome of public service provision.

1.8   The macroeconomic policy framework has successfully delivered stability and growth, proving flexible and responsive in the face of global weakness and uncertainty. The economy continues to enjoy the longest period of economic expansion on record, with employment at record levels and unemployment at its lowest for a generation. Sustained economic growth and tough decisions on taxation and spending have placed the public finances on a sustainable footing, generating additional resources for investment in public services and allowing fiscal policy to support monetary policy in limiting the impact of global weakness on the UK economy. The monetary policy framework has also ensured that inflation has remained lower and more stable than in the past.

Economic **1.9**   Since the Pre-Budget Report, geo-political risks, particularly surrounding hostilities
prospects in Iraq, have compounded global economic uncertainties. Despite recent action by policy-makers, sharp declines on equity markets and rising oil prices have prompted falls in consumer confidence and the continued deferral of business investment plans, restraining global economic activity still further. Consequently, G7 growth this year is forecast to be weaker than expected at the time of the Pre-Budget Report, with prospects for the Euro-area particularly badly affected. Following growth of 1½ per cent last year, GDP in the G7 economies is expected to grow by just 1¾ per cent this year, before accelerating to 2¾ per cent in 2004 and to 3 per cent in 2005. Growth in the Euro-area is expected to be just 1 per cent in 2003, rising to 2¼ per cent next year.

1.10   International developments continue to be a key influence on prospects for the UK economy, and persistent uncertainty and subdued global growth have affected business confidence and investment recently. Nonetheless, low inflation and sound public finances have allowed macroeconomic policy to support the economy during this period of global weakness, leaving the UK better placed than in previous world slowdowns to maintain economic stability. The economy grew by 1.8 per cent in 2002, above the Pre-Budget Report forecast and behind only North America among the G7 economies. In the Budget 2003 forecast:

- GDP is expected to grow by between 2 and 2½ per cent this year as ongoing uncertainty contributes to weaker global demand and subdued private investment in the first half of the year. Thereafter, reduced uncertainty and a subsequent strengthening of the global recovery should allow growth of 3 to 3½ per cent in 2004 and 2005 as the economy returns to trend;

- growth is expected to become steadily more balanced over the forecast period as deferred business investment is brought back on stream, exports pick up in response to stronger external demand, and private consumption growth continues to moderate;

- RPIX inflation is expected to remain close to the Government's 2½ per cent target throughout the forecast period; and

- prospects for the UK economy remain dependent on the turn of global events. The Budget forecast assumes that current economic uncertainties diminish in the second half of the year, prompting a steady recovery in business and consumer confidence. While the pace of global recovery in the short term, and of European economic reform in the medium term, will both influence the future pattern of UK growth, with sound economic fundamentals in the UK, policy remains well placed to respond to risks in either direction.

The public finances   1.11   Global uncertainty affected the fiscal balances last year, as receipts weakened due to cyclical or otherwise temporary factors and the Government made a special contingency provision of £3 billion to cover the full cost of the UK's military obligations in Iraq. The estimated outturn for the current budget in 2002-03 shows a deficit of £11.7 billion, compared with a projected deficit of £5.7 billion in the Pre-Budget Report and a surplus of £3.2 billion in Budget 2002. Net borrowing is estimated to have been £24.0 billion in 2002-03, compared with £20.1 billion projected at the time of the Pre-Budget Report and £11.2 billion in Budget 2002. The provisional outturns demonstrate that fiscal policy supported monetary policy through the operation of the automatic stabilisers, helping to maintain stability during a period of weaker global demand.

1.12   While the full amount of the Government's contingency provision for military obligations in Iraq has been allocated to 2002-03, there is considerable uncertainty over when these costs will fall. In the light of this uncertainty, and to protect committed investment while responding prudently to heightened global risks, the Government has decided to make no further allocations from the Capital Modernisation Fund (CMF). Instead, unallocated CMF funding will contribute to rebuilding the Annually Managed Expenditure margin, to ensure that the Government's public spending projections include a prudent and cautious safety margin against unexpected events.

1.13   Against this backdrop, and in addition to the steps already taken to meet international and public spending commitments, Budget 2003 announces further decisions to build a Britain of economic strength and social justice, including:

- a package of reforms to promote flexibility in labour, product and capital markets, including measures to promote enterprise, innovation and skills, and support to help people find and succeed in work;

- further steps to advance flexibility and fairness together, with a new Child Trust Fund to strengthen the saving habit of future generations, and further support for pensioners; and

- reforms to tackle avoidance and advance fairness in the tax system, to ensure that everyone contributes fairly to the public services from which they benefit.

1.14   Table 1.2 lists the key Budget policy decisions and their impact on the public finances.

1.15   Prolonged uncertainty in the world economy and the decisions taken in this Budget mean that the near-term outlook for the public finances has deteriorated slightly since the time of the Pre-Budget Report. While a current budget deficit of £8 billion is now expected this year, a decline in global uncertainty and a cyclical recovery in the world economy mean that the current budget is restored to surplus from 2005-06. The forecast demonstrates that fiscal policy is expected to continue providing support to monetary policy as the economy remains below trend.

The fiscal rules   1.16   The forecast also demonstrates that the Government remains firmly on track to meet its strict fiscal rules over the economic cycle, including in the cautious case. As shown in Table 1.1, the average surplus on the current budget since the start of the current cycle in 1999-2000 remains positive throughout the forecast period, leaving the Government on track to meet the golden rule. Public sector net debt is projected to rise slightly to just under 34 per cent of GDP by 2007-08, comfortably meeting the sustainable investment rule, and the lowest level of debt as a proportion of national income in the G7.

Table 1.1: Meeting the fiscal rules

	Outturn 2001-02	Estimate 2002-03	Projections 2003-04	2004-05	2005-06	2006-07	2007-08
					Per cent of GDP		
Golden rule							
Surplus on current budget	1.0	–1.1	–0.8	–0.1	0.2	0.4	0.6
Average surplus since 1999-2000	1.8	1.1	0.7	0.6	0.5	0.5	0.5
Cyclically-adjusted surplus on current budget	0.9	–0.5	0.2	0.5	0.4	0.4	0.6
Sustainable investment rule Public sector net debt	30.2	30.9	32.2	32.7	33.2	33.5	33.8

1.17   The public finances are also sustainable over the long term. Consistent with the requirements of the *Code for fiscal stability*, Annex A of the *Economic and Fiscal Strategy Report* presents illustrative long-term fiscal projections and examines the long-term sustainability of the public finances. The projections indicate that the UK is well placed to deal with future fiscal challenges, such as those arising from an ageing population, and that current policies impact fairly between generations.

MEETING THE PRODUCTIVITY CHALLENGE

1.18   Productivity growth, alongside high and stable levels of employment, is an important driver of long-term economic performance and rising living standards. In the modern global economy, faster productivity growth demands new flexibility in product, capital and labour markets. With global markets for business, investment and skills, governments, individuals and firms must be able to respond quickly and adapt rapidly to change. Failure to do so risks an unproductive use of resources, with long-term costs to growth, employment and prosperity. The Government's long-term goal is to raise the sustainable rate of productivity growth in the economy, closing the gap that exists between the UK and other advanced industrialised countries.

Action so far   **1.19**   The Government's strategy is described in detail in Chapter 3 and focuses on five important drivers of productivity performance:

- **improving competition** to increase flexibility in product markets and promote business efficiency and consumer choice. The Enterprise and Competition Acts, as well as substantial increases in resources for the competition authorities, have increased the powers of the Office of Fair Trading and strengthened the UK's overall competition regime. Action has also been taken to promote competition in specific markets, including small business banking and the professions;

- **promoting enterprise** by removing market barriers to entrepreneurship, especially in disadvantaged areas. Reforms to the business tax regime have increased the support to new and growing businesses and helped all businesses to compete more effectively in global markets. Two thousand Enterprise Areas have been designated in the most deprived communities in the UK, and additional support made available to help businesses in these areas start up, develop and grow. Resources have also been allocated to promote understanding of business, the economy and enterprise throughout the school and further education systems;

- **supporting science and innovation** to open up new markets and opportunities. Record increases in science spending and funding for knowledge transfer are supporting improvements in the UK science base and stronger collaboration between businesses and universities. Tax credits are also rewarding research and development by the private sector;

- **raising UK skills** to deliver a more flexible and productive workforce. Substantial increases in resources are helping to improve standards throughout the school and further education systems and to advance the Government's ambitious long-term goal to raise participation in post-16 education and training. Employer Training Pilots are testing new means of support to help those already in the workforce acquire new skills; and

- **encouraging investment** and better investment decision-making, on the basis of stronger, more efficient capital markets. Radical reform of the land use planning system and increased resources to improve the supply of housing are helping to tackle inflexibilities in the housing market, while comprehensive reviews into institutional investment and the market for long-term savings have sought to promote greater flexibility in capital markets, helping businesses to manage risk more efficiently.

Next steps **1.20**   Budget 2003 introduces further measures to promote productivity growth through a more enterprising and highly skilled economy, including:

- new proposals to promote greater flexibility in the housing market and to streamline and simplify the planning regime;

- a package of reforms to improve access to finance for small businesses, including consultation on the scope for introducing Small Business Investment Companies in the UK;

- improvements to research and development (R&D) tax credits to enable more businesses to claim a wider range of relief, and consultation on the definition of R&D to ensure it remains competitive internationally;

- deregulatory reforms to ease the regulatory burden, especially on small businesses;

- additional measures to improve skills in the UK, including the launch of six new Employer Training Pilots and a new package of training support for small businesses;

- further improvements to the Highly Skilled Migrants Programme and other migration schemes to make the UK migration system a more effective source of highly skilled labour for the UK economy;

- £16 million over two years to fund Enterprise Advisers to work alongside head teachers in around 1,000 secondary schools in deprived areas, ensuring that pupils in these areas gain a better knowledge of business and enterprise;

- an extension of 100 per cent first year capital allowances for small businesses investing in ICT, for one further year; and

- further steps to support a modern and competitive business tax system, with reforms to VAT for small business, simplification of employee share schemes, and abolition of Petroleum Revenue Tax on new third party tariffing business.

INCREASING EMPLOYMENT OPPORTUNITY FOR ALL

1.21   The Government's long-term goal is employment opportunity for all – the modern definition of full employment. Its aim is to ensure a higher proportion of people in work than ever before by 2010. Worklessness, particularly on a long-term basis, is a constraint on Britain's growth potential and a major cause of poverty and deprivation for many individuals and their families. A dynamic and flexible labour market that equips people to adapt to changes in global and domestic demand, and which has the institutional flexibility to deliver high employment and low unemployment across the economic cycle, is key to achieving the Government's goal.

Action so far **1.22**   Chapter 4 describes the steps the Government has already taken to ensure that the labour market remains dynamic and flexible and that employment opportunity is extended to all groups and regions in the country, including by:

- equipping people to cope with change through investment in skills and training and transitional help for people moving between jobs. Since 1997, the New Deal programmes have helped to deliver substantial reductions in the numbers of young and older long-term unemployed people. Employment Zones are also testing a new and innovative approach to helping long-term unemployed people back to work, by allowing jobseekers and their personal advisers to use funds with complete flexibility to overcome individual barriers to work;

- reforms to make work pay and to strengthen incentives to move into and progress within employment. Reforms to the tax and benefit system, underpinned by the National Minimum Wage and the Child and Working Tax Credits, improve work incentives for families with children, people with disabilities and those in low-paid work, helping the labour market to respond flexibly to economic shocks, while preserving a degree of stability in workers' incomes; and

- reforms to improve institutional and structural flexibility in the labour market to ensure that employment opportunity is extended to all. Over the past five years, the Government has extended assistance under the New Deal to workless benefit claimants, including lone parents, disabled people and partners of the unemployed. Action Teams have been introduced to tackle serious employment problems in some of Britain's most disadvantaged areas, while the national roll-out of Jobcentre Plus is providing work-focused support to all working age benefit recipients, whether unemployed or economically inactive.

Next steps 1.23 Building on measures to raise levels of skills in the workforce, Budget 2003 describes the additional steps the Government is taking to strengthen flexibility and fairness in the labour market to ensure it can adapt to changing circumstances and deliver high and sustainable employment, including:

- extra help for unemployed people searching for jobs, with additional interventions in the first six months;

- greater flexibility for Jobcentre Plus districts to respond to local conditions, with a new discretionary fund, more flexible options within the New Deal for young people, and greater rewards for successful managers;

- significant reform of Housing Benefit to improve financial gains to work, facilitate labour mobility, and deliver greater reliability in the service to claimants;

- extension of Employment Zones to lone parents and people returning to the New Deal for a second time, and the introduction of multiple providers;

- increases in the National Minimum Wage from October 2003 for adult and youth workers and for those in approved training;

- improved support for lone parents, with a flexible fund to improve access to debt advisory services, and pilots of a new worksearch premium to cover the extra costs of looking for work;

- an enhanced New Deal for partners from April 2004, bringing support for partners of benefit claimants into line with that available to lone parents; and

- extra support to help people from ethnic minorities, with a new £8 million policy fund for Jobcentre Plus managers, and specialist advisers in Jobcentre Plus areas with high ethnic minority populations.

BUILDING A FAIRER SOCIETY

I.24   The Government is determined to ensure that flexibility and fairness work together so that every individual has the chance to fulfil their potential, regardless of their circumstances. Policies for flexibility need not be implemented at the expense of those for fairness, but must be pursued together so that concerns about social justice are recognised and addressed. Chapter 5 describes the steps the Government is taking to eradicate child poverty and tackle pensioner poverty, extending opportunity to all children and ensuring security for all in old age. It also describes the Government's wider strategy for rewarding and encouraging saving, establishing a modern and fair tax system and promoting international efforts to reduce global poverty.

Action so far I.25   The Government has already introduced significant reforms to address its priorities, including:

- enhanced support for families with children in recognition of the costs and responsibilities that come with parenthood and to help tackle child poverty. Financial support through the tax and benefit system has been increased, with record rises in Child Benefit, improved maternity and paternity provision and the introduction of the new Child Tax Credit. To tackle the underlying causes of poverty and their effects, the Government has also delivered substantial investment in child-focused public services, including schools, preventative healthcare services and the Children's Fund;

- improved support for pensioners to tackle poverty and ensure security for all in retirement. The Minimum Income Guarantee has improved the living standards of more than two million pensioners, while the Pension Credit – delivered by a modern and integrated Pension Service – will reward saving for pensioners on low and modest incomes from October 2003. The basic state pension has risen by more than inflation in each of the last three years, and will rise by at least 2½ per cent in 2004-05. Around 11 million people aged 60 or over also benefit from winter fuel payments, worth £200 per household per year; and

- steps to encourage saving including through the introduction of stakeholder pensions and Individual Savings Accounts. The Government has also published a Green Paper setting out proposals to help those of working age plan more effectively for a secure retirement and is consulting on options for radical simplification of pensions tax. Saving Gateway pilots are testing a new approach of Government-funded matched contributions to help people on low incomes develop a regular saving habit.

Next steps I.26   Building on this comprehensive programme of reform, Budget 2003 announces further steps to promote social justice and establish a modern and fair tax system, ensuring that a flexible economy is matched by a fairer society, including:

- a new Child Trust Fund providing every child born from September 2002 with an initial endowment at birth of £250, rising to £500 for children in the poorest third of families, a reform which is progressive and universal and will strengthen the saving habit of future generations;

- an extra £100 for households with a pensioner aged 80 or over in addition to the £200 winter fuel payment, for the lifetime of this Parliament;

- extending, to 52 weeks, the period over which all pensioners in hospital receive their full state pension;

- a cross-government review of financial support for 16 to 19 year olds, including the financial incentives to participate in education or training and the case for extending the National Minimum Wage;

- a new income tax exemption for foster carers, to facilitate the recruitment and retention of these carers;

- measures to protect tax revenues, including a compliance and enforcement package for direct tax, expected to produce an additional £1.6 billion over the next three years;

- details of the modernised regime for stamp duty, announced in Budget 2002, to tackle avoidance and distortions while protecting small business and paving the way for e-conveyancing;

- further steps to ensure a fair system of alcohol and tobacco taxation;

- the abolition of bingo duty, to be replaced by a new gross profits tax on bingo companies; and

- further work to establish an International Finance Facility to secure the additional resources needed to tackle global poverty.

DELIVERING HIGH QUALITY PUBLIC SERVICES

1.27   The Government's long-term goal is to deliver world class public services through sustained increases in investment and reforms to deliver efficient and responsive services which meet public expectations throughout the country. Strong and dependable public services lay the foundations for a flexible, high productivity economy, supporting greater efficiency among businesses and adaptability within the workforce. They also promote opportunity and security for all, helping to tackle poverty and social exclusion and improving the quality of life.

Action so far   1.28   Chapter 6 describes the Government's approach to strengthening the delivery of public services, including:

- a new framework for managing public spending to ensure that resources are used as efficiently and effectively as possible. The Government's reforms to the public spending framework have removed unnecessary controls on departmental finances, strengthening incentives to plan for the long term and giving departments the freedom and flexibility they need to ensure improvements in public service delivery;

- significant extra resources for public services, consistent with the fiscal rules. The 2002 Spending Review planned an additional £63 billion of departmental spending by 2005-06 compared with 2002-03 plans, while total investment in public service infrastructure by the public and private sectors is set to rise to more than £47 billion by 2005-06 – the largest sustained increase in public sector investment for more than 20 years. Provision of £3 billion has been set aside to cover the full cost of the UK's military obligations in Iraq, while continuing to meet the fiscal rules; and

- targeting resources on priority services. Prudent management of the economy has generated savings in social security and debt interest payments and allowed additional resources to be devoted to improving front line public services. More than 75 per cent of the planned additional resources allocated in the 2002 Spending Review have been directed to the Government's priorities of education, health, transport, housing and the fight against crime.

Next steps **I.29**   Budget 2002 delivered the largest ever sustained increase in spending on the UK National Health Service (NHS) – 7.2 per cent annual average real terms growth over five years – funded by a one per cent increase in national insurance contributions (NICS) on all earnings above the NICs threshold from this month, and a freeze in the income tax personal allowance for those aged under 65 in 2003-04. Matched with comprehensive plans for reform, these resources reverse past decades of underinvestment in health and will help to secure the future of an NHS that is free at the point of use, and available to all on the basis of clinical need and not ability to pay. Budget 2003:

- **provides £332 million to invest in further counter-terrorism measures** over the next three years, to ensure that UK citizens are protected within the UK from the threat of international terrorism;

- **sets out key issues to be investigated in the run-up to the next Spending Review**, including a new study into the scope for relocating public service staff from London and the South East to other parts of the country, and an update of the long-term challenges in implementing the 'fully engaged' scenario set out in last year's Wanless Review of long-term health trends, with a particular focus on preventative health and health inequalities; and

- **provides details of the next steps in reform**, with action to increase regional and local flexibility in public service pay systems and to increase transparency about performance, including through the introduction from April 2003 of regular reporting on the Treasury website of performance against all new Public Service Agreement targets.

PROTECTING THE ENVIRONMENT

I.30   The aim of sustainable development is to ensure a better quality of life for everyone – today and for generations to come. Economic growth and social progress must go hand-in-hand with action to protect and improve the environment, and policy must balance the need to meet these separate objectives. The Government is using a range of economic instruments to address the challenge of sustainable development, tackling local environmental threats and controlling and reducing emissions of the gases responsible for climate change and poor air quality.

Action so far **1.31** Chapter 7 describes the steps the Government has already taken to deliver its environmental objectives:

- **tackling climate change and improving air quality** to ensure that the UK meets its commitments under the Kyoto Protocol. The climate change levy is encouraging business to use energy more efficiently, while the world's first economy-wide emissions trading scheme is helping companies to reduce their emissions at the lowest possible cost. Reforms to the tax system are stimulating investment in the development of environmentally-friendly fuels and technologies and promoting the take-up of cleaner fuels and vehicles;

- **improving waste management** to deliver a more environmentally-sustainable economy. The landfill tax is encouraging efforts to minimise the amount of waste generated and to develop more sustainable waste management techniques, while the landfill tax credit scheme has supported a number of community and environment projects that have improved the quality of the environment at the local level; and

- **protecting Britain's countryside and natural resources** to ensure they are sustainable economically, socially and physically. The aggregates levy and sustainability fund are helping to tackle the environmental costs of quarrying, action has been taken to limit the environmental impact of pesticides use, and increased funding has been allocated to deliver productivity increases in the farming and food industries and to improve environmental performance.

Next steps **1.32** Budget 2003 takes further steps to protect and improve the environment and to advance the Government's goals, including:

- **a package of reforms to improve waste management**, including:

  - an increase in the standard rate of landfill tax of £3 per tonne in 2005-06 and increases of at least £3 per tonne in future years, on the way to a medium- to long-term rate of £35 per tonne. The landfill tax rises to £14 in 2003-04, to £15 in 2004-05, and to £18 in 2005-06;

  - **further detailed consultation** on options to ensure that landfill tax increases are revenue neutral to business as a whole;

  - a **Waste Management Performance Fund** in England to help local authorities improve waste performance for all households; and

  - a **sustainable waste delivery programme** to reduce waste volumes and to promote recycling and new waste management technologies.

- a **freeze in the rates of the climate change levy**;

- **new enhanced capital allowances** to promote business investment in energy-saving new technologies and to encourage more sustainable water use and improvements in water quality;

- **detailed consultation** on specific measures to promote household energy efficiency;

- **deferred annual revalorisation** of the main road fuel duties until 1 October 2003, owing to the recent high and volatile level of oil prices, as a result of military conflict in Iraq;

- further steps to promote the use and development of cleaner road fuels, including new duty incentives for sulphur-free fuels and bioethanol and an increase in the duty on red diesel and fuel oil;

- a new lower rate of vehicle excise duty for the most environmentally-friendly cars with very low levels of carbon dioxide emissions; and

- a freeze in the rates of the aggregates levy.

Box 1.1: Promoting flexibility

Flexibility is the ability to respond to economic change efficiently and quickly in a way that maintains high employment, low inflation and unemployment, and growth in real incomes. In the modern global economy, flexible labour, product and capital markets are vital to ensure that the economy is responsive and that economic shocks do not have long-lasting effects, so that high and stable levels of output and employment can be maintained.

Were the UK to join EMU, the need for flexibility would be even greater, as the ability to adjust interest and exchange rates would no longer be available at the national level. In such circumstances, labour product and capital markets would need to respond dynamically to shocks, so as to avoid putting at risk high and stable levels of growth and employment.

A sufficient level of wage flexibility is vital to eliminate imbalances between supply and demand; relative price adjustment is a particularly important mechanism to allow changes in competitiveness between countries, and a flexible and integrated capital market can provide the financial instruments that help consumers and firms stabilise their consumption following a shock. These issues are addressed in detail in the preliminary and technical work supporting the five economic tests.

Building on the reforms already introduced, and summarised throughout this chapter, Budget 2003 announces new measures to improve:

- labour market flexibility, through measures to increase wage flexibility in the public sector; improve skills, particularly at the basic and intermediate level; enhance local discretion in the delivery of employment policies; and increase the supply of labour by helping people move from welfare to work and raising managed migration over the economic cycle;

- product market flexibility, with additional steps to enhance competition in specific markets; reform the planning system to make it work more quickly, predictably and efficiently; and ease the impact of regulation on small businesses; and

- capital market flexibility, through new proposals to improve access to finance for small enterprises with high growth potential, and consultation on further reform of the corporation tax system.

The Government supports policies to strengthen competition in the European Union and the Single Market. All European countries have embarked on an ambitious programme to reform labour, product and capital markets. However, more needs to be done across Europe, in particular to enhance employment flexibility, trade and the Single Market in financial services.

BUDGET MEASURES AND THEIR IMPACT ON HOUSEHOLDS

1.33   The measures introduced in this and previous Budgets support the Government's objectives of promoting work and tackling child and pensioner poverty, while laying the foundations for sustained investment in Britain's public services.

1.34   As a result of the freezing of the income tax personal allowance and the one per cent rise in national insurance contributions announced in Budget 2002, in 2003-04:

- a person on median earnings of £21,400 a year will pay an additional £3.66 a week;

- a person on 50 per cent of median earnings of £10,700 a year will pay an additional £1.61 a week; and

- a person on 150 per cent of median earnings – £32,100 a year – will pay an additional £5.72 a week.

1.35   The introduction of the Child and Working Tax Credits from this month will provide greater support for families with children and reward work. As a result of all personal tax and benefit measures taking effect in April 2003:

- a single earner family on median earnings of £21,400 and with two children will be nearly £5.00 a week better off, largely because of the new Child Tax Credit;

- 50 per cent of families with children will be better off, even after the freezing of the income tax personal allowance and the one per cent rise in national insurance contributions announced in Budget 2002; and

- a single person, aged 25 or over, and working 35 hours a week at the National Minimum Wage will be £21.75 a week better off, largely because of the new Working Tax Credit.

1.36   As a result of personal tax and benefit measures introduced since 1997[1]:

- families with children are, on average, £1,200 a year better off; and

- families with children in the poorest fifth of the population are, on average, £2,500 a year better off.

1.37   As a result of personal tax and benefit reforms since 1997, by October 2003:[1,2,3]

- households will be, on average, £775 a year better off;

- pensioner households will be, on average, £1,250 a year better off; and

- the poorest third of pensioner households will be, on average, £1,600 a year better off.

1.38   Table 1.2 lists the key Budget policy decisions and their impact on government spending and revenue. Further details are provided in Chapter A of the FSBR.

---

[1] Compared with the 1997-98 system of taxes and benefits, indexed to 2003-04 prices.
[2] The Pension Credit is introduced from October 2003.
[3] The National Minimum Wage will be £4.50 for adults from October 2003.

Table 1.2: Budget 2003 policy decisions

		(+ve is an Exchequer yield)			£ million
		2003-04 indexed	**2004-05 indexed**	**2005-06 indexed**	**2003-04 non-indexed**
MEETING THE PRODUCTIVITY CHALLENGE					
1	100 per cent first year capital allowances for ICT	−5	−160	+70	−5
2	VAT flat-rate scheme upper limit of £150,000	−15	−15	−15	−15
3	Revalorise VAT registration and deregistration thresholds	0	0	0	−5
4	VAT: simplify the treatment of business gifts	*	−5	−5	−5
5	VAT: electronically supplied services	+20	+25	+30	+20
6	Simplified import VAT accounting	−5	−20	−20	−5
7	Improvements to research and development tax credit	−20	−40	−50	−20
8	Employment benefits: deregulatory measures	−5	−5	−5	−5
9	Reform of North Sea infrastructure taxation	0	−15	−20	0
10	Life companies: change to policyholder rate and apportionment of profits	−25	−40	−40	−25
INCREASING EMPLOYMENT OPPORTUNITY FOR ALL					
11	Income tax: indexation of starting and basic rate limits	0	0	0	−400
12	Housing Benefit disregard	0	−45	−45	0
BUILDING A FAIRER SOCIETY					
Supporting families and pensioners					
13	Child Trust Fund	−350	−230	−235	−350
14	Tax exemption for foster carers	0	−5	−5	0
15	Income tax exemption for reimbursed homeworking costs	−5	−5	−5	−5
16	Extend hospital downrating exemption to 52 weeks	−30	−15	−15	−30
17	Indexation of the pension schemes earnings cap	0	0	0	−5
18	£100 payment to older pensioners	−180	−180	−180	−180
Protecting tax revenues[1]					
19	Tackling avoidance and creating a fairer system: equity remuneration	+110	+90	+95	+110
20	Chargeable gains: anti-avoidance involving second-hand life insurance policies	0	+30	+30	0
21	Capital gains tax: countering avoidance schemes through offshore trusts	0	+5	+5	0
22	Loan relationships: closing loopholes	+25	+50	+50	+25
23	Tackling avoidance through sale and repurchase agreements	+30	+50	+50	+30
24	Income tax: avoidance through relevant discounted securities	+20	+20	+20	+20
25	Service companies: closing loopholes used by domestic workers	+15	+15	+15	+15
26	VAT anti-fraud measures	+225	+230	+235	+225
27	VAT on continuous supplies	*	+15	+15	*

Table 1.2: Budget 2003 policy decisions

	(+ve is an Exchequer yield)			£ million
	2003-04 indexed	**2004-05** indexed	**2005-06** indexed	**2003-04** non-indexed
Duties and other tax changes				
28 Treatment of options for the purposes of tax on chargeable gains	0	+20	+40	0
29 Inheritance tax: indexation of threshold	0	0	0	–30
30 Electronic payment for large employers	0	+10	+10	0
31 Introduction of gross profits tax for bingo	–20	–25	–20	–20
32 Amusement machines licensing duty: freeze of rates	–5	–5	–5	0
33 General betting duty: minor amendments	+5	+5	+5	+5
34 Tobacco duties: revalorisation of rates	0	0	0	+170
35 Alcohol duties: revalorise beer and wine, freeze other rates	–35	–35	–30	+145
PROTECTING THE ENVIRONMENT				
36 Landfill tax: £3 increases from 2005-06	0	0	+140	0
37 Climate change levy: freeze rates	–20	–20	–20	0
38 Aggregates levy: freeze rates	–10	–10	–10	+10
39 Enhanced capital allowances for water-efficient technologies	–20	–30	–25	–20
40 Enhanced capital allowances for additional energy-saving technologies	–5	–5	–10	–5
Transport and the environment				
41 Company car tax: emissions level for minimum charge	0	0	+125	0
42 Fuel duties: revalorisation of rates from 1 October	–300	0	0	+300
43 Fuel duties: new duty rate for bioethanol from January 2005	0	–5	–30	0
44 Fuel duties: increase rebated oils by 1p above revalorisation	+95	+95	+100	+95
45 Air passenger duties: freeze of rates	–25	–25	–30	0
46 Changes to Vehicle Excise Duty	+30	+30	+35	–95
47 VAT: revalorisation of car fuel scale charges	0	0	0	+10
OTHER POLICY DECISIONS				
48 Recycled revenues from landfill tax increases	0	0	–140	
TOTAL BUDGET MEASURES	**–505**	**–250**	**+110**	**–45**

* Negligible

ADDITIONAL BUDGET POLICY DECISIONS

Resetting of the AME margin	+805	–980	–1,750

¹ In addition, further details of the package of measures to modernise stamp duty announced in Budget 2002 are set out in Table A2.1. The original yield set out in Budget 2002 (Tables 1.2 and A.1) has been updated, and a reduced yield (by £10 million in 2003-04, and £100 million in 2004-05) included in Budget 2003 fiscal projections.

GOVERNMENT SPENDING AND REVENUE

1.39   Chart 1.1 presents public expenditure by main function. Total public spending (Total Managed Expenditure – TME) is expected to be around £456 billion in the current financial year, 2003-04. TME is divided into Departmental Expenditure Limits (DEL) and Annually Managed Expenditure (AME). DEL spending is set out in Table C12 of the FSBR, though a number of DELs, particularly those of the devolved administrations, contribute to spending on more than one of the functions in Chart 1.1. AME components are shown in Table C11 of the FSBR and some of these, especially spending financed locally by local authorities, also cover spending on several different functions.

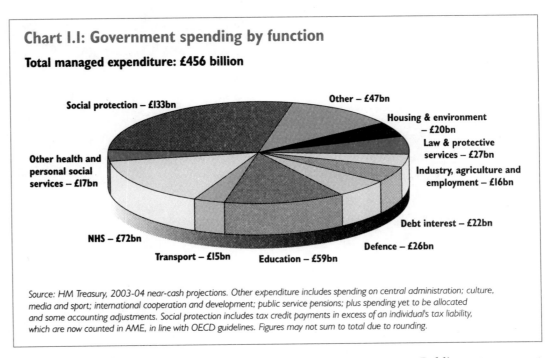

Chart 1.1: Government spending by function

Total managed expenditure: £456 billion

Social protection – £133bn

Other – £47bn

Housing & environment – £20bn

Law & protective services – £27bn

Other health and personal social services – £17bn

Industry, agriculture and employment – £16bn

Debt interest – £22bn

NHS – £72bn

Defence – £26bn

Transport – £15bn

Education – £59bn

Source: HM Treasury, 2003-04 near-cash projections. Other expenditure includes spending on central administration; culture, media and sport; international cooperation and development; public service pensions; plus spending yet to be allocated and some accounting adjustments. Social protection includes tax credit payments in excess of an individual's tax liability, which are now counted in AME, in line with OECD guidelines. Figures may not sum to total due to rounding.

1.39   Chart 1.2 shows the different sources of government revenue. Public sector current receipts are expected to be around £428 billion in 2003-04. Table C8 of the FSBR provides a more detailed breakdown of receipts consistent with this chart.

Chart 1.2: Government receipts

Total receipts: £428 billion

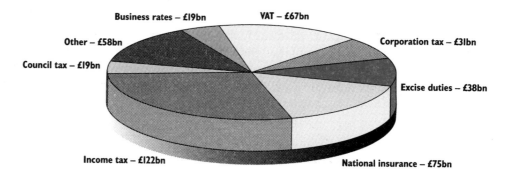

Business rates – £19bn

VAT – £67bn

Other – £58bn

Corporation tax – £31bn

Council tax – £19bn

Excise duties – £38bn

Income tax – £122bn

National insurance – £75bn

Source: HM Treasury, 2003-04 projections. Other receipts include capital taxes, stamp duties, vehicle excise duties and some other tax and non-tax receipts – for example, interest and dividends. Figures may not sum to total due to rounding.

2 MAINTAINING MACROECONOMIC STABILITY

International developments remain a key influence on the UK economy. Last year, concern over corporate accounting scandals and events in the Middle East brought uncertainty and volatility to equity and oil prices. This year, geo-political risks, particularly surrounding hostilities in Iraq, have compounded global uncertainties and further restrained global economic activity, particularly in the Euro-area. Nonetheless, the economic stability delivered by the Government's macroeconomic framework has left the UK well placed to deal with the impact of global events:

- the monetary policy framework is delivering low and stable inflation, while allowing the Bank of England's Monetary Policy Committee to respond to risks generated by weakness in the world economy; and

- the fiscal rules are delivering sound public finances and allowing the automatic stabilisers to operate freely to support monetary policy.

The immediate outlook for the world economy is now weaker than anticipated at the time of the Pre-Budget Report and prospects for the major economies, in particular the Euro-area, have been revised downwards. Growth is forecast to accelerate from the second half of 2003 and into 2004 as international uncertainty eases. UK GDP is forecast to grow by between 2 and 2½ per cent this year, and between 3 and 3½ per cent in 2004 and 2005, as the economy returns to trend.

The projections for the public finances show that the Government is firmly on track to meet its strict fiscal rules over the economic cycle, including in the cautious case, and while meeting its international and public spending commitments:

- the average current budget since the start of the current cycle in 1999-2000 is comfortably in surplus, ensuring the Government remains on track to meet the golden rule, using cautious assumptions and in the cautious case; and

- public sector net debt is projected to be low and stable throughout the next five years, stabilising at just under 34 per cent of GDP by the end of the projection period. This comfortably meets the sustainable investment rule and gives the UK the lowest level of debt as a proportion of national income in the G7.

In the short term, the operation of the automatic stabilisers means that fiscal policy is supporting monetary policy in maintaining economic stability as the economy remains below trend. In the medium term, the public finances return towards the Budget 2002 profile as economic growth strengthens. The use of cautious assumptions and the 'stress test' against the cautious case help to ensure that the public finances are sound and sustainable, despite continued international uncertainty and global economic weakness.

THE MACROECONOMIC FRAMEWORK

2.1   Compared with the Pre-Budget Report, economic growth is now expected to be weaker in the world's major economies, particularly in the Euro-area. Last year, concern over corporate accounting scandals and events in the Middle East brought uncertainty and volatility to equity and oil prices, and this has continued into 2003. Geo-political risks, most of all those surrounding the hostilities in Iraq, have compounded existing uncertainties. International developments continue to be a key influence on the outlook for the UK economy, and persistent uncertainty and subdued global growth have prompted falls in consumer confidence and further deferred business investment plans. The macroeconomic framework limits the impact of adverse global developments on the economy so that the UK can maintain high and stable levels of growth and employment.

2.2 The macroeconomic framework is designed to maintain long-term economic stability. Large fluctuations in output, employment and inflation add to uncertainty for businesses, consumers and the public sector, and can reduce the economy's long-term growth potential. Stability allows businesses, individuals and the Government to plan more effectively for the long term, improving the quality and quantity of investment in physical and human capital and helping to raise productivity.

2.3 The macroeconomic framework is based on the principles of transparency, responsibility and accountability[1]. The monetary policy framework seeks to ensure low and stable inflation, while fiscal policy is underpinned by two strict rules that ensure sound public finances over the medium term. The fiscal rules are the foundation of the Government's public spending framework, which facilitates long-term planning and provides departments with the flexibility and incentives they need to increase the quality of public services and deliver specified outcomes. These policies work together in a coherent and integrated way.

Box 2.1: Government policy on EMU

The Government's policy on membership of the single currency was set out by the Chancellor in his statement to Parliament in October 1997. In principle, the Government is in favour of UK membership, in practice, the economic conditions must be right. The determining factor is the national economic interest and whether, on the basis of an assessment of the five economic tests, the economic case for joining is clear and unambiguous.

The Government is committed to publishing a comprehensive and rigorous assessment of the five tests within two years of the start of this Parliament. If a decision to recommend joining is taken by the Government, it will be put to a vote in Parliament and then to a referendum of the British people.

The Government's preliminary and technical analysis supporting the five tests assessment and comprising 18 supporting studies will be published alongside the assessment.

The Government is also committed to ensuring that preparations are made so that the British people would be in a position to exercise genuine choice in a referendum, should the economic tests be met. The Government's National Changeover Plan describes how the UK can be ready for a smooth and cost-effective changeover should Government, Parliament and the people decide to join the single currency. The Treasury has monitored the changeover in the Euro-area to gather examples of best practice. This work has been published in the Government's sixth report on euro preparations, which also contains an update on preparations for a possible UK changeover.

The Government continues to help small- and medium-sized enterprises consider the impact of the euro on the way they do business and is committed to ensuring that UK business has access to the information it needs to take advantage of opportunities in the Euro-area.

---

[1] Further details can be found in *Reforming Britain's economic and financial policy*, HM Treasury, 2002.

Monetary policy framework   **2.4**   Since its introduction in 1997, the monetary policy framework has consistently delivered inflation close to the Government's target and allowed the Bank of England's Monetary Policy Committee (MPC) to mitigate the impact of global uncertainty on the UK economy. The framework is based on four key principles:

- clear and precise objectives. While the primary objective of monetary policy is to deliver price stability, the adoption of a single, symmetrical inflation target ensures that outcomes below target are treated as seriously as those above, so that monetary policy also supports the Government's objective of high and stable levels of growth and employment;

- full operational independence for the MPC in setting interest rates to meet the Government's inflation target. The Government is reaffirming in Budget 2003 the target of $2\frac{1}{2}$ per cent for the 12 month increase in the Retail Prices Index excluding mortgage payments (RPIX), which applies at all times;

- openness, transparency and accountability, which are enhanced through the publication of MPC members' voting records, prompt reporting of the minutes of monthly MPC meetings, and publication of the Bank of England's quarterly Inflation Report; and

- credibility and flexibility. The MPC has discretion to decide how and when to react to events, within the constraints of the inflation target and the open letter system. If inflation deviates by more than one percentage point above or below target, the Governor of the Bank of England must explain in an open letter to the Chancellor the reasons for the deviation, the action the MPC proposes to take, the expected duration of the deviation and how this meets the remit of the MPC.

2.5   These arrangements have removed the prospect of short-term political influence over monetary policy and ensured that interest rates are set in a forward-looking manner to meet the Government's symmetrical inflation target.

Fiscal policy framework   **2.6**   The Government's fiscal policy framework is based on the five key principles set out in the *Code for fiscal stability*[2] – transparency, stability, responsibility, fairness and efficiency. The Code requires the Government to state both its objectives and the rules through which fiscal policy will be operated. The Government's fiscal policy objectives are:

- over the medium term, to ensure sound public finances and that spending and taxation impact fairly within and between generations; and

- over the short term, to support monetary policy and, in particular, to allow the automatic stabilisers to help smooth the path of the economy.

2.7   These objectives are implemented through two fiscal rules, against which the performance of fiscal policy can be judged. The fiscal rules are:

- the golden rule: over the economic cycle, the Government will borrow only to invest and not to fund current spending; and

- the sustainable investment rule: public sector net debt as a proportion of GDP will be held over the economic cycle at a stable and prudent level. Other things being equal, net debt will be maintained below 40 per cent of GDP over the economic cycle.

---

[2] *The code for fiscal stability,* HM Treasury, November 1998.

2.8   The fiscal rules ensure sound public finances in the medium term while allowing flexibility in two key respects:

- the rules are set over the economic cycle. This allows the fiscal balances to vary between years in line with the cyclical position of the economy, permitting the automatic stabilisers to operate freely to help smooth the path of the economy in the face of variations in demand; and

- the rules work together to promote capital investment while ensuring sustainable public finances in the long term. The golden rule requires the current budget to be in balance or surplus over the cycle, allowing the Government to borrow only to fund capital spending. The sustainable investment rule ensures that borrowing is maintained at a prudent level. To meet the sustainable investment rule with confidence, net debt will be maintained below 40 per cent of GDP in each and every year of the current economic cycle.

Public spending framework

2.9   The fiscal policy framework also takes account of uncertainty that is inherent in projections of the public finances. The fiscal projections are based on cautious assumptions for key economic variables, including the trend rate of growth, equity prices and the level of unemployment. This cautious approach builds a safety margin into the public finances and minimises the need for unexpected changes in taxation or spending. The assumptions are audited by the Comptroller and Auditor General as part of a three-year rolling review to ensure that they remain reasonable and cautious.

2.10   To enhance the reporting of past fiscal developments, a new *End of year fiscal report* was published for the first time alongside the 2002 Pre-Budget Report. The report provides detailed retrospective information on the public finances in 2000-01 and 2001-02, supplementing the information already published under the *Code for fiscal stability* and bringing the UK into line with international best practice.

2.11   Sound public finances are a prerequisite for sustainable investment in public services. The fiscal rules underpin the Government's public spending framework and have important consequences for the structure of the budgeting regime. The golden rule increases the efficiency of public spending by ensuring that growth-enhancing public investment is not sacrificed to meet short-term current spending pressures. Departments are now given separate allocations for resource and capital spending to help ensure adherence to the rule. The sustainable investment rule sets the context for the Government's public investment targets and ensures that borrowing for investment is conducted in a responsible way. Full details of the public spending framework are set out in Chapter 6, which also provides information on the resources made available for public services in the 2002 Spending Review and on the Government's strategy for reforming public services.

THE PERFORMANCE OF THE FRAMEWORK

Monetary strategy 2.12   The Government's frameworks for monetary policy, fiscal policy and public spending form a coherent strategy for maintaining high and stable levels of growth and employment, and for minimising the harmful impact of external events.

2.13   The monetary policy framework has enhanced the credibility of policy making and continues to deliver clear benefits. Since the framework was introduced:

- RPIX inflation has fluctuated in the narrow range of 1.5 to 3.2 per cent and has averaged 2.3 per cent, close to the Government's target; and

- long-term inflation expectations, as measured by survey and financial markets data, show that inflation is expected to remain close to the Government's target, having fallen from over 4 per cent in 1997.

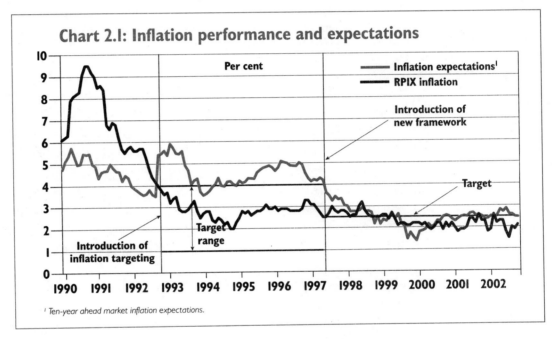

Chart 2.1: Inflation performance and expectations

[1] Ten-year ahead market inflation expectations.

2.14   The framework has also dealt successfully with unexpected economic events. The MPC responded quickly and decisively to the global slowdown during 2001 and to the events of 11 September 2001, cutting interest rates by a total of two percentage points. Interest rates were then left at historically low levels for over a year, before a further reduction in February 2003. This helped to keep output close to its trend level, while ensuring that inflation remained close to target. Long-term interest rates are around their lowest levels for over 35 years, reducing the Government's debt interest payments and freeing up resources for investment in public services.

Fiscal strategy 2.15   The Government has taken tough decisions on taxation and spending to restore the public finances to a sustainable position. Between 1996-97 and 2000-01, the fiscal stance was tightened by more than 4 percentage points of GDP, supporting monetary policy during a period when the economy was generally above trend. Public sector net debt has also been reduced from 44 per cent of GDP in 1996-97 to around 31 per cent of GDP in 2002-03 – the lowest level of debt as a proportion of national income in the G7.

2002 Spending Review 2.16 Significant investment in the reform and modernisation of public services has been delivered within this framework. The 2002 Spending Review established departmental spending plans for the three years to 2005-06, and for the five years to 2007-08 for UK spending on the NHS, consistent with the Government's strict fiscal rules. To deliver the largest ever sustained spending growth in the history of the NHS, while meeting the fiscal rules and other priorities, Budget 2002 raised national insurance contributions (NICs) by one per cent for employees, employers and the self employed on all earnings above the NICs threshold from April 2003, and froze the income tax personal allowance for those aged under 65 in 2003-04.

2.17 Total Managed Expenditure (TME) is set to rise by 4.3 per cent a year, on average, in real terms between 2002-03 and 2005-06. Within this, the Government has been able to devote additional resources to priority public services:

- over the three years to 2005-06, planned spending on education is set to grow by 5.7 per cent a year in real terms and on transport by 8.3 per cent. Over the five years to 2007-08, planned spending on health is set to grow by 7.2 per cent a year in real terms;

- social security payments, tax credits and debt interest payments will account for just 23 per cent of the additional public spending planned over the next three years, compared with 57 per cent between 1991-92 and 1996-97;

- debt interest payments are expected to have fallen by almost 7 per cent a year, on average in real terms, over the period 1996-97 to 2002-03, compared with an average annual increase of more than 7 per cent in real terms between 1991-92 and 1996-97; and

- to address the legacy of under-investment in public services, public sector net investment, already expected to be almost three times higher in 2003-04 than in 1997-98, is projected to rise still further to $2\frac{1}{4}$ per cent of GDP in 2007-08.

RECENT ECONOMIC DEVELOPMENTS AND PROSPECTS

Recent economic developments 2.18 Global economic conditions have remained challenging since the 2002 Pre-Budget Report and prospects for the world's major economies, in particular the Euro-area, have been revised downwards. Last year, concern over accounting scandals and tensions in the Middle East brought uncertainty and volatility to equity and oil prices, and this has continued into 2003. Geo-political risks, particularly surrounding hostilities in Iraq, have compounded existing uncertainties. Although oil prices have now fallen back, they have recently been at their highest level for around two and a half years and global equity markets and exchange rates have seen further turbulence since the time of the Pre-Budget Report.

2.19 International uncertainty remains a key influence on UK economic prospects. Ongoing global uncertainty, combined with an already sluggish global recovery, has kept business confidence in the UK subdued and discouraged firms from bringing deferred investment projects back on stream. Nonetheless, the Government's macroeconomic framework has continued to perform well against these global challenges and risks. Inflation has remained close to target, allowing the MPC to reduce interest rates to their lowest level in almost fifty years. Fiscal policy has continued to complement monetary policy in supporting growth.

2.20   While a number of the world's major economies were in recession in 2001, the UK economy has continued to grow throughout the recent period of protracted global uncertainty. The UK is currently experiencing its longest unbroken period of economic expansion since quarterly records began almost fifty years ago, with GDP having increased for 42 consecutive quarters.

Economic   **2.21**   Growth slowed across the G7 economies in the final months of 2002, as expected.
prospects   However, since the turn of the year, geo-political risks and volatility in equity markets prompted further sharp falls in consumer confidence and weaker than expected household consumption in most of the major economies. With business confidence remaining at low levels and further evidence that firms are continuing to defer investment decisions, global economic activity in the first few months of 2003 is now forecast to be weaker than anticipated at the time of the Pre-Budget Report. Growth is expected to strengthen from the middle of 2003 as uncertainty dissipates and the recovery in the US gathers pace.

Table 2.1: The world economy

| | Percentage changes on a year earlier | | | |
| | | Forecast | | |
	2002	**2003**	**2004**	**2005**
Major 7 countries[1]				
Real GDP	1½	1¾	2¾	3
Consumer price inflation[2]	1¾	1¼	1½	1½
Euro-area				
Real GDP	¾	1	2¼	2¾
World trade in goods and services	2½	4¾	8½	7¾
UK export markets[3]	1¾	4¼	7½	7

[1] G7: US, Japan, Germany, France, UK, Italy and Canada.
[2] Final quarter of each period. For UK, RPIX.
[3] Other countries' imports of goods and services weighted according to their importance in UK exports.

2.22   Chart 2.2 shows that, since the time of the Pre-Budget Report, Consensus Forecasts have revised down their projections for GDP growth during 2003 in each of the G7 economies, and especially in the Euro-area. However, the latest consensus forecasts also reveal that growth is expected to recover throughout the G7 during 2004, as global uncertainties ease from the second half of this year.

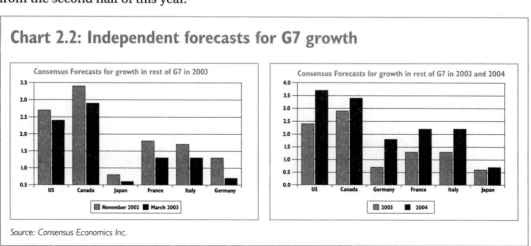

Chart 2.2: Independent forecasts for G7 growth

Source: Consensus Economics Inc.

2.23   Ongoing global uncertainty is expected to continue to subdue demand in key UK export markets and hold back business investment in the near term. UK GDP is expected to grow by between 2 to 2½ per cent this year. Growth is expected to accelerate in the second half of 2003 and into 2004, as international uncertainty eases and an anticipated gathering in the pace of the global economic recovery feeds through to the domestic economy. GDP is therefore forecast to increase by 3 to 3½ per cent both next year and the year after, with the economy returning to trend by the end of 2005.

2.24   RPIX inflation is expected to remain a little above the Government's target over the next few months, temporarily boosted by housing cost effects. Thereafter, inflation is forecast to ease back as these temporary factors unwind and slack in the economy puts downward pressure on domestic prices.

Table 2.2: Summary of UK forecast

		Forecast		
	2002	**2003**	**2004**	**2005**
GDP growth (per cent)	1¾	2 to 2½	3 to 3½	3 to 3½
RPIX inflation (per cent, Q4)	2½	2¾	2½	2½

2.25   International developments have also affected the recent pattern of economic growth. Global uncertainty has undermined business confidence and external demand, while a robust labour market, allied with strong house price rises, has given support to private consumption. Growth is expected to become more balanced over the forecast horizon as deferred business investment comes back on stream, exports pick up in response to stronger global demand, and private consumption growth moderates towards sustainable rates.

Forecast risks   **2.26**   There are both upside and downside risks to the economic outlook. On the upside, the various uncertainties currently affecting the global economy could dissipate more quickly, and confidence recover more sharply than anticipated. This would, in turn, help support a stronger than expected improvement in UK economic prospects.

2.27   A period of prolonged uncertainty, accompanied by continued volatility in financial markets, weaker equity prices and higher oil prices poses the clearest downside risk to G7 activity. The Government will remain vigilant in the face of these risks. The public finance projections will continue to be based on cautious assumptions, including for equity prices and the trend rate of growth, and 'stress tested' against the cautious case, which builds in a margin against shocks and unexpected events. The Government remains on track to meet its strict fiscal rules over the economic cycle, including in the cautious case.

The economic cycle   **2.28**   Since Budget 2000, the Government's provisional judgment has been that the economy completed a full, albeit short cycle between the first half of 1997 and mid-1999. The current economic cycle therefore began in mid-1999, with output moving slightly above trend in 2000 and the first half of 2001. This judgement does not affect the fact that the Government remains firmly on track to meet its fiscal rules over the economic cycle. The average current budget since 1999-2000 and since 1997-98 remains comfortably in surplus in every year of the projection period.

Caution and the public finances

2.29 The Comptroller and Auditor General independently audits 12 key assumptions that underpin the public finances projections on a three-year rolling programme to ensure that they remain reasonable and cautious. A complete list of these assumptions is set out in Chapter C of the *Financial Statement and Budget Report*. For Budget 2003, the existing assumptions relating to privatisation proceeds and interest rates have been audited; as set out in Chapter C, the tobacco assumption has been revised to reflect recent trends in smuggling and the success of HM Customs and Excise strategy. All were deemed to be reasonable and to have demonstrated or incorporate caution[3].

2.30 As described in Chapter 5, Budget 2003 launches a new compliance and enforcement package for direct tax and national insurance contributions. An additional £66 million is being provided to the Inland Revenue over the next three years to support implementation of the package. The package is expected to produce £1.6 billion in total additional revenue over the next 3 years, but in line with the Government's cautious approach to the public finances a lower figure of under £1.4 billion over three years, with the annual figure rising to just over £0.6 billion in 2005-06, has been included in the forecast. The Comptroller and Auditor General has audited the projections and concluded that they are based on a reasonable approach and incorporate caution.

Box 2.2: Equity prices and the public finances

The projections for the public finances are based on the cautious assumption that equity prices rise from their current levels in line with projected growth in money GDP.

The equity price assumption which underpins the Budget 2003 projections is based on the 28 March 2003 level of the FT All-Share index, which, at 1778, is 9 per cent lower than that used in the 2002 Pre-Budget Report projections. This affects receipts from capital taxes, corporation tax and stamp duty, and reduces total receipts by just under £1 billion in each year compared with the Pre-Budget Report projections. The impact on receipts of the recent stock market increases over the past week have therefore not been incorporated into the forecast published today.

The Treasury's methodology for estimating the impact of the economic cycle on the public finances is based on the average impact of the output gap on the fiscal aggregates over previous cycles. This would only capture the effect of equity prices on the public finances to the degree that movements in equity prices have been associated with past economic cycles. To the extent that this is not the case, recent falls in equity prices will not be captured in estimates of the automatic stabilisers.

Equity prices are heavily influenced by expectations about the future, making them volatile and prone to 'bubbles' and periods of over-correction. The consensus among market analysts is that equity prices are currently suppressed by unduly harsh risk premia associated with global instability, and the average of recent independent forecasts[1] suggests that equity prices will rise by 20 per cent over the coming year. This would generate a £1 billion increase in total receipts this year relative to the Budget projections. Nonetheless, consistent with its prudent approach to managing the public finances, and in the interests of stable and robust fiscal planning, the Government continues to base its projections on a deliberately cautious equity price assumption.

[1] Based on a panel of independent organisations forecasting the year-ahead level of the FTSE 100 index in March 2003.

---

[3] *Audit of Assumptions for Budget 2003*, National Audit Office, April 2003 (HC 627).

RECENT FISCAL TRENDS AND OUTLOOK

2.31 Budget 2003 presents the Government's annual fiscal forecast and updates the 2002 Pre-Budget Report interim projections which showed weaker receipts this year and over the next two years, primarily due to cyclical or otherwise temporary factors.

2.32 Continued weakness and uncertainty in the world economy and the £3 billion contingency provision to meet the full cost of the UK's military obligations in Iraq affected the fiscal balances last year. The estimated 2002-03 outturn for the public sector current budget shows a deficit of £11.7 billion, compared with a projected deficit of £5.7 billion in the 2002 Pre-Budget Report and a surplus of £3.2 billion in Budget 2002. For public sector net borrowing, the estimated 2002-03 outturn is £24.0 billion, compared with a projection of £20.1 billion in the Pre-Budget Report and of £11.2 billion in Budget 2002. However, disciplined management of the public finances means that the Government can allow the automatic stabilisers to operate during this period of global economic weakness, while remaining on track to meet the fiscal rules over the economic cycle, including in the cautious case.

2.33 Table 2.3 shows the projections for public sector net borrowing compared with those in the 2002 Pre-Budget Report. It disaggregates the changes into those attributable to the automatic stabilisers, other non-discretionary factors and discretionary measures, which include the Budget decisions set out in paragraphs 2.42 to 2.44 below.

Table 2.3: Public sector net borrowing compared with the 2002 Pre-Budget Report

£ billion	Estimate[1]	Projections				
	2002-03	2003-04	2004-05	2005-06	2006-07	2007-08
PBR 2002	20.1	24	19	19	19	20
Effect of automatic stabilisers	−1.1	2	3	1	0	0
Effect of other non-discretionary factors	3.1	1	1	1	1	1
Discretionary measures[2]	1.9	0	1	2	1	1
of which: policy measures since PBR 2002	2.0	0	0	0	−1	−1
resetting the AME margin	−0.1	−1	1	2	2	2
Budget 2003	24.0	27	24	23	22	22

Note: Figures may not sum due to rounding.

[1] The 2002-03 figures were projections in PBR 2002.

[2] This includes the £2 billion added since the Pre-Budget Report to make the contingency provision for the UK's military commitments in Iraq £3 billion in 2002-03. The allocation of resources between years will be reviewed in the light of developments.

2.34 The automatic stabilisers explain over half of the change in borrowing in 2003-04 and 2004-05. As the economy returns to trend over the medium term, so the effect of the automatic stabilisers declines. Other non-discretionary factors will capture a variety of influences on the public finances, including some temporary factors that are not picked up by the Treasury's methodology for cyclical adjustment described below, and the forecast revenue effects of the Inland Revenue compliance and enforcement package. From 2004-05, discretionary measures increase the level of borrowing, primarily as a result of the Government's decision to reset the AME margin to ensure that the public spending projections include a prudent and cautious safety margin against unexpected events. The discretionary measures line also includes the additional £2 billion added to the contingency provision in 2002-03 since the Pre-Budget Report.

2.35 The Treasury's methodology for estimating the impact of the economic cycle on the public finances is based on the average impact of changes in the output gap on the public finances over previous cycles. This means that the impact of changes in equity prices, social security payments and financial company profits are only attributed to the automatic stabilisers to the degree that changes in these have been associated with the output gap in the past. To the extent that this economic cycle differs from previous ones, temporary changes in the public finances may be ascribed to other non-discretionary effects rather than the automatic stabilisers.

2.36 An alternative disaggregation of the factors underlying the change in public sector net borrowing is shown in Table 2.4. Changes associated with the assumptions audited by the NAO help to reduce projections of net borrowing. This is primarily the result of the new assumption for anti-tobacco smuggling measures and the Inland Revenue compliance and enforcement package, partly offset by lower equity prices as described in Box 2.5. Other economic and forecasting effects includes the impact of the cycle on net borrowing to the extent that these cyclical factors are not associated with the NAO assumptions or financial company profits.

Table 2.4: Public sector net borrowing compared with the 2002 Pre-Budget Report

£ billion	Estimate[1]	Projections				
	2002-03	2003-04	2004-05	2005-06	2006-07	2007-08
PBR 2002	20.1	24	19	19	19	20
Assumptions audited by the NAO	0.0	−1	−1	−1	−2	−2
of which: equity price assumption	0.0	0	1	1	1	1
tobacco assumption	0.0	0	−1	−1	−1	−1
Inland Revenue package	0.0	0	−1	−1	−1	−1
Financial company profits	0.0	1	1	0	0	0
Other economic and forecasting effects	2.0	3	4	4	3	3
Total before discretionary measures	2.0	3	4	2	0	−1
Discretionary measures[2]	1.9	0	1	2	1	1
of which: policy measures since PBR 2002	2.0	0	0	0	−1	−1
resetting the AME margin	−0.1	−1	1	2	2	2
Budget 2003	24.0	27	24	23	22	22

Note: Figures may not sum due to rounding.

[1] *The 2002-03 figures were projections in PBR 2002.*

[2] *This includes the £2 billion added since the Pre-Budget Report to make the contingency provision for the UK's military commitments in Iraq £3 billion in 2002-03. The allocation of resources between years will be reviewed in the light of developments.*

Non-discretionary changes in receipts

2.37 Receipts are now expected to be £10.1 billion lower in 2002-03 compared with the Budget 2002 projection, and £2.7 billion lower than projected in the 2002 Pre-Budget Report. The change between Budget 2002 and the 2002 Pre-Budget Report reflects the impact of falls in equity prices and weaker financial company profits. The decline in overall receipts since the Pre-Budget Report is largely due to lower than expected receipts from income tax and national insurance contributions.

2.38 Receipts in 2003-04 are projected to be below the levels forecast in Budget 2002, and slightly lower than those in the 2002 Pre-Budget Report. Over the medium term, receipts steadily return to the levels forecast in Budget 2002. Chapter C of the Financial Statement and Budget Report provides further detail on changes to the forecast of receipts.

Non-discretionary changes in spending

2.39 The estimated outturn for Total Managed Expenditure (TME) in 2002-03 is £1.2 billion higher than projected in the 2002 Pre-Budget Report. For Departmental Expenditure Limits (DEL), the estimated outturn is £2.7 billion higher than projected in the 2002 Pre-Budget Report and Annually Managed Expenditure (AME) is expected to be £1.5 billion lower.

2.40   In subsequent years, AME is higher than forecast in the 2002 Pre-Budget Report as social security payments increase and towards the end of the projection period debt interest payments rise. Local authority self-financed expenditure is also higher at the end of the projection period, though this has a broadly neutral impact on the fiscal balances as it is matched by higher council tax receipts, which reflect the convention that projections for council tax are based on recent years' increases. AME is also projected to rise as a result of the Government's decision to reset the AME margin.

BUDGET DECISIONS

2.41   The Budget is the definitive statement of the Government's desired fiscal policy settings. In making its Budget decisions the Government has considered:

- the need to ensure that, over the economic cycle, the Government will continue to meet its strict fiscal rules;

- its fiscal policy objectives, including the need to ensure sound public finances and that spending and taxation impact fairly both within and between generations; and

- how fiscal policy can best support monetary policy over the economic cycle.

2.42   Within this disciplined framework, Budget 2003 shows the Government can meet its public spending commitments and announces further decisions to build a Britain of economic strength and social justice, including:

- a package of reforms to promote flexibility in labour, product and capital markets, including measures to promote enterprise, innovation and skills, and support to help people find and succeed in work;

- further steps to advance flexibility and fairness together, with a new Child Trust Fund to spread the benefits of asset ownership to all and further support for pensioners; and

- reforms to tackle avoidance and advance fairness in the tax system, to ensure that everyone contributes fairly to the public services from which they benefit.

2.43   Table 1.2 lists the key Budget policy decisions and their impact on the public finances. Further details are set out in Chapter A of the *Financial Statement and Budget Report.*

2.44   As described in Chapter 6, the Government has made a special contingency provision of £3 billion to ensure that resources are available to cover the full cost of the UK's military obligations in Iraq. The full amount of the provision has been allocated to 2002-03, though it is not yet clear when these costs will fall. In the light of this uncertainty and to protect committed investment while responding prudently to heightened global risks, the Government has decided to make no further allocations from the Capital Modernisation Fund (CMF). Instead unallocated CMF funding will contribute to the rebuilding of the AME margin to ensure that the public spending projections include a prudent and cautious safety margin against unexpected events. Resetting the AME margin to £1, £2 and £3 billion for the years 2003-04, 2004-05 and 2005-06, in accordance with usual practice, increases projections for TME by £1 billion in 2004-05 and by £1.8 billion in 2005-06, compared with those made in the 2002 Pre-Budget Report.

MEDIUM TERM FISCAL PROJECTIONS

2.45   Table 2.5 compares the projections for the current balance, net borrowing and net debt with those published in Budget 2002 and in the 2002 Pre-Budget Report. Changes in the fiscal balances are disaggregated into those explained by discretionary measures and those due to forecasting changes. It includes the impact of all Budget decisions in accordance with the *Code for fiscal stability*. Consistent with the presentation in the Pre-Budget Report, the table includes the impact of the windfall tax and associated spending. Further detail is provided in Chapter C of the *Financial Statement and Budget Report*.

2.46   The revised outturn for 2001-02 shows the current surplus to be £0.7 billion lower than forecast in Budget 2002 and £2.3 billion higher than in the 2002 Pre-Budget Report. The figures for public sector net borrowing are around £1½ billion lower than in both Budget 2002 and the 2002 Pre-Budget Report.

2.47   The projections for the current budget and net borrowing, which includes the £3 billion contingency provision to cover the full cost of the UK's military obligations in Iraq, show a slight deterioration in the near-term position compared with the 2002 Pre-Budget Report. Over the medium term, as the economy returns to trend, the projections move back towards the path described in Budget 2002. This slight deterioration in the short-term fiscal position leads to a modest increase in net debt which stabilises at just under 34 per cent of GDP by the end of the period, well below 40 per cent of GDP.

Table 2.5: Fiscal balances compared with Budget 2002

	Outturn 2001-02	Estimate[1] 2002-03	Projections 2003-04	2004-05	2005-06	2006-07	2007-08
Surplus on current budget (£ billion)							
Budget 2002	10.6	3.2	7	9	7	9	–
Effect of forecasting changes	–3.0	–7.9	–12	–7	–3	–1	
of which: effect of automatic stabilisers	*–0.6*	*–5.8*	*–9*	*–5*	*–1*	*0*	
effect of other non-discretionary factors	*–2.4*	*–2.1*	*–4*	*–2*	*–2*	*–1*	
Effect of policy measures	0.0	–1.0	1	0	1	1	
PBR 2002	7.7	–5.7	–5	3	5	8	10
Effect of forecasting changes	2.3	–4.1	–4	–3	–1	–1	0
of which: effect of automatic stabilisers	*0.5*	*1.1*	*–2*	*–3*	*–1*	*0*	*0*
effect of other non-discretionary factors	*1.8*	*–5.2*	*–2*	*0*	*0*	*–1*	*0*
Effect of Budget measures	0.0	–1.9	0	–1	–1	–1	–1
Budget 2003	9.9	–11.7	–8	–1	2	6	9
Net borrowing (£ billion)							
Budget 2002	1.3	11.2	13	13	17	18	–
PBR 2002							
Effect of forecasting changes	–0.2	7.8	12	6	2	1	
of which: effect of automatic stabilisers	*0.6*	*5.8*	*9*	*5*	*1*	*0*	
effect of other non-discretionary factors	*–0.8*	*2.0*	*4*	*2*	*1*	*1*	
Effect of policy measures	0.0	1.0	–1	0	–1	–1	
PBR 2002	1.2	20.1	24	19	19	19	20
Effect of forecasting changes	–1.5	2.0	3	4	3	1	1
of which: effect of automatic stabilisers	*–0.5*	*–1.1*	*2*	*3*	*1*	*0*	*0*
effect of other non-discretionary factors	*–1.0*	*3.1*	*1*	*1*	*1*	*1*	*1*
Effect of Budget measures	0.0	1.9	0	1	2	1	1
Budget 2003	–0.4	24.0	27	24	23	22	22
Public sector net debt (per cent of GDP)							
Budget 2002[2]	30.4	30.2	30.4	30.4	30.7	31.0	–
PBR 2002	30.4	31.0	32.1	32.4	32.6	32.7	33.0
Budget 2003	30.2	30.9	32.2	32.7	33.2	33.5	33.8

Note: Figures may not sum due to rounding.
[1] The 2002-03 figures were projections in Budget 2002 and PBR 2002.
[2] The 2001-02 figures was an estimate in Budget 2002.

2.48   Table 2.6 sets out the underlying structural position of the fiscal balances, adjusted for the impact of the economic cycle on the public finances. Cyclically-adjusted, the current budget and net borrowing remain close to the levels projected in Budget 2002 and the 2002 Pre-Budget Report over the medium term. In 2002-03, which includes the £3 billion contingency provision to meet the full cost of the UK's military obligations in Iraq, cyclically-adjusted net borrowing increases by $^1/_2$ per cent of GDP compared to the 2002 Pre-Budget Report, and the cyclically-adjusted current budget falls by around $^3/_4$ per cent of GDP, leading to a deficit of $^1/_2$ per cent in that year.

Table 2.6: Cyclically-adjusted fiscal balances

	Outturn	Estimate[1]	Projections				
	2001-02	2002-03	2003-04	2004-05	2005-06	2006-07	2007-08
Surplus on current budget (per cent of GDP)							
Budget 2002	1.0	0.5	0.6	0.7	0.6	0.7	–
PBR 2002	0.7	0.2	0.3	0.6	0.5	0.6	0.7
Budget 2003	0.9	−0.5	0.2	0.5	0.4	0.4	0.6
Net borrowing (per cent of GDP)							
Budget 2002	0.2	0.9	1.2	1.2	1.4	1.4	–
PBR 2002	0.2	1.2	1.5	1.3	1.5	1.5	1.5
Budget 2003	0.1	1.7	1.5	1.5	1.7	1.7	1.6

[1]The 2002-03 figures were projections in Budget 2002 and PBR 2002.

Box 2.3: International public finances

The global economic slowdown has had a significant impact on public finances throughout the world and many of the G7 economies have experienced rising debt ratios since 2000, and are expected to see further rises in the coming years. As shown in the chart below, the UK now has the lowest debt-to-GDP ratio in the G7.

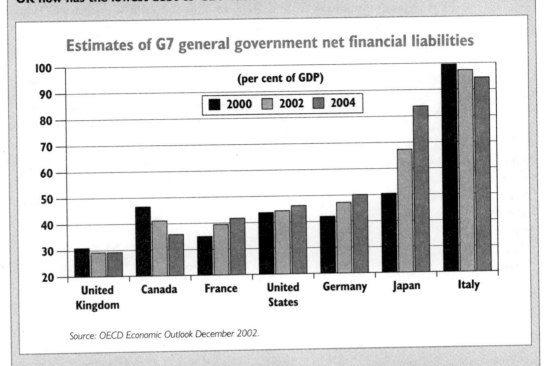

Estimates of G7 general government net financial liabilities

Source: OECD Economic Outlook December 2002.

Public sector net debt in the UK has fallen from nearly 44 per cent of GDP in 1996-97 to around 32 per cent in 2003-04. Low and stable debt levels have allowed fiscal policy to support monetary policy in limiting the impact of recent global weakness on the UK economy without threatening the long-term sustainability of the public finances.

Projections for borrowing have also been revised in the light of the recent weakness in the global economy. The table below shows how the European Commission forecasts for the 2003 general government net lending have been revised since spring 2002.

Forecasts for general government net lending for 2003

Per cent of GDP	Date of forecast		Change
	Spring 2002	Spring 2003	
Italy	−1.3	−2.3	−1.0
France	−1.8	−3.7	−1.9
US	−0.9	−4.8	−3.9
Germany	−2.1	−3.4	−1.3
Japan	−6.1	−7.0	−0.9

Source: European Commission Forecasts Spring 2002 and Spring 2003.

ADHERING TO PRINCIPLES

2.49   Table 2.7 presents the key fiscal aggregates based on the five themes of fairness and prudence, long-term sustainability, economic impact, financing and European commitments. The table indicates that, after allowing for non-discretionary changes to receipts and spending and taking into account the Budget decisions, the Government remains on track to meet both fiscal rules.

Table 2.7: Summary of public sector finances

				Per cent of GDP			
	Outturn	Estimate[1]		Projections			
	2001-02	2002-03	2003-04	2004-05	2005-06	2006-07	2007-08
Fairness and prudence							
Surplus on current budget	1.0	−1.1	−0.8	−0.1	0.2	0.4	0.6
Average surplus since 1999-00	1.8	1.1	0.7	0.6	0.5	0.5	0.5
Cyclically-adjusted surplus on current budget	0.9	−0.5	0.2	0.5	0.4	0.4	0.6
Long-term sustainability							
Public sector net debt	30.2	30.9	32.2	32.7	33.2	33.5	33.8
Core debt	30.3	30.4	30.9	30.9	31.2	31.6	32.0
Public sector net worth[2]	26.2	22.9	21.7	20.0	18.5	18.0	17.0
Primary balance	1.8	−0.6	−0.8	−0.4	−0.3	−0.1	−0.1
Economic impact							
Public sector net investment	1.0	1.2	1.7	2.0	2.1	2.1	2.2
Public sector net borrowing (PSNB)	0.0	2.3	2.5	2.1	1.9	1.7	1.6
Cyclically-adjusted PSNB	0.1	1.7	1.5	1.5	1.7	1.7	1.6
Financing							
Central government net cash requirement	0.3	2.0	3.2	2.4	2.1	2.2	1.9
Public sector net cash requirement	0.3	2.1	2.9	2.3	1.9	2.0	1.7
European commitments							
Treaty deficit[3]	0.0	2.3	2.4	2.1	1.9	1.7	1.7
Cyclically-adjusted Treaty deficit	0.1	1.7	1.5	1.4	1.7	1.7	1.7
Treaty debt ratio[4]	37.9	38.0	39.0	39.4	39.6	39.9	40.1
Memo: Output gap	−0.2	−1.1	−1.4	−0.7	−0.1	0.0	0.0

[1] The 2002-03 figures were projections in Budget 2002 and PBR 2002.
[2] At end-December; GDP centred on end-December.
[3] General government net borrowing.
[4] General government gross debt.

Golden rule 2.50   The current budget is the difference between current receipts and current expenditure, including depreciation. It measures the degree to which current taxpayers meet the cost of paying for the public services they use and is therefore an important indicator of inter-generational fairness. Lower receipts and higher spending mean that the estimated outturn for 2002-03 is a current budget deficit of 1.1 per cent of GDP. The deficit is projected to fall to 0.8 per cent of GDP in 2003-04 before the current budget approaches balance in 2004-05. Strong surpluses on the current budget are projected by the end of the period.

2.51 The golden rule is set and assessed over the economic cycle. Chart 2.3 shows that the Government is comfortably on track to meet the golden rule. The average surplus on the current budget since 1999-2000, which is the Government's provisional judgement on the start of the current cycle, is comfortably positive throughout the forecast period by at least 0.5 per cent of GDP.

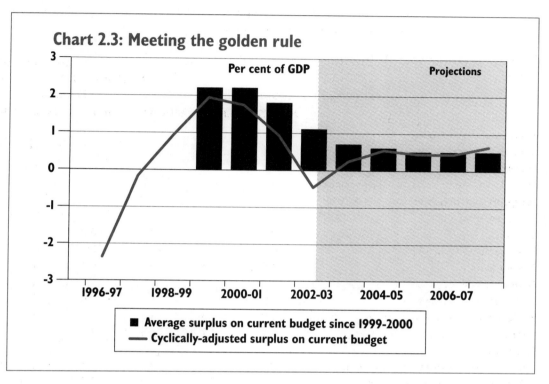

Chart 2.3: Meeting the golden rule

Sustainable investment rule **2.52** The Government's primary objective for fiscal policy is to ensure sound public finances in the medium term. This means maintaining public sector debt at a low and sustainable level. To meet the sustainable investment rule with confidence, net debt will be maintained below 40 per cent of GDP in each and every year of the current economic cycle.

2.53 Chart 2.4 shows that, despite sustained weakness in the world economy, net debt is expected to remain low and stable, rising slightly from 31 per cent to stabilise just under 34 per cent of GDP over the forecast period. This comfortably meets the sustainable investment rule by remaining well below 40 per cent.

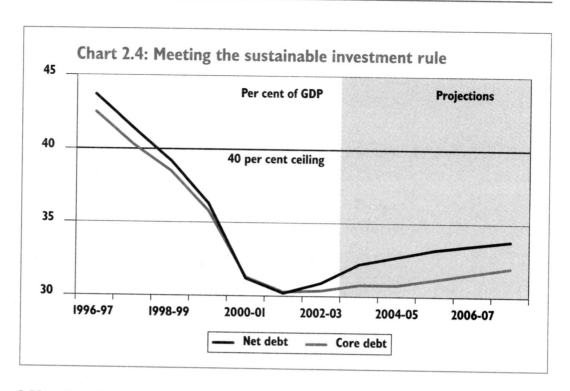

Chart 2.4: Meeting the sustainable investment rule

2.54   Sound public finances and greater economic stability have allowed the Government to increase investment in public services while maintaining a margin against unexpected economic events. Debt interest payments were around £7 billion lower in 2002-03 compared with 1996-97, freeing up resources to improve frontline public services. Public sector net investment, already planned to be around three times higher in 2003-04 than in 1997-98, is projected to rise still further to 2¼ per cent of GDP in 2007-08

2.55   Alongside net debt, Chart 2.3 also illustrates projected core debt which, excludes the estimated impact of the economic cycle on public sector net debt[4]. Underlying economic stability means that, in recent years, the levels of core debt and net debt have been very similar. Looking ahead, core debt is projected to rise slowly to 32 per cent of GDP, as a result of modest and prudent borrowing to fund increased long-term capital investment in public services. This is consistent with the fiscal rules, and with the principle of inter-generational fairness which underpins the fiscal framework.

2.56   Net worth, the difference between the total assets and liabilities of the Government, provides a further measure of fiscal sustainability, and is expected to decline gently over the projection period. At present net worth is not used as a key indicator, mainly because of the difficulties involved in measuring government assets and liabilities accurately.

Economic impact   2.57   While the primary objective of fiscal policy is to ensure sound public finances over the medium term, fiscal policy also plays an important role, supporting monetary policy in delivering economic stability over the cycle. The impact of fiscal policy on the economy can be assessed by examining changes in public sector net borrowing (PSNB), projections for which are set out in Chart 2.5.

---

[4] An explanation of the methodology was published alongside Budget 2002 in *Core debt: an approach to monitoring the sustainable investment rule*, HM Treasury, April 2002.

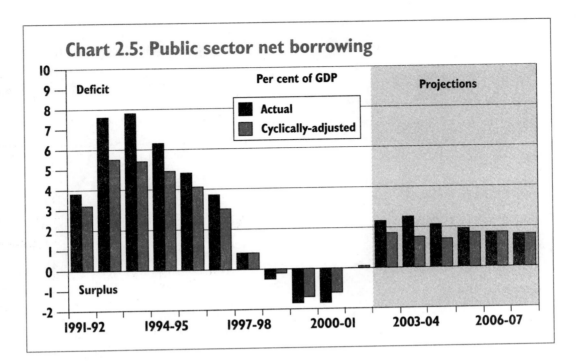

Chart 2.5: Public sector net borrowing

2.58   Modest levels of borrowing over the forecast period reflect sustained capital investment in priority public services. In addition to the operation of the automatic stabilisers over the short term, rising public spending, including investment, will support monetary policy as the economy remains below trend. Increased public investment is sustainable and fully consistent with the fiscal rules as net debt remains at a stable and prudent level over the forecast period.

2.59   The overall impact of fiscal policy on the economy is made up of changes in:

-    the fiscal stance – that part of the change in PSNB resulting from changes in cyclically-adjusted PSNB; and

-    the automatic stabilisers – that part of the change in PSNB resulting from cyclical movements in the economy.

2.60   Between Budgets, the fiscal stance can change as a result of a discretionary measure to:

-    achieve a desired change in the fiscal stance; or

-    accommodate or offset the impact of non-discretionary factors (non-cyclical or structural changes to tax receipts or public spending).

2.61   Table 2.8 explains how these concepts relate to the projections in the Budget. It shows the changes in both the fiscal stance and the overall fiscal impact between Budget 2002 and the 2002 Pre-Budget Report, and the changes since the Pre-Budget Report.

Table 2.8: The overall fiscal impact

	Outturn	Estimate[1]	Percentage points of GDP Projections				
	2001-02	2002-03	2003-04	2004-05	2005-06	2006-07	2007-08
Change from Budget 2002 to PBR 2002							
Post Budget and PBR policy decisions	0.0	0.1	−0.1	0.0	0.0	0.0	–
+							
non-discretionary factors	−0.1	0.2	0.3	0.2	0.1	0.1	–
=							
CHANGE IN FISCAL STANCE	−0.1	0.3	0.3	0.1	0.1	0.1	–
+							
automatic stabilisers	0.1	0.6	0.8	0.4	0.1	0.0	–
=							
OVERALL FISCAL IMPACT	0.0	0.9	1.1	0.5	0.2	0.1	–
Change from PBR 2002 to Budget 2003							
Budget measures	0.0	0.2	0.0	0.1	0.1	0.1	0.1
+							
non-discretionary factors	−0.1	0.3	0.1	0.1	0.1	0.1	0.0
=							
CHANGE IN FISCAL STANCE	−0.1	0.5	0.1	0.2	0.2	0.2	0.1
+							
automatic stabilisers	0.0	−0.1	0.1	0.2	0.1	0.0	0.0
=							
OVERALL FISCAL IMPACT	−0.2	0.3	0.2	0.4	0.3	0.2	0.1

[1] The 2002-03 figures were projections in Budget 2002 and PBR 2002.

2.62   Table 2.8 shows that, particularly in 2002-03 and 2003-04, fiscal policy is supporting monetary policy as the economy continues below trend. Over the medium term, the effect of the automatic stabilisers decreases as the economy returns to trend. However, the degree of caution in the assumptions underpinning the public finance projections increases over the projection period, and the actual outcomes and the effects on the economy may not necessarily reflect the projections, especially in later years.

2.63   GDP growth in 2002 was slightly higher than forecast at the time of the 2002 Pre-Budget Report and the output gap was consequently smaller. For 2002-03, the Treasury's methodology for cyclical adjustment therefore attributes less of the change in net borrowing between Budget 2002 and Budget 2003 to the automatic stabilisers. Nonetheless, fiscal policy supported monetary policy in maintaining macroeconomic stability in 2002-03.

Box 2.4: Monetary and fiscal policy in the G7 economies

During 2001 growth slowed significantly and simultaneously in the US, Europe and Asia for the first time for almost thirty years and the world's three largest economies – the US, Germany and Japan – were all in recession. For the US and the Euro-area the slowdown bought to an end a period of continuous growth stretching back to the beginning of 1993. While growth slowed in the UK, it continued and the UK has now experienced the longest unbroken economic expansion since quarterly records began.

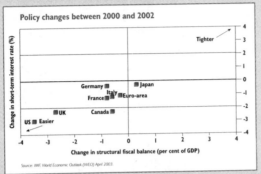
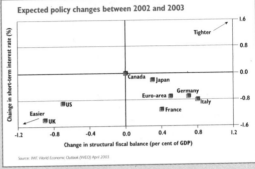

In recent years, decisive action by policy-makers, particularly in the aftermath of the events of 11 September 2001, has prevented a more severe global slowdown. The charts show that, between 2000 and 2002, all of the G7 economies except Japan benefited from a coordinated easing of monetary and fiscal policy. It also highlights that the scale of the easing was more significant in the US and the UK.

The charts also show that, against a backdrop of continued global uncertainty, monetary and fiscal policy is expected to continue supporting growth in the US and the UK during 2003. By contrast, a further expected easing of monetary policy within the Euro-area is expected to be partially offset by planned fiscal tightening in some countries.

Financing 2.64 The provisional Debt Management Report 2003-04 (DMR) was published on 20 March 2003 in advance of the Budget and in compliance with the *Code for fiscal stability*. It included a provisional financing remit for 2003-04. The forecast for the financing requirement was based on the 2002 Pre-Budget Report projection for the central government net cash requirement (CGNCR) in 2003-04. In the DMR, it was announced that a provisional net financing requirement of £49.8 billion for 2003-04 would be met by gross gilts issuance of £40.0 billion and a £9.8 billion adjustment in the net short-term debt position.

2.65 The Budget forecast for the CGNCR for 2002-03 is £21.4 billion, £2.7 billion higher than forecast at the time of the 2002 Pre-Budget Report. The forecast for the CGNCR in 2003-04 is £35.3 billion. This means that the net financing requirement, which includes £21.1 billion of redemptions, is now £54.8 billion. In line with the contingencies outlined in the DMR, these changes have been accommodated by increasing gross gilts issuance by £7.4 billion to £47.4 billion and decreasing the unwind of the Debt Management Office's net cash position by £2.4 billion to £4.2 billion. The difference between CGNCR and PSNB in 2003-04 is partly the result of cash and accrual implications of the NICs measures announced in Budget 2002, which increase accrued receipts by more than cash receipts – reducing PSNB by more than CGNCR. Full details and a revised financing table can be found in Chapter C of the *Financial Statement and Budget Report*.

European
commitments

2.66   The Budget 2003 projections meet both the EU Treaty reference values for general government gross debt (60 per cent of GDP) and general government net borrowing (3 per cent of GDP) throughout the projection period. The projections are consistent with the Government's prudent interpretation of the Stability and Growth Pact, described in Box 2.4.

Box 2.4: The Stability and Growth Pact

The Stability and Growth Pact is intended to ensure that EU Member States maintain sound public finances through the budgetary objective of 'close to balance or in surplus' over the medium term. Fiscal sustainability is a prerequisite for macroeconomic stability, and the Government agrees with the principle of a strong Pact founded on sensible fiscal policy coordination as set out in the EU Treaty.

Building on the Code of Conduct, agreed by Member States in June 2001, the Government supports a prudent interpretation of the Pact. A prudent interpretation would lock in long-term fiscal discipline and sustainability, enhancing credibility, while allowing the automatic stabilisers to smooth fluctuations in output, and allow appropriate increases in investment in public services. Specifically, it would take into account the following factors:

- **the economic cycle** – by allowing the automatic stabilisers to operate fully and symmetrically over the cycle, fiscal policy can support monetary policy in smoothing the path of the economy. It is therefore important to focus on cyclically-adjusted fiscal balances when assessing the public finances;

- **sustainability** – low debt levels enhance the sustainability of the public finances, allowing greater room for the automatic stabilisers to operate, and providing a sound basis for investment in public services. Assessment of the sustainability of public finances should also take into account the long-term budgetary impact of ageing populations, such as that set out in Annex A and in the Government's *Long-term public finance report*, published alongside the 2002 Pre-Budget Report; and

- **public investment** – against a background of sound public finances and economic stability, public investment contributes to the provision of high-quality public services and can help to underpin a flexible, high productivity economy. The 2002 Spending Review set new plans to increase public sector net investment in the UK to 2 per cent of GDP by 2005-06 – a five-fold increase compared with 1997-98 – and the projections in this Budget assume a further increase to $2\frac{1}{4}$ per cent of GDP by 2007-08. These plans are fully consistent with the fiscal rules and with the maintenance of low levels of debt.

In March 2003, the European Council fully endorsed a report agreed by EU Finance Ministers on strengthening budgetary co-ordination. The report emphasised the importance of taking into account the economic cycle, long-term sustainability, and the quality of public investment in assessing the state of public finances. It also stressed the need to apply a country-by-country approach to assessments of compliance with the medium-term fiscal objective of 'close to balance or in surplus'. This is in line with key aspects of the Government's prudent interpretation of the Stability and Growth Pact.

Dealing with uncertainty 2.67 The fiscal balances represent the difference between two large aggregates and forecasts of them are subject to wide margins of error. The use of cautious assumptions, audited by the Comptroller and Auditor General, builds an allowance into the public finances projections to guard against unexpected events. To accommodate potential errors arising from misjudgements about the trend rate of growth in the economy, the Government bases its public finance projections on a trend growth assumption that is $\frac{1}{4}$ percentage point lower than its neutral view.

2.68 A second important source of potential error results from misjudging the position of the economy in relation to this trend. To minimise this risk, the robustness of the projections are tested against an alternative scenario in which the level of trend output is assumed to be one percentage point lower than in the central case. Chart 2.6 illustrates the forecast in this 'cautious case'.

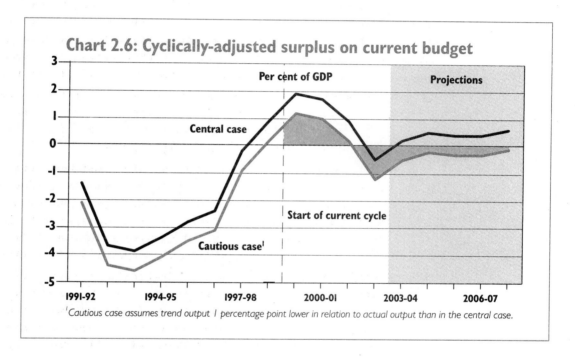

Chart 2.6: Cyclically-adjusted surplus on current budget

Cautious case assumes trend output 1 percentage point lower in relation to actual output than in the central case.

2.69 The chart shows that the cyclically-adjusted current budget in the cautious case was in strong surplus in 1999-2000, which on the Government's provisional judgement is the start of the current economic cycle, and in 2000-01. It is projected to move into deficit before returning towards balance by the end of the forecast period. The average cyclically-adjusted current budget is in surplus in the cautious case over the current economic cycle, meeting the 'stress test' of the golden rule. The Government is therefore on track to meet the golden rule over the economic cycle, including in the cautious case.

Long-term fiscal sustainability

2.70 While a key objective of fiscal policy is to ensure sound public finances over the medium term, the Government must also ensure that fiscal policy decisions are sustainable in the long term. Failure to do so would see financial burdens shifted to future generations with detrimental effects on long-term growth. This would also be inconsistent with the principles of fiscal management set out in the *Code for fiscal stability*.

2.71   An analysis of long-term fiscal sustainability is presented in Annex A. The analysis shows that, based on current policies, current consumption – spending on items such as health and education – can grow at a slightly faster rate than real GDP over the next 30 years, ensuring that resources are available to meet potential future spending pressures, such as those arising from an ageing population, while still meeting the fiscal rules. Public sector net investment can also grow broadly in line with the economy without jeopardising the sustainable investment rule.

2.72   This conclusion concurs with the detailed findings of the *Long-term public finance report*[5], published alongside the 2002 Pre-Budget Report. The Government will continue to update and report on its assessment of long-term fiscal sustainability in future Budgets and through regular publication of the *Long-term public finance report*.

MACROECONOMIC STABILITY AND THE HOUSING MARKET

2.73   Strong cycles in the housing market have been a striking feature of the UK economy over the past three decades. This volatility has affected the wider economy through private consumption, as household spending is closely linked to changes in housing wealth. Reducing volatility in the housing market will therefore promote macroeconomic stability.

2.74   A number of structural features explain high levels of housing market volatility in the UK compared to other European countries, and the strong link to consumption:

- the responsiveness of housing supply to demand pressures is particularly low in the UK. Since 1960, the UK has invested a lower proportion of its national income in housing than any other EU country. A weak supply response is largely responsible for the strong upward trend in real house prices in the UK and tends to accentuate house price volatility;

- the high level of mortgage debt and dominance of variable rate mortgages combine to explain households' interest rate sensitivity and the strong link between the housing market and consumption in the UK; and

- high levels of owner occupation, as compared to private or social renting, and the ability of households to withdraw equity from housing adds to the impact of changes in housing wealth on consumption.

2.75   The effect the housing market has on macroeconomic stability could be much more significant should the UK join EMU. The housing market forms an important part of the monetary transmission mechanism – the means by which interest rates affect the wider economy. This is the subject of a supporting study to the assessment of the five economic tests.

---

[5] *Long-term public finance report: an analysis of fiscal sustainability*, HM Treasury, November 2002.

2.76   The Government has recognised that reforms are needed to help increase the supply of housing, particularly affordable housing, and reduce volatility and promote stability in the wider economy. Reforms already announced include:

- the Deputy Prime Minister's proposals for significant development in four growth areas in the South-East, new regional housing bodies to better coordinate funding at the regional level and action in areas facing a surplus of housing, all backed by an additional £1.1 billion a year by 2005-06 to support a substantial increase in affordable housing; and

- making the planning system work more quickly, predictably and effectively by speeding-up the processing of applications, a commitment for local authorities to deliver planned increases in housing numbers, with intervention if necessary, committing to build at higher densities than the past, statutory timetables for called-in applications and £350 million extra for planning authorities over the next 3 years.

2.77   The weak responsiveness of new housing supply to rising house prices is a complex problem. In the light of its reforms to the planning system, the Government has therefore asked Kate Barker to conduct a review of issues affecting housing supply in the UK – in particular to look at the role of competition, capacity and finance of the house-building industry, and possible fiscal instruments, and the interaction of these factors with the planning system and sustainable development objectives. This review would complement the work of the Sustainable Home Ownership Taskforce announced by the Deputy Prime Minister on 18 March this year.

2.78   Building on the reforms already announced to deliver a step change in planning policy, further significant changes in the planning, supply and finance of housing will be required to address both demand and supply in the housing market to tackle market failures, significantly increase the responsiveness of supply to demand, and reduce national and regional price volatility. This includes requiring new Regional Spatial Strategies to take account of volatility in the housing market and promote macro-economic stability as part of delivering sustainable development; tough and credible measures, including intervention, where local authorities are not delivering housing numbers in high demand areas; and exploring whether, in the medium term, achieving our objectives will require a system of binding local plans. The Government's proposals are outlined in more detail in Chapter 3.

2.79   The share of variable rate mortgages in the UK is markedly higher than in many other countries. The Chancellor has asked Professor David Miles to undertake a review of the supply and demand side factors limiting the development of the fixed rate mortgage market in the UK. The review will establish why the share of fixed-rate mortgages is so low compared to the United States and many other EU countries, and examine whether there has been any market failure that has held back the market for fixed and long-term fixed-rate mortgages. It will make an interim report in autumn 2003 before reporting in full by Budget 2004.

3 MEETING THE PRODUCTIVITY CHALLENGE

Productivity growth underpins strong economic performance and sustained increases in living standards. The Government's long-term goal is that Britain will achieve a faster rate of productivity growth than its main competitors. In the modern global economy, faster productivity growth demands new flexibility in product, capital and labour markets, with government, firms and individuals able to respond quickly and adapt rapidly to change. Were the UK to join EMU, flexibility would be even more important to ensure that economic shocks could be managed and economic strength maintained. Building on reforms to the competition regime and the support for businesses already introduced, Budget 2003 sets out the further steps the Government is taking to strengthen the drivers of productivity growth, including:

- **new proposals to promote greater flexibility in the housing market, and to streamline and simplify the planning regime;**

- **a package of reforms to improve access to finance for small businesses,** including consultation on the scope for introducing Small Business Investment Companies in the UK;

- **improvements to research and development (R&D) tax credits** to enable more businesses to claim a wider range of relief, and consultation on the definition of R&D to ensure the credits remain competitive internationally;

- **deregulatory reforms to ease the regulatory burden,** especially on small businesses;

- **additional measures to improve skills in the UK,** including the launch of six new Employer Training Pilots and a new package of training support for small businesses;

- **further improvements to the Highly Skilled Migrants Programme** and other migration schemes to make the UK migration system a more effective source of highly skilled labour for the UK economy;

- **£16 million over two years to fund Enterprise Advisers** to work alongside head teachers in around 1,000 secondary schools in deprived areas, ensuring that pupils in these areas gain a better knowledge of business and enterprise;

- **an extension of 100 per cent first year capital allowances** for small businesses investing in information and communication technology for one further year; and

- **further steps to support a modern and competitive tax system,** with reforms to VAT for small business, simplification of employee share schemes, and abolition of Petroleum Revenue Tax on all new third party tariffing business.

PRODUCTIVITY IN A FLEXIBLE ECONOMY

3.1   Productivity growth, alongside high and stable levels of employment, is central to long-term economic performance and rising living standards. The UK has historically experienced low rates of productivity growth by international standards, as macroeconomic instability and market failures restricted competition, enterprise and innovation, and discouraged long-term investment in capital and skills. The Government's goal is to raise the sustainable rate of UK productivity growth through greater flexibility in product, capital and labour markets.

Box 3.1: The productivity challenge

Productivity is a measure of how effectively an economy uses resources to generate outputs. The Government's central measure of productivity is output per worker, a measure that is both relatively straightforward to quantify and is directly related to the Government's objective of raising the economy's trend rate of growth.

Latest estimates show that, on this measure, US productivity is 31 per cent higher than in the UK, and that productivity in France and Germany is 16 per cent and 4 per cent higher respectively. Measured in terms of output per hour, the gap with the US narrows to 26 per cent, while that with France and Germany widens to 33 per cent and 25 per cent respectively. The difference between the per worker and per hour measures of productivity partly reflects the fewer hours worked and longer holiday entitlements in France and Germany[1]. However, lower participation rates also explain the gap between living standards in Europe and the US. While employment rates in the UK are similar to those in the US (71 per cent and 73 per cent respectively in 2001), they are substantially lower in both France (62 per cent) and Germany (66 per cent)[2].

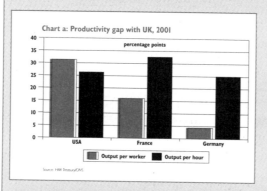

Chart a: Productivity gap with UK, 2001

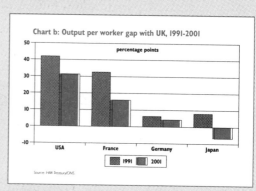

Chart b: Output per worker gap with UK, 1991-2001

Raising productivity growth is a long-term challenge, and so it is important to consider international trends over time. Chart (b) illustrates how the UK has performed over the last decade in comparison with other major economies. The gap relative to France, Germany and the US has narrowed, but Japan now has a productivity gap of 7 per cent with the UK.

International comparisons of productivity are very sensitive to statistical revision. Following Census 2001, the Treasury has estimated (as shown in the charts above) the impact of the latest ONS population estimates on the output per worker figures. Recent revisions to GDP figures and to Purchasing Power Parities have also led to a reduction in the estimated productivity gap with the G7. These indicate that the UK's productivity gap with the US is 7 per cent lower than estimated in the Pre-Budget Report, while the gap with Germany is 5 per cent lower and that with France 1 per cent higher.

[1] OECD figures show that average annual hours worked by people in employment in 2001 were 1,821 in the US, 1,711 in the UK, 1,532 in France and 1,467 in Germany.
[2] Figures are taken from the 2002 OECD Employment Outlook.

3.2 The Government is pursuing a wide-ranging strategy to tackle the barriers to productivity growth. This strategy involves maintaining macroeconomic stability to help businesses, individuals and the Government plan effectively for the long term, and implementing microeconomic reforms to remove the barriers that prevent markets from functioning efficiently.

Productivity and flexibility

3.3 In the modern global economy, faster productivity growth demands new flexibility in product, capital and labour markets. With global markets for business, investment and skills, it is important that governments, individuals and firms are able to respond quickly and adapt rapidly to change. Failure to do so risks an unproductive use of resources, with long-term costs to growth, employment and prosperity.

3.4 Flexible product markets help firms respond effectively to economic shocks and take advantage of competitive opportunities, ensuring high levels of output and maintaining employment. The Government is committed to sharpening the UK's competitive business environment and improving opportunities for entrepreneurship. Flexible capital markets play an important role in ensuring an efficient allocation of capital for investment, supplying capital for new business opportunities and helping to stabilise the economy in response to shocks – roles that would be increasingly important were the UK to join the single currency. The Government is further strengthening the flexibility of capital markets through its actions to modernise financial regulation and to improve financing options for investment and new business.

3.5 Were the UK to join EMU, these flexibilities would be even more essential, as the ability to adjust interest rates and exchange rates would no longer be available at a national level. In such circumstances, the labour, product and capital markets would need to respond dynamically so as to enhance the economy's resilience to shocks without putting at risk high and stable levels of growth and employment. A sufficient level of wage flexibility is vital to eliminate imbalances between supply and demand; relative price adjustments are a particularly important adjustment mechanism to allow changes in competitiveness between countries; and a flexible and integrated capital market can provide the financial instruments that help consumers and firms stabilise their consumption following a shock. The importance of flexibility in the UK and in the EU is considered further in the preliminary and technical work that underpins the assessment of the five economic tests.

3.6 The Government's programme of microeconomic reform seeks to address this challenge, improving the flexibility of markets and equipping people to master change. It focuses on historic weaknesses in five key drivers of productivity performance:

- enhancing **competition** to improve flexibility in product and capital markets and promote greater business efficiency and consumer choice;

- promoting **enterprise** by removing the market barriers that deter enterpreneurship and prevent new firms from developing and growing;

- supporting **science and innovation** to harness the potential of new technologies and to promote more efficient ways of working;

- improving **skills** among young people and the adult workforce to generate a flexible and dynamic labour market; and

- encouraging **investment** and better investment decision-making through stronger local and national capital markets.

3.7 In addition to the range of measures set out in Chapter 4 to promote a flexible and more dynamic labour market, this chapter describes the Government's work to strengthen product and capital markets and to improve levels of skills throughout the workforce.

Working with the CBI and TUC

3.8 While government has a key role to play in supporting productivity growth, it must work together with employers, employees and trades unions to close the productivity gap. The CBI and TUC have continued to work closely with the Government in identifying practical steps on a range of issues, and the Government has taken significant steps to implement their recommendations, including through support to address basic and intermediate skills shortages and to improve the UK's innovation performance. Following further joint working in recent months, Budget 2003 includes further measures to increase access to finance and training for small and medium-sized enterprises (SMEs), improve the operation of research and development (R&D) tax credits, and extend the current round of Employer Training Pilots.

3.9   Looking forward, the Government will continue to work with the CBI and TUC to promote productivity growth through policies designed to:

- improve the environment for business investment and promote venture capital investment throughout the UK;

- support small and growing business and an entrepreneurial culture, especially in areas of high unemployment;

- stimulate innovation and R&D across the economy;

- increase flexibility in the economy, by tackling regulation and helping the labour market to respond more quickly;

- develop a longer-term view of government procurement; and

- raise skills levels, through further evaluation of Employer Training Pilots and enhanced Modern Apprenticeships.

Productivity and flexibility in the regions   3.10   To ensure that the benefits of improved productivity are spread throughout the country, measures to raise productivity growth and promote flexible markets should also be focused at the regional or sub-regional level. The Regional Development Agencies (RDAs) are the strategic leaders of economic development and regeneration in the regions, and have an important role to play in implementing the Government's productivity strategy. To benefit from their regional perspective, the Treasury asked the Agencies to provide advice on policy relating to enterprise, innovation, regulatory reform and skills, in preparation for this Budget. Among issues raised by the RDAs were proposals to promote entrepreneurship in schools, improve opportunities for SMEs in public sector procurement, work with the Government to consider how the regulatory burden on small firms can be minimised, and create flexibility at a regional level to meet employers' skills needs. Budget 2003 announces further measures which respond to the issues raised. The Treasury will discuss with the RDAs how to further enhance their input into future Budgets.

3.11   As announced in the 2002 Spending Review, pilots in selected regions are currently providing the RDAs with a wider leadership and management role in driving forward economic development and increasing flexibility in regional markets. The pilots, which will last for two years, involve two RDAs in the management and coordination of business support services at the regional level and three RDAs in the management of regional funding for post-19 training. The North West Development Agency is conducting a joint pilot of both activities.

European economic reform   3.12   Faster productivity growth in the UK depends on economic reform in Europe, as well as at home. A more flexible, dynamic and open Europe will increase employment, fairness and growth, and will promote and facilitate the UK's efforts to boost its own productivity and economic performance. While the EU has made progress in delivering reform[1], there is much more to do. EU enlargement, monetary union, global economic uncertainty, and an ageing and contracting workforce all demand renewed effort to deliver stronger and more flexible EU markets. The Government's priorities on the European reform agenda include:

---

[1] Set out in *Meeting Europe's potential: economic reform in Europe*, HM Treasury, February 2002, and *Meeting the challenge: economic reform in Europe*, HM Treasury, February 2003.

- the development of modern social policies that promote skills, employment and labour market flexibility;

- better implementation and enforcement of improved regulation;

- a stronger and more effective competition policy that proactively seeks to raise competition rather than just react to cases;

- a modernised state aids regime and regional policy; and

- work to deliver a single market for services, including progress on the Financial Services Action Plan.

3.13   Achieving the goal of higher productivity and employment requires each EU country and region to realise its full potential. In most cases, decision-making and delivery should be devolved and decentralised as far as possible, while maintaining clear accountability and coordination. The EU must support this, for example, by ensuring that the state aids rules and their implementation support economic growth at the national and regional level.

3.14   The momentum of reform must be increased to generate a more efficient allocation of resources across Member States and regions, and to ensure that increased prosperity is delivered across an enlarged EU. On regional policy, the Government believes these goals could best be achieved through its proposed EU Framework for Devolved Regional Policy[2], and is currently consulting on whether this should form the basis for a UK position in the debate on the future of Structural and Cohesion Funds.

3.15   Efforts to improve the flexibility of product and capital markets should not stop at the EU's borders. A more flexible and dynamic Europe will be better placed to contribute to the strength and resilience of the global economy, and could play a greater role in breaking down barriers to trade and investment in the rest of the world. The EU must make every effort to ensure that trade negotiations, in the context of the World Trade Organisation Doha Development Agenda, are completed to schedule by 2005. Further work is also needed to deepen the world's largest bilateral trade and investment relationship – that between the EU and US. Strengthening the transatlantic alliance, by further liberalising trade in goods and services, would do much to benefit consumers in both Europe and the US.

Public services productivity   **3.16**   As well as creating the right environment for improved productivity in the private sector, the Government is also striving for greater efficiency in the public sector. The performance of the public sector is a major determinant of the productivity of the economy as a whole. Strong health and education systems and an integrated transport network lay the foundations for an enterprising and high productivity economy, by producing a healthier, better skilled and more mobile labour force. The Government's approach to public service reform is described in Chapter 6, and in *Public Services: meeting the productivity challenge*, published alongside the Budget.

COMPETITION

3.17   Competition is central to the creation of flexible product and capital markets, and is an important driver of productivity performance. Competitive markets provide incentives for firms to respond quickly to changes in technology and costs, to adopt more efficient ways of working, and to develop new products and services that meet the demands of consumers. This is essential if businesses are to take full advantage of the opportunities offered by the European Single Market and by free and open trade.

---

[2] *A modern regional policy for the United Kingdon*, HM Treasury, Department of Trade and Industry and Office of the Deputy Prime Minister, March 2003.

The competition regime

3.18 The Government has taken significant steps to ensure that the UK competition regime ranks among the best in the world. Over the next six months, implementation of the Enterprise Act will further strengthen the competition regime by giving full independence to the UK competition authorities, creating a new proactive role for the Office of Fair Trading (OFT), and allowing criminal sanctions to be imposed on those engaging in hard core cartels. The OFT has now appointed its Board and is currently consulting on how best to run its mergers investigation regime.

Consumers **3.19** Following radical improvements to the UK competition regime, the challenge now is to develop an equally effective consumer regime that empowers and protects consumers, boosting competition and enhancing productivity. Consumer protection enforcement has been strengthened by the introduction of Stop Now Orders in 2001 and, from June 2003, their extension in the Enterprise Act. From summer 2004, the rollout of *Consumer Direct*, a new nationwide telephone and internet advice service, will further empower consumers.

3.20 A major international study to benchmark the domestic consumer regime in relation to the UK's main competitors is now reaching its completion, and the Department of Trade and Industry (DTI) intends to publish its findings in the summer. Following this study, the DTI will review, jointly with stakeholders, the objectives of the consumer regime, and how these are delivered through the existing statutory framework, consumer education and information, redress mechanisms and enforcement. The Government's goal is to ensure that the UK has one of the best consumer and competition regimes in the world by 2006.

Promoting competition in specific markets

3.21 The OFT is successfully promoting competition in specific markets. Four market studies – on pharmacies, private dentistry, consumer IT services and extended warranties for electrical goods – have already been completed. Further studies on taxi services, estate agents and doorstep selling are ongoing. The studies on private dentistry and doorstep selling were both launched in response to super-complaints by consumer organisations.

Pharmacies **3.22** The OFT report on pharmacy entry licensing was published in January 2003. The report recommended that regulations currently controlling entry to the pharmacy market should be lifted to increase competition. The Government welcomes the OFT's analysis and agrees that the present regime governing the pharmacy market should be updated. As the OFT noted in their report, a more competitive environment might necessitate additional targeted measures to ensure that patients in all areas are able to access essential pharmacy services. In formulating its response to the OFT's report, the Government will therefore aim to develop a balanced package of measures to promote competition, new entry into the market and increased choice for consumers, alongside support for wider social and health policy objectives. Proposals for reform of the pharmacy market will be developed before the summer recess, and a report on progress will be published at the end of June All subsequent changes will be subject to full consultation.

The professions **3.23** Following the OFT's report on competition in the professions, the Government remains determined to remove all restrictions, where these do not clearly benefit the consumer or the public, on providing legal services, and to improve the regulatory framework. The Government will announce shortly its conclusions on opening up the probate and conveyancing markets and on allowing new business structures such as multi-disciplinary partnerships. The Government will announce shortly details of the review of what currently appears to be an outmoded, over-complex and in some ways ineffective regulatory framework. In addition, the Lord Chancellor has announced that he intends to consult no later than the end of July on whether the status of QC should continue to exist and if so the method of appointment.

Private dentistry   3.24   The Government welcomes the OFT's report on private dentistry. The report highlights the lack of information provided to consumers, including insufficient price transparency. It also found a lack of compliance with professional guidance and inadequate complaints procedures, and identified a need for better and more effective self-regulation and regulatory restrictions on the supply of dental services.

Payment systems   3.25   The Government looks forward to seeing the findings of the OFT's ongoing study of recent payment system developments, and will introduce legislation to give the OFT new powers to promote effective competition in payment systems as soon as parliamentary time allows.

Energy   3.26   The Energy White Paper, published in February 2003, set out a long-term strategic vision to deliver environmental, social, economic and reliability of supply goals. Liberalised, competitive energy markets are key to the implementation of the Government's strategy. Liberalisation has already delivered lower gas and electricity prices, and increased competition has reduced the need for regulation, with price controls removed from domestic gas and electricity supply in April 2002. The Government is now extending the New Electricity Trading Arrangements to the Scottish market, to create a wholesale electricity market across Britain. British Electricity Trading and Transmission Arrangements, which will be implemented by April 2005, will ensure that Scottish customers receive the benefits of a competitive market aligned with that elsewhere in Britain, while helping independent generators to get their power to market.

Box 3.2: Strengthening EU product markets

Deepening the Single Market promotes product market flexibility by removing barriers to trade, increasing competition and expanding the variety of goods and services on offer. However, further action is needed to strengthen EU product and service markets so as to deliver greater flexibility and dynamism to businesses and consumers. In a single currency, flexible product markets are vital to ensure that the economy is responsive and that shocks do not have lasting effects. The Government's priorities include:

- a more proactive European competition regime, with investigation of markets which may not be working properly and in which the full benefits of competition may not be felt by consumers;

- steps towards more rigorous assessment of EU regulation and a lighter touch approach to new legislation, especially as it affects small firms. The Government will press for an assessment by the European Commission of the impact of regulation on competition and small businesses;

- modernisation and simplification of the state aids regime to ensure that procedures are streamlined, market failures constraining productivity and employment are tackled effectively, and that the Commission and Member States focus their attention on the most significant state aids;

- measures to provide framework conditions more conducive to business investment in R&D, including high levels of competition and an effective intellectual property regime. The Government will also press for implementation as soon as possible, in a business-friendly manner, of the recently agreed Community Patent; and

- the development of a regional policy which generates a more efficient distribution of resources across Member States and regions. The Government believes that this can best be achieved through its proposed EU Framework for Devolved Regional Policy, and is consulting on whether this should form the basis of a UK position in the debate on the future of Structural and Cohesion Funds.

Water **3.27** Legislation to extend competition for non-household consumers using large quantities of water was introduced in February 2003. The Government expects further opportunities for competition to increase choice, promote efficiency and improve services.

Regulatory reform

3.28 Effective and well-focused regulation can play a vital role in correcting market failure, promoting fairness and ensuring public safety. However, unnecessary or poorly implemented regulation can be an obstacle to flexibility, restricting competitiveness and employment growth, stifling innovation and deterring investment.

Reducing regulatory burdens **3.29** The Government is taking forward a set of reforms to reduce the overall burden of regulation on business and the public sector:

- more than 500 specific deregulatory measures have been identified since February 2002, of which over a quarter have already been implemented. In future, departments will be held accountable for their performance on deregulation through annual reporting, and their performance will be taken into account in the next spending round;

- more business secondees will be brought into the Government's Regulatory Impact Unit to examine regulatory burdens on the construction, transport and environmental service sectors, and to propose measures to reduce them; and

- the Construction Industry Scheme will be reformed in April 2005 to reduce the regulatory burden on construction.

Small business regulation **3.30** Over 99 per cent of all UK businesses are SMEs, generating more than 12 million jobs. While such firms are often hit harder by regulation than larger firms, well-targeted exemptions can ease their regulatory burden and, alongside specific tax measures, help to break down the barriers to business success.

3.31 The Small Business Service (SBS) recently published a comprehensive new guide[3] to help entrepreneurs understand the regulations which apply to them and the range of government services available to help them. Budget 2003 builds on this support with a package of deregulatory reforms to ease burdens on SMEs, including raising the company law definitions of small- and medium-sized companies to the maximum possible under EU regulations. Legislation to establish the new definitions will be introduced as soon as the new EU maxima come into force[4]. As a result of this:

- all firms falling under the revised small company threshold will become subject to the existing less onerous accounting and reporting regime. The Government has also already announced its intention to introduce a simpler accounting regime for small companies in the *Modernising Company Law* White Paper;

- firms falling under the revised medium-sized company threshold will be eligible for the 40 per cent plant and machinery allowance; and

- firms also falling under the revised small company threshold will be eligible for the 100 per cent information and communication technology (ICT) allowance until it expires on 31 March 2004.

---

[3] *The no-nonsense guide to Government rules and regulations for setting up your business*, Small Business Service, March 2003.
[4] The current EU maximum threshold for small businesses is £4.8 million turnover and £2.4 million balance sheet total. This compares with current UK company law thresholds of £2.8 million and £1.4 million respectively. For medium-sized companies, the equivalent EU maximum figures are £19.6 million and £9.8 million, and under current UK company law are £11.2 million and £5.6 million.

3.32   The Government is currently reviewing the impact of the last increase in the statutory audit threshold, from £350,000 to £1 million, that benefited a further 150,000 companies, and will be consulting in summer 2003 on the potential for further increases in the audit threshold, with a decision in time for the 2003 Pre-Budget Report. In addition, the National Statistician is taking further steps to minimise the survey compliance burden on businesses, in particular through rationalisation of surveys, wider use of administrative data and greater use of new technology in data collection. To strengthen firms' input into this process and to ensure the most efficient use of data collected, the Office for National Statistics (ONS) will establish a Small Business Forum. The Information Commissioner will also produce revised and simplified guidance on the Data Protection Act – including material specifically tailored for small businesses – by the end of May.

Improving enforcement   3.33   The Government is currently consulting[5] on how to improve and monitor the performance of local enforcement bodies. The Regulatory Reform Act provides the Government with a reserve power to set out statutory codes of practice in enforcement, and the Government stands ready to exercise this power should some continue to use over-zealous means of enforcement in contravention of the Enforcement Concordat.

Improving regulatory procedures   3.34   The Government has also taken steps to improve the quality and flow of regulation within the UK and the EU. New guidance requires policy makers in the UK to consider the regulatory impact of new initiatives, particularly on small businesses, and to give consideration to alternatives. The competition authorities have also been given new powers to challenge anti-competitive regulations and to increase their scrutiny of new and existing regulation, and the OFT has already provided competition advice to the Government on more than 100 proposed regulations. As described in Chapter 4, the Government has also adopted a set of twelve principles for intervention in the labour market.

3.35   Around 40 per cent of new legislation with a non-negligible impact on UK business originates in the EU. The Government believes that rigorous assessment of European regulation is essential and welcomes new EU assessment procedures currently being phased in, with 42 proposals to be subject to review this year. The Government will push for further improvements, including that assessments at European level should include review of the impact on small businesses and competition, and will press the Commission to adopt a lighter touch approach to legislation which affects small firms.

Public sector procurement   3.36   In the 2002 Pre-Budget Report, the Government welcomed the Competition Commission's recommendations[7] to improve competition in procurement, and announced that the Office of Government Commerce (OGC) would consider steps to increase competition, and thereby value for money; and to encourage better long-term capacity planning, in markets where the Government possesses significant purchasing power. The OGC will be supported by a working group comprising the DTI, the SBS and the Treasury, and will report to ministers in the summer.

3.37   The OGC is also taking further steps to enable SMEs to compete for government contracts and deliver value for money. It has launched an internet portal[6] to advise SMEs on access to government procurement, and has simplified the financial appraisal of suppliers to make it easier for SMEs to bid. In addition, the Better Regulation Task Force's report on reducing the barriers to SMEs in doing business with the public sector, will be published during May, and will propose further important steps including:

---

[5] *Enforcement Concordat: Good practice guide for England and Wales*, Department of Trade and Industry, March 2002.

[6] www.supplyinggovernment.gov.uk

[7] *Group 4 Falck A/S and the Wackenhut Corporation: A report on the merger situation*, Competition Commission, October 2002.

- improving advice for SMEs to enable them to access public sector markets;

- working towards standard pre-qualification procurement documentation for lower value contracts across central and local government; and

- research by the OFT into markets where SMEs can have an important impact on competition, innovation and value for money in public procurement.

3.38   Where appropriate, the Government will ask the OGC, the SBS and the Local Government Procurement Forum to act on these recommendations.

ENTERPRISE

3.39   *Enterprise Britain*[8], published alongside the 2002 Pre-Budget Report, described the role of enterprise in delivering growth and flexibility in a modern economy. Ambitious, enterprising businesses drive competition, support flexible and adaptable markets, and help to support sustainable regeneration and neighbourhood renewal in disadvantaged communities. However, rates of entrepreneurial activity in Europe are typically only half the levels in the US, and variations in start-up rates between regions are even greater.

Creating an enterprise society

Enterprise and education   **3.40**   There is strong evidence to suggest that cultural and social constraints inhibit enterprise activity in the UK. The Government shares the conclusion of Sir Howard Davies' review of enterprise and education, that efforts to build a deeper and wider entrepreneurial culture must begin in schools, and is now introducing a series of measures, including:

- £16 million over two years to fund Enterprise Advisers to work alongside headteachers in around 1,000 secondary schools in deprived areas to encourage enterprise practice among teachers and pupils. These advisers will be funded from existing Learning and Skills Council resources and accessed through the network of Education Business Links Consortia;

- pilots to investigate how best to provide pupils with five days of enterprise experience in their school career. The pilots will begin in 2003 and cover around 250 secondary schools, including a number of schools in Enterprise Areas. Rigorous evaluation of these pilots will inform a national roll-out from 2005-06; and

- the establishment of a new £1 million Enterprise Promotion Fund, to support private and voluntary sector creativity in promoting enterprise awareness across schools, business and the wider non-business community. The Fund will offer resources to projects meeting specific enterprise objectives and demonstrating significant private sector support.

3.41   More people between the age of 16 and 25 years consider starting up in business than in any other age group. To meet the aspirations of young people, the Government will consider establishing a National Council for Graduate Entrepreneurship to act as a central information source for students and graduates considering starting up in business. The aim of the Council would be to engage career advisors, academics, institutions and organisations to promote and facilitate self-employment as a viable career option, including through promotional shows, networking events and mentoring opportunities.

---

[8] *Enterprise Britain: a modern approach to meeting the enterprise challenge*, HM Treasury and the Small Business Service, November 2002.

Supporting business and entrepreneurship

3.42   The Government has introduced a series of reforms to create a fertile business environment and enhance the UK's position as an internationally competitive location for business. Budget 2003 describes further steps to ensure businesses in the UK are able to develop, grow and compete effectively in global markets.

Supporting small business training   **3.43**   Research shows that businesses that obtain training and advice are more likely to succeed than others. Given their important role in communicating support to small businesses, the Government will work in partnership with high street banks to develop a new package of training and support for SMEs. The package will use the banks' existing communication networks to stimulate demand for advice and training, and make entrepreneurs more aware of their benefits. It will also include a one-stop web-based training directory to raise awareness of public and private sector training opportunities and provide access to on-line counselling and mentoring services. A steering group, chaired by Sue Brownson, chief executive of Blue Bell BMW and a member of the Small Firms Council, will oversee the management and development of the support package. The group will include banks, the SBS, Ufi/learndirect, small business organisations, and a range of entrepreneurs, will oversee the management and development of the support package. Further details of how the Government intends to involve intermediaries in supporting SME development will be set out in the Skills Strategy, due to be published in June 2003.

Improving access to finance   **3.44**   While the majority of established businesses experience little difficulty in accessing the finance they need to fulfil their potential, the same is not true for new businesses in need of start-up funding or those seeking modest amounts of risk capital to finance rapid growth. Problems also tend to be more acute for businesses operating in disadvantaged communities. Flexible capital markets that work for small businesses in all localities are vital to support enterprise, job creation and growth.

3.45   The Government has taken a number of steps to help new and growing businesses access appropriate finance. Regional Venture Capital Funds will invest up to £270 million in growing SMEs across the country, and eight of the nine funds are now up and running. For businesses requiring debt finance, eligibility for the Small Firms Loan Guarantee (SFLG) has been extended, from April 2003, to previously excluded sectors including retail and catering.

3.46   To complement existing measures, and to support an increased flow of new fund managers into the early-stage venture capital market, the Government will now consult on the scope for introducing Small Business Investment Companies (SBICs) in the UK SBICs are recognised to be one of the most important drivers behind the growth of venture capital in the US in the late 1990s. A new consultation paper, *Bridging the finance gap: a consultation on improving access to growth capital for small businesses*, is published alongside this Budget.

3.47   The paper also explores options for targeting support on those businesses most affected by the equity gap through the Enterprise Investment Scheme (EIS) and Venture Capital Trust (VCT) tax incentives. The EIS and VCT schemes have played a significant and growing role in the supply of private equity funds in recent years. Views are also invited on how to ensure that the SFLG reaches its full potential, particularly in disadvantaged communities, and the paper considers the scope for increasing flexibility in the rules governing how past SFLG-backed borrowing affects entitlement to future SFLG-backed loans.

Demand for risk capital   **3.48**   Steps to increase the level of demand for risk capital are as important as those to improve its supply. Unlike the costs incurred in raising loan finance, which are tax deductible for companies, there is currently no tax deduction for the incidental costs of raising equity finance. The consultation paper therefore invites views on whether the current tax treatment presents a further obstacle to SMEs seeking to raise equity finance and, if so, how tax relief might be implemented in practice.

Box 3.3: The equity gap

While the UK has a well developed private equity market, smaller-scale investments in growth-oriented businesses suffer from a number of constraints. There are significant transaction costs involved in identifying suitable investment opportunities, and in undertaking the necessary investment appraisal. Furthermore, while venture capital investors often devote significant resources to monitoring the ongoing performance of their investments and to providing mentoring or other management support, these costs generally do not vary in proportion to investment size, and may therefore be prohibitive for smaller transactions. Evidence also suggests that some smaller businesses and their advisers lack a clear understanding of equity finance, and investors sometimes cite poor presentation or business plans as a constraint[1].

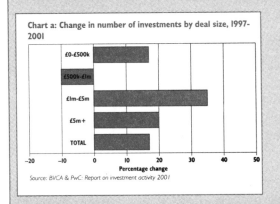

Chart a: Change in number of investments by deal size, 1997-2001

Source: BVCA & PwC: Report on investment activity 2001

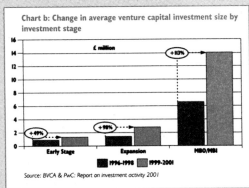

Chart b: Change in average venture capital investment size by investment stage

Source: BVCA & PwC: Report on investment activity 2001

These constraints help to explain the existence of an equity gap, which appears to be particularly acute for investments of less than £1 million. Chart (a) shows that while the overall number of private equity investments has grown significantly in recent years, the number of investments of between £500,000 and £1 million has actually fallen. Only 8 per cent of private equity funds were directed towards start-up and other early-stage businesses in 2001[2] and, for any given stage of business development, the venture capital sector appears to have gravitated towards larger individual investments, as chart (b) shows. As a percentage of GDP, total early-stage investment in the US is more than twice as high as in the UK, and that in Canada is almost four times as high[3].

[1] Designing an "investment ready" programme: some considerations, report to the Small Business Service, Mason, C. & Harrison, R, 2001.

[2] Report on Investment Activity, British Venture Capital Association, 2001.

[3] OECD Venture Capital database, 1998-2001 data.

3.49   The SBS is currently running six 'investment readiness' demonstration projects which are providing intensive education to SMEs, to raise their awareness and understanding of the different financing options available and how best to access them. The Government will consider the results of these products carefully in determining how best to move forward in this area. One approach is to make more effective use of existing intermediaries. Accountants for example, provide advice to around two-thirds of SMEs. Recognising this, a joint Government/accountants working group is being set up under the chairmanship of Michael Snyder, chair of the Finance and Resources Committee at the Corporation of London, to explore how the quality of financial advice available to all growing SMEs could be enhanced further.

Modernising and simplifying VAT

3.50   The Government has already introduced a series of measures designed to help small and newly-registered businesses reduce their VAT compliance costs, improve their cash flow and manage their entry into the VAT system. Budget 2003 consolidates and enhances this support. From April 2003:

- the VAT registration threshold will be increased in line with inflation from £55,000 to £56,000, keeping the smallest businesses out of VAT and maintaining the UK threshold as the highest in the EU;

- the optional VAT flat-rate scheme will be extended to businesses with turnover of up to £150,000, as previously announced, meaning that more than 650,000 small firms can now benefit;

- immediate entry into the annual accounting scheme will be extended to a further 15,000 businesses per year with turnover of up to £150,000, allowing small businesses to make a single annual VAT return and to spread their VAT payments across the year; and

- an incentive scheme will be launched to help small businesses trading above the registration threshold into the VAT system. In return for maintaining high compliance standards, businesses will not face late-registration penalties and may be offered limited time to pay their outstanding VAT bills.

3.51   As well as reforming VAT for small and newly-registered businesses, the Government is also taking steps to modernise and simplify the VAT system for all businesses, including by:

- allowing non-EU providers of electronically supplied services to register, account for and pay VAT electronically to ease compliance burdens and maintain the UK as a world leader in e-commerce;

- simplifying the VAT treatment of business gifts, modernising the existing rules to reduce unnecessary compliance burdens; and

- consulting on a package of measures to increase fairness in the recovery of input VAT, including a simplified 'option to tax' on commercial buildings, and fairer rules on the recovery of VAT incurred on goods and services prior to registration.

3.52   Following a period of detailed consultation, Budget 2003 also introduces from 1 December 2003 a simplified system for accounting for VAT at import, allowing approved businesses to provide reduced or zero security against deferred VAT payments and offering up to £80 million in compliance savings. Budget 2003 also introduces a system of civil penalties for minor breaches of customs law relating to the import and export of goods, and certain cases of evasion, creating a level playing field for compliant businesses while retaining criminal punishments for serious offences.

Corporation tax

3.53   The Government has recently consulted[9] on further reform of the corporation tax system to remove tax distortions to business decision-making, simplify and modernise the tax system, and ensure that the UK remains an attractive place for businesses to locate. The wide-ranging proposals explore the tax treatment of capital assets not covered by earlier reforms, rationalisation of the schedular system and the differences in the treatment of trading and investment companies. The Government has received a large number of

---

[9] *Reform of corporation tax: a consultation document*, HM Treasury and Inland Revenue, August 2002.

responses from businesses and has held a series of discussions with specific sectors. A further round of consultation will be launched in the summer, setting out the Government's strategy for taking forward the proposed corporation tax reforms. The Government will consider the reform of corporation tax in its broader international and European context.

Simplifying employee share schemes **3.54**   Employee share schemes provide employees with a real stake in the business they work for, promoting enterprise and productivity. The 2002 Pre-Budget Report announced simplified corporation tax rules for such schemes to encourage more companies to offer them to their employees. Budget 2003 builds on this reform with new measures to simplify the Share Incentive Plan and modernise Save As You Earn and the Company Share Option Plan.

Capital gains tax **3.55**   To encourage entrepreneurial activity, the Government has introduced a generous capital gains tax (CGT) taper for business assets, reducing the effective rate of tax for a higher rate taxpayer to 20 per cent for assets held for one year and to 10 per cent after only two years, making the UK regime among the most favourable in the world. To improve access to property for unincorporated traders, the Government will now extend business assets taper relief to property let to sole traders and a wider range of partnerships from 6 April 2004. Building on the changes introduced last April, Budget 2003 also further simplifies the CGT regime and reforms the CGT rules to ensure they operate more fairly in certain transactions in which the sale proceeds cannot be determined at the time of sale.

Promoting enterprise in disadvantaged areas

Enterprise Areas **3.56**   Entrepreneurial and business activity in disadvantaged areas is central to the sustainable regeneration of these communities. The 2002 Pre-Budget Report designated 2,000 Enterprise Areas on which measures to boost enterprise are being focused. These areas cover the most deprived communities across the UK, where social attitudes, the business environment and specific market failures can present significantly higher barriers to enterprise.

Starting and growing a business **3.57**   To reduce the cost to business of locating and investing in disadvantaged areas, and to support the regeneration of brownfield sites, the Government has removed stamp duty from property transactions below £150,000 in the 2,000 Enterprise Areas. Following the receipt of EU state aids approval in January, Budget 2003 announces that stamp duty will be removed from all non-residential property transactions in Enterprise Areas from 10 April.

Investing **3.58**   The Community Investment Tax Relief promotes private investment in enterprises in disadvantaged communities by offering tax relief to investors in Community Development Finance Institutions (CDFIs) which provide finance to businesses and social enterprises in deprived communities. Eleven CDFIs have now been accredited and enabled to raise around £35 million of new capital from private sector investors. Applications for accreditation from a further seven CDFIs are currently being considered.

3.59   The £40 million Bridges Community Development Venture Fund was launched in May 2002 and made its first investments at the end of last year. The Fund invests in businesses in disadvantaged areas that create local jobs, provide services to the local community or stimulate a local supply chain. The Government is currently considering the scope for investing in a second community development venture capital fund.

3.60   To encourage further business investment in Enterprise Areas, the Government is considering how enhanced capital allowances for particular types of expenditure in these areas might be used to tackle specific market failures, and the state aids aspects of any such measures.

Trading and employing   **3.61**   The comprehensive support for small businesses described earlier in this chapter, including the recently published *No-nonsense guide to Government rules and regulations*, will benefit thousands of new and growing businesses operating in deprived areas of Britain. The guide contains information on the extra support available in Enterprise Areas, to ensure that these firms are aware of it and can access it quickly. To build further on this support and tackle the higher barriers to enterprise in these areas, **HM Customs and Excise will improve its services to businesses in Enterprise Areas,** expanding the national programme of Business Advice Open Days to include a number of satellite events in Enterprise Areas. Two new types of enhanced business support provision will also be piloted in selected disadvantaged areas, complementing the assistance already available from Inland Revenue Business Support Teams and Employer Talk events. Around 1,000 employers have already attended these events.

Planning for deprived areas   **3.62**   The planning system must be transparent, accessible and affordable to businesses if they are to contribute to investment and development in deprived areas. The Government is working to identify a package of planning measures to help local authorities speed up and simplify the planning process in the most disadvantaged areas across the country. Legislation for Business Planning Zones, included in the current Planning Bill, will give local authorities the power to designate zones in which there is no requirement to apply for planning permission where predetermined criteria are met. Budget 2003 also announces that, in England, the Government will:

- set aside resources from the Planning Delivery Grant to assist authorities delivering planning for Enterprise Areas, from 2004-05;

- encourage local authorities to use Local Development Orders in Enterprise Areas, subject to forthcoming legislation, granting automatic planning permission for types of development specified in the Order; and

- work with local authorities to ensure Enterprise Areas are effectively planned for in local plans.

Enterprise at the local level

3.63   Productivity differentials are currently at least as great within regions as they are between them. A dynamic, high productivity economy requires greater flexibility in local markets and stronger local incentives to promote enterprise and encourage growth.

Local growth incentives   **3.64**   As described in Chapter 6, the Government is already offering greater freedoms and flexibilities to local authorities in return for commitments to deliver more stretching outcomes. To give a further boost to local growth and regeneration, as announced in the 2002 Pre-Budget Report, the Government also intends to allow all local authorities in England to retain some or all of any additions to business rates revenues generated by increases in local business activity. Amendments to the Local Government Bill have been introduced to provide the necessary primary legislation for the scheme. The precise details of the scheme are currently being considered and a series of options that balance simplicity, the distributional impact and the incentive effect are being developed. The Government will consult on these in the summer.

Urban   **3.65**   As announced in the 2002 Pre-Budget Report, to provide further support for
regeneration regeneration and enterprise in many of Britain's urban areas, the Government has introduced a new tax incentive to encourage business donations toward the running costs of Urban Regeneration Companies (URCs), including those operating in Enterprise Areas. The tax incentive has been available since 1 April 2003 and allows businesses to deduct expenditure on contributions, whether in cash or in kind, towards the running costs of URCs when computing their taxable profits.

Enterprise in the EU

3.66   The European Commission published a consultative Green Paper on Entrepreneurship[10] in January. While tax remains a matter for Member States, in keeping with the principle of subsidiarity, the Commission's initiative in other areas must now be translated into concrete reform. The Government is strongly supportive of action in a number of areas, including to ensure that the role of enterprise in delivering sustainable regeneration is reflected in the priorities of instruments such as the European Investment Fund Start-Up Facility.

SCIENCE AND INNOVATION

3.67   Innovation is an increasingly important source of productivity growth. New ideas generate products and markets, improve efficiency, and deliver benefits to firms, consumers and society. The UK has an excellent scientific research base, second only to the US in terms of the volume and influence of publications, but has historically been less effective than other advanced industrial economies at turning research outputs into innovations with commercial potential. The UK also has a relatively low overall level of industry-funded business R&D compared with industrial competitors, despite having high R&D intensity in particular sectors.

Science strategy   **3.68**   The Government's science strategy, *Investing in innovation*[11], was published in July 2002 and is now being implemented. Supported by the largest sustained increase in the Science Budget for more than a decade, the strategy sets out a comprehensive new approach to ensure that the UK remains competitive through investment in the UK's science base, improvements to the financial sustainability of university research and to the supply of science and engineering skills, and further steps to promote the translation of research into business innovation.

Research and   **3.69**   To promote commercial R&D in the UK, the Government has introduced tax credits
development tax for SMEs and large companies. Introduction of the tax credits has been supported by a series
credits of national roadshows designed to promote take-up and to provide a forum for exchange of views on the operation of the credits. The roadshows were attended by R&D businesses from across the country, and interest and take-up continues to increase. Around 3,000 claims for the SME tax credit for R&D activity carried out during 2001-02 are expected, leading to more than £150 million of support for innovative UK companies.

---

[10] *Green Paper Entrepreneurship in Europe*, European Commission, January 2003.
[11] *Investing in innovation: A strategy for science, engineering and technology*, Department of Trade and Industry, HM Treasury, and Department for Education and Skills, July 2002.

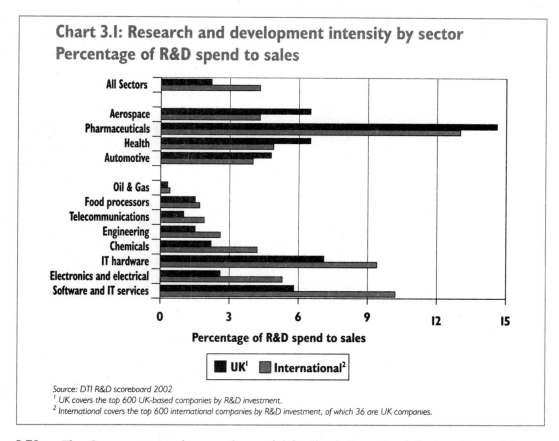

Chart 3.1: Research and development intensity by sector
Percentage of R&D spend to sales

Percentage of R&D spend to sales

UK[1] International[2]

Source: DTI R&D scoreboard 2002
[1] UK covers the top 600 UK-based companies by R&D investment.
[2] International covers the top 600 international companies by R&D investment, of which 36 are UK companies.

3.70 The Government welcomes the useful feedback it received during the roadshows. Building on this feedback, Budget 2003 introduces a series of reforms to improve the operation of the SME and large company R&D tax credits:

- reducing the minimum expenditure threshold from £25,000 to £10,000;

- extending coverage of the credits to include the costs of agency workers and, subject to consultation on the definition, of advanced software;

- simplifying the rules for apportioning staff costs so that relief is still awarded for staff performing relatively small amounts of R&D; and

- additional steps to ensure that SMEs that are currently excluded from the credits are able to claim in future.

3.71 A new definition of R&D for tax purposes was introduced in 2000 under guidelines published by the Secretary of State for Trade and Industry. Since then, business interest in this issue has grown substantially, and the Government will therefore consult on improving the definition of R&D to ensure that it remains consistent with technological developments and competitive internationally. Any broadening of the definition would be subject to affordability, and the Government will consider the extent to which any changes might initially be limited to the SME scheme.

Scientific **3.72** As announced in the 2002 Pre-Budget Report, the Government is also reviewing the
Research tax exemption for Scientific Research Organisations (SROs), to ascertain whether existing tax
Organisations rules could be improved to allow SROs to undertake a wider range of R&D activities while still maintaining their current tax exempt status.

Capital allowances for ICT
3.73 Budget 2000 introduced temporary 100 per cent first year capital allowances for small businesses investing in ICT. The allowances provide a favourable and stable environment for businesses seeking to invest in technology that promotes greater efficiency and enables them to deal faster and more effectively with Government and other businesses. Budget 2003 extends the allowances for one further year. In future years, small employers will have financial incentives to organise their payroll via the Internet. The amendment to the company law definition of small businesses will increase the number of businesses eligible for the allowance.

Knowledge transfer
3.74 The Government is taking a number of steps to promote the translation of research into business innovation, including through the £187 million Higher Education Innovation Fund (HEIF). In the next round of the HEIF, for investment between 2004 and 2006, universities will be invited to present new strategies for building links with businesses, in particular SMEs, and RDAs will play an enhanced role in directing resources so that they contribute most effectively to regional economic growth. RDAs are also engaged in their own knowledge transfer initiatives to promote regional innovation. In support of this work, the Secretary of State for Trade and Industry has asked Sir Tom McKillop, as chair of the first Regional Science and Industry Council, to work with the RDAs to ensure that best practice in promoting innovation and knowledge transfer is shared and spread rapidly between the regions. The Government also continues to support the commercialisation of science and technology from Public Sector Research Establishments and NHS Trusts. Funding of £15 million will be allocated this year to help catalyse this activity, building on previous policy reforms and funding.

DTI innovation review
3.75 Building on the Government's science strategy and the growing level of resources for DTI innovation programmes, the Secretary of State for Trade and Industry has launched a wide-ranging review of business innovation and its contribution to UK productivity growth. The review will set out a clear strategy for improving the UK's comparative innovation performance across products, processes, services and business practices. It will report in summer 2003 on how to improve the effectiveness of innovation policies at both national and regional level.

Review of business-university collaboration
3.76 In the 2002 Pre-Budget Report, the Government commissioned Richard Lambert to conduct an independent review into how the long-term links between business and British universities can be strengthened to improve the UK's innovation and productivity performance. The review will focus on how business can best exploit the technologies and skills under development in the university sector, to the mutual advantage of both sectors. The review team are currently consulting widely with business, universities and national and regional administrations in the UK and overseas. The review will complement and feed into the DTI's innovation review, and will report to ministers in late summer 2003.

Innovation and R&D in the EU
3.77 Building on the call for the creation of a European Research and Innovation Area by EU leaders, in March 2002 the Barcelona European Council concluded that spending on R&D and innovation in the EU should increase to approach 3 per cent of GDP by 2010, with two-thirds of new investment coming from business. Achieving this target will require framework conditions conducive to business investment in research and innovation, including high levels of competition, accessible capital markets, appropriately skilled labour, and an effective intellectual property regime. The Government will press for these ideas to be taken forward in the Commission's forthcoming Action Plan on R&D and will also press for implementation as soon as possible, in a business-friendly manner, of the recently agreed Community Patent.

SKILLS

3.78   The quantity and quality of skilled labour in an economy are important determinants of economic performance and productivity growth, and the adaptability of the UK labour market is central to the flexibility of the economy as a whole. Skilled workers often adapt faster and more effectively to change, allowing firms to update products and working practices at the rate demanded by rapidly changing markets. International evidence suggests that the UK suffers from significant skills shortages, especially at the lower-intermediate level. To raise UK skills levels and increase productivity, the Government is therefore acting to improve the skills of young people entering the workforce and to increase the opportunities available to those already in the workforce to acquire new skills.

Skills Strategy   **3.79**   The Government is planning to publish a Skills Strategy in June 2003, setting a framework for action by government, individuals and employers to tackle deficiencies in the UK's skills base. The Strategy will propose measures to support employers facing barriers in raising skills levels, improve vocational opportunities for young people, engage more low-skilled adults in training, and make further education funding and qualification structures more responsive to the needs of the economy. The Strategy will also include the findings of a review of funding of adult learning, including proposals to ensure that the funding of further education provides incentives for individuals and employers to engage in training and to make training provision more responsive to the needs of the economy.

Developing the skills of young people

Primary and secondary education   **3.80**   The Government is determined to raise pupil attainment across the education system. Between 1997 and 2002, the proportion of 11 year-olds reaching expected levels in reading and maths rose by 12 per cent and 11 per cent respectively. The proportion of 16 year-olds achieving five A*-C grades at GCSE also rose, from 45 per cent in 1997 to 51 per cent in 2002.

3.81   Local and national policy is focused on the achievement of a range of targets to ensure that the education system meets the needs of all. Minimum attainment targets provide a framework within which local authorities and schools can exercise increased autonomy and freedoms in the provision of local education services. Reforms to the funding of Local Education Authorities will help to support increased local reforms, and the new Leadership Incentive Grant will help secondary schools in challenging areas to develop excellent leadership. The newly acquired ability for every school to benchmark its expenditures and outcomes against schools with a similar pupil intake is also strengthening local accountability and transparency, enhancing local decision-taking and serving to support existing inspection arrangements.

Modern Apprenticeships   **3.82**   Modern Apprenticeships (MAs) provide a nationally recognised programme of work-based training, understood by young people, their parents and employers. Since 1997, the number of young people participating in MAs has increased dramatically, from 76,000 to 220,000. The Government is now expanding the programme to meet the target that, by 2004, 28 per cent of 22 year-olds will have entered an apprenticeship, with plans that, by 2006, an estimated 320,000 young people will be participating in an MA.

3.83   A new employer-led National Modern Apprenticeship Taskforce was launched in February 2003. Chaired by Sir Roy Gardner, CEO of Centrica, the taskforce will seek to increase further the number of apprenticeship opportunities available for young people, and to ensure that the design of MAs meets the needs of young people and employers. In its first year, it will encourage more employers to provide MAs and increase the diversity of those who do, with a focus on smaller employers. The taskforce will also provide a number of sector reports, with an initial focus on the construction and retail industries.

Post-16 participation

3.84   As the UK moves towards a high-skilled economy, young people who leave formal learning at 16 are much less likely to gain long-term employment. Prior attainment is a key driver of post-16 participation in learning. Despite a marked increase in attainment at GCSE, more must be done to increase levels of participation towards those seen in comparable countries.

3.85   To increase the number of young people entering higher education or skilled employment, the Government intends to make the learning choices available to young people more appealing. A working group, led by Mike Tomlinson, will report to Department for Education and Skills ministers in summer 2004 on work to strengthen the structure and content of full-time vocational programmes and offer greater coherence in learning programmes for all young people throughout their 14 to 19 education. The review will make recommendations about a unified framework of qualifications that recognise different levels of achievement. The national roll-out of the Connexions Service and Education Maintenance Allowances (EMAs) will increase the support and guidance available to young people making the transition into post-16 education and learning. EMAs and the wider system of financial support for 16 to 19 year olds are discussed in Chapter 5.

Higher education

3.86   The January 2003 White Paper, *The future of higher education*, set out a range of proposals to widen participation in higher education and to ensure that universities are equipped to compete in the world economy, including:

- major improvements in the funding of research and knowledge transfer;

- measures to support participation by those from disadvantaged backgrounds; and

- a new Graduate Contribution scheme from 2006.

Improving workforce skills

3.87   While measures to increase the skills of young people will lay the foundations for long-term improvements in the UK's skills base, their effect will only be gradual. Two-thirds of today's workforce will still be in the labour market in 2020 and more than one-third have qualifications below level 2. An increase in the number of people participating in workplace training has been achieved through voluntary approaches. However, despite these efforts, they have not been sufficient given the scale of the problem. The Government is therefore seeking to develop policy that will help employers, individuals and government to better address this problem. It is the shared responsibility of government, employers and individuals to tackle this problem, recognising and addressing the barriers which prevent both individuals and businesses from taking up the training they need to develop and progress.

3.88   The case for helping individuals to acquire level 2 skills is particularly strong. Level 2 skills are both important in their own right and provide an essential platform for progression to higher skill levels. Evidence shows that market failures are particularly acute at level 2, and that adults who have reached this level are much more likely to undertake further training on their own initiative or to receive training from their employers and gain higher-intermediate level skills. The Government is therefore considering how best to focus resources on areas where the market failures are greatest, such as training for a first level 2 qualification.

Increasing the demand for training   **3.89**   Employer Training Pilots (ETPs), launched in September 2002 in six local Learning and Skills Council (LSC) areas, are exploring ways to counter the financial barriers, time constraints and information failures which currently exclude people and businesses from the training they need to develop and progress. Across the six pilots, firms offer low-skilled workers paid time off to train and the Government is testing the impact of subsidies to cover the costs involved, together with free training courses up to NVQ level 2, and information and guidance on training.

3.90   Initial results suggest that the pilots are successfully engaging firms and individuals with little prior involvement in training. Within the first six months of operation, 1,500 employers had joined the scheme and more than 5,600 employees had begun training towards a basic skills or level 2 qualification. The pilots are helping to tackle the particular barriers to training faced by small firms – over 70 per cent of participating businesses employ fewer than 50 people – and are reaching other groups, such as part-time workers, that have previously had little opportunity to improve their skills during working hours. Early indications are that completion rates by learners are high, and both businesses and individuals are positive about the benefits of their involvement.

3.91   As announced in the 2002 Pre-Budget Report, the Government is providing £130 million in England to enable Employer Training Pilots to be extended for a second year and to around one quarter of local LSC areas. New pilots will operate from summer 2003 in Berkshire, East London, Kent, Leicester, Shropshire and South Yorkshire, helping to strengthen evaluation of the scheme. The extension will allow the Government to test the impact of elements within the model, such as the level of compensation to employers, more thoroughly, and will ensure that pilot areas can explore further the means of increasing the capacity of local training providers and engaging employers in the scheme. The extension will provide important evidence to inform the development of national policy, complementing work in other areas.

Union Learning Fund

3.92   Since 1998, the Union Learning Fund (ULF) has supported over 350 projects ranging from tackling basic skills needs to continuing professional development. The ULF has also helped to establish and train a national network of over 4,500 Union Learning Representatives who promote learning in the workplace, particularly among those with basic skills needs. The Government has decided to increase funding for the ULF from £11 million in 2003-04 to £14 million in 2004-05 and 2005-06.

Professional and other bodies

3.93   Building on the measures already described, the Government also intends to review the tax treatment of fees and subscriptions to professional and other approved bodies, to see how it can further strengthen and support the provision of workforce education and skills.

Management

3.94   Effective management makes a significant contribution to productivity growth. To improve understanding of the relationship between management and economic performance, Professor Michael Porter was asked by the DTI and the Economic and Social Research Council (ESRC) to oversee a short research project as part of a broader study into UK competitiveness. Professor Porter concluded that the UK has a managerial skills deficit among lower and middle management levels, reflecting the overall skills gap in the UK labour force. The ESRC has a £17 million research budget to take forward research in this area, building on the analysis in the report.

Migration

3.95   Migration is a long-standing source of skills and labour in Britain, and over time has helped to raise productivity, boost economic growth and mitigate domestic skills shortages. The Government has taken a number of steps to maximise the contribution of migration to a skilled and flexible workforce and to help employers facing specific recruitment difficulties. The Highly Skilled Migrant Programme (HSMP), introduced in 2002, has proved successful in enabling highly-skilled individuals to enter the UK to seek and take up work. Around 1,300 people entered through this route in the first year of operation, demonstrating their eligibility through educational qualifications, work experience, achievements in their field and past income. Applications renewing HSMP status to date have been approved on the basis of very strong labour market performances.

3.96   The work permit system now provides a flexible and effective service for employers who are unable to fill positions through domestic recruitment. Over 95 per cent of permits are processed within 24 hours, and Work Permits UK expect to receive some 200,000 applications in the coming year. As confirmed in the 2002 Pre-Budget Report, a Small Business Unit has been established within Work Permits UK to ensure that all employers are able to use the work permit system effectively to meet their skills needs.

3.97   Building on the success of recent initiatives, the Government is taking further steps to facilitate migration as a source of skills and labour in the economy. To maximise the economic contribution of high-skilled migration, the Government will strengthen the Highly Skilled Migrants Programme by adjusting the threshold eligibility criteria, introducing a new category for younger applicants, and taking partners' achievements into account in assessing individual applications. The new criteria will take effect from August 2003.

3.98   Overseas students can help to relieve UK shortages in the supply of science, technology, engineering and mathematics skills, and the Government is committed to encouraging them to utilise their skills in these subject areas after they graduate. The Government will, therefore, introduce a new entitlement for foreign students beginning or continuing courses in these subjects to work in the UK for 12 months following graduation from a UK institution. This will apply to students completing courses from summer 2004.

3.99   The Work Permit system is proving effective in alleviating employers' recruitment difficulties at NVQ level 3 and above, across a wide range of sectors. New schemes for lower skilled migration will also operate from May 2003 to alleviate labour shortages in the food processing and hospitality sectors. Employers will be able to apply for 12 month permits from an initial annual quota of 10,000 migrants per sector, and will be expected to provide suitable accommodation and support for their employees. Evaluation of these schemes will provide valuable evidence on the potential benefits of low-skilled migration in meeting employer demand and tackling illegal working.

3.100   However, acute shortages of intermediate, NVQ level 2 vocational skills remain in certain sectors, such as the construction industry. The Government will therefore consult in summer 2003 on how best to address intermediate vocational skills shortages in these sectors, including consultation on lowering the minimum qualification for work permit occupation on a sector specific basis.

3.101   The Government is also introducing changes to the Working Holidaymakers Scheme, under which young Commonwealth citizens can work in the UK for up to two years, to make it more flexible and responsive to labour market needs. Working Holidaymakers will in future be able to take up work in any sector, move freely between employers, and switch into work permit employment after one year in the UK.

3.102   The Home Office is also taking steps to ensure that employers and individuals have access to appropriate information on UK migration routes, to improve the effectiveness of the system and aid the integration of recent migrants. The Home Office will review its website provision and establish a dedicated site for legal economic migration to the UK by autumn 2003.

Immigration into the EU   **3.103**   Migration is also key to the EU's ability to meet the challenges and opportunities posed by an ageing population and a contracting workforce. The Spring European Council in March 2003 concluded that migration should be considered in the context of skills shortages and demographic challenges across the EU as a whole. The Government welcomes the Commission's intention to produce a Communication on the relationship between immigration, integration of migrants in EU society and employment.

INVESTMENT

3.104   Alongside a skilled labour force, investment in physical capital is vital to support a flexible and productive economy. In the past, the capital stock of firms and the stock of public infrastructure in the UK has fallen well below the levels in other industrial countries, impairing the UK's labour productivity performance. The Government is taking important steps to reverse this trend, improving the environment for private investment and investment decision-making through macroeconomic stability and greater flexibility in capital markets, taking forward investment plans in transport infrastructure, and addressing failures in the property market.

Improving investment decision-making

3.105   Efficient and flexible capital markets have a vital role in allocating capital in the economy, promoting growth and productivity. Capital markets help businesses manage risk, while integrated international markets improve the flow of capital and reduce costs. The effective combination of high, robust standards of corporate governance and strong shareholders is the essential underpinning for efficient, flexible markets in a modern global economy.

3.106   The Government takes a broad approach to reform of capital markets, to ensure that the chain of savings, investment and governance works efficiently and effectively to create wealth and long-term value for savers, companies and the economy. This approach operates at a number of levels. At the level of the company, there is a need to promote the interests of shareholders and to ensure that they have access to timely and accurate financial reporting. This in turn requires a set of external stakeholders whose actions promote and reinforce good governance: institutional shareholders that are responsive to the needs and interests of their ultimate customers and accountable for the ownership rights they exercise; independent auditors; comprehensive and robust accounting standards; and fair and timely commentary from analysts and ratings agencies.

3.107   The Government has therefore commissioned a number of strategic reviews. The Cruickshank, Myners and Sandler reports investigated competition in banking, institutional investment and retail savings products. The Higgs review of the role and effectiveness of non-executive directors, the Coordinating Group on Audit and Accounting Issues, and the Smith group recommendations on guidance for audit committees together provided an overarching approach to reforming the governance and financial reporting of companies. These, in turn, require effective exercise by institutional shareholders of their ownership rights, an important theme of the Myners review.

The Myners   **3.108**   The Myners review of institutional investment in the UK was published in March
review of   2001. In October 2001, the Government confirmed that it would take forward all of the
institutional   recommendations of the review, including revised Codes of Investment Principles to
investment   encourage diversity in investment approaches. Since then:

- the Institutional Shareholders' Committee (ISC) has published guidance for fund managers on Shareholder Activism, helping them to maximise the value of their clients' equity holdings and the productivity of the companies they own. In 2004, the Government will review the extent to which the ISC's statement of principles has been successful in delivering behavioural change;

- the December 2002 Pensions Green Paper restated the Government's commitment to legislate to require more expertise of Pension Scheme Trustees. This will improve the investment decisions taken for the huge blocks of capital controlled by the occupational pension scheme sector;

- the Government has launched a major review, to run until the end of 2003, of the effectiveness of the Myners principles in driving change in investment decision-making by occupational pension schemes. The review will inform future decisions on the need for further action to improve the operation of the institutional investment market; and

- the Financial Services Authority is now consulting on proposals on soft commission and the 'bundling' of transaction costs by brokers, following discussion of these issues in the Myners report.

Accountancy and audit   3.109   Corporate crises in the US have highlighted the vital importance of strong frameworks for financial reporting and audit regulation, and corporate governance in underpinning efficient and flexible national and international capital markets. The final report of the Coordinating Group on Audit and Accounting Issues was published in January 2003. The Government endorses the recommendations set out in the report, including that enforcement of accounting standards should become more proactive and risk-based. The report also recommended that steps be taken to strengthen auditor independence, including through:

- strengthened requirements on the rotation of audit partners, and greater restriction on the provision of non-audit services;

- an enhanced role for audit committees in appointing and overseeing auditors. The group endorsed new guidance for audit committees proposed by Sir Robert Smith; and

- the transfer of responsibility for setting standards for auditor independence to a body independent of the professional accountancy bodies, as part of a wider restructuring of the regulation of the accountancy profession.

The Higgs review of non-executive directors   3.110   Effective non-executive directors have a central role to play in raising standards of corporate governance and performance. In April 2002, the Government appointed Derek Higgs to review the role and effectiveness of non-executive directors. The report was published in January 2003 and concluded that the existing framework of corporate governance, though sound in its essentials, should be progressively strengthened. The 'comply-or-explain' nature of the Combined Code has been successful in raising corporate governance standards, and the report recommends that the existing Combined Code be updated to include the following provisions:

- half of a listed company's board should be independent of management;

- the roles of chairman and chief executive should be separated;

- the chief executive should not go on to become chairman of the same company;

- disclosure of the role that non-executives perform, the time they commit, and their attendance at board meetings should be significantly increased;

- there should be closer relationships between non-executive directors, including the senior independent non-executive director, and shareholders, building on the conclusions of the Myners Review of institutional investment and developing shareholder activism as proposed by the ISC;

- there should be formal performance evaluation of the board as a whole, and of individual directors; and

- the role of chairman should be strengthened, recognising their pivotal role on the board.

3.111   The Government welcomes the conclusions of the report. It is now for the Financial Reporting Council (FRC) to update the Combined Code in the light of its recommendations and those of Sir Robert Smith's group on audit committee best practice. The Government welcomes the FRC's intention to amend the Combined Code after a short consultation period so that the new Code is in place to report in future years, beginning 1 July 2003. When the new Code is in place, the test will be the extent to which the business and investment communities rise to the challenge that has been laid down. The Government therefore welcomes Derek Higgs' recommendation for a two-year review of progress against his conclusions. It also believes that effective implementation of the Higgs recommendations will both assist and depend on active shareholder engagement, consistent with the principles set out by the Institutional Shareholders' Committee.

Shareholder Executive   3.112   Government-owned businesses also have an important role to play in raising UK productivity. As announced in the Pre-Budget Report, the Government has decided to create a Shareholder Executive located in the Cabinet Office to allow it to fulfil better its role as shareholder in those businesses. An early priority for the Chief Executive and their team will be to assess the current shareholder performance of government. Following this review, and within the first six months, the Shareholder Executive will define best practice standards and processes for all shareholding departments, develop action plans to enable the main shareholding departments to improve their shareholder performance, and help departments to implement those action plans. Departments will be held accountable for their shareholder capability and processes, and their effective use of the Shareholder Executive and implemention of its recommendations, in the next Spending Review.

Box 3.4: Strengthening EU capital markets

The creation of a genuine single market in financial services is a cornerstone of EU economic reform. A single financial services market will make it easier for European businesses to raise finance, and benefit consumers by giving them a wider choice of competitively priced products. The European Financial Services Action Plan is intended to create a single market by removing barriers to its development. However, further efforts are required to improve the flexibility of capital markets and to ensure that these do not stop at the EU's borders. Flexible capital markets are especially important in the context of Economic and Monetary Union. The Government's priorities include:

- increasing competition within EU capital markets. As described earlier in this chapter, the Government encourages the Commission to investigate whether there are barriers to competition in specific sectors;

- ensuring effective and efficient corporate governance. The Government strongly supports efforts to improve corporate governance across the EU, and calls on the Commission to ensure that the forthcoming Corporate Governance Action Plan focuses on agreeing high-level principles to underpin a framework of mutual recognition between Member States; and

- improving EU-US regulatory dialogue and mutual recognition. A more intensive EU-US regulatory dialogue should encourage cooperation and facilitate the mutual recognition of EU and US regulatory systems. As a first step, the Government calls for the commissioning of a report to assess the potential benefits of EU-US mutual recognition. The Government would like to see this initiative extended to other non-EU markets.

Encouraging North Sea Investment

3.113   Budget 2002 introduced necessary changes to ensure that North Sea taxes raise a fair share of revenue and encourage investment, helping to create a stable fiscal regime for the longer term. Within that framework the Government wants to achieve maximum value from scarce oil and gas resources by encouraging optimum use of North Sea infrastructure and the development of all commercially viable reserves. The Government therefore intends to abolish, from 1 January 2004, Petroleum Revenue Tax on all new third party tariffing business under contracts completed on, or after, Budget day relating to use of pipelines and other infrastructure in the UK and on its continental shelf. This change is the result of constructive dialogue between the Government and industry, who have made it clear that the benefits of the change will be passed on to infrastructure users. The Government wishes to continue this dialogue through the establishment of a consultation group to examine the issue of current low levels of exploration, working in parallel with PILOT, the industry task force. Over the next six months, the group will consider whether there are cost-effective, targeted measures that could improve this situation and help maximise economic recovery of North Sea oil and gas.

Investing in transport

3.114   A modern and reliable transport network fosters labour mobility and provides businesses with access to markets, a pool of available labour and new investment opportunities. The Government's Ten-Year Plan for Transport sets out plans for public and private investment in excess of £180 billion to create a modern transport network across the UK. The Department for Transport is currently conducting a review to assess how best to roll forward the Ten-Year Plan into the next decade, as part of which it will also review existing support for local bus services to ensure that these are effectively targeted on the Government's objectives. The Government is also engaged in a national consultation on UK airport capacity. Further detail is set out in Chapters 6 and 7.

Housing, property and planning

3.115   On 5 February, the Deputy Prime Minister set out the Government's new approach to creating and maintaining sustainable communities in a growing and changing economy[12]. The Government's strategy places key housing, planning and regeneration policies in the context of wider requirements for sustainable communities, including jobs, quality public services, transport, a safe and healthy local environment, and sound local government.

Housing 3.116   A stable and flexible housing market is essential to a healthy economy and housing market imbalances are a potential brake on economic development (see Box 3.5). Strong cycles in the housing market have been a striking feature of the UK economy over the past three decades. This volatility has affected the wider economy through private consumption, as household spending is closely linked to changes in housing wealth. Reducing volatility in the housing market will therefore promote macroeconomic stability. The Government has recognised that reforms are needed to help increase the supply of housing, reduce volatility and promote stability in the wider economy. The effect the housing market has on macroeconomic stability wil be much more significant should the UK join EMU. The housing market forms an important part of the monetary transmission mechanism – the means by which interest rates affect the wider economy. This is the subject of a supporting study to the assessment of the five economic tests.

3.117   Poor quality and abandoned housing is strongly linked to social disadvantage and has a detrimental impact on investment. In areas of high demand, an inadequate supply of affordable housing also affects the supply of skilled workers, such as nurses, teachers and police officers, who deliver the UK's essential services. The Government recognises both the

---

[12] *Sustainable communities: building for the future*, Office of the Deputy Prime Minister, February 2003.

need to provide an adequate supply of new homes and jobs in areas of the country experiencing high growth and to combat the decline of other areas where there is a surplus of housing stock. The programme will establish a series of 'pathfinders', financed by £500 million of new resources, to deal with declining areas suffering severe abandonment of housing, and an ambitious three-pronged strategy will be launched for areas in the South East, East and East Midlands regions experiencing high demand:

- bringing the number of homes built up to planned levels in all local authority areas;

- focusing additional housing development in selected growth areas; and

- delivering a new corridor of growth in the Thames Gateway. The scale of the brownfield development opportunity will give it a major role in providing for sustainable growth in London and the South East.

Box 3.5: Flexibility and the housing market

A flexible and mobile workforce plays an important role in matching people to jobs and, in particular, matching those with specific skills to appropriate jobs. Current evidence suggests that while increased labour mobility can make a significant contribution to increasing employment, it can make an even greater impact on improving productivity. However, labour mobility in the UK is low in comparison with the US and lower than in most other northern European countries.

One barrier to labour mobility is variation in house prices and house price to earnings ratios, which can prevent people moving from low to high price areas. For instance, in the UK these differences can prevent people from migrating into high demand areas such as London and the South-East. The chart below shows the variation between house prices and house price to earnings ratios across the UK's regions. These variations can create labour shortages and put upward pressure on wages in both private and public sectors.

Source: Halifax

Owner-occupiers face higher costs of moving than private renters, an issue that is exacerbated in the UK due to its high level of owner-occupiers. In addition, the UK's large social housing sector has, historically, been immobile. The Government is now taking steps to address this through Housing Benefit reform and restructuring social rents. Transaction costs incurred in buying or selling property can also reduce labour mobility. In the UK overall transaction costs are very low compared to most other European countries.

3.118　To help address these issues, £22 billion will be invested over the next three years in housing, planning and regeneration, £5 billion of which will be made available for affordable housing, including at least £1 billion for housing for keyworkers. Some £446 million will be invested in the Thames Gateway, in addition to resources from other programmes, and a further £164 million will be invested in the other growth areas.

3.119　The Government will work closely with regional and local partners to deliver infrastructure, economic development and regeneration in growth areas, and will strengthen local delivery mechanisms in support of this goal. In the Thames Gateway, the Government intends to establish two new Urban Development Corporations – one in the London Gateway and the other in Thurrock – and will consult on the latter shortly. The Government will also bring forward proposals for special delivery vehicles in other areas, which it will discuss with delivery partners.

3.120　The Government is also committed to ensuring, through intervention if necessary, that local authorities in high demand areas deliver housing numbers set out in Regional Planning Guidance. Local authorities should not just be operating the planning system, but also ensuring that the necessary level of house building happens. There will be a new role for the Audit Commission to assess authorities' performance in this area, while the new Comprehensive Performance Assessment (CPA) system for local authorities, described in Chapter 6, will appraise the performance of authorities in delivering the right sort of housing in the right quantities and the right places. Performance against this criterion will influence local authorities' CPA assessments as well as the allocation of resources recommended by Regional Housing Boards for new affordable housing.

3.121　As described in Chapter 2, the Government has also commissioned a review of the factors affecting the elasticity of housing supply in the UK.

3.122　The land-use planning system has an important impact on many property investment decisions, including housing. The Government is committed to a faster, more transparent and more effective planning system to support macroeconomic stability and flexibility, particularly within the housing and retail sectors, and the delivery of infrastructure to support sustainable growth.

Planning　3.123　The Government's proposals for reform of the planning system were set out by the Deputy Prime Minister in July 2002[13]. The 2002 Spending Review allocated an additional £350 million over the next three years to help local planning authorities make improvements to their planning services. The reforms, which are designed to promote better infrastructure and investment decisions, include:

- the first Planning Bill for more than a decade;

- the creation of statutory Regional Spatial Strategies to guide the pattern of development at a regional level;

- the abolition of county structure plans to remove an entire tier of plan-making;

- the introduction of a more flexible local development plans system;

- statutory timetables for called-in applications;

- reviews of national Planning Policy Guidance (PPG); and

- the introduction of Business Planning Zones.

[13] *Sustainable communities: delivering through planning*, Office of the Deputy Prime Minister, July 2002.

3.124   However, the Government wants to go further to improve the planning system. Building on the reforms already announced to deliver a step change in planning policy, further significant changes in the planning, supply and finance of housing will be required to address demand and supply in the housing market to tackle market failures, significantly increase the responsiveness of supply to demand, and reduce national and regional price volatility. It is vital that planning underpins a flexible housing market, responds better to the needs of deprived areas, and is better aligned with transport objectives. These objectives will not be delivered without a change in the culture of the planning system. Budget 2003 announces measures to respond to these challenges.

Supporting the delivery of new housing

3.125   The predictability and consistency of the planning system is key to the flexibility and stability of the housing market. The Government will vigorously pursue its target that 60 per cent of new housing should be built on brownfield land, and issued policies in 2000 on planning for housing (PPG3), designed to maximise the use of brownfield land and ensure that new housing is suitably located and built at higher densities than in the past. While the Government is committed to these policies, there is evidence that some planning authorities are implementing the guidance in ways which lead to a shortfall in overall housing supply compared with regional targets. To support better implementation by planning authorities the Government will:

- state that its overriding policy objective is that local authorities should deliver agreed housing numbers;

- help ensure the delivery of housing numbers by preventing the arbitrary use of local authority phasing policies to delay otherwise suitable housing developments allocated in plans;

- ensure that local authority plans make provision for at least 10 years' potential supply of housing, while continuing to prioritise 'brownfield' development and drive up density;

- propose that local authorities should allow land allocated for industrial or commercial use in their development plans, and redundant commercial buildings, to be used for housing or mixed use development unless a convincing case for retention can be made;

- offer greater help to planning authorities in negotiating planning obligations to ensure a more professional and consistent approach;

- as part of the Planning Delivery Grant, continue to offer extra resources to local planning authorities in the growth areas;

- set out, before the summer, measures to improve the performance of planning authorities that are not delivering an adequate supply of new housing – including incentives, support, and engagement – followed, where necessary, by intervention;

- be prepared to call in proposed major housing developments for decision where local authorities are not delivering housing numbers and where intervention will speed up delivery; and

- review the application of PPG3 this year to ensure that it is having the desired effect.

3.126   To address problems in delivering new housing, the Government will also:

- increase certainty for applicants by issuing new guidance requiring expectations for planning obligations – including affordable housing agreements – to be set out in policies in their plans;

- take forward the existing reviews of regional plans covering the high demand growth areas in the South East as the means for realising the additional growth potential of 200,000 homes identified in *Sustainable communities – building for the future*;

- require the Regional Planning Bodies to consider the case for additional growth in the longer term when preparing new Regional Spatial Strategies, and to take account of volatility in the housing market and the need to promote macro-economic stability as part of delivering sustainable development. The Government will publish region-by-region analysis of these issues for consultation by the end of 2003;

- explore whether, in the medium term, achieving the Government's objectives will require a system of binding local plans to increase certainty and ensure the stability of the housing market;

- building on the development of a register of surplus public sector land being developed by English Partnerships, consider how surplus central and local government landholdings can contribute to the delivery of corporate Government objectives, including housing supply, and clarify the scope for public bodies to take account of these broader interests; and

- consider ways to encourage a greater range of private sector involvement in both the financing and provision of affordable housing.

Improving retail planning   **3.127**   Productivity in the UK retail sector lags that in competitor economies. The planning system may be one of the factors affecting productivity if it restricts competition, innovation and choice. The Government is committed to ensuring the viability and vitality of town centres, and will review its guidance on planning for retail development to ensure that this is achieved alongside improvements in productivity. Revised guidance will encourage proactive planning for town centres and multi-level retail development to reduce land take. The Government will also ask Regional Planning Bodies to consider the need for, and broad location of, major new retail and distribution facilities in Regional Spatial Strategies.

Delivering infrastructure and land 3.128   The delivery of sustainable communities will require major new development, supported by appropriate infrastructure and land assembly processes. Land use and transport strategies need to be woven together at the national, regional and local levels. The Government will therefore:

- conduct, by the end of 2003, a wide-ranging review of the links between transport and land-use planning;

- radically simplify the compulsory purchase process and make it easier to use, subject to legislation;

- provide extra resources to planning authorities to incentivise better performance, particularly in handling major planning applications, as part of the Planning Delivery Grant;

- review whether the compensation offered for the indirect and nuisance effects of infrastructure development is appropriate, building on the work of the Law Commission; and

- explore whether the Government's proposals to conduct planning inquiries in concurrent sessions can be extended to other types of inquiry to save time.

Changing the culture of planning 3.129   Too often the planning system is seen as reactive and regulatory rather than as a positive tool for change. The Government has already introduced in the Planning Bill a duty for regional and local plans to support sustainable development. To further promote culture change, the Government will work with stakeholders to develop a wide programme of action, including:

- inviting Sir John Egan, President of the CBI, to develop a skills and training strategy for economic development, regeneration and planning to deliver sustainable communities, building on the efforts of the Royal Town Planning Institute to examine its own structure and the educational requirements leading to a planning qualification;

- piloting a new Planning Advisory Service, which will seek to use business experience of process management to help local authorities improve the way they handle planning applications;

- issuing a new draft version of its key planning policy guidance note (PPG1) for consultation in the autumn, setting out the key principles guiding plans and development control decisions; and

- holding a conference in the autumn to promote a positive vision for planning, focused on delivering increased productivity and economic development in support of *Sustainable communities.*

Commercial property 3.130   Commercial property is an important factor of production, contributing directly to economic growth and regeneration in towns and cities. However, inflexible lease terms can restrain business growth and expose them to undue risk. The Government is working with all parts of the industry to promote a voluntary Code of Conduct on Commercial Leases to improve lease flexibility. The effectiveness of the Code is being independently evaluated. Should the interim independent evaluation of the Code show that there has been little progress in the commercial lease market towards greater flexibility, the Government will consult later this year on possible legislative options to ameliorate the situation.

3.131 Tax distortions can be a further source of structural problems in the commercial property market. Chapter 5 outlines a series of reforms to stamp duty to tackle avoidance and reduce distortions to commercial decision-making. Tax reforms may also have a role to play in enhancing the property investment market. The Government will discuss with the industry the appropriate tax treatment of new property derivative products. Consultation on corporation tax reform also provides an opportunity to consider the tax treatment of commercial property. The Government also wishes to explore with the industry the evidence for further measures to improve the efficiency and flexibility of the commercial property market.

3.132 Building on the reforms to the planning regime and to raise levels of skills in the workforce described in this chapter, the next chapter sets out in detail the Government's wider strategy to create a dynamic and flexible labour market.

INCREASING EMPLOYMENT OPPORTUNITY FOR ALL

> The Government's long-term goal is employment opportunity for all – the modern definition of full employment. Its aim is to ensure a higher proportion of people in work than ever before by 2010. Worklessness, particularly on a long-term basis, is a constraint on the economy's growth potential and a major cause of poverty and deprivation. A dynamic and flexible labour market, that equips people to adapt to changing economic conditions, and which has the institutional flexibility to deliver high employment and low unemployment across the economic cycle, is key to achieving the Government's goal. Any decision to join the single currency would place a further premium on UK labour market flexibility, as well as other flexibilities, just as it does for existing members. Budget 2003 describes the action the Government is taking to increase flexibility in the labour market, including:
>
> - **extra help for unemployed people searching for jobs**, with additional interventions in the first six months;
>
> - **greater flexibility for Jobcentre Plus districts** to respond to local labour market conditions, with a new discretionary fund, more flexible options within the New Deal for young people, and greater rewards for successful managers;
>
> - **significant reform of Housing Benefit** to improve financial gains to work, facilitate labour mobility, and deliver greater reliability in the service to claimants;
>
> - **extension of Employment Zones** to lone parents and people returning to the New Deal for a second time, and the introduction of multiple providers;
>
> - **increases in the National Minimum Wage** from October 2003 for adult and youth workers and for those in approved training;
>
> - **improved support for lone parents**, with a flexible fund to improve access to debt advisory services and pilots of a new worksearch premium to cover the extra costs of looking for work;
>
> - **an enhanced New Deal for partners** from April 2004, bringing support for partners of benefit claimants into line with that available to lone parents; and
>
> - **extra support to help people from ethnic minorities**, with a new £8 million policy fund for Jobcentre Plus managers, and specialist advisers in Jobcentre Plus areas with high ethnic minority populations.

INTRODUCTION

4.1   The Government's long-term goal is to ensure a higher proportion of people in work than ever before by 2010. Worklessness, particularly on a long-term basis, is a constraint on Britain's growth potential – the strength of the economy depends on how many people are in work and on how productive they are. It is also a major cause of poverty and deprivation – for most families and individuals, employment is the single most effective means of avoiding poverty. The Government's strategy for delivering employment opportunity for all – the modern definition of full employment – involves maintaining macroeconomic stability and ensuring a dynamic and flexible labour market that equips people to adapt to change.

Labour market flexibility

4.2   There are many aspects to labour market flexibility, including the speed with which the labour market can adjust to economic shocks, the structural and institutional factors that influence wage setting and supply and demand in the labour market, and the equilibrium unemployment rate. While these aspects are interrelated, a flexible labour market can be defined as one that has the ability to adjust to changing economic conditions in a way that maintains high employment, low inflation and unemployment, and continued growth in real incomes.

4.3   An efficient and flexible labour market, that creates jobs, increases competitiveness, and raises productivity, is essential to the UK, whether or not it is a member of Economic and Monetary Union (EMU). Any decision to join the single currency would place a premium on adjustment mechanisms, which in the labour market equates with wage flexibility. While EMU membership has the potential to create more jobs, through greater trade opportunities and market integration, sufficient flexibility in wages, as well as other forms of flexibility, would be necessary to realise those gains. The preliminary and technical analysis supporting the five tests assessment includes an analysis of labour market flexibility which will be published as a supporting study alongside the assessment.

Flexibility and fairness

4.4   The UK labour market generally exhibits a high degree of flexibility and this has helped to deliver a strong performance in recent years, despite uncertain global conditions. With the right type of flexibility in British and European labour, capital and product markets, economic efficiency, employment opportunity and fairness can advance together. In the UK, as in the rest of the EU, labour markets must foster job creation and provide the right work incentives, while maintaining minimum standards in work and providing security for those who cannot work. However, significant sources of inflexibility remain, and this chapter explains how the Government is working to advance flexibility and fairness in the labour market by:

- ensuring that people are equipped to adapt to changing economic circumstances;

- providing adequate rewards from work while promoting stability in workers' incomes; and

- creating the institutional and structural flexibility needed to deliver high and sustainable employment.

Principles of intervention in the labour market

4.5   The Government believes that intervention to deliver a more effective, efficient, flexible and fair labour market must be driven by a set of key principles, described in Box 4.1. Key Government reforms exemplify principles-driven intervention. For example, the National Minimum Wage was introduced in response to the long-standing economic and social problem of low paid work, is kept under review by the Low Pay Commission and has successfully raised the incomes of low paid workers without jeopardising employment growth or wage stability. Similarly, the Working and Child Tax Credits were introduced to tackle poverty and improve gains to work following extensive consultation, a full Regulatory Impact Assessment and careful study of similar polices in other countries. The Government will continue to apply these principles as it considers future employment policies. The principles commit the Department of Trade and Industry to implement changes to employment regulation only in April and October, unless European obligations require otherwise. Where appropriate, other government departments will adopt the same approach.

Box 4.1: Key principles of intervention in the labour market

In a globally competitive environment, full employment can be achieved only by creating a more flexible and dynamic economy in which firms and individuals are equipped to respond quickly and easily to change. Flexibility and fairness in the labour market are not opposites but complements; labour market policy can and must promote both. Measures to ensure well-functioning markets must incorporate a social dimension, just as social objectives are most effectively realised when based on well-functioning markets. Intervention should be driven by the following principles:

- intervention only where there is a recognised and significant problem requiring a government response;

- full consideration of policy alternatives, to keep distortions and regulatory burdens to a minimum;

- benchmarking of new proposals against existing requirements in other OECD countries;

- assessment of the consequences for small firms in particular, and consideration of small firms' exemption where appropriate;

- testing for the impact on labour flexibility and employment opportunities, especially among disadvantaged or vulnerable groups;

- testing for the impact on productivity and growth;

- intervention will be subject to cost-benefit analysis and, for regulation, Regulatory Impact Assessment;

- proper consultation in compliance with the Government's code on written consultation, prior to a decision being taken;

- the Department of Trade and Industry will implement changes to employment regulations only in April and October each year, unless European obligations require otherwise;

- information and support packages for firms, for all measures which have a potentially large impact on businesses. This will include a strategy to help businesses comply with any new legal duties;

- promotion of alternative means of resolving employment disputes; and

- where EU regulation might affect competitiveness, evaluation by the Competitiveness Council prior to a decision being taken to ensure proposals are not harmful to economic and employment objectives.

The Government will present a submission to the EU Employment Taskforce, led by Wim Kok, setting out in detail this principled approach to labour market intervention.

4.6   At an EU level, labour market policy must also take account of the principle of subsidiarity – intervention should be undertaken at national level where possible, and at EU level where necessary. If institutions, social and legal frameworks and individual preferences vary substantially across Member States, EU level legislation removing existing flexibilities that help the labour market work more efficiently can harm the employment chances of those that it seeks to protect. Over-rigid legislation capping working time, for example, may not be the most appropriate means of protecting workers from the obligation to work excessive hours. As well as failing to target the problem, such an approach could constrain choice over working arrangements and income and, by adding to the regulatory burden, damage employment growth. Progress at an EU level towards more principles-based intervention, such as the Commission's commitment to impact assessment and consultation, is welcome but must be built upon.

4.7   EU Member States share common economic ambitions – high productivity and full employment – and a common commitment to social values. The Lisbon economic reform agenda recognises the multi-faceted economic, social and environmental nature of policy-making. While appropriate intervention in the labour market serves both economic and social goals, poorly targeted policy which distorts employer and employee decisions may lead to lower employment and increased duration of unemployment, thereby putting at risk both the EU's employment objectives and the longer term aim of employment opportunity for all. Since the Lisbon employment targets were agreed, the EU has created five million new jobs. However, much more progress is still needed:

- reaching the 70 per cent overall employment target requires the creation of a further 15 million jobs;

- meeting the 60 per cent goal for female employment requires a further 6 million jobs for women; and

- meeting the 50 per cent employment target for older workers would require at least 5 million more jobs for older people.

4.8   To ensure that labour market policy across the EU promotes flexibility and fairness, the Government will present a submission to the new Employment Taskforce setting out a principled approach to intervention in the broader context of a full employment strategy for Europe. The Employment Taskforce – launched at the March 2003 European Council, and chaired by the former Prime Minister of the Netherlands, Wim Kok – has been mandated to report by spring 2004 on the practical steps that Member States might take to achieve the Lisbon employment targets. The Government strongly welcomes this important and imaginative initiative, and looks forward to giving the Taskforce its full support.

Box 4.2: Delivering full employment in the European Union

The European Union contains 15 diverse labour markets, with different cultures, traditions, frameworks and institutions, but one common goal – employment opportunity for all. The EU has three employment targets for 2010: 70 per cent total employment, 60 per cent female employment, and 50 per cent employment among older workers. While the UK currently meets all of these targets, the labour market performance of other Member States has been less strong, and the EU as a whole falls short of meeting each target. A step change in the pace of reform is essential if these targets are to be met.

The European Employment Strategy (EES) is the key vehicle for labour market reform in the EU. The Government welcomes the recent agreement to align the new EES with the Lisbon 2010 timeframe and to incorporate within it the 2010 employment targets. The revised Strategy should focus on promoting employability and removing obstacles to work, and should be simplified with fewer guidelines.

Labour market reform is essential to achieve the EU's common goals, but must not come at the expense of those on the margins of the labour market. All employees should have a right to decent minimum standards in work and should not suffer unfair discrimination or inequality of opportunity. The challenge facing EU labour markets is to raise employment and increase social cohesion by making labour markets respond more efficiently to changes in economic conditions. Flexible working patterns and working hours are an important first step back into the labour market for vulnerable groups, such as lone parents and older workers, and enable firms to respond to difficult economic conditions. Badly targeted legislation on the other hand can reduce labour market flexibility and damages prospects of achieving the EU's employment targets.

EQUIPPING PEOPLE TO COPE WITH CHANGE

4.9   In an uncertain global environment it is more important than ever that labour markets are flexible enough to respond quickly to change. New technologies, changing consumer preferences, and evolving demands for particular skills require businesses and individuals to adapt so that resources remain in productive use and high employment can be maintained. Earlier this year, EU Member States agreed that measures to address change and promote adaptability, while ensuring a proper balance between flexibility and security, should be a priority area for reform across the EU[1].

4.10   Faced with economic shocks, regions or countries must have labour markets in which local wage setting is characterised by a low degree of rigidity, the institutional labour market framework is supportive of adjustment and job creation, and workers have opportunities to train and acquire new skills. Labour market flexibility helps particular regions, industries, and groups of workers to adapt to changing economic circumstances, preventing pockets of high and persistent unemployment emerging in the face of negative shocks. Flexibility also improves the ability of the economy to take advantage of the opportunities generated by positive shocks arising from changing consumer preferences, falling input prices, or the impact of innovation. A decision to join the single currency would place a premium on adjustment mechanisms, such as wage flexibility, that allow the labour market to respond rapidly to shocks.

---

[1] Employment Committee of the Employment, Social Policy, Health and Consumer Affairs Council, February 2003.

Functional flexibility

4.11   The ability of individuals to undertake a wide range of tasks – functional flexibility – allows people to adapt to changing patterns of demand and production techniques, promoting employment and productivity by ensuring that resources shift rapidly to more efficient roles. In a dynamic labour market, such as that in the UK, functional flexibility also ensures that those who become unemployed are able to return rapidly to employment. It will tend to be higher if there are more skilled people in the workforce and if active labour market policies are effective at re-attaching people to the labour market.

Workforce skills   **4.12**   The quantity and quality of skilled labour in an economy are important determinants of economic performance. Skilled workers often adapt faster and more effectively to change, making the labour market and the economy more flexible. International evidence suggests that the UK suffers from skills shortages, especially at the lower-intermediate level, and other EU Member States, such as Sweden, have demonstrated what can be achieved through a focus on skills and lifelong learning. As described in Chapter 3, the Government is taking action to raise levels of skills in the workforce, including through:

- the introduction of Enterprise Advisers and school pilots to promote enterprise learning throughout the education system and strengthen the links between education, enterprise and employment;

- the launch of a new employer-led National Modern Apprenticeship Taskforce to help increase the number of apprenticeship opportunities available for young people;

- the extension of Employer Training Pilots, to tackle the barriers which exclude people from the training they need to develop and progress; and

- a package of measures to facilitate migration as a source of skills and labour in the economy, building on previous reforms.

Active labour   **4.13**   The performance of the labour market over recent years has been strong by
market policies   international and historical standards. At 5.0 per cent, UK unemployment on the International Labour Organisation (ILO) definition is the lowest among the G7 economies. Claimant count unemployment has fallen by more than 700,000 since 1997 to levels last seen a generation ago, and since the start of 2001 has remained consistently below one million – the first time this has happened since 1975. Employment is currently at record highs, having risen by nearly 1.5 million since spring 1997. Labour market policies, including the New Deal and the Jobseeker's Allowance regime, which balance rights and responsibilities, have enabled the labour market to function better and are likely to have increased its flexibility.

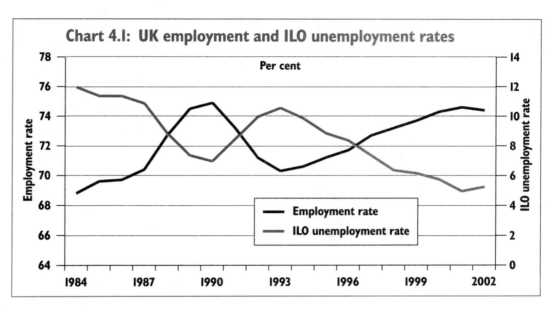

Chart 4.1: UK employment and ILO unemployment rates

Jobseeker's Allowance

4.14 The Jobseeker's Allowance (JSA) regime helps the labour market to adjust to changing economic conditions, by re-allocating labour as relative demand changes. Delivered through Jobcentre Plus, JSA provides individuals who are out of work and actively seeking employment with the advice and support they need to find jobs, helping to ensure that, for the majority of claimants, unemployment is a short-term experience. Compared with 1997, when nearly 40 per cent of claims lasted for more than a year, 69 per cent of JSA claims are now of less than six months duration. However, nearly 300,000 current JSA claims have lasted for over six months, and further support is therefore needed to ensure that a greater number of claimants find work earlier.

4.15 Budget 2003 introduces a series of reforms to build on the success of the JSA regime in maintaining low levels of unemployment, and to improve its effectiveness at helping people adapt to changing conditions. From April 2004, the reforms will:

- increase the minimum number of steps that JSA claimants are required to take to search for jobs, strengthening the emphasis on jobsearch; and

- increase the number of interventions in the first six months, with weekly signing for six weeks after the existing 13 week interview for all JSA claimants.

Welfare to Work

4.16 For those who remain unemployed for longer, the Government's Welfare to Work strategy ensures that they remain attached to the labour market, helping to sustain a dynamic and flexible labour market. The strategy seeks to tackle long-term unemployment by equipping people with the skills and opportunities they need to compete successfully for the vacancies generated by the labour market.

4.17 The New Deal for young people (NDYP), for 18 to 24 year olds, and the New Deal for those aged 25 and over (ND25+), provide a range of support for young and older long-term unemployed jobseekers. These programmes involve comprehensive support for jobsearch and have helped to deliver significant reductions in long-term and youth long-term unemployment. Almost 415,000 long-term unemployed 18 to 24 year olds have found jobs through NDYP, while ND25+ has helped more than 135,000 older people back into work. Independent research confirms the positive impact of the New Deal[2]. In addition, the New Deal for over 50s, introduced nationally in 2000, has helped to increase the employment rate of those aged between 50 and state retirement age to 69 per cent from 65 per cent in 1997.

---

[2] See, for example, *The New Deal for young people: implications for employment and the public finances*, National Institute of Economic and Social Research, December 2002; and *New Deal for young people: national follow through*, National Centre for Social Research, April 2000.

Local flexibility **4.18**   To deliver full employment throughout the country, local and regional economies must be equipped to adjust and respond to change. While the national New Deal programmes have successfully led to increases in overall employment, as shown in Chart 4.2, local concentrations of unemployment persist. Local staff are often best placed to identify the needs of local labour markets, and to adapt programmes to provide local solutions to employment problems in specific areas. Flexibility in regional and local employment policies can therefore help to ensure that people move back into employment quickly and are able to change jobs in response to changing local conditions, advancing the Government's goal to reduce the persistent gap in growth rates between different regions and localities.

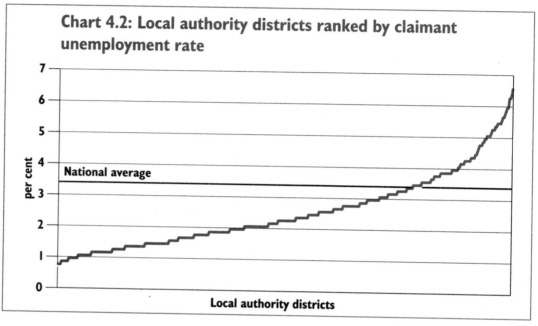

Chart 4.2: Local authority districts ranked by claimant unemployment rate

4.19   The Rapid Response Service (RRS) provides enhanced support to help local areas adapt to large-scale redundancies. While all areas will naturally experience and absorb flows in and out of work, areas with existing high unemployment or that are heavily dependent on one industry can suffer long-term damage when redundancies occur. The RRS seeks to address localised employment problems by offering flexible help tailored to meet the needs of individuals, employers, and the local economy.

4.20   Budget 2003 takes further steps to enhance flexibility in local employment policies. From April 2004, Jobcentre Plus districts will be given greater flexibility and discretion to increase their effectiveness in moving people quickly into work:

- a new discretionary fund will give District Managers enhanced flexibility to direct resources, including to address specific barriers to work affecting the local community;

- advisers will have greater discretion over which clients qualify for early entry to the New Deal;

- districts will be able to adopt a more flexible approach to the length and design of the options within the New Deal for young people, with the minimum length of options reduced from 26 weeks to 13 weeks;

- Jobcentre Plus will develop a partnership strategy to work more closely with private recruitment agencies; and

- with immediate effect, managers in the most successful districts will receive greater rewards, while those who fail to deliver a high standard of service will be replaced.

Employment   **4.21**   Alongside the New Deal, Employment Zones are testing an innovative approach to
Zones   helping long-term unemployed people aged 25 and over back into work. Currently operating in 15 areas of England, Scotland and Wales, Employment Zones allow jobseekers and their personal advisers to use funds with complete flexibility to overcome individual barriers to work. The Government is taking further steps to extend the help provided by Employment Zones more widely and to encourage innovation among providers:

- from October 2003, the Employment Zone approach will be extended to people who would otherwise return to the New Deal for young people for a second or subsequent time in existing Employment Zone areas;

- from April 2004, multiple providers will be introduced in the five London Employment Zones, as well as in the Birmingham, Liverpool and Glasgow Zones. Multiple providers will each be allocated a random cross-section of clients with similar characteristics so that performance can be compared on a like-for-like basis; and

- from April 2004, Employment Zones will replace the New Deal for lone parents (NDLP) in the five London Zones, and will replace the NDLP for lone parents returning for a second or subsequent work-focused interview in the other Zones.

Labour market   **4.22**   Access to good quality information about local labour markets can help people to
information   make well-informed decisions about their employment choices and respond to changes in local conditions. To improve the availability of such information, the Department for Work and Pensions and the Department for Education and Skills, working with local, regional and national partners, will publish an action plan later this year, setting out proposals to improve collation of the numerous sources of labour market information that exist, and to make these accessible to a wide range of users.

Geographic labour mobility

4.23   Geographic labour mobility refers to the ability and willingness of workers to commute or move location to find employment. The extent of geographic mobility depends on a range of factors, including the flexibility of the housing market, the ease of commuting, and the degree to which economic migrants are attracted to, and able to move to, high demand areas. In the UK, as elsewhere in Europe, geographic mobility tends to be relatively low. However, Government policies aim to exert a positive impact on mobility and make it easier for people to move location in response to change, including through:

- an increase in the area over which JSA claimants are expected to travel in order to find work, from one hour to one and a half hours travelling time, after 13 weeks on JSA;

- reforms to facilitate migration as a source of skills and labour in the UK. As described in Chapter 3, Budget 2003 introduces new measures to maximise the economic benefits of migration and to help employers facing recruitment difficulties, building on the success of the Highly Skilled Migrant Programme and the Work Permits system;

- new proposals to increase flexibility in the housing market, through a step change in housing provision and reforms to the planning system described in Chapter 3. Reforms to Housing Benefit, described later in this chapter, will also help people move between different jobs and localities; and

- a review of Government support for local bus services, described in Chapter 7, to ensure that these better meet the needs of local people and communities.

Employment flexibility

4.24   Employment flexibility is the ability, or willingness, of employers and employees to adjust working patterns to meet new challenges. Flexible working patterns that allow people to balance work with other responsibilities can have a positive influence on the overall supply of labour, encouraging people to take up jobs they might not otherwise have done. The UK labour market exhibits a significant degree of employment flexibility, with a high incidence of part-time working and widespread adoption of flexible working practices, generally as a result of workers' choices. Around 25 per cent of total UK employment is part-time and the distribution of hours worked is far wider than in most other EU countries. The Government believes that the European regulatory framework should continue to support individual choice over flexible working patterns and hours.

4.25   The Government has taken steps to improve levels of employment flexibility in the UK. As described in Chapter 5, reforms to the tax and benefit system since 1997, including the introduction of the Child and Working Tax Credits and new maternity, paternity and adoption leave rights, are helping to deliver a step change in choice and support for parents, increasing the flexibility of the labour market. Chapter 5 also describes the Government's strategy[3] for enhancing this support, in particular by supporting parents to secure the benefits of more flexible working arrangements.

Flexibility in wage setting

4.26   A dynamic and flexible labour market requires wages to respond flexibly to shocks and to imbalances between supply and demand. Adjustment of wages would be even more important within a single currency since changes in external competitiveness would be driven by inflation differentials alone. Historically, real wage flexibility has appeared relatively low in the UK and may have contributed to the high levels of unemployment experienced in the 1980s and early 1990s. Real wages have tended to be rigid in the face of high levels of unemployment but have grown strongly when unemployment has fallen. The preliminary and technical analysis supporting the five test assessment of labour market flexibility includes an analysis of wage flexibility.

4.27   Relative wage flexibility – the extent to which wages vary between different sectors or regions in response to changing conditions – also needs to be sufficiently high to provide incentives for labour to move in response to changes in demand between industries and sectors. Flexible relative wages reduce the likelihood of mismatch between labour supply and demand occurring at the sectoral or regional level.

4.28   Evidence suggests that wages in the UK do tend to adjust across regions and across skills. There is considerable scope for variation in wage settlements between individual industries and regions, and this responsiveness appears to have increased over time.[4]

Public sector wage flexibility   **4.29**   However, while relative wage flexibility is generally high in the private sector, where wage setting is highly decentralised, institutional constraints remain. The Government's cross-cutting review of the public sector labour market, conducted as part of the 2002 Spending Review, found that public sector wages vary far less by region compared with those in the private sector, with relatively little variation between regions outside London. The review concluded that there was significant scope to increase the flexibility and responsiveness of the public sector labour market through the setting of pay and workforce conditions.

---

[3] *Balancing work and family life: enhancing choice and support for parents*, HM Treasury and the Department of Trade and Industry, January 2003.

[4] See, for example, *Wage Flexibility and EMU*, Chapter 4 in UK Selected Issues, IMF Staff Country Report No. 00/106, IMF (2000).

4.30   To recognise local and regional conditions in pay, especially for the low paid, the Government will therefore make sure that the remit for the Pay Review Bodies and for public sector workers includes a stronger local and regional dimension. Further information on public sector pay and workforce initiatives is set out in Chapter 6.

MAKING WORK PAY

4.31   A flexible and dynamic labour market requires work incentives that make it worthwhile for all individuals to compete in the labour market. In March this year the European Council agreed on the need for EU-wide reform of tax and benefit systems in Europe in order to increase work incentives across the Union. In Britain, with the introduction of tax credits, the Government has already made the shift from a benefit system that created barriers to work to a system that advances labour market flexibility by providing greater rewards from work while promoting stability in incomes. The Government's strategy to make work pay tackles two problems:

- the unemployment trap, when those without work find the difference between in-work and out-of-work income too small to provide an incentive to enter the labour market. The unemployment trap reduces labour market flexibility as people choose not to take jobs even if vacancies are available; and

- the poverty trap, when those in work are discouraged from working longer hours or from taking a better paid job because it may leave them little better off. The poverty trap restricts functional and employment flexibility since workers see little gain from adjusting their working patterns.

National Minimum Wage   **4.32**   The National Minimum Wage provides fair minimum incomes from work, while allowing wages to respond to labour market conditions. In March 2003, the Government published the Fourth Report from the Low Pay Commission (LPC). The Report found that the National Minimum Wage had no discernible negative impact on overall employment, inflation or the wider economy. The LPC also found that the increase in the National Minimum Wage in October 2001 had particularly benefited disabled people and women and had helped to make flexible working patterns more attractive – they estimate that 70 per cent of employees benefiting from the increase were women, 13 per cent were disabled, and two-thirds worked part-time.

4.33   In the light of these findings, the rate for adult workers aged 22 or over will be increased to £4.50 an hour from October 2003 and, subject to consideration of the LPC's review early next year, to £4.85 from October 2004. The youth and development rate, for workers aged between 18 and 21 or in approved training, will also rise, to £3.80 from October 2003 and to £4.10 from October 2004. The increased differential between the adult and youth rates will help to address the problem of low pay among adult workers, who are more likely to face in-work poverty or poor work incentives, while providing flexibility for employers to hire less experienced younger workers. The LPC estimates that at least 1.3 million low paid workers will benefit from the new rates of the National Minimum Wage in October 2003, and that at least 1.7 million will benefit in October 2004.

4.34   As described in Chapter 5, the Government has also agreed that the LPC should look into the advantages and disadvantages of a minimum wage for 16 and 17 year olds and will conduct a wider, cross-government, review of financial support for 16 to 19 year olds, including the financial incentives for young people to participate in education and training and the interaction between this support and any new minimum wage for 16 and 17 year olds. The review will report in spring 2004.

The Working Tax Credit 4.35   The tax and benefit system also influences the extent to which the labour market responds to economic shocks. Building on the success of earlier reforms, Budget 2002 introduced a new system of support to help families, tackle child poverty and make work pay. Paid from this month, **the Child and Working Tax Credits consolidate and improve existing streams of child and in-work support**. Details of the Child Tax Credit are set out in Chapter 5.

4.36   The Working Tax Credit is designed to help tackle poor work incentives and persistent poverty among working people, providing support on top of the guarantee provided by the National Minimum Wage. It replaces the adult elements of the Working Families' Tax Credit and the Disabled Person's Tax Credit and extends in-work support to workers aged 25 or over without children or disabilities working 30 or more hours a week. The Working Tax Credit also replaces the New Deal 50+ Employment Credit, by including a return-to-work element for people aged 50 or over who have received certain out-of-work benefits for at least six months.

Tackling the unemployment trap 4.37   Table 4.1 shows how, since the introduction of the National Minimum Wage in April 1999 and the Working Families' Tax Credit in October 1999, the Government has increased the minimum income that people can expect when moving into work, including through increases in the National Minimum Wage in October 2003.

Table 4.1: Weekly minimum income guarantees

	April 1999	October 1999	October 2003
Family 1 child, full-time work (35 hours)	£182	£200	£241
Family 1 child, part-time work (16 hours)	£136	£144	£184
Single person, no children, 25 or over, full-time work (35 hours)	£113	£113	£158
Couple, no children, 25 or over, full-time work (35 hours)	£117	£117	£187

Note: assumes prevailing rate of National Minimum Wage and that the family is eligible for the Working Families' Tax Credit and, from April 2003, the Working Tax Credit/Child Tax Credit.

4.38   The Government's reforms, including the introduction of the Child and Working Tax Credits, have increased the gains to work for households with children. Chart 4.3 shows the effect on households with one child.

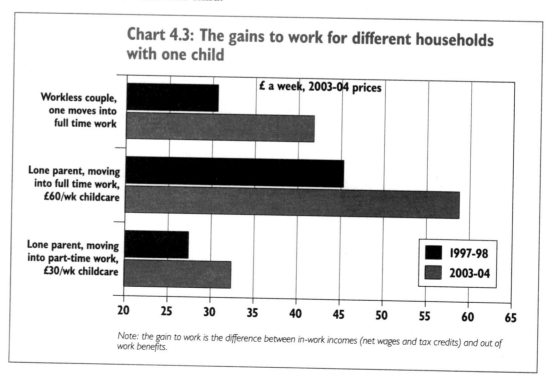

Chart 4.3: The gains to work for different households with one child

£ a week, 2003-04 prices

- Workless couple, one moves into full time work
- Lone parent, moving into full time work, £60/wk childcare
- Lone parent, moving into part-time work, £30/wk childcare

1997-98
2003-04

20 25 30 35 40 45 50 55 60 65

Note: the gain to work is the difference between in-work incomes (net wages and tax credits) and out of work benefits.

4.39   The Working Tax Credit improves work incentives for workers aged 25 and over without children. From October 2003, a couple aged 25 and over in full-time work without children or a disability will be guaranteed at least £187 per week. This represents an increase in gains to work to £40 per week, compared with £15 per week before the introduction of the Working Tax Credit. The reforms also mean that a single person aged 25 or over without children working full-time on the National Minimum Wage will be more than £25 a week better off from October 2003 compared with the previous system – an 18 per cent increase in income.

Tackling the poverty trap

4.40   While improved gains to work are tackling the unemployment trap, the Government also wants to ensure that workers have incentives to move up the earnings ladder. Tackling the poverty trap improves labour market flexibility by providing stronger incentives for people to respond to the opportunities generated by change – for example, by adjusting their working patterns, or moving into better paid jobs. Marginal deduction rates measure the extent of the poverty trap by showing how much of each additional pound of gross earnings is lost through higher taxes and withdrawn benefit or tax credits. As a result of the Government's reforms, over half a million fewer low-income households now face marginal deduction rates in excess of 70 per cent than did so in April 1997. The increase in the number of households facing marginal deduction rates of between 60 and 70 per cent is primarily due to the introduction of tax credits, and more recently the extension of support to workers aged 25 or over without children.

Table 4.2: The effect of the Government's reforms on high marginal deduction rates

Marginal deduction rate [1]	Before Budget 1998	2003-04 system of tax and benefits
Over 100 per cent	5,000	0
Over 90 per cent	130,000	30,000
Over 80 per cent	300,000	135,000
Over 70 per cent	740,000	185,000
Over 60 per cent	760,000	1,490,000

[1] Marginal deduction rates are for working households in receipt of income-related benefits or tax credits where at least one person works 16 hours or more a week.

Note: Figures are cumulative. Before Budget 1998 based on 1997-98 estimated caseload and take-up rates; the 2003-04 system of tax and benefits is based on 2001-02 caseload and take-up rates, and projected caseload estimates of Working Tax Credit and Child Tax Credit in 2003-04 based on 1999-2000 caseload and take-up rates.

Income stability

4.41   The Government's reforms are designed to advance flexibility and fairness together, providing people with incentives to adapt to change while tackling the insecurities that surround it. The National Minimum Wage and the Child and Working Tax Credits guarantee a minimum income from work, helping to tackle the unemployment trap and ensuring that work pays more than benefits. The National Minimum Wage and the tax credits also interact to help the labour market respond flexibly to economic shocks, while preserving a degree of stability in workers' incomes.

4.42   The National Minimum Wage sets a floor to earnings at a cautious level, preventing the worst instances of low pay. Above that level, the tax credits respond to changes in income, cushioning the effect that temporary fluctuations in earnings have on overall income while preserving incentives to work. For example, if a family with one child, in receipt of the new tax credits and earning £12,000 a year, faced a £3,000 reduction in their gross earnings in a given tax year, the level of support provided through the Working Tax Credit would adjust to provide an additional £20 a week, offsetting some of the reduction in income. However, if the same family saw their earnings rise by £3,000, the level of support provided through the Working Tax Credit would fall by a much smaller amount, since the new tax credits respond only to rises in income of more than £2,500 in the current tax year.

FULL EMPLOYMENT IN A FLEXIBLE LABOUR MARKET

4.43   As well as adjusting rapidly to changing economic conditions, a dynamic and flexible labour market must also have the institutional and structural flexibility to deliver sustained high employment and low unemployment across the economic cycle.

4.44   The UK labour market has historically suffered from important structural inflexibilities. Macroeconomic instability during the 1980s and early 1990s left large numbers of people detached from the labour market, while institutional barriers and the tax and benefit system provided insufficient incentives and support to help people return to work. Offered too little help, many who lost their jobs drifted into economic inactivity, often on disability-related benefits. The failure of the labour market to adapt to changing conditions in the short term reduced employment opportunities for many over the longer term.

4.45   While the performance of the labour market has improved markedly in recent years, areas of concern remain – in particular, to address persistent levels of economic inactivity. Inactivity is as much of a constraint on the economy's growth potential as unemployment and, in contrast to previous economic cycles, has not fallen as unemployment has declined in recent years. A disproportionate number of the inactive are found in particular groups of the population, including lone parents and the long-term sick and disabled. Tackling inactivity is therefore key to improving the employment prospects of these groups. Some areas also have persistently high levels of unemployment, inactivity and deprivation and have failed to share in the rising national prosperity that economic stability has brought. The remainder of this chapter sets out the next steps in the Government's strategy to address the structural and institutional inflexibilities that stand in the way of its ambition to deliver employment opportunity for all.

Reforming Housing Benefit

4.46   Housing Benefit provides help with rental costs for low income tenants in and out of work. Around 3.8 million tenants rely on it for help with their rent. Box 4.3 shows how the design and administration of Housing Benefit can create powerful disincentives to move into work and constrain flexibility in the labour market.

4.47   The Government is determined to alleviate the problems associated with Housing Benefit in order to reduce its capacity to act as a barrier to work. It has already published detailed proposals to reform the administration and design of Housing Benefit[5] and from October 2003, will pilot a new standard local housing allowance for tenants in the private sector in ten Pathfinder areas. This will ensure that private sector tenants know how much Housing Benefit they will be entitled to in advance of signing a tenancy agreement, regardless of the accommodation they choose to live in. The Government intends to introduce the flat rate system in the private sector throughout the country as soon as possible, giving all private sector tenants greater choice and information when taking decisions about where to live. This reform will also promote improved labour mobility by making it easier for tenants to move localities in response to changing labour market conditions.

---

[5] *Building choice and responsibility: a radical agenda for Housing Benefit*, Department for Work and Pensions, October 2002.

Box 4.3: Housing Benefit – the need for reform

The current system of Housing Benefit is complex and difficult to administer, and performance in delivering a quick and efficient service is highly variable. The requirement on claimants to submit new claims each time they find a job leads many claimants to worry that their benefit payments will be interrupted if they move into work. Moreover, claimants in the private rented sector often do not know the level of their entitlement until they have signed a tenancy agreement, with 70 per cent of private tenants subsequently finding that their rental costs are not fully covered by their benefit payment. These factors inhibit labour market flexibility by discouraging people from moving to areas of higher employment to look for work.

The interaction of Housing Benefit and Council Tax Benefit with tax credits can also erode financial incentives to work. For each additional £1 of income earned through work or tax credits, entitlement to Housing Benefit and Council Tax Benefit is withdrawn at a rate of 85 pence, restricting financial gains to work to just 15 pence in the pound. Areas with high rental costs are particularly affected, as Housing Benefit continues to be payable on relatively high incomes. The chart below demonstrates how gains to work are diminished under the existing system.

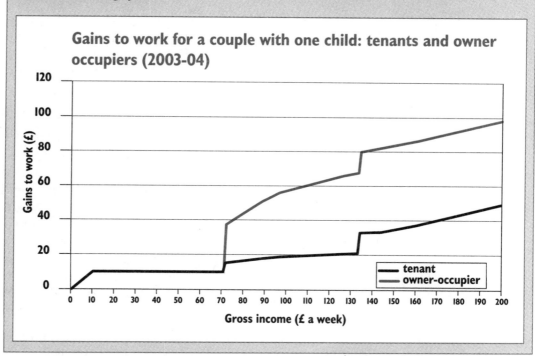

Gains to work for a couple with one child: tenants and owner occupiers (2003-04)

4.48   Claimants should also expect a swift and reliable service regardless of where they make their claim. To reduce variations in service and errors in processing, the Government therefore intends to implement a series of radical reforms to simplify the administration of Housing Benefit. From April 2004:

- claimants will no longer be required to submit a new claim each time they return to work and will need only to report their change in circumstances to the local authority instead. Housing Benefit will be paid at their previous out-of-work rate until the new benefit level is recalculated, even if this goes beyond the four-week run-on period;

- claimants will no longer be required to reclaim Housing Benefit periodically;

- claimants of Incapacity Benefit or Severe Disablement Allowance will be treated in the same way as JSA and Income Support claimants when they return to work and will benefit from the Housing Benefit run-on; and

- the calculation of Housing Benefit will disregard the first £11.90 of earnings for all tenants who are claiming, or are entitled to claim, the Working Tax Credit, rather than the current disregard of the 30 hour premium. This will improve gains to work for tenants with children or a disability working between 16 and 30 hours per week, replacing the current disregard of the 30 hour premium. For a typical lone parent working part-time at the National Minimum Wage and renting their property, this change will mean that their weekly income will be at least £40 more than they could expect to receive if claiming benefits.

4.49   In addition, as described in Chapter 5, from May 2003 the period over which hospital inpatients receive most benefit entitlements, including Housing Benefit, will be extended to 52 weeks.

Reform in the social sector   **4.50**   Tenants in the social sector should benefit from having the same fair and transparent help with housing costs as those in the private sector, and should also be able to make decisions based on value and price when choice is available to them. The process of restructuring rents in the social sector in England is well underway and will be substantially completed by 2011. Restructuring will ensure that the pattern of social housing rents represents more closely the relative attractiveness of properties to tenants. The Government's targets to ensure that 25 per cent of local authorities adopt some form of choice-based letting scheme by 2005, and that all local authorities offer choice to applicants by 2010, will complement and reinforce this process.

4.51   The Government therefore intends to implement a flat rate Housing Benefit system in the social sector, similar to that anticipated in the private rented sector, as soon as rent restructuring and increased choice create a better market. In extending the flat rate system to the social sector the Government will take into consideration a number of factors, including:

- the fact that social sector rent levels vary significantly between localities;

- differences in rents and occupancy restrictions between those social tenants housed by Registered Social Landlords and those housed by local authorities;

- the fact that social housing, unlike private accommodation, is partly funded through capital subsidies;

- the need to ensure adequate protection of the most vulnerable groups, such as pensioners and people with disabilities; and

- the need to ensure overall comparability of treatment between tenants in the social and private rented sectors.

Further reform **4.52**   The Government is committed to further structural reform of Housing Benefit in order to ease the transition to work for all working age tenants and ensure that they see appropriate gains to work as they progress within employment. Such action will address the problem of steep benefit withdrawal rates in order to deliver a more effective system of housing cost support that works with, rather than against, the new tax credits. The Government will look at ways of aligning the rules of Housing Benefit and tax credits – in particular, with regard to the way they treat child maintenance.

Tackling wider worklessness

4.53   The Government's strategy to improve structural flexibility in the labour market has delivered important reductions in worklessness. The number of workless households has fallen by over 350,000 from its peak of almost $3^1/_2$ million in 1995, while the proportion of children living in workless households has fallen from over 19 per cent to less than 16 per cent in the same period.

4.54   Nonetheless, there are still more than $4^1/_4$ million people of working age living in households in which no-one is working, and in many workless households there is at least one person claiming an inactive benefit. The delivery of effective, work-focused support to all working age benefit recipients is key to ensuring that employment opportunity is extended to all and to tackling child poverty.

Jobcentre Plus **4.55**   The creation of Jobcentre Plus brings together the Employment Service and those parts of the Benefits Agency dealing with working age people to provide inactive benefit claimants with the same level of work-focused support available to other benefit claimants. Anyone making a claim for benefit at a Jobcentre Plus office receives a meeting with a personal adviser to discuss the opportunities available for work and can access job vacancies, advice, training and support. This balancing of rights and responsibilities is central to the Government's strategy of work for those who can and security for those who cannot. Jobcentre Plus also helps employers find the right employees for their vacancies, enabling the labour market to adjust to changes in the pattern of employment more quickly.

4.56   Since its launch in April 2002, more than 200 new Jobcentre Plus offices have opened and the Government aims to have opened more than 500 offices in total by April 2004, completing the nationwide roll out in 2006. While levels of customer satisfaction are already high, the Government continues to seek improvements in the performance and accountability of Jobcentre Plus as it rolls out new offices nationwide, and has begun publishing quarterly district performance tables on the Jobcentre Plus website to encourage such improvements.

4.57   Budget 2003 announces plans to enhance the relationship between Jobcentre Plus and employers, in order to provide employers with increased help to find suitable candidates for their vacancies. Steps being taken include:

- specialist sector managers to provide a highly responsive job placement service to ten key industrial sectors;

- specialist managers to develop an enhanced relationship with small businesses, and to increase co-ordination of Jobcentre Plus activities across small business networks; and

- detailed advice to employers on the supply of labour in their local area.

Helping lone parents

4.58 Over the last 20 years increases in participation among women, especially among mothers, have contributed significantly to labour supply. However, lone parent employment rates have lagged substantially behind those of mothers in couples. Lone parents face particularly difficult choices when seeking to balance work and caring responsibilities. The overwhelming majority of lone parents want to work and helping them to find employment is key to reducing the number of workless households and the incidence of child poverty. The Government's target is to ensure that 70 per cent of lone parents are in work by 2010.

New Deal for lone parents

4.59 The New Deal for lone parents (NDLP) provides a comprehensive package of support, including access to a personal adviser; help with training, education and childcare; and advice on benefits, in-work financial support and self-employment. Eligibility for NDLP has been extended to all lone parents who are either not working or who work less than 16 hours a week, and more than 175,000 lone parents have moved into work with its support. Employment among lone parents has risen substantially, from just over 40 per cent throughout the early 1990s to 54 per cent in spring 2002, while the number of lone parents claiming Income Support has fallen by almost one-fifth since 1997. Evaluation evidence[6] confirms the overwhelmingly positive impact of NDLP in helping lone parents into work and suggests that the programme more than doubles the employment chances of participants.

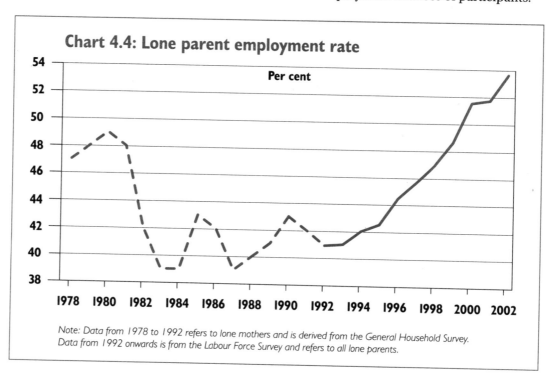

Chart 4.4: Lone parent employment rate

Per cent

Note: Data from 1978 to 1992 refers to lone mothers and is derived from the General Household Survey. Data from 1992 onwards is from the Labour Force Survey and refers to all lone parents.

4.60 Despite the significant progress made so far, the Government recognises that it must continue to improve and enhance the help it offers to lone parents to ensure that the 2010 target is met. The Government therefore intends to enhance the level of work-focused support provided through Jobcentre Plus and NDLP, improve incentives for lone parents to work, and increase access to good quality and affordable childcare.

---

[6] *New Deal for lone parents: findings from the quantitative survey*, Department for Work and Pensions, March 2003.

Enhancing work-focused support 4.61   The delivery of work-focused support to lone parents through Jobcentre Plus is central to the Government's strategy. Compulsory personal adviser meetings already ensure that most lone parents are aware of the help available to them and have access to this support when they need it. These meetings have significantly increased the take-up of NDLP – more than a quarter of lone parents who attend a meeting decide to join the programme. The Government seeks continuously to improve the quality of personal adviser meetings, to ensure that they meet the needs of lone parents, even as their circumstances change. As announced in Budget 2002, from April 2004, the requirement to attend a personal adviser meeting will be extended to lone parents on Income Support with children under the age of five, completing the extension of compulsory adviser meetings to all lone parents.

4.62   Following the success of recent pilots, the Government has begun introducing a new national mentoring service for lone parents, to provide confidential advice and support on a wide range of issues and increase the help available to those who wish to make the transition to work.

4.63   As announced in the 2002 Pre-Budget Report, the Government has also asked the National Employment Panel to consult leading employers on how they might help lone parents into employment. A group chaired by Ben Verwaayen, chief executive of British Telecom, and involving representatives of leading employers and lone parents' interest groups has now reported. In line with the recommendations of the group, the Government now intends to:

- pilot immediately a new communications and outreach strategy in six cities with high lone parent populations, working closely with employers;

- pilot a Discovery Week in the same six cities from autumn 2003 to boost soft skills, such as confidence, and increase the familiarity of lone parents with the help and support available to them. British Telecom has already agreed to work with Jobcentre Plus on the first Discovery Week, in London;

- pilot childcare tasters from April 2004 to allow lone parents on NDLP to access formal childcare for up to one week to test whether it suits their needs; and

- encourage employers to consider flexible working arrangements, recruitment and staff benefit packages, so that a broader range of people, including lone parents, consider work opportunities in a wider range of occupations.

Help with the costs of finding work 4.64   For many lone parents, the costs involved in looking for work act as a disincentive to worksearch. To help overcome this problem, the Government intends to provide additional support to those lone parents who are actively searching for a job. From October 2004, a new worksearch premium of £20 per week, paid on top of normal benefit entitlements, will be available in eight pilot areas to lone parents who have been on Income Support for more than one year and who voluntarily choose to actively search for a job. The premium will be continued at the higher rate of £40 per week for the first year in work. In a further four pilot areas, the in-work element will be tested separately.

Improving incentives to work   **4.65**   Reform of the tax and benefit system, including the introduction of tax credits, has helped to make work pay for lone parents and enabled many to adopt flexible working arrangements without losing out financially. Nonetheless, the transition from welfare to work can be an uncertain time and the Government recognises that there is a need for further action. Budget 2003 therefore introduces a new flexible fund for Jobcentre Plus managers to improve access to debt advisory services in areas where provision is limited from April 2004. This will allow lone parents and other benefit claimants to access advice on debt issues before they take up work, helping to ensure that employment is financially sustainable.

Help with childcare   **4.66**   For many working families, and for lone parents in particular, access to good quality and affordable childcare is key to participation in the labour market. Financial support to help low- and middle-income working parents meet the costs of childcare is now provided through the Working Tax Credit. As described in Chapter 5, eligibility for the childcare element of the Working Tax Credit has also been extended to include those who use approved childcare in their own home.

4.67   The Government is also investing record amounts to help meet the growing demand for childcare, and has supported the creation of places that have helped more than 1.1 million children since 1997. To increase access to affordable and good quality childcare, the level of funding for childcare will more than double in real terms between 2002-03 and 2005-06, as part of an increase in the budget of the Sure Start Unit to £1.5 billion. These additional funds are designed to:

- ensure the creation of at least 250,000 new childcare places by 2006, including childcare provided directly in Children's Centres; and

- support the creation and operation of Children's Centres in disadvantaged areas, building, where possible, on Sure Start local programme facilities and other existing provision. By 2006, an additional 300,000 children will have access to Children's Centre services.

4.68   As described in Chapter 5, the Government is also consulting[7] on a series of proposals to encourage more employers to help their staff meet the costs of safe, good quality childcare.

Help for partners

4.69   Women in couples with a partner claiming benefit have much lower levels of labour market participation than those in couples where the partner is in work. Even in the 1990s, the benefit system treated partners of unemployed people – overwhelmingly women – as 'adult dependants' of the claimant – overwhelmingly men – offering them no help in accessing opportunities in the labour market. The 1980s and early 1990s also saw a rise in the number of workless households, as the tax and benefit system failed to provide incentives for either partner to move into work. The overall effect was to constrain labour supply, reducing flexibility in the labour market.

4.70   Everyone who is workless should have access to the work-focused support provided by Jobcentre Plus. The Government's long-term aim is to extend rights and responsibilities in the benefit system further, so that all partners of benefit claimants have access to the help and support they need and are not excluded from support as they have been in the past.

---

[7] *Employer supported childcare*, Inland Revenue and HM Treasury, February 2003.

4.71   Steps have already been taken to extend the rights and responsibilities of JSA claimants to partners on an equal basis and childless partners of the unemployed, where at least one partner was born after 1957, are now joint JSA claimants. As announced in the 2002 Pre-Budget Report, the Government also intends to introduce **compulsory work-focused interviews for partners of all new benefit claimants and existing claimants without children** from April 2004, beyond those having joint claim status for JSA. This will be extended to existing claimants with children once the roll out of Jobcentre Plus is complete. The Government is currently considering whether further changes could be made to the benefit system to provide additional support to workless households, building on the success of joint claims for JSA.

New Deal for partners   4.72   Targeted support for households in which both partners are workless is provided through the New Deal for partners – a personal adviser service for partners of benefit claimants. To improve the support offered under the programme, **the New Deal for partners will be enhanced from April 2004**, to coincide with the introduction of compulsory work-focused interviews. The enhanced New Deal will provide the same package of support as that currently available to lone parents, including a training allowance and help with childcare. Partners will also be eligible for the enhanced Job Grant from October 2004.

Help for people with disabilities

4.73   Despite the strong performance of the labour market in recent years, inactivity rates among people with disabilities have been slow to fall. While annual flows onto incapacity-related benefits have fallen by nearly a quarter since 1996, the average length of claim for those with claims lasting over a year has increased to eight years. As a consequence, more than 2.7 million people are now in receipt of incapacity-related benefits – many more than the combined total of lone parents and unemployed people on benefit.

New Deal for disabled people   4.74   The New Deal for disabled people (NDDP) was introduced nationally in 2001. NDDP engages those moving onto incapacity-related benefits and provides a national network of innovative job brokers to help disabled people locate and move into secure employment. Around 9,000 people have been helped into work through the programme.

Support in work   4.75   The Government also provides financial support to help disabled people meet the additional costs they face when in work. Last year, almost 40,000 people received in-work support through the Disabled Person's Tax Credit (DPTC) – more than double the number who received Disability Working Allowance at its peak in June 1999. From this month, financial support for disabled people in work is provided through the Working Tax Credit which increases the guaranteed minimum income for a single disabled person working 35 hours to £194 a week – £19 a week more in real terms than in April 2002.

Next steps   4.76   The Government is considering the scope for further action to help people with health problems and disabilities find work and will **pilot a series of measures from October 2003** to provide new recipients of incapacity-related benefits with greater support earlier in their claims. The 2002 Spending Review allocated £97 million over three years to support the new pilots, which will test the effectiveness of more responsive work-focused interviews, rehabilitation measures, and a return to work payment of £40 per week for 52 weeks. The measures will also be available to current recipients of incapacity-related benefits. Details of the pilots were set out in the November 2002 Green Paper.[8] The Government will publish its response to the consultation on the Green Paper proposals shortly.

---

[8] *Pathways to work: helping people into employment*, Department for Work and Pensions, November 2002.

Box 4.4: Work and income security for disabled people

Transforming disability into ability, an OECD report into work and income security for disabled people, was published in February 2003. The report made a series of policy recommendations designed to help people with disabilities into work:

- disability status should be recognised as independent of the claimant's work and income situation, and be the basis for benefits that are designed to compensate for the extra costs of medication, care or mobility needs. It should be paid only for as long as these additional costs arise, and eligibility should be reassessed regularly. Some countries unbundle disability status and benefit receipt – for example, in Denmark, pensions are allowed to "rest" while claimants work, while in Sweden, disability pensions are "frozen". In the UK, "linking rules" allow people in receipt of Incapacity Benefit to try out work, returning to the same level of benefit if they lose their job within a year;

- in return for benefits, claimants should have an obligation to participate in activities deemed appropriate by the State so as to prevent isolation and exclusion from society. Several countries, including Denmark, Austria and Sweden, require claimants of disability benefits to participate in vocational rehabilitation schemes, with receipt of a disability settlement conditional upon completion of this process. In most cases however, this obligation is subject to a high degree of flexibility and discretion, depending on, for example, the age and work experience of the disabled person. Conditionality in Germany and Norway operates in a moderated way. In the UK, disabled people will be required to participate in work-focused interviews, but involvement in rehabilitation and NDDP is voluntary;

- work and benefit packages should be individually designed, and should include rehabilitation, vocational training and work experience. In the UK, NDDP offers vocational training experience, while those on Incapacity Benefit can try out work for up to a year;

- early intervention is the most effective means of insuring against long-term benefit dependence. In the UK, the Government is consulting on a proposal to introduce intensive work-focused interviews for new claimants, before they become benefit dependent;

- existing employer-employee relationships should be utilised by establishing positive incentives and legal obligations. In Italy, employers have been made responsible for assigning people who become disabled tasks equivalent to their previous role, or a lower-grade role, under the same terms and conditions. In the UK, new pilot schemes are testing a variety of measures to improve job retention and rehabilitation, while, from October 2004, the Disability Discrimination Act will require all employers to make reasonable adjustments to enable people with disabilities to work; and

- benefit systems should be restructured to remove the disincentives to work that can occur as a result of income replacement benefits, with claimants instead offered financial incentives to return to work. In the UK, the Working Tax Credit includes an element to support workers with a disability and the Government intends to pilot a new £40 a week return to work credit for people who have claimed incapacity-related benefits for three months or more.

Ethnic minority employment

4.77   The labour market position of ethnic minority groups tends to be worse than that of the rest of the population. With concentrations in areas of Britain with the highest levels of worklessness, unemployment rates among ethnic minorities can be up to four times higher, and employment rates significantly lower.

4.78   The Government has taken steps to improve the employment prospects of people from ethnic minorities. Action Teams have been introduced in 63 disadvantaged areas of Britain, many of which contain large ethnic minority communities, and a new outreach service is now operating in five urban areas that are home to three quarters of Britain's ethnic minority population. This outreach service aims to attract people to mainstream services, improve the links between communities and employers, and provide specialist training where it may help individuals to find work. The Jobcentre Plus target system is also being re-structured to re-direct funding towards areas with both higher unemployment and high ethnic minority populations.

4.79   The Government is, however, determined to go further and has accepted all of the recommendations of the recent Cabinet Office Strategy Unit report[9] on steps to improve the position of ethnic minorities in the labour market. Building on the conclusions of the report, Budget 2003 therefore introduces further support, including:

- from April 2004, specialist advisers in Jobcentre Plus districts with high ethnic minority populations; and

- from April 2004, a new policy fund of £8 million over the next two years will be available to Jobcentre Plus managers to provide innovative solutions to helping people from ethnic minorities into work.

Local worklessness

4.80   Rising concentrations of worklessness have given rise to communities in which worklessness is no longer the exception, but the norm. Local areas that suffer from low employment rates often do not simply lack jobs. Many combine high vacancies with low employment or are found alongside other districts with large numbers of vacancies. A high proportion of residents may face multiple barriers to work.

4.81   As announced in the 2002 Pre-Budget Report, the Government therefore intends to pilot a programme of intensive support in neighbourhoods with very high concentrations of worklessness. Starting in April 2004, the pilots will focus on 12 of the most deprived neighbourhoods of the country, offering intensive support to help local residents access the jobs that are often found within travelling distance of where they live.

4.82   In each pilot area, residents claiming JSA will benefit from accelerated access onto the New Deal after just three months of unemployment. More frequent work-focused interviews will also be introduced for partners and lone parents, and new Incapacity Benefit claimants will be given more help to ensure that employment opportunities and barriers to work are regularly discussed. Each neighbourhood will also receive a discretionary fund, allowing personal advisers to tackle the substantial and varied barriers that prevent residents from returning to work. The fund will provide personal advisers, working in cooperation with Local Strategic Partnerships, with flexibility to deliver services in ways that best meet the needs of the local community.

---

[9] *Ethnic minorities and the labour market,* Cabinet Office Strategy Unit, March 2003.

Helping ex-offenders back to work

4.83 The Government is taking steps to extend employment opportunity to ex-offenders, recognising that work is often the best route away from crime. From later this year, Jobcentre Plus will offer dedicated employment and benefit surgeries in prisons across England, Scotland and Wales. These surgeries will ensure that ex-offenders are aware of the work opportunities available ahead of their release, and will be followed by a guaranteed Jobcentre Plus appointment after release to enable jobsearch to start immediately. The Government also intends to offer jobs in a wide range of sectors to young offenders across the country who have successfully undertaken training in prison, building on an existing successful private sector initiative.

Funding for Welfare to Work

4.84 The Welfare to Work programme has been funded by the one-off Windfall Tax on the excess profits of the privatised utilities. The majority of the Welfare to Work programme is delivered by the DWP, and the associated resources are generally now included within its Departmental Expenditure Limit (DEL). The 2002 Spending Review allocated extra resources to Welfare to Work programmes, including the national roll-out of Jobcentre Plus.

Table 4.3: Allocation of the Windfall Tax

£million	1997-98	1998-99	1999-00	2000-01	2001-02	2002-03²	2003-04³	TOTAL
Spending by programme¹								
New Deal for young people⁴	50	200	310	300	240	270	200	1570
New Deal for 25 plus	0	10	90	110	200	240	180	830
New Deal for over 50s	0	0	5	20	10	10	10	60
New Deal for lone parents	0	20	40	40	40	80	80	300
New Deal for disabled people⁵	0	5	20	10	10	30	30	100
New Deal for partners	0	0	5	10	10	10	10	40
Childcare⁶	0	20	10	5	0	0	0	35
University for Industry⁷	0	5	0	0	0	0	0	5
Workforce development⁸	0	0	0	0	0	30	170	200
ONE pilots⁹	0	0	0	5	5	0	0	10
Action Teams	0	0	0	10	40	50	50	150
Enterprise development	0	0	0	10	20	10	0	40
Modernising the Employment Service	0	0	0	40	0	0	0	40
Total Resource Expenditure	50	260	480	560	570	730	730	3380
Capital costs¹⁰	90	270	260	750	450	0	0	1820
Estimated Windfall Tax Margin								0
Windfall Tax receipts	2600	2600						5200

¹ Rounded to the nearest £10 million, except where expenditure is less than £5 million. Constituent elements may not sum to totals because of rounding. Figures include Windfall Tax spending in Annually Managed Expenditure omitted at Budget 2002, and exclude resources from mainstream employment programmes in DEL included at Budget 2002.
² Figures for 2002-03 and 2003-04 are provisional.
³ Windfall Tax expenditure is significantly reduced in 2003-04 as Windfall Tax resources are exhausted. Remaining in-year expenditure will be topped up with general government revenues.
⁴ Includes funding for the Innovation Fund.
⁵ Includes £10 million in 1999-2000, an element of the November 1998 announcements on welfare reform.
⁶ Includes £30 million for out-of-school childcare. The costs of the 1997 Budget improvements in childcare through Family Credit are included from April 1998 until October 1999, after which the measure was incorporated within the Working Families' Tax Credit.
⁷ Start up and development costs. Other costs of the University for Industry are funded from within Departmental Expenditure Limits.
⁸ Includes funding for the second year of the Employer Training Pilots.
⁹ Funding for repeat interviews. Other funding is from the Invest to Save budget.
¹⁰ Includes capital spending on renewal of school infrastructure, to help raise standards.

5 BUILDING A FAIRER SOCIETY

The Government is determined to ensure that flexibility and fairness are advanced together so that everyone can share in rising national prosperity. Reform of the welfare state, including the launch of the Child and Working Tax Credits and the Pension Credit, is at the heart of the Government's strategy for tackling child poverty, supporting families with children and providing security for all in old age. A modern and fair tax system, which encourages work and saving and ensures that everyone pays their fair share of tax, underpins this programme of reform. Budget 2003 announces further steps to promote fairness with flexibility, including:

- **a new Child Trust Fund** providing every child born from September 2002 with an initial endowment at birth of £250, rising to £500 for children in the poorest third of families, a reform which is progressive and universal and will strengthen the saving habit of future generations;

- **an extra £100 for households with a pensioner aged 80 or over in addition to the £200 winter fuel payment** for the lifetime of this Parliament;

- **extending to 52 weeks the period over which all pensioners in hospital receive their full state pension;**

- **a cross-government review of financial support for 16 to 19 year olds,** including the financial incentives to participate in education or training and the case for extending the National Minimum Wage;

- **a new income tax exemption for foster carers,** to facilitate the recruitment and retention of these carers;

- **measures to protect tax revenues,** including a compliance and enforcement package for direct tax, expected to produce £1.6 billion over the next three years;

- **details of the modernised regime for stamp duty,** announced in Budget 2002, to tackle avoidance and distortions, while protecting small businesses and paving the way for e-conveyancing;

- **further steps to ensure a fair system of alcohol and tobacco taxation;**

- **the abolition of bingo duty, to be replaced by a new gross profits tax on bingo companies;** and

- **further work to establish an International Finance Facility** to secure the additional resources needed to tackle global poverty.

INTRODUCTION

5.1   Since 1997, the Government has placed reform of the welfare state at the heart of its strategy for promoting social inclusion. The new tax and benefit system puts into practice the principles of progressive universalism, with support for all, and more help for those who need it most, when they need it most. Modern, high quality and integrated services, such as Jobcentre Plus and the Pension Service, will offer advice and support tailored to people's circumstances, removing the inflexibilities of the old system.

5.2   Fewer families will suffer from very high marginal deduction rates when they move into work or increase their hours, improving flexibility in the labour market and providing opportunities for people to lift themselves out of poverty. Where appropriate, financial support will be delivered through the tax system to reduce stigma, and there is a particular focus on children and pensioners.

5.3   This chapter describes the Government's reforms to tackle child and pensioner poverty, promote saving throughout life, provide support for people with disabilities, and advance the Millennium Development Goals for reducing global poverty. It also sets out how this ambitious programme of reform is underpinned by wider action to establish a modern and fair tax system which encourages work, saving and investment, raises sufficient revenue to pay for public services, and towards which everyone – individuals and businesses alike – contributes their fair share.

SUPPORT FOR FAMILIES AND CHILDREN

Tackling child poverty   5.4   Every child deserves the best possible start in life, to be supported as they develop and to be given opportunities to achieve their full potential. Children who grow up in poverty experience disadvantage that affects not only their own childhood, but also their experience as adults and the life chances of their own children. Support for today's disadvantaged children will therefore help to ensure a more flexible economy tomorrow.

5.5   The Government's objective is to halve child poverty by 2010 and to eradicate it by 2020. As a first step towards achieving its long-term goal, the Government is committed to a Public Service Agreement (PSA) target for 2004-05, to reduce by one quarter the number of children living in low-income households compared with 1998-99. The Government's strategy for tackling child poverty was set out alongside the 2001 Pre-Budget Report[1]. This strategy involves:

- helping to ensure decent family incomes, with work for those who can and support for those who cannot;

- support for parents, so that they in turn can provide better support for their children;

- delivering high quality public services in all neighbourhoods, with targeted interventions for those with additional needs; and

- harnessing the power and expertise of the voluntary and community sectors, promoting innovation and good practice.

5.6   Between 1998-99 and 2001-02 the numbers of children in low-income households[2] fell by 400,000 after housing costs and by 500,000 before housing costs from 4.2 million and 3.1 million respectively. The Government is therefore around halfway to meeting its 2004-05 PSA target in half of the time. On one measure – before housing costs – it is over halfway, while on the other – after housing costs – it is slightly less than halfway.

5.7   These data show that steady progress has been made in reducing child poverty during a period of high growth in income. In contrast, between 1979 and 1987, median income grew strongly, while the proportion of children in relative low-income households almost doubled. Moreover, these data do not reflect the impact of recent policies, including the Child and Working Tax Credits, paid from this month.

5.8   The Government estimates that, in 2003-04, there will be 1.5 million fewer children living in relative low-income households than there would otherwise have been, had the Government done no more than index 1997 policies to prices. This comprises both the number of children living in households now lifted above the relative income level and the number of children who would otherwise have fallen below that level as median real income and earnings rose, demonstrating the full impact of the Government's policies.

---

[1] *Tackling child poverty: giving every child the best possible start in life*, HM Treasury, December 2001.

[2] Defined as having an income below 60 per cent of the contemporary median. Data from *Households Below Average Income 1994-95 to 2001-02*, Department for Work and Pensions, March 2003.

5.9   A number of initiatives are underway which will help to achieve the Government's long-term goal of eradicating child poverty. The Department for Work and Pensions (DWP) has recently consulted on a range of options for building on its existing poverty indicators with a measure of child poverty that reflects the complexity of the issues, makes sense to people who experience poverty, allows the public to hold the Government to account and leads to the most effective policy decisions. DWP will publish its initial conclusions shortly. Any change will not relate to the 2004-05 PSA target. As announced in the 2002 Pre-Budget Report, the Government will also publish shortly a Green Paper on children at risk, which will examine how to make mainstream services more preventative and more responsive to the needs of children at risk of a range of adverse outcomes.

5.10   The Government wants to ensure that it tackles child poverty in the most effective way so as to achieve its long-term goals to halve and then eradicate child poverty. It will examine, for Budget 2004 and the next Spending Review, both the welfare reform and public service changes needed to advance faster towards these goals. In pursuing its goals, the Government will continue to work closely with outside organisations.

Financial support for families and children

5.11   The Government is reforming the tax and benefit system to guarantee decent family incomes and tackle child poverty. The reforms ensure that support is available to all families with children and that those who need the most help, including families on lower incomes, receive the greatest support, when they need it most.

Child Benefit   **5.12**   In April 2003, the rates of Child Benefit were increased in line with prices from £15.75 to £16.05 a week for the first child in every family, and from £10.55 to £10.75 a week for subsequent children. The rate for the first child is now 25 per cent higher in real terms than it was in 1997.

The Child Tax Credit   **5.13**   As part of the next steps in tax and benefit reform, Budget 2002 introduced two new tax credits for families and those on low incomes. Paid from this month, the Child and Working Tax Credits provide a new system of support to help families, tackle child poverty and make work pay. The Working Tax Credit, which makes work pay for low-income households and includes an element to support the costs of eligible childcare, is described in Chapter 4.

5.14   The Child Tax Credit provides a single, seamless system of income-related support for families with children, replacing the child elements of the Working Families' Tax Credit (WFTC), the Disabled Person's Tax Credit (DPTC), Income Support or Jobseeker's Allowance, and the Children's Tax Credit. Building on the foundation of universal Child Benefit, the Child Tax Credit provides:

- a secure stream of income for families with children which does not depend on the employment status of the parents;

- a system in which all support for children is paid direct to the main carer in the family – usually the mother, as in Child Benefit;

- a common framework for assessment, so that all families are part of the same system and poorer families do not suffer any stigma;

- a more responsive system, in which a family's tax credit award can be adjusted to reflect changes in their income and circumstances; and

- a simpler and more streamlined annual renewal process.

5.15   The Child Tax Credit is available to nine out of ten families with children. Additional help is available for some families, including free school meals, free prescriptions and the Sure Start Maternity Grant. This help is linked to the tax credit award, depending on the needs and income of individual families.

5.16   Paid on top of Child Benefit, the Child Tax Credit provides:

- a family element of £545 a year – doubled to £1,090 for families with a child under the age of one – for all families with incomes of less than £50,000, gradually withdrawn for those with incomes above this amount; and

- a child element of £1,445 a year for each child or young person in families with incomes of up to around £13,000 a year, gradually withdrawn for families with higher incomes. Families caring for disabled children receive increased child elements to reflect their greater needs. From April 2004, the child element will be uprated at least in line with earnings rather than prices for the rest of the Parliament.

5.17   Table 5.1 shows the levels of support that the Child Tax Credit and Child Benefit provide for families. The precise amount a family receives depends on their income and circumstances, with support reduced as income rises.

Table 5.1: Levels of support for families from April 2003

| Family income (£ a year) | less than £13,000 | less than £50,000 | all families |
Per cent of families	25	85	100
1 child	£2,825	£1,375	£830
2 children	£4,830	£1,935	£1,390
3 children	£6,835	£2,495	£1,950

5.18   Around 5³/₄ million families with children are expected to benefit from the Child Tax Credit. In 2003-04, around 1.3 million families will receive amounts equivalent to the Child Tax Credit through their Income Support or Jobseeker's Allowance, before being transferred automatically onto the Child Tax Credit between April and October 2004. The Inland Revenue has now received over 3.9 million claims. For those who have not yet claimed, claims can be backdated for up to three months, so families will receive their full entitlement provided they claim before 6 July 2003. People can call the tax credits freephone response line – 0800 500 222 – to request a claim pack, or can log on to the tax credits website – www.inlandrevenue.gov.uk/taxcredits – which enables families to calculate their entitlement and make a claim online.

5.19   To ensure that families understand the changes and claim what they are entitled to, the Government has:

- issued claim forms to all recipients of existing tax credits;

- launched a £12 million nationwide awareness campaign, involving national television advertising, supported by radio, press and online publicity, and including advertising focused on ethnic minority communities;

- worked with intermediary organisations, such as Citizens Advice, the Child Poverty Action Group and the National Council for One Parent Families, to provide information, training and support to help them communicate with their client groups;

- held a series of tax credit road-shows throughout the country and hosted seminars aimed at particular groups, such as employers and those who work with students or people with disabilities; and

- initiated two four-month pilot projects to communicate information on the new tax credits to those with whom the Government currently has little or no contact. The pilots utilise networks established by voluntary and community groups and are being run by the Inland Revenue with Community Links in the London Borough of Newham and in Keighley, West Yorkshire. Both pilots have generated additional claims.

Box 5.1: Transferring support for children from fathers to mothers

Support for children through tax credits used to be paid through the wage packet to the main earner in the family, often the father. Under the Child Tax Credit, support is now paid into the bank account of the main carer, usually the mother. This means that up to £2 billion will be transferred to mothers, with around 2.5 million fathers losing between £10 and £60 per week, and more in some cases, from their wage packet. ICM research polling in January 2003 supports the decision to pay financial support for children direct to the main carer:

- 65 per cent of people polled believed that all support for children should be paid to the mother, with just one per cent preferring payment to the father;

- the majority of men polled – 64 per cent – also believed that all support to children should be paid to the mother;

- 70 per cent of those polled felt that mothers were most likely to ensure that the money went towards the needs of the children; and

- only 2 per cent thought that fathers would be most likely to ensure that financial support was of direct benefit to children.

Effects of measures to support families with children

5.20   As a result of the Government's personal tax and benefit reforms since 1997[3] including the changes to national insurance contributions (NICs) and the freezing of the income tax personal allowance announced in Budget 2002, from April 2003:

- families with children are, on average, £1,200 a year better off, while those in the poorest fifth of the population are, on average, £2,500 a year better off in real terms;

- a single-earner family on half average earnings of £14,300 with two young children is £3,430 a year better off in real terms; and

- a single-earner family on average earnings of £28,600 and with two children is £275 a year better off in real terms.

5.21   Chart 5.1 shows the impact by decile, since 1997, of the Government's reforms for families with children.

---

[3] Compared with the 1997-98 system of taxes and benefits, indexed to 2003-04 prices.

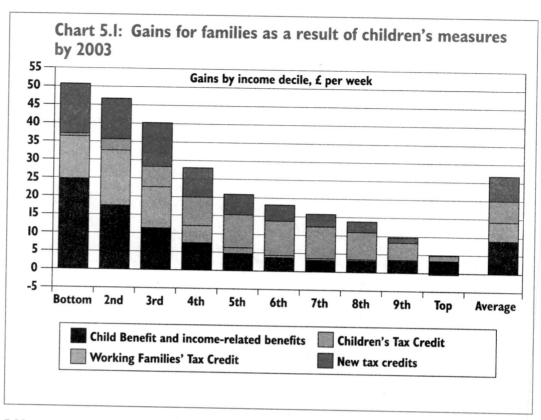

Chart 5.1: Gains for families as a result of children's measures by 2003

Gains by income decile, £ per week

Legend:
- Child Benefit and income-related benefits
- Working Families' Tax Credit
- Children's Tax Credit
- New tax credits

The Social Fund

5.22   The Social Fund is an important source of support for people on low incomes. As announced in the 2002 Pre-Budget Report, from April 2003, £90 million will be added to the budget of the Discretionary Social Fund over the three years to 2005-06 and the maximum payment for the fixed element of the funeral grant rises from £600 to £700. Combined with administrative improvements, this investment will enhance the Fund's ability to help those on low incomes manage their finances. The Government is considering the case for further reform of the Social Fund.

Support for young adults

5.23   A decent education builds employment opportunity and enhances the well-being of people throughout their lives. In the past, too few people have aspired to continue in learning after the statutory school-leaving age, often because of a lack of financial support. In recognition of these financial barriers, Education Maintenance Allowances (EMAs) will be introduced across England from September 2004. EMAs will enable more young people from poorer families to pursue education beyond the age of 16 by providing up to £1,500 a year, depending on household income.

5.24   From 2004, the improved package of financial support for 16 to 19 year olds and their families will enable more young people to remain in full-time education. However, other young people may choose the vocational pathway of training combined with work. The Government has agreed that the Low Pay Commission should look at the advantages and disadvantages of a minimum wage for 16 and 17 year olds, but believes that this issue should be considered alongside other financial incentives and support for young people in this age group. The Government will therefore establish a wider cross-government group to examine the overall system of financial support for 16 to 19 year olds. The review will report in spring 2004 and will examine:

- the financial incentives for young people to participate in education and training and the interaction between this support and any new minimum wage for 16 and 17 year olds;

- the financial support for young people and their parents or carers, including those who are living independently and those in very low paid employment; and

- how the system of financial incentives and support could be rationalised, given the variety of channels through which it is currently delivered.

Adoption and foster carers   **5.25**   The Government recognises the important contribution made by parents who foster or adopt children. As announced in the 2002 Pre-Budget Report, payments to adoptive families under the Adoption and Children Act 2002 will continue to be free of tax. These arrangements will benefit all adoptive families who receive financial support to help them meet the extra costs they face when they adopt a child.

5.26   The Government has also considered how the tax system might facilitate the recruitment and retention of foster carers and will introduce, from April 2003, an income tax exemption for foster carers receiving less than £10,000 a year per residence plus an additional amount per child. This will ensure that benefits for these carers are applied consistently across the UK, and that they are not unfairly taxed upon the legitimate expenses they incur.

Supporting parents: balancing work and family life

5.27   The Government is determined to advance flexibility and fairness in the labour market together, allowing more men and women to secure the benefits of being able to balance their work and family responsibilities, while ensuring that firms have the flexible working patterns they need to become more productive. The Government's strategy was set out in *Balancing work and family life: enhancing choice and support for parents*, published in January[4]. This involves:

- supporting parents' choices;

- tailoring financial support to families' circumstances;

- enhancing access to good quality childcare and parenting services; and

- working in partnership with business to promote the benefits of flexible working and to support the take up of best practice approaches.

Enhancing choice and support for parents   **5.28**   A package of measures introduced this month will provide parents with more choice and support than ever before, benefiting employers, employees and their children. By protecting families from fluctuations in income, the new Child and Working Tax Credits make it easier for one parent in a family to remain at home and care for their children if they choose to do so. By improving work incentives for second earners, providing more flexible childcare support, and enabling parents to combine their hours to qualify for enhanced support, the new tax credits also give families more choice about how they structure their work and caring responsibilities.

5.29   The childcare element of the Working Tax Credit responds to changes in the costs of childcare, giving parents greater flexibility to change their childcare arrangements to suit their needs. Parents can also now claim support for the costs of using approved childcare in their own home. At present, only existing registered childminders can become approved home childcarers, but the Government will consult in the early summer on proposals to widen this to those wishing to become childcare workers and to those already working in the childcare sector.

---

[4] *Balancing work and family life: enhancing choice and support for parents*, HM Treasury and the Department of Trade and Industry, January 2003.

5.30 The Government has also introduced new rights this month to help working mothers and fathers meet their work and childcare responsibilities. Parents of young and disabled children can apply for flexible working in the knowledge that their employers have a legal duty to consider their requests seriously. The flat rate of Statutory Maternity Pay (SMP) is now £100 a week and expectant and new mothers can take 26 weeks Ordinary Maternity Leave and a further 26 weeks unpaid Additional Maternity Leave, providing up to one year's maternity leave in total. Adoptive parents now have comparable rights and, for the first time, new fathers also have the right to take two weeks paternity leave, paid at the same flat rate as SMP.

5.31 These changes build on the success of the Working Families' Tax Credit (WFTC) and the Disabled Person's Tax Credit (DPTC), together with the childcare element of WFTC, which reached over £1 million a day to help working parents. Record amounts are being invested to support new childcare places, and places for over 1.1 million children have been created since 1997, advancing the Government's target to create 1.6 million places by 2004 and 2 million places by 2006. This investment will be supported by a transformation in the way in which services respond to the needs of children and parents, including through new Children's Centres and extended schools.

Further support with childcare **5.32** Budget 2003 announces further measures to support parents:

- from April 2004, the Government will remove the restrictions in the childcare element of the Working Tax Credit that prevent mothers on paid maternity leave receiving help with the costs of childcare for their new babies. This will enable parents to settle their new baby into childcare before returning to work; and

- as set out in Chapter 4, from April 2004, new childcare taster sessions will be introduced for lone parents on the New Deal for lone parents, allowing them to access formal childcare for up to one week to assess whether it suits their needs.

Working with business **5.33** Employers have an important role in helping employees to balance their work and family lives and can benefit from doing so, including through improved recruitment and retention, staff morale and organisational performance. To support this employer-employee relationship, Budget 2003 abolishes, from April 2003, the income tax charge that arises where employers contribute to additional household costs incurred by employees working at home. The Government is also consulting[5] on proposals to encourage more employers to help their staff meet the costs of safe, good quality childcare. These proposals include extending the current tax exemption to cover any formal registered childcare contracted for by the employer, a new tax exemption for childcare vouchers, and a rule to ensure that schemes should be generally accessible to all employees. The proposals will extend choice for parents and employers whose needs are not met by workplace nursery schemes.

Next steps **5.34** Although much progress has been made, balancing work and family life remains a key challenge in the twenty-first century. Today, there are more dual-income households, more single parent households and many more women in employment. In recognition of these challenges, the Government's strategy document invited views on possible next steps, once the measures introduced this month have bedded down. The Government would particularly welcome views, by 31 August 2003, on the options set out in Box 5.2, and on which of them should be considered priorities.

5.35 As described in Chapter 6, to prepare the ground for the next Spending Review, the Government will also examine the further steps needed to ensure an adequate supply of good quality childcare, building on the inter-departmental childcare review and the 2002 Spending Review.

---

[5] *Employer supported childcare: improving the tax and national insurance exemptions*, Inland Revenue and HM Treasury, February 2003.

Box 5.2: Helping parents to balance work and family life

In the light of new measures coming into effect this month, time is needed for the new framework to bed down. Looking further ahead, the Government will monitor the impact of new and existing reforms and will also consider:

- how well support for childcare costs within the tax credit system is working, including the effect of increased flexibility on parents' ability to adjust their childcare arrangements to suit their needs;

- the case for counting unpaid maternity leave as being 'in work' for the purposes of tax credits, to enable families to continue receiving support during this period;

- allowing parents to use their full parental leave as one block at the end of maternity, paternity or adoption leave;

- whether to allow fathers time off to attend ante-natal care;

- whether to extend the period of paid paternity leave and/or to introduce unpaid paternity leave;

- the case for extending paid paternity leave in case of multiple births and disabled children; and

- the impact of the maternity, paternity and adoption leave provisions. The Government is already committed to reviewing, in three years' time, the employers' duty to consider requests for flexible working.

Public services to tackle child poverty

5.36   The 2002 Spending Review provided substantial new investment for child-focused public services, including an extra £14.7 billion a year for education by 2005-06, £570 million over three years to support the roll-out and operation of Children's Fund partnerships, and increased resources to help tackle health inequalities and establish better preventative healthcare services. All children will benefit from this additional support, while targeted interventions will ensure that those most in need receive the greatest help. Children living in deprived neighbourhoods will also benefit from a strengthened set of deprivation-related PSA floor targets, setting out how outcomes for those living in the poorest areas should improve.

Children at risk   **5.37**   As part of the 2002 Spending Review, the Government conducted a cross-cutting review into the delivery of programmes and services to help children at risk of poor outcomes in areas such as health, education and employment. The review examined best practice in local partnership delivery of integrated children's services and identified a number of barriers to improved coordination.

5.38   Building on the analysis set out in the review, as mentioned earlier in this chapter, the Government will publish shortly a Green Paper on services for children and young people at risk. The Green Paper will examine how to increase the preventative nature of mainstream services and make them more responsive to the needs of children at risk of a range of adverse outcomes, including educational under-achievement; poor physical, mental or sexual health; victimisation, bullying and abuse; and offending. It will also look at the provision of specialist services. The focus will be on ensuring that investment in services for children is matched by reform, and that reform is organised around the needs of children and young people.

FAIRNESS FOR PEOPLE WITH DISABILITIES

5.39   The Government is determined to increase opportunities for people with disabilities to lead independent and fulfilling lives. The recent Green Paper, *Pathways to work: helping people into employment*, set out how the Government intends to use the resources allocated in the 2002 Spending Review to trial earlier and more intensive employment support for disabled people who are able to work, building on the assistance available through the New Deal for disabled people. The Working Tax Credit also includes an element of support for people with disabilities, in recognition of the additional costs they face when in work. These measures are described in Chapter 4.

5.40   People with disabilities who are unable to work should have financial security and support. The Disability Income Guarantee ensures that severely disabled people under 60 years of age and on income-related benefits receive a guaranteed minimum income of at least £144.45 a week for single people, and £189.95 a week for couples. In recognition of the fact that families with disabled children often need extra help, the disabled child premium or disability element was also increased in April 2003 to more than £40 a week on top of basic Income Support or tax credits, benefiting around 88,000 children.

Tackling discrimination and exclusion   **5.41**   Fairness for disabled people requires an end to discrimination in the workplace and beyond. The Government is committed to extending rights and opportunities for disabled people and will publish shortly a draft Disability Bill with the intention that it should undergo pre-legislative scrutiny before being taken forward as part of the Government's legislative programme later in this Parliament. The draft Bill will include new measures proposed by the Disability Rights Task Force, including changes to the Disability Discrimination Act (DDA) affecting the public sector, transport and premises, and an extended definition of disability. The Government also intends to cover membership of larger private clubs in the DDA, and will consult widely on how and when the practical changes involved should take effect.

FAIRNESS FOR PENSIONERS

5.42   A fair society guarantees security in old age. The Government is committed to tackling pensioner poverty so that all pensioners can share in rising national prosperity. This means ensuring security for all pensioners, with extra help for those who need it most and reward for those who have saved modest amounts. It also means helping today's workers to plan more effectively for a secure retirement, through the range of proposals set out in the Government's Pensions Green Paper[6] and consultation on simplifying the taxation of pensions[7]. The Government provides a foundation of support for retirement income. Above this, individuals, where possible supported by their employers, are responsible for determining the level of income on which they wish to retire, and for planning their saving and working patterns accordingly.

---

[6] *Simplicity, security and choice: working and saving for retirement*, the Department for Work and Pensions, HM Treasury and Inland Revenue, December 2002.

[7] *Simplifying the taxation of pensions: increasing choice and flexibility for all*, HM Treasury and Inland Revenue, December 2002.

Security for all pensioners

5.43   To ensure that today's pensioners have security in retirement, the Government has:

- increased the basic state pension by more than inflation in each of the last two years. In April 2003, the full basic state pension was increased further to £77.45 a week for single pensioners and to £123.80 a week for pensioner couples – an annual increase of more than £100 for single pensioners and more than £160 for couples;

- guaranteed that the basic state pension will rise in future years by 2.5 per cent or the increase in the September Retail Prices Index, whichever is higher;

- introduced winter fuel payments, worth £200 per household each year for people aged 60 or over for the remainder of this Parliament. In addition, Budget 2003 announces an additional £100 for households with a pensioner aged 80 or over, on top of the £200 winter fuel payment for the lifetime of this Parliament; and

- introduced free TV licences for households containing someone aged 75 or over and free eye tests for all those over 60.

Tackling pensioner poverty

5.44   The Government has also taken steps to help those pensioners in greatest need. Reforms to Income Support for pensioners with a more generous Minimum Income Guarantee (MIG) now benefit over two million pensioners. Since its introduction, the level of the MIG has been increased at least in line with earnings so that, from April 2003, no single pensioner need live on less than £102.10 a week and no pensioner couple on less than £155.80 a week. As a result, the proportion of pensioners living in low-income households, measured after housing costs, is now at its lowest level since the mid-1980s[8].

Help for those in hospital   5.45   Since the introduction of the welfare state, hospital inpatients have had their benefits reduced after a certain length of stay. This can lead to financial insecurity and distress, particularly among pensioners who currently have their State Retirement Pension reduced after just six weeks. The problems are exacerbated by complexity in the current rules, and delays in notifying the Government of time spent in hospital can often result in benefit and pension entitlements being adjusted in the months after a patient returns home.

5.46   To provide greater financial security and reduce anxiety for those who experience longer stays in hospital, all pensioners in hospital will in future receive their full state pension for stays of up to 52 weeks. The change will be introduced as soon as possible and will apply to pensioners and to those of working age entering hospital. Those already in hospital for less than 52 weeks will have their benefits increased from the date of change.

---

[8] Defined as having an income below 60 per cent of contemporary median.

The Pension Credit: rewarding low and modest-income pensioners

5.47 To advance its goal of tackling pensioner poverty and to reward saving for retirement, the Government is introducing the Pension Credit from October 2003. Around half of all pensioner households stand to gain an additional £400 a year on average under the Pension Credit, with some gaining up to £1,000 a year. As a result of the MIG and the introduction of the Pension Credit, the poorest third of pensioners will be about £600 a year better off on average than had the equivalent amount been spent on raising the basic state pension.

5.48 Delivered by the new Pension Service, the Pension Credit will replace the MIG, bringing pensioners' incomes up to a guaranteed minimum entitlement. The minimum entitlement will be linked to the growth in average earnings throughout this Parliament, ensuring that more pensioners are able to share in rising national prosperity.

5.49 The Pension Credit will also ensure that millions of pensioners who have saved modest amounts for their retirement gain from having done so. From the of age 65, single pensioners with incomes of up to £139 a week will be rewarded with up to £14.79 a week. Pensioner couples with incomes of nearly £204 a week will see rewards of up to £19.20 a week. The current MIG capital regime will be revised and the MIG's weekly means test abolished for the vast majority of pensioners. For those aged 65 and over, adjustments to awards will be made only when circumstances change significantly, although recipients will be able to request a reassessment should their circumstances mean that they are entitled to an increase. People on Housing Benefit or Council Tax Benefit will be protected to ensure that they receive the full benefit of the Pension Credit.

Box 5.3: Pension Credit: "pick it up, it's yours"

Around half of all pensioner households will be entitled to the Pension Credit following its introduction from 6 October 2003. The Government is determined that at least three million households should receive the Credit by 2006 – the first time a Government target has been set for the take-up of an entitlement.

The Government, through the new Pension Service, is taking important steps to raise awareness of the Pension Credit and ensure that pensioner households understand what they are entitled to. Advance applications for the Pension Credit have been taken since 7 April 2003, and all applications received before October 2004 will be backdated to the start of the Pension Credit where eligible. The Government is pursuing a comprehensive strategy to maximise take-up, including:

- the distribution of personal direct mail packs to every pensioner household, tailored to the individual circumstances of each household;

- MIG customers have been written to, advising them that they will automatically receive their Pension Credit entitlement from October 2003;

- widespread and high-profile advertising campaigns will run from late summer 2003 to raise general awareness of the Pension Credit among pensioners, their friends and their families; and

- the Pension Service will work with local pensioner groups to provide the information and support necessary to promote take up in their communities, and particularly among harder-to-reach groups.

Effects of measures to support pensioners

5.50   From 2004-05, following the introduction of the Pension Credit, the Government will be spending around £9.2 billion more in real terms on pensioners as a result of measures introduced since 1997. It is £5.7 billion more than the cost of indexing the basic state pension to earnings.

5.51   Compared with the 1997 system[9], as a result of the Government's measures including the Pension Credit, on average, from October 2003:

- pensioner households will be £1,250 a year better off in real terms – around £24 extra a week; and

- the poorest third of pensioner households will have gained £1,600 a year in real terms.

5.52   Chart 5.2 shows the distributional impact, in current prices, of the Government's measures to support pensioners introduced before April 2004, including the Pension Credit.

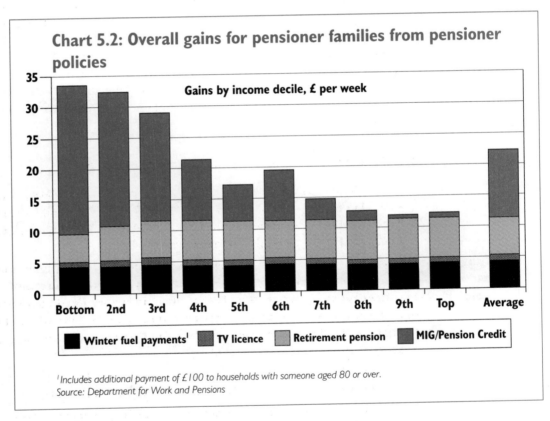

Chart 5.2: Overall gains for pensioner families from pensioner policies

Gains by income decile, £ per week

Legend: Winter fuel payments[1] · TV licence · Retirement pension · MIG/Pension Credit

[1] Includes additional payment of £100 to households with someone aged 80 or over.
Source: Department for Work and Pensions

Support for pensioners who pay tax

5.53   While most pensioners have no income tax to pay, for those who do, the age-related personal allowances in 2003-04 rise to £6,610 for people aged between 65 and 74 and to £6,720 for those aged 75 or over. This represents an increase of £400 and £240 a year respectively over the amount that would have resulted from statutory indexation, and will ensure that no pensioner aged 65 or over pays tax on income of less than £127 a week. The age-related personal allowances will be raised at least in line with earnings rather than prices for the remainder of this Parliament.

---

[9] Compared with the 1997-98 system of taxes and benefits, indexed to 2003-04 prices.

Supporting tomorrow's pensioners

The Pensions Green Paper   **5.54**   Building on the foundation of the Government's reforms to state provision, including increases in the basic state pension, the introduction of the State Second Pension, the Minimum Income Guarantee, and, from October 2003, the Pension Credit, the Green Paper set out a range of proposals to enable those of working age to plan more effectively for a secure retirement. The proposals seek to renew the partnership between the Government, individuals, employers and the financial services industry, which has long been a strength of the UK pensions system, by:

- helping people to make better informed choices about their retirement, including through the extension of pensions forecasts which provide information tailored to individual circumstances;

- reaffirming the role and responsibilities of employers in the pensions partnership, improving saving throughout the workplace through major regulatory simplification and increased member protection;

- encouraging the development of simple and flexible savings products and improving access to financial help through generic healthcheck products and workplace advice; and

- facilitating extended working lives, eroding the cliff edge between work and retirement by enabling flexible retirement and offering fair increases for deferring state pensions.

5.55   The Government has consulted widely on the proposals set out in the Green Paper, organising a series of seminars and events to discuss the issues with key stakeholders. Around 750 organisations and individuals, including members of the public, submitted responses which the Government will now consider. The Government has also established a new Pensions Commission to examine the regime for UK private pensions and long-term savings and to assess the effectiveness of the voluntarist approach. The Commission expects to publish its work programme shortly.

Simplifying the taxation of pensions   **5.56**   The Government has also published proposals for radical simplification of the taxation of pensions. The proposals sweep away the complexity of the current system, replacing the existing eight different tax regimes for pensions with a single lifetime limit on the amount of pension saving that can benefit from tax relief.

5.57   In the past, people with occupational pensions have been subject to absolute limits on their annual pension savings based on their earnings, which have been subject to a cap since 1989. The proposed lifetime limit is broadly equivalent to the maximum pension that individuals earning at or above the level of the current earnings cap – £99,000 – could have built up under these limits, and 99 per cent of people will be able to save more under the new rules. As stated in the consultation document, *Simplifying the taxation of pensions*, the small minority in uncapped regimes that have managed to accumulate a pension entitlement worth more than the lifetime limit – around 5,000 people – will have their existing rights guaranteed.

5.58   All pension savers will benefit from greater clarity and transparency about the amount of tax-favoured savings they can make, more choice over when and how they retire and how they draw benefits from their pension, and, in many cases, a larger tax-free lump sum. Simplification will also reduce administrative burdens for employers and pension providers, lowering costs and delivering better value for all savers. Initial estimates put these cost savings at £80 million a year.

5.59   The proposals have been well received, including at a number of consultation events. The consultation period ends on 11 April and the Government intends to publish its plans for legislation in the summer.

PROMOTING SAVING AND ASSET OWNERSHIP

5.60   Savings and assets provide people with security in times of adversity, long-term independence and opportunity and comfort in retirement. The Government's strategy for promoting saving and asset accumulation focuses on:

- improving the environment for saving, with macroeconomic stability and an efficient and well-regulated market in financial services;

- creating the right incentives for saving by ensuring that the tax and benefit system does not unfairly penalise savers and by assisting those on lower incomes;

- empowering individuals with financial information, improved access to advice, and simpler and easier to understand savings products; and

- developing savings products suitable for each stage in a person's life cycle. As the scale of saving increases, proceeds from one product may be rolled into the next, helping people to progress up the savings ladder.

The Child Trust Fund   **5.61**   The Government is committed to strengthening the saving habit of future generations and ensuring that all children have a stake in the wealth of the nation. Budget 2003 therefore introduces a new Child Trust Fund (CTF), with entitlement backdated to include children born from September 2002 to align payments with the school year. The CTF will provide an endowment for every child at birth, with those from the poorest families receiving the largest amounts.

5.62   Following extensive consultation, the key features of the Child Trust Fund announced in Budget 2003 are:

- an initial Government endowment of £250. This will rise to £500 for children from low-income families who also qualify for the full Child Tax Credit – around one third of all children;

- additional contributions can be made by parents, other family members or friends up to an annual limit of £1,000;

- access to assets in the fund, including any additional contributions, will be permissible only upon account maturity at the age of eighteen. There will be no restriction on the use of assets at maturity, at which point funds could be rolled over into other savings products; and

- provision of CTF accounts, expected to be available by 2005, will be by open market competition – any authorised provider will be able to enter the market, subject to meeting the conditions of the CTF.

5.63   This structure will provide the foundation on which the Government will build in future Budgets and Spending Reviews. The Government will publish its full proposals for the Child Trust Fund in summer 2003 including product specifications, sales regulation, limits on investment risk, the default investment option and the extent of any incentives for contributions into the CTF. This will ensure that providers and other stakeholders have the opportunity to comment on the detailed implementation plans.

The Saving Gateway **5.64** The Saving Gateway is designed to be an ideal starting point for many younger or low-income individuals who would otherwise have difficulty starting on the savings ladder. The Saving Gateway would encourage saving by means of a Government-funded match of all money saved, up to a limit. Tailored financial information and education is provided alongside Saving Gateway accounts to help individuals make informed saving choices. The account would also provide an effective bridge to other forms of saving, such as Individual Savings Accounts (ISAs).

5.65 The Government is currently piloting the Saving Gateway in Cambridgeshire, Cumbria, Gorton, Hull and Tower Hamlets, in conjunction with the Community Finance and Learning Initiative, led by the Department for Education and Skills. As of 31 March 2003, around 700 pilot accounts had been opened at the five nominated Halifax branches, with total contributions of nearly £38,000. The pilots, which end in February 2005, have been designed to provide a regular stream of information and will be evaluated to assess their impact on saving behaviour. Further development of the Saving Gateway, including the appropriate level of the match rate and the criteria to be used to determine eligibility, will follow in light of evaluation evidence.

Individual Savings Accounts **5.66** Individual Savings Accounts (ISAs) are the Government's primary vehicle for tax-advantaged saving outside pensions. They have helped to make saving, and the benefits of saving, simple for ordinary investors to understand. Over 14 million people – around one in four adults – now have an ISA and over £105 billion has been subscribed to ISAs since their launch in 1999.

The Sandler review of retail savings **5.67** In June 2001, the Government appointed Ron Sandler, former CEO of Lloyd's of London, to conduct a review of the medium- and long-term savings industry. The review reported in July 2002 and made six major recommendations aimed at improving competitive intensity in the retail savings market, including through the development of a suite of simple, low cost and risk-controlled 'stakeholder' investment products aimed at low- and medium-income investors and sold through a simplified sales regime. The Treasury is currently consulting[10] on the design of these products, and has commissioned independent research into how best to cap product charges. The Financial Services Authority (FSA) is also consulting[11] on the sales regime for any future 'stakeholder' products and on the separate Sandler recommendation relating to the reform of with-profits policies.

5.68 In the 2002 Pre-Budget Report the Government announced that it would consider further Sandler's proposals relating to the taxation of life insurance policies. The Government welcomes Sandler's emphasis on minimising tax-generated distortions and agrees with his stress on the desirability of a more level tax playing field in this area. At the same time, industry representatives have argued that the Government should look at Sandler's tax proposals in the wider context of other tax issues affecting the market for life insurance and other pooled investment products such as unit trusts. The Government agrees, and will consider these recommendations further within a wider framework that takes account of ongoing regulatory change and other developments such as corporation tax reform.

---

[10] *Proposed product specifications for Sandler 'stakeholder' products*, HM Treasury and the Department for Work and Pensions, February 2003.

[11] *Options for regulating the sale of simplified products (Discussion paper 19)*, Financial Services Authority, January 2003.

SUPPORTING VOLUNTARY AND COMMUNITY ACTIVITY

5.69   Voluntary and community activity plays a valuable role in building strong communities, fostering socially responsible businesses, and delivering high quality public services in partnership with government.

5.70   The Government has demonstrated its commitment to the voluntary and community sector since 1997. Following last year's cross-cutting review, £93 million has been allocated to implement a new framework for service delivery between the Government and the voluntary and community sector. As described in Chapter 6, the Government is also investing £125 million over three years in a new *future*builders fund to assist voluntary and community sector organisations in their public service delivery work, £25 million over three years in a new Parenting Fund, and further developing the Community Interest Company model to complement government services at the community level.

5.71   Fiscal incentives to promote giving are also now in place, and tax reliefs are currently worth around £2 billion a year to charities. To strengthen these incentives, from April 2004, self-assessment taxpayers will be able to direct tax repayments to nominated charities. The Government has also allocated £3 million to establish *Guidestar* – a comprehensive new information base designed to boost charitable giving by improving access to information about charities and their activities.

5.72   The December 2002 discussion document, *Next steps on volunteering and giving in the UK*[12], set out the Government's plans to consolidate support for the sector in the coming years, and to ensure this support is reflected across society.

Corporate Challenge   **5.73**   The Government appreciates the value of corporate community involvement and is currently consulting on proposals for a new Corporate Challenge designed to increase corporate involvement in charitable and voluntary activity. The Challenge will seek to increase the numbers of employees engaged in volunteering activity and in Payroll Giving, by facilitating and encouraging corporate provision and promotion of these opportunities. The Challenge will be launched later in the year.

Young Volunteer Challenge   **5.74**   The Government is also committed to supporting volunteering in communities across the UK, and recognises that people benefit from opportunities to volunteer from a young age. From May 2003, a new Young Volunteer Challenge scheme will be piloted to encourage young people from lower income backgrounds to volunteer in community projects. This innovative scheme will work initially with 1,200 young people in ten urban and rural areas across the UK as they take a gap between school, college or training and further learning.

Sports clubs   **5.75**   Sport at grassroots level has an important role to play in promoting the health and cohesion of local communities. The Government has already committed £20 million a year to stimulate the creation of a national network of community amateur sports clubs. It now looks to the sector to provide stronger analysis and evaluation of the impact of existing support to help to inform any future decisions in this area.

Museums   **5.76**   The Government is also committed to improving access to items of cultural and historical significance. Budget 2001 introduced a new scheme to refund national museums and galleries the VAT they incur on purchases when they allow free admissions to the public. The Government will now review the options available for improving support to regional and national museums to enable them to acquire and make works of art and culture accessible to all.

---

[12] *Next steps on volunteering and giving in the UK*, HM Treasury and the Home Office, December 2002.

DELIVERING A MODERN AND FAIR TAX SYSTEM

5.77 A modern and fair tax system encourages work and saving, keeps pace with developments in business practice and the global economy and raises sufficient revenue to fund the Government's objective to build world-class public services. To ensure that the burden of tax does not fall unfairly on compliant taxpayers, loopholes giving scope for unfairness and economic distortion must be closed. Taxpayers who contribute their fair share have a right to expect that others will do so as well, and that the Government will take action against those who abuse the system, ensuring a level playing field for compliant taxpayers.

Protecting tax revenues

Direct tax compliance
5.78 To promote fairness in the tax system, Budget 2003 launches a new compliance and enforcement package for direct tax and NICs. Additional Inland Revenue staff, backed up by new IT and specialist expertise, will be deployed in three areas where significant risks to revenue have been identified:

- protecting the Exchequer from non-payment of tax and NICs debts and from failure to file tax returns;

- tackling fraud involving concealment of undeclared income or profits offshore; and

- countering avoidance of corporation tax and of NICs and tax on employment income.

5.79 An additional £66 million is being provided to the Inland Revenue over the next three years to support implementation of the package. The package is expected to produce at least an additional £1.6 billion in revenue over the next three years, but in line with the Government's cautious approach to the public finances a lower figure of under £1.4 billion over three years, with the annual figure rising to just over £0.6 billion in 2005-06, has been included in the forecast. The Comptroller and Auditor General has audited the projections and concluded that they are based on a reasonable approach and incorporate caution.

5.80 The package is the first step in a new Inland Revenue compliance strategy. This will cover all compliance activities, from supporting those who want to meet their obligations to taking action against those who do not. The aim is to ensure that a strategic approach is taken to the analysis of risks to revenue, to the deployment of resources, and to monitoring the outcomes of compliance work.

Protecting direct tax revenues
5.81 The compliance package also complements and reinforces ongoing Government work to protect direct tax revenues. In addition to the new package, Budget 2003 takes further action to tackle instances of direct tax avoidance and reduce burdens on compliant taxpayers. Chapter A of the Financial Statement and Budget Report gives details of the full range of measures, which will protect around £250 million per annum in future years, and include:

- action to prevent tax and NICs avoidance through the payment of share-based remuneration;

- action to close loopholes in the chargeable gains regime for second-hand life policies and to prevent avoidance of capital gains tax through complex transactions using offshore trusts;

- new measures to close loopholes in the loan relationships and derivative contracts regimes;

- reforms to tackle avoidance through sale and repurchase agreements; and

- action to counter tax avoidance using relevant discounted securities and to prevent exploitation of the 100 per cent information and communications technology allowances for small firms, as previously announced.

5.82   In order to ensure that tax revenues are protected, the Government also needs to be ready to respond to emerging developments, particularly in fast-moving financial markets. Financial market and regulatory changes are leading to the development of debt instruments economically equivalent to equity, which create particular challenges for the tax system. The Government will continue to monitor developments closely and, if appropriate, consider with the industry what changes might be necessary to the tax treatment of such instruments.

5.83   The Government is also determined to protect the corporation tax system against legal challenges under European law, particularly where these challenges have the potential to undermine international agreements. The continuing consultation on corporation tax reform, described in Chapter 3, will provide an opportunity for the Government to discuss with business legislative options to ensure that the UK regime remains robust.

Tackling indirect   **5.84**   The Government's work to protect direct tax revenues complements that aimed at
tax losses   tackling losses in the indirect tax regimes. *Protecting indirect tax revenues*[13], published alongside the 2002 Pre-Budget Report, reported on the progress the Government had made to stop the growth in tobacco smuggling and to reduce revenue lost through cross-Channel passenger smuggling of alcohol and tobacco by more than 80 per cent. To consolidate and improve further these results, HM Customs and Excise will consult in the spring on regulatory measures to reduce opportunities for alcohol fraud.

VAT fraud and   **5.85**   The Government is applying its approach to tackling tobacco and other excise fraud
avoidance   to countering fraud, avoidance and non-compliance in the VAT system. The Government's strategy was described in detail in *Protecting indirect tax revenues* and is designed to produce more than £2 billion in additional revenues by 2005-06. In support of this strategy, Budget 2003 introduces further targeted measures to reduce instances of VAT fraud and avoidance, including:

- a new provision for joint and several liability for VAT due from missing traders, with safeguards to protect those innocently involved;

- extended powers for HM Customs and Excise to require security from businesses that consistently trade in supply chains involving missing traders or those who become insolvent leaving VAT unpaid;

- a provision to deny input tax recovery to traders that do not hold a valid tax invoice and cannot provide further evidence to support the bona fide nature of a transaction, where supplies are subject to widespread fraud;

- immediate legislation to prevent avoidance in relation to the private and non-business use of land and buildings; and

- in the light of consultation, action to ensure that VAT is accounted for where appropriate on the sale of face value vouchers and at least once a year on certain ongoing supplies between connected businesses.

---

[13] *Protecting indirect tax revenues*, HM Customs and Excise, November 2002.

Modernising and simplifying the tax system

Stamp duty   **5.86**   Budget 2002 announced a major reform of stamp duty on UK land and buildings to close loopholes and remove distortions in the system and to modernise administration and enforcement. Following consultation, **Budget 2003 sets out further details of the modernised stamp duty regime which will be introduced from December 2003.**

5.87   The modernised regime will generate a more streamlined process for ordinary homebuyers, paving the way for the development of e-conveyancing. It will also introduce fairer treatment for purchases funded by certain types of financing arrangement.

5.88   The main focus of the reform affects commercial property. In Budget 2002, the Government signalled its commitment to ensure that the charge applies fairly to all relevant transactions in UK land and buildings. The existing regime allows many transactions to take place without incurring a stamp duty charge, placing an additional burden on other taxpayers. The Government is also concerned that commercial decision making is being distorted by widespread tax planning, giving rise to complex and artificial arrangements to transfer the rights to property.

5.89   As a response to widespread avoidance, the reform includes comprehensive powers that are proportional to the scale of the problem. These encompass effective enforcement and compliance powers, commensurate with those that already exist for other taxes; comprehensive measures to target stamp duty-free transfer of property through the use of corporate vehicles; and the power to make in-year changes to counter any further avoidance.

5.90   As an element of stamp duty reform, the Government has also consulted on modernisation of the charge applying to new leases, addressing tax distortions between purchasing and leasing and in the structure of leasehold contracts. **The Government believes that the existing charge, which varies according to the length of the lease, should be replaced with a single one per cent charge on the total net present value of rental payments. The Government also proposes to lift 60 per cent of commercial leasehold contracts out of the charge altogether, through a new exempt threshold of £150,000.** The Government will move ahead with reform along these lines, for introduction alongside the modernised charge from December 2003, unless further consultation with business demonstrates that the Government's objective of securing a fair amount of tax from lease contracts can be better met by an alternative approach.

5.91   In securing the right amount of tax, the Government has also sought to protect small businesses, and where possible to reduce the burden on them. **Budget 2003 therefore increases the exempt threshold for commercial property to £150,000 from December,** lifting many small business purchases out of stamp duty altogether. This builds on the exemptions in Enterprise Areas described in Chapter 3 and will ensure that the modernised tax is better targeted at those who can best afford to pay. The stamp duty reforms also involve significant deregulation, by taking non-land transactions, except shares, out of stamp duty altogether.

5.92   Given the scale of this reform, the Government intends to continue consulting up to and beyond implementation. In particular, there will be further consultation on new arrangements to ensure that the charge is levied fairly on complex commercial developments and financing transactions, and on property held through partnerships. In examining the need for future changes, and as a result of improvements to the administration of stamp duty and data collection, the Government will be able to differentiate between the commercial and residential markets, in order to take into account significant differences in the economic circumstances of the two sectors and the need to ensure fairness between taxpayers.

Residence and domicile
5.93 The 2002 Pre-Budget Report gave further details of the Government's review of the residence and domicile rules. The Government is today publishing a background paper, *Reviewing the residence and domicile rules as they affect the taxation of individuals*, which takes forward continuing work in this area. The paper describes the current rules and their historical perspective, analyses international experience, and develops the principles that the Government believes should underpin any modernisation of the system. The paper will provide a framework for further analysis and discussion and ensure that any specific options for reform of the current rules are based on the widest possible understanding of their effect.

Tobacco duties
5.94 Smoking is the single greatest cause of preventable illness and premature death in the UK, killing 120,000 people every year. Research has consistently shown that the demand for cigarettes is affected by their price, and that high tax levels can play an important role in reducing overall tobacco consumption. Maintaining the real price of tobacco helps to encourage existing smokers to smoke less or quit, and to discourage young people from taking up the habit. Tobacco duty will therefore be increased in line with inflation from Budget day.

Alcohol duties
5.95 The Government is committed to delivering a fairer balance in the burden of taxation falling on different alcoholic drinks and different types of drink producer. To increase fairness in the alcohol duty regime:

- the duty on spirits will be frozen for the sixth Budget in a row – the longest freeze since the 1950s and equivalent to a cut in the tax on a standard bottle of 92 pence in real terms since 1997;

- the duty on beer and wine will be increased in line with inflation, adding one penny to a pint of beer and four pence to a standard 75 cl bottle of wine, maintaining revenue; and

- the duties on cider and sparkling wine will be frozen.

Gambling taxation
5.96 In recent years, the Government has modernised the structure of gambling taxation, the design of which had remained largely unchanged since the 1960s. Reforms to general betting duty and to pools betting duty have reduced administrative complexity, improved efficiency and helped the UK gambling industry to compete more effectively in an increasingly global marketplace. Evaluation of the new tax on bookmakers' gross profits confirms the success of the Government's reforms, which have contributed to strong growth in the industry, lower prices for consumers, and the creation of more than 2,000 new jobs. A full evaluation report will be published later in the spring.

5.97 As announced in Budget 2002, the Government has also consulted on the scope for replacing bingo duty with a tax on bingo companies' gross profits. In the light of consultation, Budget 2003 abolishes bingo duty and replaces it with a 15 per cent tax on the gross profits of bingo companies. This will benefit players, through higher prizes or lower prices, and bingo clubs, by promoting increased participation in bingo. The tax will be introduced from 4 August 2003.

5.98 As the next stage in the modernisation of gambling taxation, the Government will consult shortly on the scope for reform of Amusement Machine Licence Duty (AMLD). As with previous reforms, the Government aims to ensure that AMLD is fair and efficient and makes a sustainable contribution to government revenues while supporting the competitiveness of the industry. The Government also intends to ensure that reform of gambling taxes moves forward in concert with potential changes to the regulatory regime for gambling following the White Paper, *A safe bet for success*.[14]

TACKLING GLOBAL POVERTY

5.99 The Government is at the forefront of international efforts to reduce global poverty and achieve the Millennium Development Goals (MDGs) – shared international commitments to halve the proportion of people living in extreme poverty, reduce child and maternal mortality, achieve universal primary education, and reverse the spread of HIV/AIDS, malaria and other killer diseases by 2015.

5.100 Meeting these goals requires a significant increase in resources for development and further improvements in aid effectiveness. Best available estimates suggest that an extra $50 billion a year of development assistance is needed to meet the MDGs by 2015, and the Government has proposed an International Finance Facility, described in Box 5.4, to raise the resources required. The Government believes that meeting these ambitious targets require a new Marshall plan for the global economy with all countries meeting their shared obligations. This involves:

- an improvement in the terms on which the poorest countries participate in the global economy, with all countries pursuing agreed codes and standards of fiscal and monetary policy transparency;

- the adoption of high corporate standards by the international business community for engagement as reliable partners in the development process, and the creation in developing countries of the right domestic conditions for business investment;

- the sequenced adoption of an improved regime for trade that allows developing countries to benefit from and participate on fair terms in the world economy; and

- further improvements in aid effectiveness and a substantial increase in global aid flows through an International Finance Facility.

5.101 At their meeting in February 2003, G7 Finance Ministers affirmed their duty and responsibility for the prosperity and sustainable development of the world and pledged to address rigorously the challenge of global poverty. This includes a continued focus on financing the MDGs with a view to making further progress by the G8 Heads of State Summit in June 2003. The Government strongly supports this commitment and is determined to play a leading role in the development of further international efforts to meet the MDGs by 2015.

---

[14] *A safe bet for success*, Department for Culture, Media and Sport, March 2002.

Box 5.4: International Finance Facility

The international community is in danger of failing to achieve its shared objective to achieve the Millennium Development Goals. Despite recent progress, on current trends around 100 million children - 80 million in Africa alone - will still be denied schooling in 2015 and 47 out of 48 sub-Saharan countries will fail to meet targets for reduced maternal mortality. Half of the world's population still lives on less than two dollars a day.

Last year, the international community signed up to the first increase in official development aid for 20 years - an additional $12 billion a year by 2006. Nonetheless, the World Bank and the United Nations estimate that an additional $50 billion in aid from the international community is needed each year if the MDGs are to be met. This reality imposes a pressing need on the international community to deliver additional finance for development and further improvements in the effectiveness of aid, so that no country genuinely committed to poverty reduction and to meeting the MDGs should be denied the chance of achieving its goals through lack of resources.

To raise the additional finance needed to address the injustice of global poverty, the Chancellor and the Secretary of State for International Development have proposed the creation of a new International Finance Facility (IFF). The founding principle of the IFF is that, in return for action by developing countries to tackle corruption and establish stable conditions for equitable and sustainable economic growth, developed countries will increase aid from $50 billion a year today to $100 billion a year up to 2015.

The Facility would deliver this significant increase in resources by locking in long-term commitments to increased aid flows by donor countries. On the basis of these commitments, the Facility would secure additional finance from international capital markets, frontloading long-term aid flows for more immediate disbursement to ensure maximum impact towards meeting the MDGs. Additional resources would be disbursed mainly in the form of grants, including debt relief, and targeted at low-income countries through existing, effective bilateral and multilateral mechanisms. This means that the Facility would neither create new debt for poor countries nor introduce cumbersome bureaucracies that divert funds away from essential investments in poor countries. Full details of the Government's proposal were published in January 2003[1].

The Government has held positive discussions with other countries and international organisations on this proposal and will continue to press the case for an IFF as a matter of urgency. The Government's aspiration is to secure agreement to the establishment of an IFF at the G8 Heads of State Summit in June 2003. To make this a reality, it is essential that the business community and civil society help make the case for an IFF and convince others of the pressing need to take action.

[1] *International Finance Facility*, HM Treasury and the Department for International Development, January 2003.

The UK's commitment

5.102   A solution to the urgent problem of global poverty requires a substantial increase in aid to those nations most in need and willing to focus on the fight against poverty. The 2002 Spending Review announced the largest ever increase in UK aid, raising aid commitments to developing countries from 0.32 per cent of national income in 2002-03 to 0.4 per cent by 2005-06. This represents a near doubling of aid resources in real terms since 1997 and fulfils the UK's obligation under the EU's commitment to reach an aid ratio of 0.39 per cent by 2006. The UK also remains on track to reach the United Nations target of 0.7 per cent.

Improved aid **5.103**   The Government's intention is that the International Finance Facility will provide a
effectiveness   framework for increased aid effectiveness, by committing aid in a predictable way over the
long term so as to provide better value for money. Aid effectiveness requires greater
coordination between donors, and better harmonisation of the activities of international
institutions and the Regional Development Banks in the poorest countries. Crucially, it
provides the right incentives for developing countries to fulfil their responsibility to improve
governance and implement sound policies. More predictable aid to the poorest, based on
clear, country-owned poverty reduction strategies, will enable developing countries to deliver
the sustained investment in health and education necessary to meet the MDGs.

5.104   Reform and better allocation of aid must also include implementation of the
European Commission's proposals on untying aid and the refocusing of assistance on poorer
countries, which could make its aid 50 per cent more effective in reducing poverty.

Debt relief **5.105**   The Government continues to be a leading advocate of debt relief through the Heavily
Indebted Poor Countries (HIPC) initiative. Twenty-six countries will benefit from debt relief
worth $62 billion already committed under the initiative, reducing their debt payments by
around $1.3 billion each year. Eight of these countries have reached Completion Point and
have had their debts irrevocably cancelled. Mali and Benin reached Completion Point in
March 2003, and Niger and Rwanda could also reach their Completion Points shortly. The UK
already provides 100 per cent debt relief to those countries that have demonstrated a
commitment to poverty reduction and has provided $375 million to multilateral institutions
to support the HIPC initiative.

5.106   The Government believes that the provision of debt relief at Completion Point should
be flexible and take account of exogenous shocks, such as reduced export earnings resulting
from falls in commodity prices to ensure a sustainable exit from debt. At the Annual Meetings
of the World Bank and the International Monetary Fund in September 2002, the Government
helped to secure agreement to the need for additional funds, of up to $1 billion, and has
already pledged its full share of up to $120 million. It is important to recognise that resources
applied for further debt relief are truly additional. The Government has therefore proposed
that the International Finance Facility be able to make disbursements by way of debt relief as
well as grants.

Tackling the diseases of poverty   **5.107**   International commitments to the Global Health Fund for HIV/AIDS, malaria and tuberculosis now stand at $3.37 billion. The Government has so far pledged $200 million over five years of which $80 billion has now been disbursed. The Department for International Development (DFID) has also agreed new bilateral commitments worth over £1.5 billion to help strengthen the capacity of health systems in poor countries. Building on existing tax reliefs for research and development (R&D), Budget 2002 introduced a new tax relief to encourage R&D into vaccines and medicines for the prevention and treatment of specific diseases threatening lives in the poorest countries.

Universal primary education   **5.108**   Since 1997, DFID has committed over £700 million to help deliver universal primary education in developing countries. The Government will expand this support by a further £1.3 billion over the next five years, with the objective of helping developing country governments to place an extra 20 million children into school by 2006. Donors should help governments to develop sound sector plans within the framework of Poverty Reduction Strategy Programmes, and harmonise and simplify their support for these plans. The Government continues to work with its existing commitments and by seeking to raise additional funds through the International Finance Facility to help deliver on the collective pledge at Dakar three years ago to ensure that no sound plans to deliver education for all are left unfunded.

Trade   **5.109**   Progress on trade could be worth three times the development aid currently received by the poorest countries. Trade can be a powerful engine for growth. The elimination of barriers to merchandise trade in both industrialised and developing countries could result in welfare gains up to $620 billion annually. One third to one half of the gains would accrue to developing countries. Liberalisation in developing countries must be appropriately sequenced, integrated into country-owned poverty reduction strategies and supported by poverty and social impact analysis. Complementary policies must be in place to support the poor through any transitional disruption. Developed countries must continue to support developing countries in building up their capacity to negotiate internationally and their ability to produce goods and services efficiently and to get them to international markets. Increased aid – including through mechanisms such as an International Finance Facility – will play an essential part in this support, helping developing countries to take advantage of their trading opportunities. Full global trade liberalisation could lift at least 300 million people out of poverty by 2015.

5.110   The Government strongly supports the agreement reached in Doha to launch a new round of trade negotiations, which clearly prioritise the needs of developing countries within the international trading system. It continues to work closely with international partners to ensure that all countries, and particularly the most developed, deliver on the commitments made. Progress on agriculture is especially important. Developed country subsidies to agriculture amount to $1 billion a day – seven times the level of overseas development assistance – and the Government is therefore pressing for significant reform of the EU's Common Agricultural Policy in the current review. The Government is also working to secure provisions in the World Trade Organisation which will improve access to medicines for the poorest people in the world.

Box 5.4: Post-conflict support for Iraq

The Government, working alongside its international partners, will be fully involved in any humanitarian and reconstruction work in Iraq and will seek to engage the United Nations (UN) and the International Financial Institutions early on in this process. The Government has made no final estimate of the likely costs of humanitarian and reconstruction needs in Iraq and will want to draw on the expertise of the international community before firm conclusions can be reached. However, a total of £240 million has so far been set aside for humanitarian assistance in Iraq, including $100 million for UN-led assistance. In addition, the Government is setting aside a further $100 million to back up the UN and the work of reconstruction and international development.

The Government will promote and participate in various methods of international support, including a fair and sustainable solution to Iraq's debt problems, aid flows appropriate to Iraq's needs and resources, technical expertise to help Iraq achieve its economic potential, and a swift end to sanctions once Iraq is in compliance with United Nations demands, including freeing up assets held by Saddam Hussein's regime so that they may in future be used for the benefit and welfare of the Iraqi people.

Chapter 6 sets out further details of the resource allocations the Government has made in response to the developing situation in Iraq.

6 DELIVERING HIGH QUALITY PUBLIC SERVICES

The Government's goal is to build a stronger, more flexible economy and a fairer society. World class public services are crucial to this goal. A healthy and educated workforce, modern and reliable transport network, and adequate supply of affordable housing promote productivity and flexibility and help to ensure opportunity and security for all. The Government's strategy is to deliver improvements in public services through sustained investment and reform to ensure that taxpayers receive value for money.

The 2002 Spending Review set departmental spending plans for the three years up to 2005-06, and five years for the NHS, consistent with the fiscal rules. These plans deliver substantial extra investment in public services, with:

- current expenditure set to rise by 3.1 per cent a year in real terms in 2004-05 and 3.8 per cent in 2005-06 and public sector net investment projected to rise to 2 per cent of GDP by 2005-06 and to $2\frac{1}{4}$ per cent of GDP by 2007-08;

- more than 75 per cent of planned additional spending allocated to the key priorities of health, education, criminal justice, housing and transport; and

- UK NHS spending plans rising by 7.2 per cent a year in real terms over the five years to 2007-08, with substantial investment in IT, buildings and equipment.

To deliver the largest ever sustained spending growth in the history of the NHS while meeting the fiscal rules and other priorities, Budget 2002 raised national insurance contributions by one per cent on all earnings above the threshold from April 2003, and froze the income tax personal allowance for those aged under 65 in 2003-04. Budget 2003:

- **provides £332 million to invest in further counter-terrorism measures** over the next three years, to ensure that UK citizens are protected within the UK from the threat of international terrorism;

- **sets out key issues to be investigated in the run-up to the next Spending Review,** including a new study into the scope for relocating public service staff from London and the South East to other parts of the country, and an update of the long-term challenges in implementing the 'fully engaged' scenario set out in last year's Wanless Review of long-term health trends, with a particular focus on preventative health and health inequalities; and

- **provides details of the next steps in reform,** with action to increase regional and local flexibility in public service pay systems and to increase transparency about performance, including through the introduction from April 2003 of regular reporting on the Treasury website of performance against all new Public Service Agreement targets.

INTRODUCTION

6.1   The Government's long-term goal is to deliver world class public services through sustained increases in investment and reforms to deliver efficient and responsive services which meet public expectations throughout the country. Strong and dependable public services lay the foundations for a flexible, high productivity economy, supporting greater efficiency among businesses and adaptability within the workforce. They also promote opportunity and security for all, helping to tackle poverty and social exclusion and improving the quality of life. For example:

- a healthy, educated and highly skilled workforce allows businesses to update products, services and working practices at the rate demanded by rapidly changing global markets and tastes;

- a modern and reliable transport network extends workers' travel-to-work horizons, helping them to access jobs in areas beyond where they live, and provides businesses with access to markets, a pool of available labour and new investment opportunities;

- an adequate supply of affordable housing in all regions ensures that people are able to move easily between jobs and localities in response to changing local labour market conditions; and

- responsive public sector pay systems that reflect differences in regional and local labour markets provide incentives for labour to move in response to changes in demand, reducing the likelihood of imbalances between supply and demand in sectors or regions.

6.2   The Government is committed to ensuring that the public services support wider efforts to promote flexibility and fairness. Sound macroeconomic management has enabled the Government to release significant extra resources to increase investment in public services, while ensuring that the fiscal rules are met. The 2002 Spending Review announced departmental spending plans for the next three years, with additional resources focused on the priority services of health, education, transport, housing and criminal justice.

6.3   These extra resources are being accompanied by wide-ranging reforms to ensure that they are used efficiently and effectively and that taxpayers receive value for money from their investment. A framework of national standards for the quality of public service provision accompanied by robust accountability and audit arrangements is allowing increasing devolution of responsibility away from central government and towards local service providers. This chapter describes how, across the public services, increased resources and ambitious reforms are helping to deliver results.

RESOURCES

6.4   Sound public finances lay the foundations for economic stability and for sustainable investment in public services. The fiscal rules, described in detail in Chapter 2, underpin the Government's public spending framework, ensuring that the public finances are sustainable over the economic cycle and that taxation and spending impact fairly between generations. The rules have important consequences for the way in which the Government budgets for public spending, removing past disincentives to invest and ensuring that borrowing for investment is conducted in a responsible way.

6.5   To help departments plan their spending programmes for the medium term the Government has introduced a system of firm and fixed Departmental Expenditure Limits (DELs) for departmental spending stretching over three years, and reviewed every two. Expenditure items that are large, potentially volatile and demand-led – such as social security benefits and debt interest payments – are collectively known as Annually Managed Expenditure (AME), and are subject to rigorous scrutiny twice a year as part of the Budget and Pre-Budget Report process. Taken together, DEL and AME add up to Total Managed Expenditure (TME), the Government's measure of total public spending.

Military conflict in Iraq   **6.6**   The 2002 Pre-Budget Report confirmed the Government's plans for public spending in 2002-03. The Pre-Budget Report also made a special contingency allocation of £1 billion to ensure that resources were available for the UK's international defence and security needs. These resources allowed the UK's armed forces to prepare, on a contingency basis, for the event that the Iraqi regime failed to comply with the conditions set down in United Nations (UN) Security Council resolution 1441.

6.7   The failure of the Iraqi regime to comply with the will of the international community as expressed in resolution 1441 led to the commencement in March of coalition military action to enforce these conditions. The Government has therefore increased its contingency provision to £3 billion to ensure that resources are available to cover the full cost of the UK's military obligations.

6.8   While the full amount of this provision has been allocated to 2002-03, there is considerable uncertainty over when these costs will fall. In the light of this uncertainty, and to protect committed investment while responding prudently to heightened global risks, the Government has decided to make no further allocations from the Capital Modernisation Fund (CMF). Instead unallocated CMF funding will contribute to the rebuilding of the AME margin to ensure that the public spending projections include a prudent and cautious safety margin against unexpected events. Resetting the AME margin to £1, £2 and £3 billion for the years 2003-04, 2004-05 and 2005-06, in accordance with usual practice, increases projections for TME by £1 billion in 2004-05 and by £1.8 billion in 2005-06, compared with those in the 2002 Pre-Budget Report.

6.9   In addition, as described in Chapter 5, the Government has also allocated £240 million towards the costs of humanitarian assistance in Iraq, including $100 million for UN-led assistance. In addition, the Government is putting aside a further $100 million to back up the UN, and the work of reconstruction and international development.

Domestic security   **6.10**   The Government is committed to ensuring that UK citizens are protected within the UK from the threat of international terrorism. Building on the significant increase in resources for counter-terrorism and security requirements allocated in the 2002 Spending Review, Budget 2003 allocates a further £332 million over the next three years to invest in new counter-terrorism measures that will enhance the security of the UK and the ability of the emergency and other services to counter the terrorist threat.

The 2002
Spending Review

6.11   Prudent management of the economy and the public finances means that the overall spending 'envelope' set in Budget 2002 and confirmed in the 2002 Spending Review remains sustainable and fully consistent with the fiscal rules. This 'envelope' allows:

- current spending to rise in total by 3.1 per cent a year in real terms in 2004-05 and 3.8 per cent in 2005-06;

- public sector net investment to rise from its target of 1.8 per cent of GDP in 2003-04, to 2 per cent of GDP by 2005-06 and to $2\frac{1}{4}$ per cent by 2007-08, continuing to address the legacy of under-investment in public infrastructure, while meeting the sustainable investment rule; and

- planned UK spending on the NHS to increase by an average of 7.2 per cent a year in real terms over the five years to 2007-08.

6.12   With TME set to rise by 4.3 per cent a year in real terms between 2002-03 and 2005-06, new resources are being targeted at front line public services where they can be used most effectively. While spending on debt interest and social security is forecast to grow in real terms by only 2.5 and 2.3 per cent a year respectively over the next three years, planned spending on education is set to grow by 5.7 per cent a year and on transport by 8.3 per cent. Over 75 per cent of the planned increase in DEL and locally-financed expenditure over the coming three years is being targeted at the Government's key priorities of health, education, personal social services, transport, housing and criminal justice.

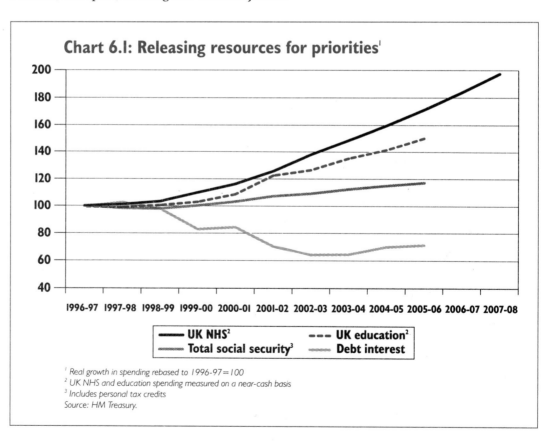

Chart 6.1: Releasing resources for priorities[1]

—— UK NHS[2]	- - - UK education[2]	
~~ Total social security[3]	~~~~ Debt interest	

[1] Real growth in spending rebased to 1996-97 = 100
[2] UK NHS and education spending measured on a near-cash basis
[3] Includes personal tax credits
Source: HM Treasury.

Public **6.13** A prerequisite for delivering high quality public services is having the right public
investment service infrastructure in place. In 1997, public sector net investment stood at just £4.9 billion
– 0.6 per cent of GDP – the lowest level for over a decade. Investment in public services had
been on a declining trend since the mid-1970s, resulting in more than twenty years of falling
standards in the quality of schools, hospitals and other public service assets. This reflected a
budgeting system which encouraged short-termism and a bias towards spending on current
pressures rather than on capital investment.

6.14 The Government is committed to reversing this under-investment in public service
infrastructure. Public sector net investment (PSNI) is now expected to rise to 2 per cent of
GDP by 2005-06. Total investment, which includes PSNI, depreciation, recycled proceeds
from asset sales and private sector investment through Public Private Partnerships and the
Private Finance Initiative, is set to rise to over £47 billion by 2005-06 in the largest sustained
increase in public sector investment for over twenty years.

6.15 As shown in Chart 6.2, within the increased level of resources devoted to investment,
the Government has focused on the four priority areas of education, transport, health and
housing:

- capital spending on health in the UK is set to grow by an average of 15 per cent
  a year in real terms between 1997-98 and 2005-06;

- capital spending on education in England will rise on average by 18 per cent a
  year in real terms between 1997-98 and 2005-06;

- investment in transport in the UK will grow from £3.8 billion in 1997 to over
  £7.2 billion by 2006; and

- investment in housing will increase from £2.1 billion in 1997-98 to £4.9 billion
  by 2005-06. Over the six years to 2005-06 capital investment is set to grow on
  average by over 10 per cent a year in real terms.

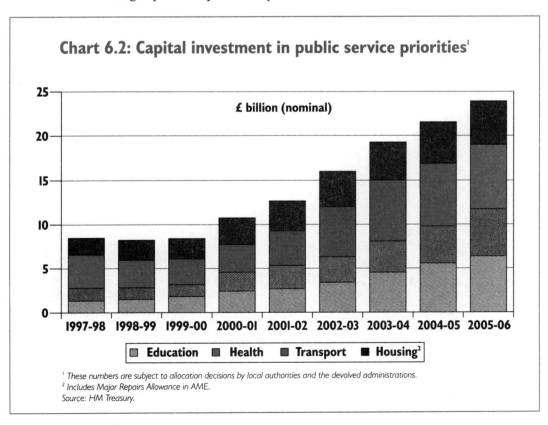

Chart 6.2: Capital investment in public service priorities[1]

[1] These numbers are subject to allocation decisions by local authorities and the devolved administrations.
[2] Includes Major Repairs Allowance in AME.
Source: HM Treasury.

Reforming the **6.16** Increased resources will only lead to improved public services if they are allocated
public spending and used efficiently and effectively. Since 1997, wide-ranging reforms to the public spending
framework framework have removed unnecessary central controls on departmental finances and given
departments the freedom and flexibility they need for successful delivery. The reforms
include:

- firm and fixed resource and capital DELs for spending on departmental
  services stretching over three years, with longer-term budgets for health and
  transport of five and ten years respectively. 2003-04 sees the introduction of
  full resource budgeting, with DELs for the first time reflecting the full
  economic costs of delivering services. This will provide improved incentives
  for the management of public assets and investment, and will increase
  transparency by providing better information to managers and the public
  about the true costs of providing public services;

- end-year flexibility (EYF), which allows departments to carry forward
  resources and capital not fully spent at the end of any financial year into
  future years. This helps departments to plan their programmes more
  effectively and removes any incentive for wasteful end-year surges in
  spending. Most departments with responsibility for agencies or non-
  departmental public bodies are cascading EYF, thus ensuring that the full
  benefit of this budgetary freedom is realised. In 2002-03 departments chose to
  draw down £5.0 billion of EYF to add to their authorised spending limits. As
  has been the case in previous years, the Government expects this net addition
  to be more than offset by under-spends elsewhere within DEL. For future
  years it is assumed that resource and capital DELs are fully spent; and

- a National Asset Register[1] to improve the way in which the public sector asset
  base is managed. The Register helps departments to use their assets more
  effectively and to reach better judgements as to whether individual assets are
  still required.

---

[1] *The National Asset Register*, HM Treasury, July 2001.

REFORMING THE PUBLIC SERVICES

6.17 The Government's goal is to build a stronger, more flexible economy and a fairer society, with opportunity and security for all. Advancing this goal implies different responsibilities for individuals, markets and communities, including government, each of which has a role to play in the delivery of fair and efficient outcomes. While markets on their own or with limited government regulation are in principle well placed to deliver many goods and services fairly and efficiently, there may often be an important role for government in helping markets to work better. Chapter 3 describes how the Government is seeking to improve the functioning of markets to deliver a more flexible and productive economy. In the case of some services however, the level of government regulation that would be required to deliver fair and efficient outcomes can be so high that the public sector is better placed to fund and manage delivery. In these circumstances, the Government's role is to improve the public sector's potential to deliver successful outcomes through investment and reform, and thereby to advance the public interest.

Delivering public service reform **6.18** The Government's programme of public service reform seeks to ensure that, where in principle the public sector is best placed to advance the public interest through the delivery of services, in practice this potential is realised. The Government's public service reforms aim to deliver efficient, responsive public services, with high standards achieved across the country, through:

- clear, long-term, outcome-focused goals, set by the Government;

- devolution of responsibility to public service providers themselves, with maximum local flexibility and discretion to innovate and incentives to ensure that the needs of local communities are met;

- independent and effective arrangements for audit and inspection to improve accountability; and

- transparency about what is being achieved, with better information about performance both locally and nationally.

6.19 The public sector is a major presence in the economy, and its productivity reinforces the productivity of the wider economy. The Government's framework for raising public service productivity, which complements its approach to raising productivity in the private sector, is set out in a new discussion paper, *Public services: meeting the productivity challenge*, published alongside this Budget.

Setting long-term goals **6.20** A crucial prerequisite for delivering better public services is clarity about the objectives which the Government is seeking to achieve. Public Service Agreements (PSAs) provide this clarity and are central to the Government's strategy for public service reform and improved delivery. First introduced in the 1998 Comprehensive Spending Review and covering the whole range of the public services, PSAs set targets for the outcomes that each department is committed to achieving. As such, they form an integral part of the Government's public spending framework, relating resource inputs to the outcomes that matter to the public, such as better health, improved education performance, and lower levels of crime.

6.21   The targets set out in PSAs have contributed to a genuine shift in departmental culture away from inputs and processes and towards the delivery of outputs and results. They provide:

- a clear sense of direction and ambition. The aim, objectives and targets in each PSA provide a clear statement around which departments can mobilise their resources. This helps in business planning and in communicating a clear message to staff and to the various public bodies which contribute to delivering each department's programme;

- a focus on delivering results. By starting from the outcome the Government is trying to achieve, the targets encourage departments to think creatively about how their activities and policies contribute to delivering those results. They also encourage departments to look across boundaries to build partnerships with those they need to work with to be successful. Departments prepare delivery plans for each of their targets, providing clarity to those responsible for delivery about what needs to be done. The Prime Minister's Delivery Unit and the Treasury help departments plan and monitor progress with implementation;

- a basis for monitoring what is and is not working. Clarity about aims, and tracking progress in achieving them, allows departments to guage whether what they are doing is working. If it is, this success can be rewarded; if it is not, poor performance can be tackled; and

- better public accountability. Targets are meant to be stretching so not all will be met. But regular reporting of progress against targets allows everyone to see what progress is being made.

6.22   Since 1998, the overall number of PSAs has been reduced substantially to an average of less than seven per department, helping departments to focus on the Government's key priorities. The quality of the targets has also improved, as demonstrated by a National Audit Office study[2] which showed that the proportion of outcome-focused targets rose from 16 to 68 per cent between the 1998 and 2000 Spending Reviews. The 2002 Spending Review took the process of improving targets further. For example:

- education floor targets are now focused on the school rather than the local authority level;

- the Department for International Development's PSA has been restructured to align it directly with the international community's Millennium Development Goals, its own organisational structure, and partner countries' priorities and plans; and

- the Office of the Deputy Prime Minister's target to improve social housing conditions has been broadened to include the private sector.

---

[2] *Measuring the performance of Government departments*, National Audit Office, March 2001.

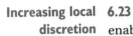

Increasing local   **6.23**   PSAs allow for increased devolution of responsibility to front line service providers,
discretion   enabling the Government to remove itself from old fashioned command-and-control
methods of public sector management. Those at the front line of service delivery are often
best placed to assess and respond to local conditions and to meet changing customer needs.
By setting targets for local delivery bodies, consistent with the national standards set out in
PSAs and with appropriate accountability arrangements in place, departments can now
empower local organisations with the freedom and flexibility they need to provide high
quality and responsive services. This helps to ensure that local services are built around the
needs of local people, while maintaining a focus on the achievement of national standards
across the country.

Box 6.1: Public sector pay and workforce – supporting better public services

Delivering high quality public services demands that the best use is made of the public
sector workforce. This means the responsible deployment of the significant resources
directed to public sector pay and careful consideration of workplace conditions to enable
the public sector to recruit, retain and reward a responsive and motivated workforce with
the right skills.

The Government aims to use pay as part of its package of reforms to improve public
service delivery. In reaching decisions on pay, the right balance needs to be struck between
rewarding people appropriately for their skills and setting pay at responsible rates that are
consistent with economic stability. Many recent public sector pay settlements have
reflected these principles – in particular, the decisions of the Pay Review Bodies – by
establishing greater links between pay and reform, increasing the focus on rewarding skills
and performance, and directing pay to address local recruitment and retention needs.
Departments are also taking a more strategic approach to pay and workforce issues,
linking these directly to delivery requirements.

To recognise local and regional conditions in pay, such as the extra costs for retention and
recruitment that arise in London and the South East, especially for the low paid, the
Government will also make sure that the remit for the Pay Review Bodies and for public
sector workers, including the civil service, includes a stronger local and regional dimension.

Enhancing   **6.24**   Independent and effective arrangements for audit and inspection are essential if
accountability   departments and agencies are to be held properly accountable for performance against their
targets. There should be separate responsibility for setting standards from responsibility for
assessing whether they are being achieved. Such arrangements are being implemented across
a range of public services. For instance:

- the role of the new Police Standards Unit is being consolidated and developed,
  working alongside Her Majesty's Inspectorate of Constabulary; and

- a single housing inspectorate has been established to drive up performance
  for all types of social landlord, replacing the current separate inspection
  regimes.

6.25 The Government is committed to providing public access to regular and reliable information about performance against PSA targets to increase transparency and improve public accountability. Departments now publish details of progress against their targets twice a year, in the autumn as well as in spring departmental reports. This information is supported by the publication of departmental Technical Notes and Service Delivery Agreements, which set out respectively how performance is measured and the key steps that departments will take to ensure that targets are met, and by the release of Departmental Investment Strategies, which set out departments' investment plans and how these contribute to the achievement of objectives. The Treasury website now provides a link[3] to this full range of performance information, ensuring that the public can gain access to it from a single portal.

6.26 In a further major innovation, representing a step-change in the level of transparency and public accountability, regular web-based reporting against all the new PSA targets will be introduced on the HM Treasury website from April 2003, making all the latest performance information accessible to the public in a single place. Departments will continue to publish performance data in the usual way, and the website will be regularly updated to reflect any changes.

6.27 In March 2002, the Government invited the Comptroller and Auditor General to externally validate the data systems underlying PSA targets, drawing on the work, and recognising the independence and authority, of the National Statistician and the Audit Commission. Over the past year the National Audit Office (NAO) has undertaken a number of short validation trials. These will be completed by the end of April and lessons from the trials will be drawn on by the NAO as it implements plans for the validation of data systems underpinning all PSAs.

Implementing reforms, delivering results

6.28 New investment is being coupled with reform across the public services, and a transparent approach to reporting performance is enabling the public to see the progress that is being made. The following section describes how resources and reform are driving delivery across a range of public service priority areas, and sets out some of the key challenges ahead. The final section describes the Government's strategy for delivering a world class healthcare system for the 21st century.

6.29 The Government's Leadership Incentive Grant is already helping to ensure that no school is held back through weak leadership. All 1,400 eligible secondary schools in poorer areas have now developed plans for improved leadership, and a new set of leadership criteria, developed as part of this process, is to become an integral part of the OFSTED inspection process.

---

[3] See www.hm-treasury.gov.uk/performancedocs

6.30   The Government has also initiated a major programme of reform in further education, to raise standards and improve performance across the sector. The 2002 Spending Review allocated an additional £1.2 billion to further education, to be invested over the next three years. To facilitate better planning, the Department for Education and Skills has cascaded three-year budgets and full 100 per cent end-year flexibility to the Learning and Skills Council (LSC), to be devolved in turn to local LSCs and learning providers. New approaches to funding will reward colleges that deliver on minimum floor and performance improvement targets for participation, success rates and employer engagement. The higher education White Paper[4] published earlier this year set out plans for reform in universities and higher education colleges.

6.31   Progress has been made in all areas to improve standards of attainment in education. In 2002, over half of all 16 year olds achieved five A* to C grades at GCSE, exceeding the target set in the 1998 Comprehensive Spending Review. The percentage of pupils achieving five or more GCSEs at grades A* to C has now increased by more than six percentage points since 1997, from 45 to over 51 per cent of pupils. Between 1997 and 2002, the proportion of 11 year-olds reaching expected levels in English and maths rose by 12 percentage points and 11 percentage points respectively, to 75 and 73 per cent. The lowest achieving Local Education Authority (LEA) is now performing at around the level of the average LEA of five years ago and the percentage of schools achieving below 65 percent in English and maths has been roughly halved since 1998. The key challenge ahead for schools is to ensure that rising standards for the majority are sustained, while ensuring that all LEAs and schools are able to reach minimum attainment levels.

Local government   **6.32**   Local government provides a range of essential public services, including schools and care for the elderly, and therefore has a vital role to play in delivering higher quality and more efficient public services. In line with the Local Government White Paper[5], the Government has taken action to promote local autonomy in service delivery by reducing Whitehall controls for all local authorities. The amount of central government revenue and capital support that is ring-fenced will be reduced, giving all councils greater control over their spending. The Government will also reduce by 75 per cent the number of plans that councils must produce, and all future inspection activity will be carried out on a coordinated and targeted basis.

6.33   The Local Government Bill currently passing before Parliament will further increase the freedoms available to local authorities. The Bill introduces a new prudential regime for borrowing that will make local authorities' capital investment more transparent and provide a framework for greater financial flexibility to deliver local priorities. It will also include provisions for a new scheme to allow local authorities to retain some or all of any increases in business rates revenue generated by increases in local business activity, as described in Chapter 3.

---

[4] *The Future of Higher Education*, Department for Education and Skills, January 2003.

[5] *Strong local leadership – quality public services*, the Office of the Deputy Prime Minister, December 2001.

6.34 The first Comprehensive Performance Assessment (CPA) for single-tier and county authorities was published in December 2002. The CPA represents a step-change in the reporting of local government performance, bringing together for the first time all available information on the performance of councils to help improve accountability to local people. Single-tier and county authorities that achieved an 'excellent' rating in the CPA will benefit from the removal of all revenue and capital ring-fencing, except for direct grants to schools. In future, they will be required to produce just two plans – a Best Value Performance Plan and a Community Strategy – and will be exempt from most inspection activity for a three-year period. Over half of all local authorities have been rated good or excellent, and will therefore benefit from increased freedoms and flexibilities.

6.35 In the first CPA, under ten per cent of authorities have been judged poor. The Government is engaging with these authorities and requires them to implement effective recovery plans that provide communities in these areas with the high quality public services they deserve. CPA will be extended to all lower-tier councils over the coming 18 months.

Criminal justice   **6.36** The Government is determined to cut crime and the fear of crime, and the Home Office, Lord Chancellor's Department and Crown Prosecution Service are working together to meet challenging targets in this area. Improved police performance, based on increased investment matched with wide-ranging reform, will be crucial to deliver a step change in performance. With police numbers now at a record high, the Government is therefore:

- delivering the three-year National Policing Plan, which establishes a clear national framework for raising the performance of all police forces, and indicators against which performance will be judged;

- increasing transparency and accountability through the introduction of Police Performance Monitors, allowing the public to compare the performance of their local police force with that of similar forces for the first time;

- implementing the recommendations of the Bureaucracy Taskforce to ensure police officers' time is used effectively;

- implementing pay reform for police, including an element for good performance;

- allocating £50 million a year direct to Basic Command Units in high crime areas for use in innovative schemes; and

- allocating a further £174 million over three years for correctional services in England and Wales.

6.37   Overall crime has fallen by 28 per cent since 1997, but in the last year has remained flat. Since 2000, there has been a 23 per cent reduction in vehicle crime and a 27 per cent reduction in domestic burglary, though vehicle crime and burglary levels have remained broadly the same over the past year. Recorded robberies have increased by 28 per cent in the year to March 2002. Since the start of the Street Crime Initiative (SCI) in April 2002 they have fallen by 25 per cent in the ten SCI areas. But the overall target of a 14 per cent reduction between 1999-00 and 2005 remains challenging.

Housing   6.38   In February, the Deputy Prime Minister set out a detailed programme of action to improve delivery in housing, planning and regeneration[6]. The programme includes stock renovation, the provision of new affordable housing and measures to address imbalances in regional housing markets. To support delivery, the Deputy Prime Minister also established Regional Housing Boards that are producing housing strategies for their regions and will deploy resources from a single regional housing investment pot, thereby linking housing delivery with planning and wider regional economic strategies. Chapter 2 gives details of a new review into the factors affecting the supply and responsiveness of housing.

6.39   Good progress is being made in improving the quality of life in urban areas and other communities and in reducing social exclusion and fuel poverty and regenerating deprived neighbourhoods through the availability of decent social housing. The Government is on course to bring a third of non-decent social housing – around 500,000 homes – up to a decent standard by 2004 and is introducing new measures to deliver its target to make all social housing decent by 2010. Up to 22,000 affordable homes will also be built through the Housing Corporation in 2003–04. To improve the sustainability of new housing development, 61 per cent of all new dwellings in 2001 were provided on previously developed land or through the conversion of existing buildings, meeting the target of 60 per cent six years early. Significant challenges for the future include achieving a better balance between housing availability and demand in all English regions and tackling low demand and abandonment in parts of the North and the Midlands.

Transport   6.40   A modern and reliable transport network is key to a flexible and high productivity economy, helping to improve labour mobility and providing businesses with access to new markets and investment. The Department for Transport is currently conducting a review of the Ten Year Plan for Transport to assess how best to roll it forward in response to the challenges that need to be met up to 2015 and beyond.

6.41   Among the issues to be considered by the review are:

- addressing the challenge of higher forecasts for road congestion, driven in part by higher economic growth, including through focused action and making better use of the existing network;

- connecting national targets with local delivery; and

- improving investment appraisal across transport programmes.

6.42   On the railways, the creation of Network Rail, coupled with a strengthened Strategic Rail Authority, has created an improved structure for the rail industry. The challenge is now to deliver improvements in performance, efficiency and cost control. The rail industry and the rail regulator are working together to achieve this.

---

[6] *Sustainable communities: building for the future*, Office of the Deputy Prime Minister, February 2003.

6.43   The Department for Transport is making progress against its targets in a number of key areas. The number of deaths or serious injuries from road accidents in 2001 was 15 per cent lower than the average between 1994 and 1998, against a target reduction of 40 per cent by 2010. Accidents involving children have fallen by 27 per cent against a target of 50 per cent. In addition, passenger use of railways had risen by 2.5 per cent by the end of 2002 compared with 2000-01, against a target increase of 50 per cent by 2010. While London Underground has made good progress in increasing network capacity and reducing journey times, the consequences of the Chancery Lane derailment mean that targets in these areas are unlikely to be met this year. Bus and light rail use has risen by 1 per cent in each of the last two years, against a new combined local public transport target of a 12 per cent increase by 2010.

Box 6.2: *futurebuilders*

It is now widely recognised that the voluntary and community sector can add significant value to the delivery of public services, whether operating across geographical and administrative boundaries or by reaching out to some of the most vulnerable and disadvantaged people in society. Many voluntary and community organisations wish to develop their service delivery role and the Government wants to help them do so.

To take forward its commitment, the Government is investing £125 million in a new *futurebuilders* fund to assist voluntary and community sector organisations in their public service work. Funding will be directed to those organisations involved in delivering front line public services in health and social care, crime and social cohesion, education and learning, and services which support children and young people. *futurebuilders* complements the new framework for service delivery between the Government and the voluntary and community sector, agreed as part of last year's cross-cutting review into the role of the voluntary sector in delivering services. The Government is working in partnership with the voluntary and community sector to design the fund and will consult shortly on specific proposals for how funding should be used.

The Government now intends to build on the cross-cutting review with a study of departmental involvement with the voluntary and community sector in local service delivery, and the potential for going further, to inform the next Spending Review. In particular, the Government will seek to develop further the Community Interest Company (CIC), an entirely new legal form designed for socially responsible enterprises. The Government does not intend that CICs should deliver essential public services such as schools or hospitals. However CICs have a clear role to play in complementing government services at the community level in areas such as childcare provision, community transport or leisure.

Next steps

6.44 The Government is determined that every pound of public spending should deliver the best possible return in high quality services. This means focusing on the drivers of performance and efficiency, and redoubling efforts to achieve consistent standards and to tackle inequalities, including looking at ways of better integrating funding streams. To make the best of funding allocated in the 2002 Spending Review and to prepare the ground for the next Spending Review, the Government will investigate a number of key issues including:

- tackling child poverty – to examine how public services and welfare reform can most effectively tackle child poverty, further integrate services for the under 5s, and improve the prospects of work and opportunity for families, especially in deprived areas;

- devolving decision making from the centre – to examine how best to achieve decentralised delivery and responsive local and regional services in a way that is consistent with equity and efficiency, against a clear framework of national standards. This will consider the way in which targets are set and the flow of information on performance;

- engaging the voluntary and community sector – to assess the progress made by departments in encouraging the involvement of the voluntary and community sector in local service delivery and the potential for going further; and

- delivering better childcare – building on the inter-departmental childcare review, to focus on the further steps needed to ensure an adequate supply of good quality childcare, as part of the wider consideration, announced in January, of possible next steps to help parents balance work and family life.

6.45 In addition the Government will be examining the scope for relocating civil service and other public service staff from London and the South East to other parts of the country, to improve cost effectiveness and achieve a better regional balance of government activity. This study will be led by Sir Michael Lyons. The Government will also be reviewing new ways of providing departments, their agencies and other parts of the the public sector with incentives to exploit opportunities for efficiency savings, and so release resources for front line public service delivery.

A HEALTHCARE SYSTEM FOR THE 21ST CENTURY

6.46   The Government's goal is to deliver a world class health service, available to all on the basis of clinical need rather than ability to pay, as a vital component of a flexible, dynamic and productive economy. Over the past 30 years the UK has consistently invested a smaller share of its national income in healthcare than comparator countries. As a consequence, the UK has fewer doctors, nurses, beds and items of diagnostic equipment per head of the population than in comparable economies. Historical underinvestment has resulted in long waiting lists and, on most measures, poorer health outcomes than the EU average.

6.47   Because a market-based approach would lead to unacceptable health outcomes in terms of both efficiency and equity, the Government is committed to public funding of health services matched by public provision, combining fairness and efficiency in the pursuit of opportunity and security for all. To address historical underinvestment in the provision of health services, Budget 2002 announced the largest ever sustained spending growth in the history of the National Health Service (NHS), with additional resources linked to a substantial package of reforms to strengthen the local delivery of services, promote accountability and patient choice, and provide for greater contestability to drive efficiency and reward innovation.

The Wanless Review of long-term health trends

6.48   In Budget 2001, the Chancellor commissioned Derek Wanless, former Group Chief Executive of NatWest Bank, to undertake an independent review of the long-term trends that will affect the resource needs of the health service in the UK over the next 20 years. The final report, published at the time of Budget 2002, concluded that in order to deliver a high quality health service the UK would need to devote a substantially larger share of its national income to health over the next 20 years. To ensure that additional resources are used to maximum effect, the Review also recommended a series of reforms to address the strategic issues facing the NHS in the coming years, including:

- the importance of setting national standards for clinical care and integrated information and communication technology systems;

- the significant scope to give more discretion to those delivering care at the local level, helping to drive up performance across the board;

- the need for a mechanism to ensure regular and rigorous independent audit of all health care spending;

- the vital interface between health and social care, and the need for similar quality improvements in the social care sector; and

- the need for public engagement to increase health awareness, based on a better understanding of rights and responsibilities.

Providing resources

6.49   The Review concluded that the resources needed to deliver a high quality health service over the next 20 years would depend on developments in the demand for and supply of health services, including the health needs and demands of the population, technological developments, workforce issues and productivity. The Review set out three scenarios – 'solid progress', 'slow uptake' and 'fully engaged' – to illustrate how different developments in these areas would affect the resources needed. For each of the scenarios, the period of fastest growth in spending is in the early years, enabling improvements in standards to be delivered as quickly as possible. The Review concluded that the 'fully engaged' scenario was the least expensive although it delivered the best health outcomes.

6.50   The Government accepted the conclusions of the Wanless Review. In line with its recommendation that the fastest period of spending growth should occur in the early years, UK NHS spending plans will grow by 7.2 per cent a year in real terms over the five years to 2007-08, from £68.1 billion in 2002-03 to £109.4 billion in 2007-08. By 2007-08, total UK health spending is projected to reach 9.4 per cent of GDP, above the EU average but still lower than in Germany and France, thereby addressing the consistent underinvestment in health relative to comparable economies that has characterised the UK over the past 30 years. The new plans include substantial increases in capital for investment in modern IT, buildings and equipment as well as record investment in the NHS workforce.

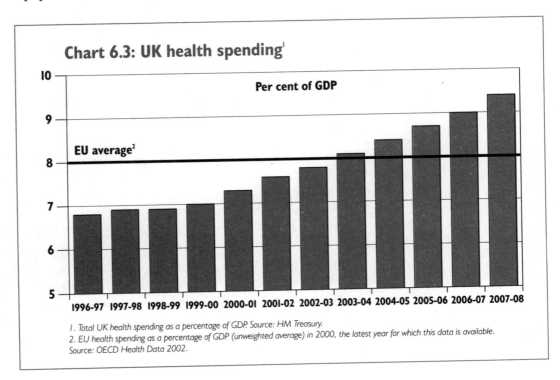

Chart 6.3: UK health spending[1]

Per cent of GDP

EU average[2]

1. Total UK health spending as a percentage of GDP. Source: HM Treasury.
2. EU health spending as a percentage of GDP (unweighted average) in 2000, the latest year for which this data is available. Source: OECD Health Data 2002.

Box 6.3: Funding long-term improvements in healthcare

General taxation and NICs provide affordable, comprehensive cover for healthcare as the costs are spread as widely and fairly as possible. They allow the Government to fund healthcare that is free at the point of use and accessible to all, irrespective of income. Because the range of medical treatments is growing, and some are more expensive than ever, the costs of health care are increasing around the world and the risks to family finances and to business would be greater than ever if the costs were met from charges or private insurance payments:

- charges would mean the sick paying for being sick. The experience of other countries is that charges deter the sick from seeking treatment – in the US one in four adults report that they have gone without medical care because they could not afford it;

- administrative costs mean that private insurance tends to be more expensive than the alternatives – in the US, half of all bankruptcies result from inability to pay medical costs;

- private insurance may not be affordable to those in the greatest need. In the US, where private insurance is the dominant method of financing health care, over 40 million people are uninsured, including around 18 per cent of non-elderly adults and 14 per cent of children;

- in social insurance systems, there is the potential for schemes to deny the full range of benefits to individuals, or for a two-tiered system to develop, as in Germany, where some people seek additional private insurance to supplement the basic insurance. As a result, the share of health spending borne by general taxation in France is increasing, to improve access for the poor and widen the revenue base; and

- the costs of social insurance can also fall disproportionately on employers – in France, employers rather than employees pay the majority of the premium.

As well as helping to ensure fairness in the provision of health services, public funding is consistent with economic efficiency. The Wanless Review concluded that there was no alternative financing method to that currently in place in the UK that would deliver a given level and quality of health care at lower cost to the economy.

To deliver the largest ever sustained spending growth in the history of the NHS, while meeting the fiscal rules and other priorities, Budget 2002 raised national insurance contributions (NICs) by one per cent for employers, employees and the self-employed on all earnings above the NICs threshold from April 2003, and froze the income tax personal allowance for those aged under 65 in 2003-04.

While the NHS has always been, and will continue to be, funded in part from NICs, the Government does not support the hypothecation of revenues to the NHS or other public services, since it would make their provision subject to the ups and downs of the economic cycle and unpredictable changes in revenues. Hypothecation would not provide what the NHS needs: a sound long-term and sustainable stream of funding.

Reforming the NHS

6.51   While public provision is in principle the most fair and efficient means of delivering health services, reform is essential to ensure that the public sector is able to meet its potential and that increased resources deliver results. Increased investment in the NHS since 1997 has therefore been matched with extensive reform, including:

- the devolution of commissioning power to local Primary Care Trusts (PCTs), run by front line doctors and nurses;

- the introduction of star ratings to improve performance, linking increased freedoms to better results;

- the establishment of a Modernisation Agency to identify and spread good practice and drive performance improvement;

- National Service Frameworks (NSF) for cancer, coronary heart disease, older people, mental health and diabetes, setting out national standards for treatment and services that should be available within the NHS;

- the establishment of the National Institute for Clinical Excellence (NICE) to assess the clinical cost-effectiveness of drugs and treatments and to tackle the postcode lottery; and

- improvements to patient access through the NHS Direct helpline, which handles over 100,000 calls a week, and through 42 walk-in centres across the country.

6.52   Over the next five years, extra resources will be matched by a renewed focus on reform to ensure that the priorities set out in the Department of Health's PSA are achieved. Consistent with the reform principles described above, there will be:

- devolution of power to front line organisations;

- new financial incentives for better performance;

- the separation of the standard-setting role of the Department of Health from the delivery role of the NHS;

- two new independent regulators to improve accountability in health – the Commission for Healthcare Audit and Inspection – and social services – the Commission for Social Care Inspection; and

- a more responsive health service providing better information and more choice to patients.

Devolving power to the front line   **6.53**   Resources and responsibility for delivery have been and will continue to be progressively devolved to local organisations, with the greatest freedoms and flexibilities going to the highest performing organisations. PCTs are central to the Government's strategy for decentralising and devolving power in the NHS to local communities. Run by GPs, nurses, other health and social care professionals, and representatives of patients and the community, PCTs are responsible for determining the health needs of local people and for commissioning the right mix of services to meet them. They are also responsible for integrating health and community health services to ensure that both systems work together for patients. From 2003-04, local PCTs will control 75 per cent of NHS resources and will be able to use them to commission care from a range of providers, delivering high quality services to patients in both community and hospital settings.

Rewarding performance   **6.54**   A new set of performance improvement incentives will underpin the devolution of resources and responsibilities, including a new system of financial flows that will encourage and reward efficient use of resources. High performing organisations will also benefit from less monitoring and inspection, improved access to capital and increased operational freedoms.

Box 6.4: Financial flows in the NHS

A new system of financial flows is being introduced across the NHS, which will encourage and reward the efficient use of resources by directing more funding to hospitals that treat more patients. Previously, the use of block contracts has meant that hospitals have not been rewarded for using their spare capacity to treat more patients. The new system will reward strong performers with additional resources to treat more patients.

The new system of financial flows works by grouping together activities that use similar resources into Health Resource Groups (HRGs). A new single national tariff is then set for each of these HRGs. Hospitals will be paid according to the mix of services they deliver.

This type of case-mix based payment system was developed in the US in the 1960s and 1970s, and many OECD countries have now introduced similar systems. The evidence from their introduction in Australia and the US suggests that this payment method has helped increase output and minimise costs by reducing patients' length of stay and fostering a shift from inpatient to day-patient and ambulatory care.

The Government's objective is to ensure that providers are paid fairly and transparently for the services they deliver and that the new financial flows regime supports patient choice, rewards efficiency and quality, matches demand to capacity, and promotes a shift away from price negotiation to a focus on quality and delivery. By 2005-06, almost all NHS Trust activity will be commissioned on the basis of HRGs.

6.55   NHS Trusts and social services are now able to earn autonomy through the star ratings system. For the highest performers there are increased freedoms, including extra discretion over the use of capital and performance fund money, and a reduced burden of inspection.

6.56   Building on the model of greater flexibility and reduced bureaucracy already established for high performing local authorities, the Government is also planning to introduce NHS Foundation Trusts which will provide additional financial and operational freedoms for hospitals with a track record of success. These freedoms will be balanced against the need to:

- deliver better treatment for all NHS patients;

- safeguard the Government's absolute commitment to NHS care free at the point of use determined on the basis of need and not ability to pay;

- prevent any perverse incentives to expand private provision or undermine investment in NHS capacity; and

- safeguard taxpayers' money.

Strengthening accountability and increasing choice

6.57   The role of the streamlined Department of Health will be to set standards and hold the NHS to account for delivery. Day-to-day management of the NHS will become the responsibility of the 28 new strategic health authorities, who will hold local services to account, build capacity and support performance improvement.

6.58   Accountability will be strengthened by the establishment of two new inspectorates for health – the Commission for Healthcare Audit and Inspection – and social services – the Commission for Social Care Inspection. The inspectorates will be independent of government and will have a range of responsibilities, including value for money audit and inspections, the publication of an annual report to Parliament on performance and use of resources in the NHS and social services, the publication of star ratings, and independent scrutiny of patient complaints.

6.59   Accountability to the public will also be reinforced by greater choice for patients. As capacity expands, NHS patients will have more choice over where and when they are treated, with booked appointments for all hospital admissions. Patients and their GPs will also receive independently validated information about hospital performance to help them make informed choices

Integrating health and social services

6.60   A modern and integrated healthcare system requires effective provision of social care services. Social services capacity has already increased significantly in recent years. Between 1999-2000 and 2002-03, 3,300 intermediate care beds have been created. Between 2000-01 and 2001-02, the number of households receiving intensive home care has risen by over 5,000, with 16,000 more households now benefiting from this service than in 1998. In view of the importance that the Wanless Review attached to investment in social services, plans for spending on social services in England rise by 5.9 per cent a year on average in real terms between 2002-03 and 2005-06. This investment will support the 10-year NSF for older people, which sets new standards and service models of care for all older people, whether they live at home, in residential care or are being cared for in hospital. The Government is also piloting Children's Trusts that will enable local partners jointly to plan, commission, finance and deliver social services for children.

6.61   The Government is taking steps to improve integration between health and social care services by introducing strong financial incentives for local authorities to assess individuals who are in hospital and make provision for any community care services they may need as quickly as possible.

Delivering results

6.62   Between 1996-97 and 2002-03, expenditure on the NHS in England has increased by about 40 per cent in real terms. There is now more capacity in the health service, activity levels have risen, waiting lists are down and good progress is being made on health outcomes.

6.63   There are already 10,000 more doctors, almost 50,000 more nurses and 8,400 more therapists working in the NHS today than in 1997. Last year over 23,000 students started nurse or midwifery training, an increase of over 50 per cent on 1996-97. The Government's health spending plans for the next five years will deliver further increases in capacity. By 2008, there will be over 20,000 more GPs and consultants, 44,000 more therapists and scientists, and 66,500 more nurses, midwives and health visitors than in 1997. Eight thousand more nurses will leave training each year and there will be an extra 1,900 medical school graduates a year compared with 2001-02. Improvements in working practices stemming from pay reform will also serve to increase NHS capacity.

6.64   The largest ever hospital building programme in the history of the NHS is also underway. In 2000, over half of the existing stock of NHS buildings had been built before 1973, and one third pre-dated 1948. Since 1997, 29 new hospital developments have been completed and are fully operational. By 2010, over 100 new hospitals will have been built since 1997. More surgery will take place in new freestanding diagnostic and treatment centres, with 250,000 patients on course to be treated in such centres by 2005. Over the next three years, £2.3 billion will be invested in IT, improving the ability of the NHS to deliver change and reform, while enhancing the patient experience and the quality of care.

6.65   Increased investment and reform is enabling the Department of Health to make good progress against its PSA targets and deliver results which matter to the public:

- there are now 130,600 fewer patients waiting for treatment than in 1997, and the number of patients waiting more than one year for an operation has fallen by 78 per cent;

- good progress is being made in reducing the number of people delayed in hospital, with delays among those aged over 75 down from 5,100 in December 2001 to 3,500 in December 2002;

- over 98 per cent of patients with suspected cancer are now seen by a specialist within two weeks;

- as a result of more effective prescribing driven by the NSF for cancer, statins – life saving drugs that reduce the level of cholesterol in the blood – now save as many as 6,000 lives a year; and

- 31,000 patients are benefitting from new anti-cancer drugs following NICE appraisal.

6.66   The further expansion in capacity and activity that will be possible as a result of sustained increases in investment over the next five years will enable the NHS to continue to deliver improvements in standards, with better access and improved health outcomes. The Department of Health's PSA sets out the key objectives that investment and reform are set to deliver, including:

- guaranteed access to a primary care professional within 24 hours and to a primary care doctor within 48 hours from 2004;

- hospital appointments that are booked for the convenience of the patient by the end of 2005;

- maximum waiting times of three months for outpatients and inpatients by 2008;

- substantial reductions in mortality rates from the major killers, including a reduction of 40 per cent for heart disease in people under 75 and a reduction of at least 20 per cent in cancer for people under 75 by 2010; and

- a 10 per cent reduction in health inequalities as measured by infant mortality and life expectancy at birth by 2010.

Reviewing progress

6.67   Budget 2002 announced that the Government would invest an additional £40 billion a year in the NHS by 2008 in line with the recommendations of the Wanless Review. Seventy five per cent of NHS funding has been allocated directly to PCTs for the next three years – the largest allocation to front line services in the history of the NHS. This investment is coupled with reform to deliver a world class health service for the 21st century.

6.68   The Government is determined to press ahead in matching new investment with reform in the NHS, to deliver a world class health service. In addition, as is usual with external reviewers, Derek Wanless, against a background of progess made, and given the public expenditure implications after 2008, will provide an update of the long-term challenges in implementing the "fully engaged" scenario set out in his report on long-term health trends – with a particular focus on cross-departmental work on preventative health and health inequalities. He will provide his update to the Government early next year.

7 PROTECTING THE ENVIRONMENT

Sustainable development is vital to ensure a better quality of life for everyone, today and for generations to come. Economic growth and social progress must be balanced with action to protect and improve the environment. The Government is using a range of economic instruments to address the many challenges posed by sustainable development, tackling local environmental threats and controlling and reducing emissions of the gases responsible for climate change and poor air quality. Budget 2003 describes the next steps in the Government's strategy, including:

- a package of **reforms to improve waste management,** including:

  - **an increase in the standard rate of landfill tax** of £3 per tonne in 2005-06 and increases of at least £3 per tonne in future years, on the way to a medium- to long-term rate of £35 per tonne. The landfill tax rises to £14 in 2003-04, to £15 in 2004-05, and to £18 in 2005-06;

  - **further detailed consultation on options to ensure that landfill tax increases are revenue neutral to business as a whole;**

  - **a Waste Management Performance Fund** in England to help local authorities improve waste performance for all households; and

  - **a sustainable waste delivery programme** to reduce waste volumes and promote recycling and new waste management technologies.

- **a freeze in the rates of the climate change levy**

- **new enhanced capital allowances** to promote business investment in energy saving new technologies and to encourage more sustainable water use and improvements in water quality;

- **detailed consultation on specific measures to promote household energy efficiency;**

- **deferred annual revalorisation of the main road fuel duties** until 1 October 2003, owing to the recent high and volatile level of oil prices as a result of military conflict in Iraq;

- **further steps to promote the use and development of cleaner road fuels,** including new duty incentives for sulphur-free fuels and bioethanol and an increase in the duty on red diesel and fuel oil;

- **a new lower rate of vehicle excise duty** for the most environmentally-friendly cars with very low levels of carbon dioxide emissions; and

- **a freeze in the rates of the aggregates levy**.

INTRODUCTION

7.1   The Government's sustainable development strategy aims to deliver a better quality of life for everyone, today and for future generations. Economic, social and environmental progress must go hand-in-hand, and policy should take account of the inter-relationship between different objectives. Energy, transport, waste and agriculture all have important environmental impacts as well as economic and social dimensions. The Government's strategy seeks to balance these factors to address the challenges of climate change, poor air quality and environmental degradation in urban and rural areas.

A strategy for
environmental
taxes

7.2   Taxes and other economic instruments can provide incentives for behaviour that protects or improves the environment, helping to achieve environmental goals at the lowest cost and in the most efficient way. By internalising environmental costs into prices, they help to signal the structural economic changes needed to move to a more sustainable economy. They can also encourage innovation and the development of new technologies.

7.3   The Government's approach to environmental taxation was set out in *Tax and the environment: using economic instruments*, published alongside the 2002 Pre-Budget Report. In general, markets provide the best means of allocating an economy's resources in the private sector, and this is as true for environmental resources as for others. However, when markets do not price environmental costs properly, economic instruments, such as environmental taxes or tradable permits, can be used to improve price signals, recognising the dynamic and long-term nature of responses within markets.

7.4   The Government's strategy document also reaffirmed its commitment to the 1997 Statement of Intent on environmental taxation. It provides a framework for developing and implementing environmental economic instruments, through extensive consultation before decisions are made and by giving early signals about the need to act so that households and businesses have sufficient opportunity to plan changes and invest appropriately. Wherever possible, the Government will explore the development of revenue-neutral proposals for reform to reduce excessive impacts on businesses and specific groups and reinforce responses.

TACKLING CLIMATE CHANGE AND IMPROVING AIR QUALITY

Tackling climate
change

7.5   There is strong evidence that global temperatures are rising. 1998 was the warmest year since records began, while nine of the ten hottest years on record fell between 1990 and 2002. No country can be immune to these trends and there is already evidence that the UK's climate is changing. In central England, the 1990s were exceptionally warm by historical standards and about 0.6 degrees Celsius (°C) warmer than the 1961-1990 average. Climate change scenarios[1], published by the Department for Environment, Food and Rural Affairs (DEFRA) in April 2002, show that average annual temperatures across the UK could rise by between 2 and 3.5°C by the end of the century.

7.6   The UK Climate Impacts Programme provides an emerging picture of how a changing climate might affect lives and livelihoods in the UK:

- more severe storm surges could increase the risk of flooding in lowland areas. Use of the Thames Barrier has already risen in frequency, from once every two years during the 1980s to an average of six times a year in the past five years;

- increased water demand and more frequent droughts could generate water supply problems in several parts of England; and

- increased weather variability might impose new costs on business, while the insurance industry could face higher pay-outs due to property damage. Weather-related economic losses to communities and businesses have increased ten-fold over the last 40 years.

---

[1] Full details of the scenarios are available from the UK Climate Impacts Programme at http://www.ukcip.org.uk/scenarios.

7.7   The Government is committed to controlling and reducing emissions of the gases responsible for global warming. The Kyoto Protocol commits the UK to reduce greenhouse gas emissions by 12.5 per cent below 1990 levels between 2008 and 2012. The Government's own Climate Change Programme is designed to take the UK well beyond its Kyoto target and towards the more demanding goal of a 20 per cent reduction in carbon dioxide emissions by 2010. Provisional data for 2002 point to a reduction of UK carbon dioxide emissions of 3.5 per cent between 2001 and 2002. Total greenhouse gas emissions in 2002 are estimated to have been between 14 and 15 per cent below the 1990 level, taking this provisional data for carbon dioxide into account. Chart 7.1 shows historic emissions of carbon dioxide and other greenhouse gases, set against the UK's Kyoto and domestic targets.

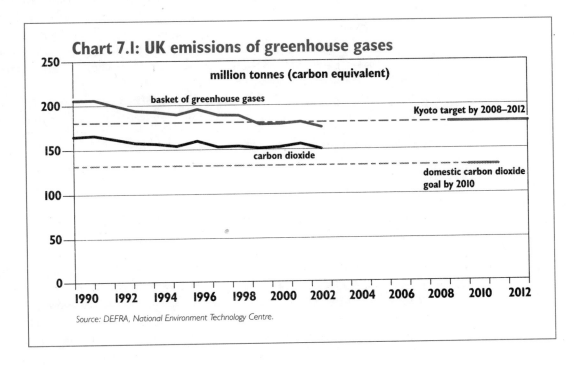

Chart 7.1: UK emissions of greenhouse gases

Source: DEFRA, National Environment Technology Centre.

Improving air quality

7.8   Poor air quality poses risks to the natural environment and to human health. It continues to be associated with an unacceptable number of hospital admissions and premature deaths every year. UK air quality is generally improving, especially in urban areas, due to the introduction of European emissions and fuel quality standards for road vehicles and reduced emissions from industry. For example, provisional results show that the average number of days a year with moderate or high air pollution decreased from 24 to 14 at urban sites and from 30 to 23 at rural sites between 2001 and 2002. Nonetheless, further improvements are needed if the UK is to meet its National Air Quality targets.

> **Box 7.1: The Energy White Paper**
>
> The Government's Energy White Paper was published in February 2003. The White Paper defines a long-term strategic vision for energy policy and establishes four key goals for energy policy, covering the environment, reliability of supply, competitive markets and social factors. On the environment, the White Paper sets out the Government's ambition that the world's developed economies should cut emissions of greenhouse gases by 60 per cent by around 2050 and puts the UK on a path towards cutting carbon dioxide emissions by 60 per cent by 2050, with real progress by 2020. Consistent with the principles set out in *Tax and the environment: using economic instruments*, the Government will aim to achieve this reduction as efficiently as possible, using instruments such as emissions trading and tax measures which allow the price mechanism to signal environmental costs.
>
> The White Paper also provided a further £60 million for renewable energy projects bringing total support for renewables to around £350 million between 2002-03 and 2005-06. It also announced a series of reforms to unblock planning obstacles to renewable energy, speed up changes to Building Regulations, and improve electrical equipment standards to encourage greater energy efficiency by businesses and households.

Business

7.9 Business has an important role to play alongside government and households in helping to achieve the UK's emissions reduction targets.

Climate change levy

7.10 The climate change levy (CCL) and its associated measures seek to encourage business to use energy more efficiently and to reduce emissions of carbon dioxide. The package is broadly revenue neutral for business, with CCL revenues recycled back to business by means of a 0.3 percentage point reduction in employer national insurance contributions (NICs) and support for energy efficiency and low-carbon technologies. **Budget 2003 freezes the rates of the CCL.**

Negotiated agreements

7.11 Forty-four energy intensive sectors of industry that have entered into negotiated agreements to improve their energy efficiency and reduce emissions are eligible for an 80 per cent discount from the CCL. DEFRA has now completed its initial assessment of the performance of these sectors against their first targets and good progress has been made. The sectors covered by the agreements have reduced emissions by 13.5 million tonnes of carbon dioxide – 3.7 million tonnes carbon – per annum against a 2000 baseline, almost three times above target. Although the majority of this has come from one sector – steel – the remaining sectors have exceeded their targets by almost one million tonnes of carbon dioxide. The performance of the energy intensive sectors in meeting their targets was also indicated by a CBI/EEF survey[2] in 2002 which showed that 87 per cent of firms covered by the agreements had taken action to improve energy efficiency or were planning to do so.

---

[2] *The climate change levy: first year assessment*, Confederation of British Industry and Engineering Employers Federation, October 2002.

7.12   As set out in the 1999 Pre-Budget Report, the Government is willing to consider alternative criteria for defining energy intensive sectors of industry eligible for entry into negotiated agreements. However, any criteria must meet the four tests which were set out when the levy was initially announced: they must have a clear rationale, and be administratively simple, legally robust, and consistent with EU state aid rules. The Government is currently exploring with business whether criteria can be identified which meet the four tests and which would enable agreements to be extended to other energy intensive sectors subject to international competition, as part of its strategy for developing and enhancing the levy to improve its environmental effectiveness.

CCL exemptions   **7.13**   Sources of energy generation with environmental benefits are exempt from the CCL and a new exemption for electricity generated from combined heat and power plants sold via licensed electricity suppliers was introduced on 1 April 2003, following receipt of state aid approval. The Government is optimistic that its proposed exemption for electricity generated from coal mine methane will also receive state aid approval from the European Commission.

> **Box 7.2: The EU Energy Products Directive**
>
> Political agreement was reached on the EU Energy Products Directive in March 2003. The Directive will, from 1 January 2004, increase the existing Community minimum rates of duty on oils, with a second increase on diesel from 1 January 2010, and provide a Community framework, with minimum rates of duty, for the taxation of other energy products, including electricity, natural gas, coal and other solid fuels. Those Member States which do not currently tax these fuels will be required to introduce such taxes.
>
> The Directive meets all of the UK's main objectives. In particular, the minimum rates in the Directive will not affect UK's rates of climate change levy and hydrocarbon oils duties, while the UK's right to exempt domestic and charity non-business use of energy from the climate change levy will be preserved. The Energy Products Directive will be formally adopted by the Council of Ministers once consultation with the European Parliament and with accession countries has been completed.

Investment in energy-saving technologies   **7.14**   Enhanced capital allowances (ECAs) for investments in approved energy-saving technologies were introduced in 2001 and currently cover more than 2,500 approved products. Administration of the ECA scheme is managed by the Carbon Trust, an independent company funded principally from revenues recycled from the CCL. The Government is committed to the continued development of the scheme, and will introduce further ECAs for investments in automatic metering and monitoring equipment. Further technologies are also being added to the existing boiler, compressed air and refrigeration categories. Work to define precise performance standards for these technologies is continuing and the Government expects to add these groups to the lists of qualifying technologies during the summer, subject to state aid approval. The addition of these groups will be worth £5 million during their first full financial year, 2004-05.

Emissions trading

7.15   The UK Emissions Trading Scheme (ETS) – the world's first economy-wide scheme – was launched in April 2002 and has made an encouraging start. Thirty-two direct participants in the scheme have committed to reduce carbon emissions by 1.1 million tonnes overall in return for an incentive worth £30 million per year after tax. Over 1,000 groups of facilities covered by CCL negotiated agreements have also used the scheme to purchase allowances in order to meet their emissions reduction targets at the lowest possible cost. Nearly 600,000 allowances have been bought by companies covered by the agreements and around four million allowances have been allocated to companies that have beaten their targets, for sale or to be ring-fenced for later use, subject to verification. Companies participating in the scheme now face an economic cost for every tonne of carbon they emit and this will play an important role in ensuring that environmental impact is taken into account in future financial and investment decisions.

7.16   The Government intends to develop further entry routes to the scheme during 2003. These include a 'new direct participant' route, which will allow organisations to join the scheme by voluntarily agreeing to meet absolute emissions targets, as well as a pilot project entry route to allow organisations to generate emissions allowances from specific emissions reduction projects.

7.17   The Government strongly supports the introduction of an EU-wide emissions trading scheme and welcomes the fact that initial agreement has now been reached on the design and coverage of a scheme to begin in 2005. The Government envisages that the scheme will play an important role in helping to deliver the emissions reduction ambition set out in the Energy White Paper. Having gained valuable experience from the operation of the UK scheme, UK industry and the City of London will be well placed to take advantage of a wider emissions trading market.

7.18   The Government will consider further the relationship between tax and tradable permit schemes as it prepares proposals for allocating emissions targets to installations covered by the EU trading scheme. The Government will aim to ensure that environmental costs can be internalised as efficiently as possible, irrespective of whether the instruments are international or domestic. It will seek to ensure a smooth transition to the new arrangements, with minimum compliance costs for business. It will also take account of the potential impact of combined measures on business competitiveness and fuel poverty.

Renewable energy

7.19   The Government is committed to ensuring that 10 per cent of electricity is supplied from renewable sources by 2010 and, as announced in the Energy White Paper, an aspiration to double the proportion of electricity generated from renewable energy between 2010 and 2020. The Energy White Paper announced a further £60 million of funding for capital grants to support renewable energy. These resources are additional to those allocated in the 2002 Spending Review. Total renewables support is now worth around £350 million between 2002-03 and 2005-06. Most forms of renewable energy are also exempt from the CCL.

7.20 The Renewables Obligation for England and Wales and the comparable Scottish Obligation require electricity suppliers to supply 4.3 per cent of their output from renewable sources in 2003-04. This is forecast to rise to 10.4 per cent of all licensed electricity sales by 2010-11, by which time the market incentive provided is expected to be worth around £780 million per year. Similar arrangements for Northern Ireland will be in place early next year.

Households

7.21   The Government recognises that energy-efficiency improvements in the domestic sector are key to reducing carbon emissions and alleviating fuel poverty. The Energy Efficiency Commitment, the Warm Front Scheme, the Affordable Warmth Programme and product energy labelling and efficiency requirements all provide help for domestic consumers to improve their energy efficiency and play an important role in ensuring that households contribute to economy-wide efforts to achieve the UK's emissions reduction targets.

Economic instruments   **7.22**   The Government has introduced reduced rates of VAT on the installation of a range of energy-saving materials in the home, including insulation, hot water and central heating system controls and solar panels. The European Commission is expected to publish proposals for a review of the provisions in European law governing the use of reduced rates of VAT during 2003. The Government will continue to press for a reduced rate for DIY energy-saving materials.

7.23   The Government also consulted on the potential for using additional economic instruments to improve household energy efficiency[3]. In the light of this initial consultation, the Government will shortly undertake further detailed consultation on specific measures to encourage household energy efficiency.

Transport

7.24   A safe, clean and efficient transport system is crucial to sustaining economic growth, generating higher productivity and safeguarding the environment. Over recent decades, rising economic activity and incomes have increased the demand for personal travel and the transport of goods and services. The Government has taken a number of steps to advance its environmental objectives, encouraging take-up of the best widely available fuels and vehicles and the development of greener forms of transport in the future. The Government's long-term goal is to support the switch to a low-carbon economy, including zero emissions transport.

Fuel duties   **7.25**   Decisions on fuel duties must take account of environmental, economic, and social factors. Owing to the recent high and volatile level of oil prices as a result of military conflict in Iraq – oil prices have fluctuated between $24 and $33 per barrel in the last four weeks – Budget 2003 defers the annual revalorisation of the main road fuel duties until 1 October 2003, at which time the duty on ultra-low sulphur petrol and diesel will rise by 1.28 pence per litre.

Sulphur-free fuels   **7.26**   Sulphur-free fuels offer further environmental benefits over ultra-low sulphur fuels, delivering greater long-term reductions in carbon dioxide emissions when used in new engine technologies, and further air quality improvements. The Government has discussed with representatives of the oil industry and vehicle manufacturers the optimum date of introduction of a duty differential to maximise environmental benefits. In the light of these discussions, the Government will introduce a duty differential for sulphur-free fuels of half a penny per litre relative to the rates for ultra-low sulphur fuels from 1 September 2004, to bring forward the availability of this fuel. Further details will be announced in due course.

---

[3] *Economic instruments to improve household energy efficiency: a consultation document,* HM Treasury and the Department for the Environment, Food and Rural Affairs (DEFRA), July 2002.

Box 7.3: Delivering low-sulphur fuels

The Government has frequently used duty differentials to encourage the take-up of more environmentally-friendly fuels. Budget 2003 introduces a new duty differential for sulphur-free petrol and diesel to encourage their early take-up. This will continue the progress the Government has already made toward lowering the sulphur content of fuels:

- between 1997 and 1999, and as documented alongside the 2000 Pre-Budget Report[1], a duty differential in favour of ultra-low sulphur diesel persuaded oil companies to produce and supply this fuel and achieved an almost complete conversion of the diesel market in just two years – enabling the UK to meet the EU's proposed 2005 diesel standards six years ahead of schedule; and

- duty differentials in favour of ultra-low sulphur petrol encouraged oil companies to convert unleaded petrol sales to ultra-low sulphur petrol by June 2001, making the UK one of the first EU countries to complete this transition.

[1] *Using the tax system to encourage cleaner fuels: the experience of ultra-low sulphur diesel*, HM Customs and Excise, November 2000.

Biodiesel 7.27   A new duty rate for biodiesel, set at 20 pence per litre below the rate for ultra-low sulphur diesel, was introduced in July 2002, to allow the UK to benefit from the reduced greenhouse gas emissions that this fuel can offer. Biodiesel production is continuing to increase strongly across the country; more than 400,000 litres are now being sold every month – a seven-fold increase in sales since the introduction of the duty incentive – and industry is making multi-million pound investments in biodiesel production plants. To maintain the current differential with ultra-low sulphur diesel, Budget 2003 raises the duty rate for biodiesel by 1.28 pence per litre from 1 October 2003.

Bioethanol 7.28   The 2002 Pre-Budget Report announced that the Government would introduce a new duty differential of 20 pence per litre for bioethanol. This differential will help to offset the additional production costs of bioethanol and allow the UK to benefit from the reduction in greenhouse gases and local pollution that it can offer. To ensure that industry is in a position to take advantage of this incentive, and has sufficient time to make the investment needed, the Government has discussed with stakeholders the optimum date of introduction. Following these discussions, Budget 2003 announces that the new rate of duty for bioethanol will become effective from 1 January 2005. The Government is also considering how best to give further support to bioethanol produced from ligno-cellulosic feedstocks, which offer even greater environmental benefits, and would welcome views on how any such support might be structured.

Road fuel gases 7.29   Road fuel gases offer reductions in particulates and nitrogen oxide emissions compared with conventional fuels. Following progressive duty reductions, liquefied petroleum gas is now supplied at over 1,100 forecourts, and a number of haulage operators are using lorries fuelled by natural gas. The Government is committed not to increase the duty on road fuel gases in real terms until 2004 and is currently considering how best to continue support beyond then. It will therefore consult key stakeholders on how best to ensure that future support for road fuel gases continues to reflect environmental and other policy objectives, with a view to announcing decisions on future duty rates and other forms of support in the 2003 Pre-Budget Report. Budget 2003 freezes the duty on road fuel gases.

Hydrogen   **7.30**   Hydrogen has the potential to lead to zero-emissions transport and will be an important fuel for the future. The Government will discuss with stakeholders the issues raised by the taxation of hydrogen fuel production for road transport, with a view to taking decisions on the fiscal framework for hydrogen in the future. As announced in Budget 2002, subject to the outcome of a Green Fuel Challenge pilot project, the Government also intends to exempt hydrogen from fuel duty for a limited period in the future to encourage further development and early take-up.

Red diesel and fuel oil   **7.31**   Budget 2003 increases the duty on rebated gas oil – red diesel – and fuel oil by one penny per litre above revalorisation from Budget day. Duty incentives have been effective in encouraging an early switch to environmentally-friendly road fuels, but rebated gas oil and fuel oil continue to contribute to local air quality problems. Rebated gas oil has a much higher permitted sulphur content than the main road fuels, but is taxed at a fraction of the road fuel rate. Fuel oil is taxed below the red diesel rate, but has an even higher permitted sulphur content. The Government will consult producers, distributors and users of red diesel and fuel oil, as well as environmental groups, to establish whether preferential duty rates for rebated oils with a lower sulphur content would deliver worthwhile environmental benefits.

Vehicle excise duty   **7.32**   The Government has reformed vehicle excise duty (VED) to provide incentives to motorists to choose the least polluting vehicles. To strengthen incentives for motorists to choose the least polluting cars, Budget 2003 introduces a new low carbon VED band for cars with carbon dioxide emissions of 100 grammes/kilometre (g/km) or less. Car and van VED rates are revalorised and rounded up to the nearest £5, in line with established practice. These changes will take effect on licences that start on or after 1 May. Motorists will now be able to save up to £110 in VED each year by choosing the most efficient and least polluting cars. An evaluation of the impact and effectiveness of the graduated VED system will be undertaken shortly. To ensure that consumers have access to information about the fuel-efficiency and environmental impact of cars on sale, the Government is also piloting a comparative colour-coded environmental label for cars based on the EU A-G banded energy label. Budget 2003 freezes VED rates for motorcycles and lorries.

7.33   The Government aims to introduce e-licensing and telephone licensing by 2005, enabling vehicle keepers to pay their VED in more convenient ways. E-licensing for cars and vans less than two years old will be introduced in February 2004. Electronic links with insurance and MoT databases will ensure that valid insurance and roadworthiness certification remains in place. Existing counter services through Post Offices and DVLA Local Offices will also remain.

Company car tax   **7.34**   Since April 2002 the system of company car taxation has been based on carbon dioxide emissions. Budget 2000 announced the levels of emissions qualifying for the minimum charge in 2002-03. It also announced that this level would be reduced by 10 grammes per kilometre (g/km) each year until 2004-05. The Government has decided that the level of emissions qualifying for the minimum charge in 2005-06 will be 5 g/km lower, at 140g/km.

7.35   A comprehensive Government evaluation programme to establish the environmental impact of this reform is underway. The evaluation will inform decisions on the level of future reductions and the Government aims to use the results to provide longer-term certainty of the charge. Early findings from the evaluation show that the reform is already having a positive influence on behaviour. Over half of employers who provide company cars have already changed their policies as a result and 85 per cent of employers providing company cars have said that they support the environmental principles behind the reform. Most company car drivers are aware of the reform and the majority of these understand that the charge is now based on carbon dioxide emissions. Independent surveys and opinion polls support the conclusion that the reforms are leading to significant reductions in carbon dioxide emissions from company cars.

Fuel scale charges   **7.36**   As announced in Budget 2002, the fuel scale charge that applies to employees who receive free fuel for private use in a company car was changed on 6 April 2003. The charge is now related to carbon dioxide emissions and includes the same discounts for cleaner fuels and premiums as the company car tax system. This change is revenue-neutral and will make the system more environmentally-friendly. The reform allows a proportionate reduction in the annual charge if an employee receiving free fuel decides to opt out during the course of the year.

Company vans   **7.37**   Budget 2002 also announced that the Government would review the tax treatment of the private use of vans provided by employers, taking into account environmental benefits, fairness and modern working practices. Following initial discussions with industry and other key stakeholders, the Government will now consult formally on the tax treatment of company vans, with a view to deciding how best to simplify the legislation for shared vans and to encourage use of more environmentally-friendly vans. A consultation document will be published shortly after the Budget.

Lorry road-user charging   **7.38**   Road haulage plays an important role in a successful and high-productivity economy. The Government is committed to helping the haulage industry become more competitive and less environmentally damaging. It believes that all lorry operators using UK roads should make a fair contribution towards the costs they impose, irrespective of nationality. As announced in Budget 2002, and subject to the outcome of discussions with potential suppliers, the Government aims to introduce, by 2006, a lorry road-user charge based on distance travelled. An initial progress report was published in April 2002 and a second report will be published towards the end of this month, setting out further details of the administrative arrangements for the charge. This report will also describe the nature of offsetting tax cuts for the industry, which will be introduced alongside the introduction of the charge itself.

Review of bus subsidies   **7.39**   The Government believes that buses have a crucial part to play in delivering its transport objectives. Buses also help to achieve environmental and social inclusion objectives and improve the productivity of the economy, by helping to tackle congestion, increase labour market flexibility, and widen employment opportunities.

7.40   Budget 2002 announced a review of bus subsidies to consider how best to use the over £1 billion of annual revenue support for local bus services in England to achieve the Government's objectives of reducing the impact of transport on the environment, bus patronage growth, modal shift from cars to buses, increasing social inclusion and improving the quality of bus services.

7.41   As part of the wider review of the Transport Ten Year Plan, now in progress, the Government will continue this work, with the aim of ensuring that public funding delivers the best possible local bus services and targets the Government's transport objectives as effectively as possible. Further work will be guided by the need to:

- ensure that bus services better meet the needs of local people and communities;

- make effective use of public subsidy to deliver public aims; and

- not reduce the level of Government support for bus transport overall or for older and disabled bus users.

7.42   In the meantime, in order to provide certainty to local authorities and bus operators, the Government will extend the Rural Bus Subsidy Grant until 2005-06. The scheme will also be modified so that the grant is available to a wider range of services, including demand-responsive and taxi-based services.

Aviation   **7.43**   Aviation offers significant economic benefits to the UK and global economy. Thousands of jobs depend on the industry and businesses rely on air links to provide access to markets and to bring in investment. The Government is currently consulting[4] on the implications of future demand for air travel on air services and new airport infrastructure. The Government's objective is to maximise the economic benefits of aviation, while meeting its environmental objectives in the most efficient way possible.

7.44   The 2002 Pre-Budget Report announced that the Government would discuss with stakeholders the most effective economic instruments for ensuring that the aviation industry is encouraged to take account of, and where appropriate reduce, its contribution to global warming and to local air and noise pollution. A Government discussion document, *Aviation and the environment: using economic instruments*[5], was published last month, setting out details of the environmental impact of aviation and describing the principles of the Government's approach in this area. A series of discussion meetings with key stakeholders will take place from April and the Government intends to set out its views in the Air Transport White Paper, due to be published later in the year. Budget 2003 freezes the rates of air passenger duty.

---

[4] *The future development of air transport in the UK*, the Department for Transport, July 2002; South East consultation document, second edition, February 2003.
[5] *Aviation and the environment: using economic instruments*, HM Treasury and the Department for Transport, March 2003.

> **Box 7.4: Aviation and the environment**
>
> Aviation imposes a series of negative environmental impacts. The recent Government discussion document, *Aviation and the environment: using economic instruments*, describes the nature of these impacts in more detail:
>
> - greenhouse gas emissions from aircraft have a significant and growing impact on climate change. Estimated in monetary terms, the cost to climate change of flights to and from UK airports amounted to £1.4 billion in 2000, and could rise to £4.8 billion by 2030. These costs take account of aviation's largest impacts on climate change – the release of nitrogen oxides at altitude and contrail formation – as well as emissions of carbon dioxide. Aviation's share of total UK carbon dioxide emissions alone is projected to increase from 5 per cent in 2000 to 10-12 per cent in 2030;
>
> - noise from aircraft is an important public concern and can affect the quality of life around airports. Current valuations imply that the total cost of noise disturbance at all UK airports amounted to £25 million in 2000; and
>
> - local air quality is affected by emissions produced by aircraft during take-off and landing. Independent research puts the total cost to local air quality of flights to and from UK airports at between £119 million and £238 million.

IMPROVING WASTE MANAGEMENT

Waste strategy   7.45   Efficient use of resources and the effective management of waste are essential features of an environmentally-sustainable economy. The waste stream contains resources which can be reused or recycled to deliver economic value, resulting in greater resource efficiency. Waste also has important impacts on the environment, both at a global level, due to emissions of greenhouse gases, and at the local level. The UK needs to reduce its dependence on landfill for disposing of waste.

Landfill tax   7.46   The landfill tax encourages efforts to minimise the amount of waste generated and to develop more sustainable waste management techniques. It contributes to the achievement of the Government's waste strategy targets through the diversion of waste away from landfill. In line with the five-year escalator announced in 1999, the landfill tax rate for active waste was increased from £13 to £14 per tonne on 1 April 2003 and will be increased to £15 per tonne from 1 April 2004. As announced in the 2002 Pre-Budget Report, following consultation, the standard rate of landfill tax will subsequently be increased by £3 in 2005-06 to £18 per tonne, and by at least £3 per tonne in the years thereafter, on the way to a medium- to long-term rate of £35 per tonne.

Recycling revenue to business   7.47   As stated in the 2002 Pre-Budget Report, increases in the standard rate of landfill tax will be introduced in a way that is revenue neutral to business as a whole. Discussions with business and other stakeholder groups have indicated that there is broad support for a package of measures, including some tailored support to those sectors facing the greatest waste management challenges. The Government will pursue this through further development of options and further consultation with stakeholders. Decisions on a package of measures will be announced in the 2003 Pre-Budget Report.

Improving local waste management   7.48   The 2002 Pre-Budget Report also announced the creation of a short-term Ministerial group, chaired by the Economic Secretary to the Treasury, to oversee work on waste across government. Reporting to the Chief Secretary to the Treasury and the Secretary of State for the Environment, Food and Rural Affairs, the group was specifically asked to focus on options to reform the central-local government performance framework. In doing so, the Group considered a range of issues, including how best to ensure that landfill tax increases are revenue neutral to local government while providing incentives for landfill diversion, and the work needed to build a more effective municipal waste performance framework in cooperation with local government, and consistent with the Government's new localism agenda. The group has also contributed to the finalisation of the sustainable waste delivery programme of additional public spending, and agreed the terms of reference of the review of the health and environmental effects of waste management and disposal options.

7.49   As a first step, and consistent with its commitment to empowering local government, the Government has decided that the Waste Minimisation and Recycling Fund should be reformed into a local authority Waste Management Performance Fund in England. The new Fund will provide non-ringfenced incentives for local government to deliver a step change in sustainable waste performance for all households. Final decisions on the start date of the Performance Fund, and its operational details, will be announced following further consultation with local government stakeholders. Decisions on how the landfill tax increases will be made revenue neutral to local government will be taken at the same time.

Landfill Tax Credit Scheme   7.50   The Government is committed to ensuring that sustainable alternatives to landfill disposal are widely available. As announced in the 2002 Pre-Budget Report, the Landfill Tax Credit Scheme has been reformed, and a proportion of the funding for the scheme – £100 million in 2003-04 and £110 million in 2004-05 and 2005-06 – redirected to public spending on a new sustainable waste delivery programme. The spending programme in England, to be managed by DEFRA, will seek to help households reduce the amount of waste they produce, increase access to doorstep collection of materials for recycling, promote the development of new and viable waste management technologies, and provide local authorities with the support they need to deliver best practice. Details of the programme will be announced by DEFRA.

7.51   To minimise disruption to existing waste and recycling projects under the Landfill Tax Credit Scheme, and ensure that planned project work can be completed during the coming year, funding in 2003-04 includes transition funding for ongoing waste projects in 2003-04.

7.52   A successor tax credit scheme will maintain funding at current levels of around £47 million per year for local community environmental projects. Following discussion with stakeholders, the Government will introduce regulations by the summer to extend the scope of the scheme to include habitat creation projects on land that need not have public access, in order to support biodiversity. The Government will also continue work with Entrust, the regulator of the scheme, and other stakeholders to improve the scheme's operation. Administration of the scheme will be simplified through a reduction in the level of information required from projects and through the use of common systems wherever possible. Better information will be recorded on project funding and audit processes will be improved. The Government will also improve monitoring and evaluation of the scheme and develop measures of value for money. These changes will be finalised by the summer.

Review of environmental and health effects   7.53   The Government has commissioned a review of the environmental and health effects of all waste management and disposal options. It aims to report on the findings of this review later in the year. The case for using economic instruments for incineration will be considered in light of this work, and in consultation with other stakeholders. The Government is also considering how the use of economic instruments could be extended further.

Household incentive schemes

7.54   The Government has ruled out a national tax on household waste. Further work is needed before any decision can be taken on whether to extend the powers of local authorities and introduce pilot household charging schemes. In cooperation with the Local Government Association and other stakeholders, work will be undertaken to consider the practicalities of operating any such schemes and how potential disadvantages might be overcome. This will take account of international experience on the operation and effectiveness of such schemes.

PROTECTING BRITAIN'S COUNTRYSIDE AND NATURAL RESOURCES

7.55   The Rural White Paper and the recently published Strategy for Sustainable Farming and Food[6] set out the Government's rural policy framework for delivering a countryside that is sustainable – economically, socially and environmentally. In tackling environmental threats to the countryside, the Government is applying the same principles as those which underpin its wider environmental strategy, addressing market failures through a range of economic instruments. This section describes the action the Government is taking to:

- reduce the environmental impact of aggregates extraction;

- reduce water use and improve water quality; and

- minimise the environmental impact of agriculture.

Aggregates extraction

Aggregates levy

7.56   The extraction of aggregates imposes a range of environmental costs. Introduced in April 2002, the aggregates levy seeks to incorporate these costs into the price of virgin aggregate and encourages the use of alternative materials, such as wastes from construction and demolition, that would otherwise be disposed of to landfill. It also promotes greater efficiency in the use of virgin aggregate and the development of alternative materials, such as waste tyres. In the light of independent research, the levy was initially set at a rate of £1.60 per tonne on virgin aggregate commercially exploited in the UK. Budget 2003 freezes the rate of aggregates levy.

7.57   The Government is also examining industry proposals for delivering additional environmental benefits through the aggregates levy by encouraging the positive use of aggregates waste. A consultation exercise ended on 10 March, and the Government is now considering the responses it received, with a view to announcing decisions later in the year.

7.58   The levy for aggregates used in processed products in Northern Ireland is being phased in, given the special circumstances of this sector. The rate for aggregates used in these products has been set at zero for the first year of the levy, and will be 20 per cent of the full rate in 2003-04. It will continue to rise by 20 percentage points each year until the full rate is reached. The Government is continuing to review the impact of the phasing-in of the levy in Northern Ireland.

---

[6] *The Strategy for Sustainable Farming and Food*, DEFRA, December 2002.

Sustainability Fund
7.59   To support businesses and communities affected by aggregates extraction, the introduction of the aggregates levy was accompanied by a new Aggregates Levy Sustainability Fund (ALSF) and a 0.1 percentage point reduction in employer NICs. The ALSF in England was launched in April 2002 and its work to date has concentrated on reducing the demand for primary aggregates, promoting environmentally-friendly extraction and transport, and reducing the local impact of aggregates extraction.

Water quality

7.60   Despite significant improvements in recent years, further effort is needed to enhance the ecological and microbiological quality of water, especially where this is affected by diffuse pollution. The Government's strategy for water policy takes account of economic, social and environmental objectives and seeks to ensure effective integration with other policies. Details of the Government's priorities for water policy in England were published recently and the views of stakeholders are now being sought[7].

Enhanced capital allowances
7.61   The Government has received a series of proposals under the Green Technology Challenge for tax incentives to encourage more sustainable water use and improvements in water quality. Following detailed consideration of these proposals, Budget 2003 introduces enhanced capital allowances for investments in five groups of technologies. The Government anticipates that the list of eligible technology groups will be published following Royal Assent of the Finance Bill and that capital allowances may be claimed for qualifying investments made on or after 1 April 2003.

Agriculture

7.62   Agriculture, like many other forms of business, is associated with a range of environmental issues, including nutrient and microbiological pollution of water. An initial review of the environmental impact of agriculture and the case for using economic instruments to tackle them was published in December 2002[8]. The Government is considering the options for using economic instruments to address the most pressing environmental issues associated with agriculture and will consult further with stakeholders in 2003. As part of this work, DEFRA is currently conducting a review of diffuse water pollution from agriculture and will consult on this issue during the coming year.

7.63   The Strategy for Sustainable Farming and Food sets out the Government's vision for the future of the farming and food industries in England alongside proposals to help realise this vision. The 2002 Spending Review allocated £500 million over three years to implement the strategy, including through pilots of an entry-level agri-environment scheme, a new network of demonstration farms, and new structures to encourage cooperation in agriculture and the dissemination of research results. These measures will help to deliver productivity increases in the farming industry and improve environmental performance.

---

[7] *Directing the flow: priorities for future water policy*, DEFRA, November 2002.

[8] *Using economic instruments to address the environmental impacts of agriculture*, DEFRA, December 2002.

Pesticides **7.64** The Government is committed to reducing the adverse environmental impact of pesticides use, and to discouraging use of those pesticides with the greatest potential to cause harm, consistent with adequate crop protection. An industry-led voluntary initiative on measures to reduce the environmental damage caused by agricultural use of pesticides was launched in April 2001. The Government values the work already completed by the signatories and will continue to press for more rapid progress. Provided this voluntary initiative is fully implemented, the Government believes it should be the most effective way of reducing the environmental impact of pesticides and remains committed to this approach.

7.65 The Environmental Audit Committee published a report on the initiative in November last year. In its response, the Government agreed the need for more rapid progress, especially on the issuing of targets, the development of Crop Management Plans and increasing farmer take-up of the initiative. The Government also announced details of work to develop a national plan for pesticides. In taking this forward, the Government will assess those policies that can contribute to the sustainable use of pesticides, including the role of the voluntary initiative, and identifying ways in which policies can most effectively be used together. The Government is also pursuing work on options for a tax or other economic instrument, should the voluntary initiative fail to deliver its agreed objectives within a reasonable timescale.

Sustainable **7.66** As announced in the 2002 Pre-Budget Report, the Government has commissioned a
forestry review of the economic rationale underpinning policy goals for forestry in England and the role of forestry in the Government's sustainable development strategy. An independent analysis of the economics of forestry policy has now been completed and the review steering group will shortly produce provisional recommendations for institutional structures and relationships to deliver forestry policy more effectively and efficiently. The recommendations will be considered alongside Lord Haskins' wider review of the delivery of environmental and rural policies.

Housing **7.67** As described in Chapter 2, Budget 2003 also launches a new review of the factors affecting the supply and responsiveness of housing. The review will consider, among other issues, the interaction between housing supply and sustainable development objectives. The Government will also continue to consider the use of economic instruments to support regeneration and encourage brownfield development

ENVIRONMENTAL APPRAISAL OF POLICY MEASURES

7.68 The Government is committed to appraising the environmental impact of Budget measures and will continue to make available the methodology underpinning the figures presented in the appraisal tables. Table 7.1 shows how Budget measures sit alongside other policies as part of the Government's approach to the environmental elements of sustainable development. Table 7.2 sets out the environmental impact of measures introduced in recent Budgets which have a significant effect on the environment or which serve an environmental purpose. The Government aims to ensure that policy design, appraisal and evaluation take account of costs and benefits, the precautionary principle, and the need to internalise costs by making the producer pay.

7.69 To increase transparency and public reporting of key performance indicators, the environmental appraisal tables are now available on the Treasury website. The tables will be updated regularly to reflect ongoing monitoring of environmental indicators and further evaluation of specific schemes.

Table 7.1: The Government's policy objectives and Budget measures

Policy objective	Sustainable development indicator[1]	Data indicating recent trends	Recent Government measures
Tackling climate change and improving air quality.	Emissions of greenhouse gases.	Based on provisional data for 2002, carbon dioxide emissions decreased between 2001 and 2002. Since 1990, total greenhouse gas emissions are estimated to have been between 14 and 15 per cent below the 1990 level[2].	*Other Government measures* • Climate Change Programme, DETR November 2000. • Emissions Trading Scheme, DEFRA August 2001. • Air Quality Strategy for England, Scotland, Wales and Northern Ireland, DETR January 2000 and Addendum, February 2003, DEFRA.
	Days when air pollution is moderate or higher.	Number of days with moderate or high air pollution decreased from 24 to 14 in urban sites and from 30 to 23 in rural sites between 2001 and 2002.	• Ten Year Plan for Transport, DETR July 2000. • Powering Future Vehicles, DfT et al July 2002. • Energy White Paper, DTI February 2003.
	Road traffic.	Between 1998 and 2002, total traffic volume rose by nearly 6 per cent, however, road traffic intensity (vehicle kilometres per GDP) fell by 4 per cent between 1990 and 2001.	*Budget measures* • Climate change levy package. • Reduced rate of VAT on the installation of energy saving materials. • Road fuel duty. • Green Fuel Challenge. • Reforms to car, lorry, van and motorcycle VED. • Company car tax and fuel scale charge reform, and authorised mileage allowance payments. • 100 per cent first-year allowances for cars with low carbon dioxide emissions, and hydrogen and natural gas refuelling infrastructure. • Green travel plans – using tax incentives to promote their development.
Improving waste management.	Household waste and all waste arisings and management.	Household waste not recycled or composted rose from 435 to 447 kilograms per person, or by 3 per cent, between 1997/8 and 2000/1. However, the proportion of household waste being recycled was over 11 per cent in 2000/1, an increase of 1 per cent over the previous year[3].	*Other Government measures* • Waste Strategy 2000, DETR May 2000. *Budget measures* • Landfill tax and landfill tax credit scheme. • Landfill tax increases. • Reforms to the Landfill Tax Credit Scheme. • New spending programmes on waste.
Regenerating Britain's towns and cities.	New homes built on previously developed land.	In 2001, 61 per cent of new housing was on previously developed land, increasing from around 54 per cent in the early 1990s.	*Other Government measures* • Urban White Paper, DETR November 2000. • Package of measures to tackle abandoned vehicles. *Budget measures* • Capital allowances for flats over shops. • Tax relief for cleaning up contaminated land. • Stamp duty exemption for disadvantaged areas. • Reforms to the VAT treatment of conversion and renovation activity.
Protecting Britain's countryside and natural resources.	Populations of wild birds.	In 2000 the decline in farmland birds – almost halving since 1977 – continued to level off. Woodland birds increased to their highest level since 1990.	*Other Government measures* • Rural White Paper, DETR November 2000. • Strategy for Sustainable Farming and Food, DEFRA December 2002. *Budget measures* • Aggregates levy and Sustainability Fund.
	Chemical river quality and biological river water quality.	By 2001, 95 per cent of UK rivers were of good or fair chemical quality and about 95 per cent were of good or fair biological quality in 2000.	

[1] *Achieving a Better Quality of Life, DEFRA January 2002 – latest data from www.sustainable-development.gov.uk.*
[2] *The main six greenhouse gases are carbon dioxide, methane, nitrous oxide, hydrofluorocarbons, perfluorocarbons, sulphur hexafluoride.*
[3] *Municipal Waste Management Survey, 2000-01, DEFRA. As the headline waste sustainable development indicator has not yet been updated this currently relates to the core indicator on household waste.*

Table 7.2: The environmental impacts of Budget measures

Budget measure	Environmental impact[1]
• Climate change levy package and rates.	Freezing the CCL will reduce savings by 0.05 MtC[2] per year. Overall, the CCL package is estimated to lead to savings of around 5 MtC per year by 2010[3,4].
• Road fuel duty differentials[5].	Deferred revalorisation until 1 October 2003 will lead to a small increase in carbon dioxide emissions and local air pollutants in England of 0.01 to 0.2 per cent in 2010.
	The duty differential for sulphur-free fuels will lead to a reduction in emissions of carbon dioxide and local air pollutants.
	The shift to ultra-low sulphur petrol from ordinary unleaded is estimated to have reduced nitrogen oxide emissions by 1 per cent, carbon monoxide emissions by 4 per cent and emissions of volatile organic compounds by 1 per cent per year between 2001 and 2004.
	The shift to ultra-low sulphur diesel from ordinary diesel is estimated to have reduced emissions of particulates by 8 per cent and nitrogen oxides by up to 1 per cent per year between 2001 and 2004.
	The reduced rate for biodiesel could save up to 0.2 MtC per year by 2010[6].
	The reduced rate for bioethanol could save a total of 0.5 MtC by 2010.
	The road fuel gas differential will result in a reduction in emissions of particulates and nitrogen oxides.
	The increase in duty on red diesel and fuel oil will lead to improvements in air quality and some reduction in carbon dioxide emissions.
• Green Fuel Challenge.	Identify fuels which could result in reductions in emissions of carbon dioxide and local air pollutants. Potential waste policy benefits.
• Reforms to car, lorry, van and motorcycle VED.	Reductions in emissions of carbon dioxide and local air pollutants.
• Company car tax reform.	The reduction in the level of emissions qualifying for the minimum charge in 2005-06 is expected to lead to a reduction in carbon, increasing, over time, to around 0.1 MtC[7].
• Fuel scale charge reform.	Programme of five-year increase in the fuel scale charge is estimated to have reduced the number of drivers in receipt of free fuel by over 150,000[8]. Expected to reduce carbon dioxide and local air pollutant emissions.
	Restructuring the fuel scale charge in 2003 to relate it to carbon dioxide emissions and to include the same discounts and premiums as in the company car tax system will reduce emissions of carbon dioxide and local air pollutants.
• 100 per cent first-year allowances for cars with low carbon dioxide emissions, and hydrogen and natural gas refuelling infrastructure.	Reductions in emissions of carbon dioxide and local air pollutants.
• Air passenger duty (APD).	The freeze in rates will lead to a small increase in emissions of carbon dioxide and local air pollutants.
• Capital allowances for flats over shops.	Bringing empty space over shops back into the residential markets, helping to create greater urban diversity while reducing the pressure for new greenfield development.
• Tax relief for cleaning up contaminated land.	Increases in the clean up of contaminated land.
• Stamp duty exemption for disadvantaged areas.	Regeneration and improved functioning of property markets in Britain's most disadvantaged areas.
• Reforms to the VAT treatment of conversion and renovation activity.	Reduced pressure on greenfield site development due to the better use of existing buildings.

Table 7.2: The environmental impacts of Budget measures *continued*

Budget measure	Environmental impact[1]
• Aggregates levy and Sustainability Fund.	Reductions in noise and vibration, dust and other emissions to air, visual intrusion, loss of amenity and damage to wildlife habitats.
• Landfill tax including increase in the standard rate to £35 per tonne in the medium- to long-term; new Waste Management Performance Fund in England; and new sustainable waste delivery programme.	Encourages waste producers and the waste management industry to reduce dependence on landfill and encourage greater waste minimisation, reuse and recycling and the development of alternative disposal methods.
• Landfill tax credit scheme.	A scheme aimed at improving the environment in the vicinity of landfill sites.

[1] *These estimates are subject to a wide margin of error.*

[2] *Million tonnes of carbon.*

[3] *There are a number of difficulties involved in estimating the emissions savings from the individual components of the climate change levy, including the need to avoid double counting. Of the 5MtC per year by 2010; the levy and exemptions account for 2.0 MtC, the negotiated agreements account for 2.5 MtC and energy efficiency measures account for 0.5 MtC. A related measure, the emissions trading scheme, is forecast to save 1.1 MtC per year by 2006.*

[4] *Based on the DTI energy model.*

[5] *Using NETCEN emissions models – further detail on the methodology used is provided in NETCEN's January 2000 report UK Road Transport Emissions Projections. Between 1997 and 1999, the fuel duty escalator is forecast to have reduced emissions by 1 to 2.5 MtC per year by 2010. The reductions in fuel duty in Budget 2001 are estimated to have increased emissions by between 0.1 and 0.2 MtC per year by 2010.*

[6] *DfT modelling.*

[7] *Based on Inland Revenue modelling.*

[8] *Based on Inland Revenue modelling.*

ILLUSTRATIVE LONG-TERM FISCAL PROJECTIONS

The budgetary decisions of the Government should be compatible with sustainable public finances over the long term and impact fairly between generations. The illustrative long-term fiscal projections presented in this annex provide an assessment of the long-term sustainability of the Government's fiscal policies over the period up to 2033, in line with the requirements of the *Code for fiscal stability*. The key findings are:

- given the projected profile for tax revenue and transfers, current consumption can grow slightly faster than assumed GDP growth in the long run while meeting the Government's golden rule;

- public sector net investment can grow close to the economy's growth rate over the projection period without jeopardising the sustainable investment rule. The net debt to GDP ratio is projected to remain below 40 per cent by the end of the projection period; and

- the Government is well placed to deal with potential future spending pressures, for example due to an ageing population.

This conclusion concurs with the findings of the *Long-term public finance report*, published alongside the 2002 Pre-Budget Report. The *Long-term public finance report* examined a number of long-term challenges to the public finances, and used a range of techniques to assess long-term sustainability. The report found that based on current policies, the fiscal position is sustainable in the long term, there is a high degree of inter-generational fairness, and the UK's fiscal position is relatively strong compared to other countries facing similar challenges from ageing populations.

INTRODUCTION

A1   The Government's fiscal policy framework, guided by the *Code for fiscal stability*, is designed to ensure transparent, long-term decision-making. Fiscal policy is set to ensure sustainable public finances, with consideration to the short, medium and long term. Long-term fiscal sustainability helps to promote long-term economic growth by ensuring that financial burdens are not shifted to future generations.

Illustrative long-term fiscal projections   **A2**   To assess the sustainability and inter-generational impact of fiscal policy, the Code requires the Government to publish illustrative long-term fiscal projections covering a period of at least 10 years. In practice, a 30-year horizon has been adopted. The projections published in Budgets between 1999 and 2002 showed that the UK's long-term fiscal position was relatively favourable and that, as a result, current consumption could grow at a faster rate than projected economic growth without jeopardising the fiscal rules.

A3   To enhance analysis of long-term fiscal sustainability, a new *Long-term public finance report*[1] was published for the first time alongside the 2002 Pre-Budget Report. The report examined a number of long-term challenges to the public finances and updated the illustrative long-term projections provided in Budget 2002. The projections set out in this annex provide a further update, incorporating the Budget 2003 medium-term spending and revenue forecasts. The underlying assumptions and the methodology used remain broadly unchanged from previous years.

---

[1] *Long-term public finance report: an analysis of fiscal sustainability*, HM Treasury, November 2002.

DEMOGRAPHIC TRENDS

A4   In common with other European Union (EU) and Organisation for Economic Cooperation and Development (OECD) countries, the UK's population is projected to age more rapidly over the coming decades than in the recent past[2]. In November 2002, the Government Actuary's Department (GAD) published its latest set of population projections for the UK. The projections, which incorporated the results of the 2001 census, show that life expectancy at birth is expected to rise from 75.8 years in 2002 to 79.5 years in 2033 for males, and from 80.3 years to 83.7 years for females. The median age is projected to rise to nearly 43 years in 2033 – around five years higher than in 2002. Chart A1 shows the UK's age pyramid in 2002 and at the end of the projection period presented in this annex, 2033.

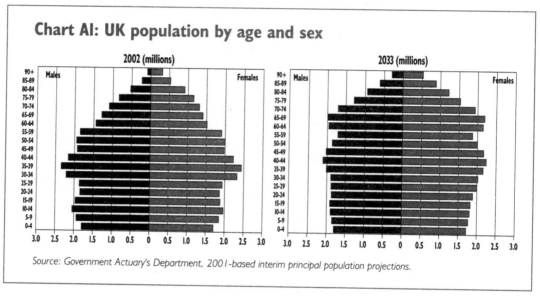

Chart A1: UK population by age and sex

Source: Government Actuary's Department, 2001-based interim principal population projections.

A5   The UK's population is ageing less rapidly than that in most other EU countries. The latest United Nations projections, published in early March, show that the UK's old-age dependency ratio (the number of people aged 65 and over as a percentage of those aged 15 to 64) could rise from 24 per cent in 2000 to 37 per cent in 2035, compared with a rise from 24 per cent to 45 per cent in the EU as a whole. However, there is no room for complacency. While the UK faces a smaller demographic challenge than many other European countries, and the impact of an ageing population on the public finances is expected to be manageable, demographic developments will continue to have implications for government spending and revenue, underlining the importance of a sound long-term strategy for the public finances.

METHODOLOGY AND ASSUMPTIONS

A6   The methodology for producing the long-term fiscal projections presented in this annex determines the rate at which current consumption (current spending on items such as health and education) can grow while the Government meets its fiscal rules. This is achieved by projecting the evolution of tax receipts, transfer payments (such as pensions) and capital consumption (depreciation) over the coming decades. Subtracting transfers and capital consumption from tax revenues provides a measure of the financial resources available for current public consumption. This methodology is unchanged since Budget 1999 and was described in detail in Budget 2000[3].

---

[2] The *Long-term public finance report* contains an in-depth discussion of long-term challenges, including demographic changes.

[3] See Box A1 of Budget 2000 (page 129).

A7   The projections are based on prudent and cautious economic assumptions and on existing policies. They are based on the fiscal forecasts and assumptions presented in Chapter C of the Financial Statement and Budget Report (FSBR), up to and including 2007-08, the end of the medium-term forecast period. Unless stated otherwise, the Government is assumed to leave these policies unchanged in 2008-09 and future years. The projections cannot, and do not, attempt to pre-empt future policy decisions.

Economic assumptions

A8   Table A1 sets out the economic assumptions that underlie the long-term fiscal projections after 2007-08[4]. The greater degree of uncertainty involved in projecting long-term trends means that the assumptions used in this exercise are particularly cautious. Hence, productivity is assumed to grow by 2 per cent a year between 2008-09 and 2012-13, and then by $1^3/_4$ per cent a year between 2013-14 and 2032-33. While there is no indication that productivity growth will slow in the long run, and the Government is pursuing policies to improve the UK's productivity performance, the slower rate of productivity growth assumed over the later projection years reflects this greater use of caution.

Table A1: Real GDP growth and its components in the baseline scenario

Year	2008-09 to 2012-13	2013-14 to 2022-23	2023-24 to 2032-33
Productivity	2	$1^3/_4$	$1^3/_4$
Employment	$^1/_4$	$^1/_4$	$-^1/_4$
Real GDP	$2^1/_4$	2	$1^1/_2$

A9   The employment assumptions are driven by demographic trends, as projected by GAD's 2001-based interim principal population projections. The overall employment rate is assumed to remain constant from 2007-08 onwards, so that changes in employment levels reflect changes in the working-age population[5]. Chart A2 illustrates GAD's principal projections, which suggest that the working-age population might increase from just over 36 million in 2001 to around 39 million in 2020, before falling to below 38 million by 2033. The rise between 2010 and 2020 is due to the increase in the female state pension age from 60 years in 2010 to 65 years by 2020. Chart A2 also shows how the working-age population might evolve were the female state pension age to remain constant at 60. In this scenario, the population of working age might remain relatively stable at around 37 million between 2013 and 2021, before falling to below 36 million by 2031.

---

[4] For the period up to and including 2007-08, the projections presented in Chapter C of the FSBR are used.

[5] All males between 16 and 65 years and all females between 16 and 60 years, rising to 65 years by 2020. This assumption does not take into account the effect of the increase of the state pension age for females between 2010 to 2020, due to uncertainty on how the employment rate would be affected. See, for example, page 31 of the *Long-term public finance report*, November 2002.

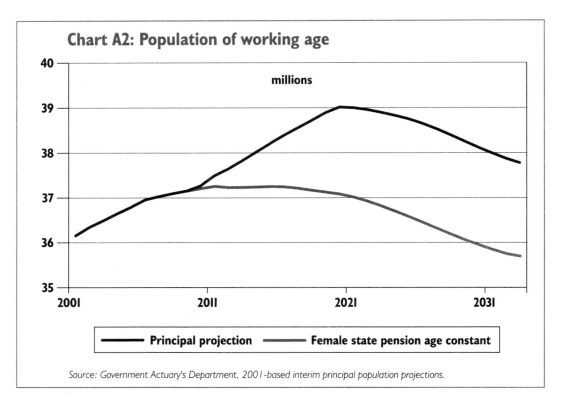

Source: Government Actuary's Department, 2001-based interim principal population projections.

A10 Given the assumed growth rates for productivity and employment described above, Gross Domestic Product (GDP) growth is derived from 2008-09 onwards.

Taxation and **A11** As described above, for the period up to and including 2007-08 the illustrative long-
spending term fiscal projections are based on the forecasts and assumptions presented in Chapter C of
assumptions the FSBR. Unless stated otherwise, policy settings in 2007-08 are then assumed to continue throughout the rest of the projection period. From 2008-09, total tax revenues therefore grow in line with GDP, so that the Government is assumed to raise the same amount of revenue as a proportion of GDP as in 2007-08, offsetting possible changes in tax bases by changing policy in a revenue neutral way. Tax revenues are also assumed to be equal to total current spending from 2008-09 onwards. This implies that the golden rule is met with the current budget in balance at all times.

A12 Current public consumption is calculated as the difference between tax revenues and other current spending which comprises transfers and capital consumption. Transfers include items such as social security transfers and interest payments. Social security transfers include the basic state pension and the long-term costs of the Pension Credit[6]. The calculation of interest payments is based on assumptions about interest rates and the level of investment. As in the medium-term forecast, interest rates are based on market expectations and the existing spread of financial assets to which those rates apply. Under the assumption that the current budget is in balance, the growth of public sector net debt reflects growth in public sector net investment. As in previous long-term fiscal projections, the share of public sector net investment in GDP is assumed to be re-set at 1.8 per cent until the end of the projection period.

A13 The forward profile for investment shows additions to the capital stock, and is used to calculate capital consumption. Consumption of both the existing stock of assets and these new additions is then calculated on the assumption that future public-sector asset lives are broadly similar to those evident in the past.

---

[6] Calculated in conjunction with the Department for Work and Pensions. The social security transfer projections are based on the latest demographic projections by GAD.

THE BASELINE PROJECTIONS

AI4   Chart A3 shows the projected evolution of total current spending, transfers, current consumption and net debt between 2002-03 and 2032-33, given the baseline assumptions. As a percentage of GDP, total current spending is projected to increase between 2002-03 and 2007-08, mainly reflecting the outcome of the 2002 Spending Review. Transfers as a share of GDP are projected to fall slightly from 2002-03 to 2032-33. Net debt is predicted to rise gradually over the projection period, rising towards 40 per cent of GDP by 2032-33, consistent with the sustainable investment rule. Current consumption is projected to rise from 20.1 per cent of GDP in 2002-03 to 23.0 per cent in 2022-23, before falling marginally to 22.5 per cent by 2032-33. Despite this, current consumption as a percentage of GDP in 2032-33 will be higher than in 2002-03. This relative expansion reflects the fact that current consumption can grow at a marginally faster average annual rate than real GDP while still meeting the fiscal rules.

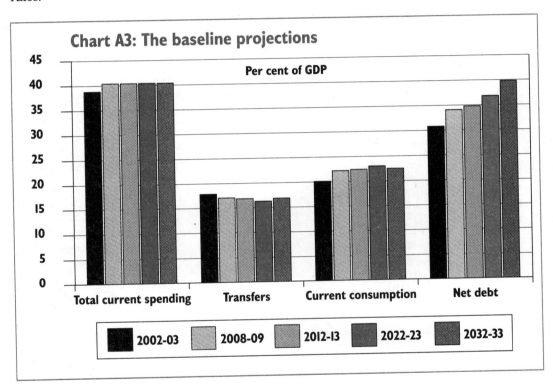

AI5   The projected changes in net debt emphasise the importance of ensuring sound public finances in the short term to prepare for future developments. On current projections, net debt will rise gradually to reach 39.8 per cent of GDP in 2032-33 given the baseline growth and investment assumptions.

Long-term public finance report **AI6**   The illustrative long-term fiscal projections presented here yield similar conclusions to those presented in the Government's *Long-term public finance report*, which used a broader range of techniques to assess long-term sustainability, including fiscal gap modelling, bottom-up projections and generational accounting techniques[7]. Using each technique, the report demonstrated that the fiscal position is sustainable in the long term, on the basis of current policies and on a range of plausible assumptions. The report also found a high degree of inter-generational fairness in current policies, in that current financial burdens are not being shifted unfairly to future generations, nor is an excessive level of assets being accumulated for future generations.

---

[7] Chapter 4 of the *Long-term public finance report* describes these different methodologies in more detail.

A17 The report also examined various international studies of fiscal sustainability[8]. International comparisons show that the UK's fiscal position is relatively strong compared with other developed countries facing similar challenges from ageing populations. The UK also has a substantially higher degree of inter-generational fairness than many other developed countries.

ALTERNATIVE SCENARIOS

A18 This section analyses the sensitivity of the projections to GAD's different population variants[9]. The variants considered here include high fertility, high net migration and high life expectancy. Each generates slight differences in population growth over the projection period, with the high life expectancy variant leading to somewhat less rapid growth than either the high fertility or high migration cases.

A19 The composition of the population – in particular the population of working age – also differs significantly in each of the three variant scenarios. This is illustrated in Chart A4. Assumed higher net migration makes an immediate, positive impact on the working-age population, and this effect continues, and becomes more pronounced, throughout the projection period. The impact of higher fertility on the working-age population is not realised until around 2020, given the time it takes for additional newborns to reach working age. Higher life expectancy has little effect on the working-age population, as this generally affects those above working age.

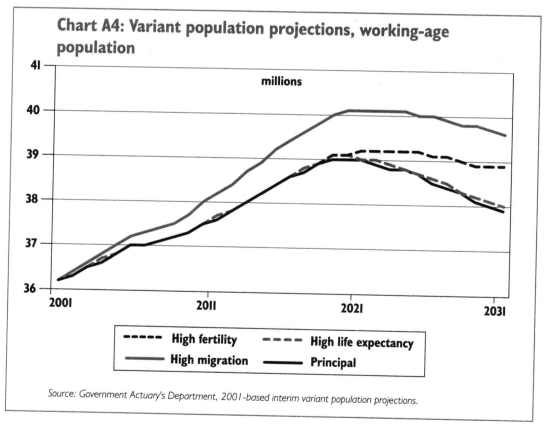

Chart A4: Variant population projections, working-age population

Source: Government Actuary's Department, 2001-based interim variant population projections.

[8] See Chapter 6 of the *Long-term public finance report*.

[9] Alternative scenarios presented in previous Budgets have studied the effects of assuming stronger economic growth and higher public sector net investment, a higher labour market participation rate, lower social transfers, and higher productivity growth.

A20   Using the methodology developed for the baseline scenario, projected GDP growth is affected by the impact on the working-age population of the variant scenarios. Table A2 summarises the GDP growth assumptions under the three population variants. All other assumptions are unchanged. However, the social security projections are modified to take account of the different population structures in the three variants. The methodology implies that migrants are assumed to have the same labour market characteristics as the resident population.

Table A2: Real GDP growth in the variant scenarios

Year	2008-09 to 2012-13	2013-14 to 2022-23	2023-24 to 2032-33
Principal	2¼	2	1½
High fertility	2¼	2	1¾
High migration	2½	2¼	1¾
High life expectancy	2¼	2	1½

A21   The alternative projections suggest that higher fertility and net migration could generate slightly greater financial resources for current consumption. By contrast, higher life expectancy could reduce the amount available for current consumption on account of higher pension and other social security spending on the elderly as a share of GDP. Instead of rising by 2.4 percentage points between 2002-03 and 2032-33, the share of current consumption in GDP with higher life expectancy could rise by 2.1 percentage points. Chart A5 shows the differences between the baseline projections and the high life expectancy variant projections.

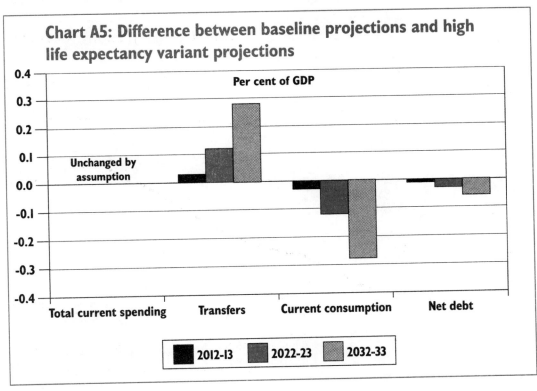

Chart A5: Difference between baseline projections and high life expectancy variant projections

A22   The alternative scenarios also show that the Government's public finances are robust to changes in the population assumptions. The net debt to GDP ratio is projected to be marginally lower in the three alternative variants than in the baseline projections, reflecting slightly faster GDP growth.

CONCLUSIONS

A23   The fiscal projections presented in this annex show that the UK's public finances are broadly sustainable over the long term, confirming the detailed findings presented in the November 2002 *Long-term public finance report*. Current consumption can grow slightly faster than assumed real GDP in the baseline case, ensuring that resources are available to meet potential future spending pressures. The golden rule and the sustainable investment rule are both met throughout the projection period, with net debt projected to be below 40 per cent of GDP in the long run. Public sector net investment can grow more or less in line with the economy without jeopardising the sustainable investment rule. The three alternative scenarios, each based on variant population projections, confirm the findings of the baseline case.

A24   However, notwithstanding the use of prudent and cautious assumptions, a wide range of unforeseen developments and spending pressures could arise over the projection period. The Government will therefore continue to update and report on its assessments of long-term fiscal sustainability, both through regular publication of the *Long-term public finance report* and through the illustrative long-term fiscal projections presented with each Budget, so as to ensure that all fiscal policy decisions are set within a sustainable long-term framework.

Financial Statement
and Budget Report

BUDGET POLICY DECISIONS

INTRODUCTION

The Economic and Fiscal Strategy Report (EFSR) explains how the measures and other policy decisions taken in the Budget build on those already introduced to advance the Government's long-term goals:

- raising the sustainable rate of productivity growth through reforms to enhance the flexibility of product and capital markets and to promote enterprise, innovation and skills;

- sustaining a higher proportion of people in work than ever before on the basis of a flexible labour market that adjusts rapidly to changing conditions and delivers employment opportunity for all;

- creating a fairer, more inclusive society with opportunity and security for all, eradicating child poverty and tackling pensioner poverty;

- establishing world class public services to underpin a flexible and high productivity economy through investment and reform; and

- tackling the global challenges of poverty and climate change through steps to achieve the Millenium Development Goals and to deliver the UK's commitments under the Kyoto Protocol.

This chapter of the Financial Statement and Budget Report (FSBR) brings together in summary form all the measures and decisions announced in Budget 2003 that affect the Budget arithmetic, giving their estimated effect on government revenue or spending up to 2005-06.[1] It includes those measures announced since Budget 2002, including in the 2002 Pre-Budget Report. The chapter also sets out how the Budget measures affect the tax and benefit system and government spending. This includes a summary of the main rates and allowances for the personal tax and benefit system, the business tax system, Value Added Tax (VAT), environmental taxes, and other indirect taxes and duties, following the Budget.

The appendices to this chapter provide background information on the Budget measures:

- Appendix A1 provides details of tax changes and other policy decisions which were announced in Budget 2002 or earlier, but which take effect from or after April 2003;

- Appendix A2 explains in detail how the effects of the Budget measures on government revenues are calculated; and

- Appendix A3 provides estimates of the revenue costs to the Government of some of the main tax allowances and reliefs.

BUDGET POLICY DECISIONS

Table A.1 summarises the Budget measures and sets out their effects on government revenue and spending. These include tax measures, national insurance contribution measures, measures that affect Annually Managed Expenditure (AME), and additions to Departmental Expenditure Limits (DEL). Measures that are financed from existing DEL provisions are not included.

[1] The contents of the brackets after each measure in this chapter refer to the line in Tables A.1 and A.2 where its cost or yield is shown. The symbol '-' means that the proposal has no Exchequer effect. The symbol '*' means that the effect is negligible, amounting to less than £3 million a year.

Table A.1: Budget 2003 policy decisions

		(+ve is an Exchequer yield)			£ million
		2003-04 indexed	2004-05 indexed	2005-06 indexed	2003-04 non-indexed
MEETING THE PRODUCTIVITY CHALLENGE					
1	100 per cent first year capital allowances for ICT	−5	−160	+70	−5
2	VAT flat-rate scheme upper limit of £150,000	−15	−15	−15	−15
3	Revalorise VAT registration and deregistration thresholds	0	0	0	−5
4	VAT: simplify the treatment of business gifts	*	−5	−5	−5
5	VAT: electronically supplied services	+20	+25	+30	+20
6	Simplified import VAT accounting	−5	−20	−20	−5
7	Improvements to research and development tax credit	−20	−40	−50	−20
8	Employment benefits: deregulatory measures	−5	−5	−5	−5
9	Reform of North Sea infrastructure taxation	0	−15	−20	0
10	Life companies: change to policyholder rate and apportionment of profits	−25	−40	−40	−25
INCREASING EMPLOYMENT OPPORTUNITY FOR ALL					
11	Income tax: indexation of starting and basic rate limits	0	0	0	−400
12	Housing Benefit disregard	0	−45	−45	0
BUILDING A FAIRER SOCIETY					
Supporting families and pensioners					
13	Child Trust Fund	−350	−230	−235	−350
14	Tax exemption for foster carers	0	−5	−5	0
15	Income tax exemption for reimbursed homeworking costs	−5	−5	−5	−5
16	Extend hospital downrating exemption to 52 weeks	−30	−15	−15	−30
17	Indexation of the pension schemes earnings cap	0	0	0	−5
18	£100 payment to older pensioners	−180	−180	−180	−180
Protecting tax revenues[1]					
19	Tackling avoidance and creating a fairer system: equity remuneration	+110	+90	+95	+110
20	Chargeable gains: anti-avoidance involving second-hand life insurance policies	0	+30	+30	0
21	Capital gains tax: countering avoidance schemes through offshore trusts	0	+5	+5	0
22	Loan relationships: closing loopholes	+25	+50	+50	+25
23	Tackling avoidance through sale and repurchase agreements	+30	+50	+50	+30
24	Income tax: avoidance through relevant discounted securities	+20	+20	+20	+20
25	Service companies: closing loopholes used by domestic workers	+15	+15	+15	+15
26	VAT anti-fraud measures	+225	+230	+235	+225
27	VAT on continuous supplies	*	+15	+15	*

Table A.1: Budget 2003 policy decisions

	(+ve is an Exchequer yield)			£ million
	2003-04 indexed	2004-05 indexed	2005-06 indexed	2003-04 non-indexed
Duties and other tax changes				
28 Treatment of options for the purposes of tax on chargeable gains	0	+20	+40	0
29 Inheritance tax: indexation of threshold	0	0	0	–30
30 Electronic payment for large employers	0	+10	+10	0
31 Introduction of gross profits tax for bingo	–20	–25	–20	–20
32 Amusement machines licensing duty: freeze of rates	–5	–5	–5	0
33 General betting duty: minor amendments	+5	+5	+5	+5
34 Tobacco duties: revalorisation of rates	0	0	0	+170
35 Alcohol duties: revalorise beer and wine, freeze other rates	–35	–35	–30	+145
PROTECTING THE ENVIRONMENT				
36 Landfill tax: £3 increases from 2005-06	0	0	+140	0
37 Climate change levy: freeze rates	–20	–20	–20	0
38 Aggregates levy: freeze rates	–10	–10	–10	+10
39 Enhanced capital allowances for water-efficient technologies	–20	–30	–25	–20
40 Enhanced capital allowances for additional energy-saving technologies	–5	–5	–10	–5
Transport and the environment				
41 Company car tax: emissions level for minimum charge	0	0	+125	0
42 Fuel duties: revalorisation of rates from 1 October	–300	0	0	+300
43 Fuel duties: new duty rate for bioethanol from January 2005	0	–5	–30	0
44 Fuel duties: increase rebated oils by 1p above revalorisation	+95	+95	+100	+95
45 Air passenger duties: freeze of rates	–25	–25	–30	0
46 Changes to Vehicle Excise Duty	+30	+30	+35	–95
47 VAT: revalorisation of car fuel scale charges	0	0	0	+10
OTHER POLICY DECISIONS				
48 Recycled revenues from landfill tax increases	0	0	–140	
TOTAL BUDGET MEASURES	**–505**	**–250**	**+110**	**–45**

* *Negligible*

ADDITIONAL BUDGET POLICY DECISIONS

Resetting of the AME margin	+805	–980	–1,750

¹ *In addition, further details of the package of measures to modernise stamp duty announced in Budget 2002 are set out in Table A2.1. The original yield set out in Budget 2002 (Tables 1.2 and A.1) has been updated, and a reduced yield (by £10 million in 2003-04, and £100 million in 2004-05) included in Budget 2003 fiscal projections.*

Table A.2 summarises the impact on government revenue and spending of other measures introduced since Budget 2002, including those announced in the 2002 Pre-Budget Report.

Table A.2: Other measures announced since Budget 2002

			(+ve is an Exchequer yield)			£ million
			2003-04 indexed	2004-05 indexed	2005-06 indexed	2003-04 non-indexed
MEETING THE PRODUCTIVITY CHALLENGE						
a	†	Share schemes – statutory corporation tax deduction	+5	−45	−75	+5
INCREASING EMPLOYMENT OPPORTUNITY FOR ALL						
b		Housing benefit: standard rate Pathfinders	−5	−20	−30	−5
c	†	Transition to work: extending the Job Grant	0	−15	−15	0
BUILDING A FAIRER SOCIETY						
d	†	Income tax: indexation of aged income limits and other allowances	0	0	0	−20
e	†	Freeze of class 2 national insurance contributions	−5	−5	−5	0
f	†	Extension of the Payroll Giving supplement for one year	−10	0	0	−10
g		VAT exemption for services provided by state regulated welfare agencies	−35	−35	−35	−35
h	†	Abolition of North Sea Royalty from 1 January 2003	−180	−180	−150	−180
i	†	Increase in the Social Fund budget	−25	−35	−45	−25
j		VAT on privately operated tolls	+10	+10	+10	+10
Anti-avoidance measures						
k	†	Abuse of Employee Benefit Trusts	+315	+425	+435	+315
l	†	Claims for unfairly accelerated capital allowances	+25	+30	+30	+20
m		Life assurance companies: anti-avoidance	+60	+80	+80	+60
n		Derivative contracts: closing loopholes	+300	0	0	+300
o	†	Controlled foreign companies: anti-avoidance measures	0	+50	+170	0
p	†	Avoidance of VAT on sales of freehold buildings	+165	+165	+165	+165
q		Controlled foreign companies: removing Ireland from excluded countries list	+15	+15	+15	+15
PROTECTING THE ENVIRONMENT						
r	†	Replacement of Landfill Tax Credit Scheme	+100	+110	+110	+100
s		Registered dealers in controlled oils	−10	−5	0	−10
ADDITIONAL POLICY DECISIONS						
	†	Additional waste spending in DEL	−100	−110	−110	
TOTAL POLICY DECISIONS			**+625**	**+435**	**+550**	**+705**

† Announced in 2002 Pre-Budget Report.

Note: As required by the Code for Fiscal Stability, the 2002 Pre-Budget Report economic and fiscal projections were based on, and included the impact of, all Government decisions and all other circumstances where the impact of these decisions could be quantified with reasonable accuracy by the day the projections were finalised.

PERSONAL TAXES AND SPENDING MEASURES

Income tax

Bands, rates and personal allowances

As announced in Budget 2002, the personal allowance is frozen at £4,615. The personal allowance for people aged 65-74 increases to £6,610 and for those aged 75 or over it increases by £240 above statutory indexation to £6,720. The income limit for age-related allowances, blind person's allowance and the married couple's allowance all rise in line with statutory indexation. Budget 2003 announces that the starting and basic rate limits are increased in line with statutory indexation, and there are no changes to the income tax rates. (d, 11)

The maximum earnings for which pension provision may be made with income tax relief (the "earnings cap") is increased in line with statutory indexation to £99,000. (17)

Childcare element of the Working Tax Credit

From April 2004, the restrictions will be removed in the childcare element of the Working Tax Credit that prevent mothers on paid maternity leave receiving help with the costs of childcare for their new babies. (*)

Reimbursed homeworking expenses

From 6 April 2003, employers will be able to meet additional homeworking costs incurred by employees who work at home without it giving rise to an income tax charge. (15)

Foster carers

From 6 April 2003, the income of foster carers will be exempt from income tax beneath a fixed threshold amount of £10,000 a year per residence plus an amount per child of £200 a week for each child under 11, and £250 a week for each child aged 11 or over. (14)

Adoption allowances

As announced in the 2002 Pre-Budget Report, a measure will be introduced to ensure that financial support to adopters under the Children and Adoption Act 2002 continues to be free from tax. (-)

Personal pensions

A measure will be introduced to remove any doubt that employer and member contributions to personal pension schemes are subject to the earnings cap. (-)

Life insurance

Fully retrospective measures will be introduced to ensure that any charge by the insurer for an exceptional risk of disability or critical illness is disregarded when determining whether a life policy is a qualifying policy, and to exclude certain group life policies from the chargeable events regime. A further measure, taking effect from 9 April 2003, will correct anomalies in the taxation of life insurance policies held by charitable trusts and of annuity contracts sold by friendly societies. (*)

A measure will be introduced, with effect from 6 April 2004, to reduce to 20 per cent the amount of tax treated as paid on gains by individuals and trustees. This measure reflects a reduction in the rate of tax to be charged on certain profits made by life insurance companies. (10)

Claims at end of enquiries

Self Assessment taxpayers will be given rights to make, amend and withdraw claims and elections at the end of an enquiry into a return in line with the rights they enjoy where a 'discovery' assessment is made. The measure will apply to enquiries concluded from Royal Assent. (*)

Employment benefits

Some of the monetary limits in exemptions for minor employment benefits will be increased later this year. (8)

Table A.3: Bands of taxable income 2003-04

2002-03	£ a year	2003-04	£ a year
Starting rate 10 per cent	0 - 1,920	Starting rate 10 per cent	0 - 1,960
Basic rate[1,2] 22 per cent	1,921 - 29,900	Basic rate[1,2] 22 per cent	1,961 - 30,500
Higher rate[2] 40 per cent	over 29,900	Higher rate[2] 40 per cent	Over 30,500

[1] The rate of tax applicable to savings income in Section 1A ICTA 1988 remains at 20 per cent for income between the starting and basic rate limits.

[2] The rates applicable to dividends are 10 per cent for income up to the basic rate limit and 32.5 per cent above that.

Table A.4: Income tax allowances 2003-04

		£ a year	
	2002-03	2003-04	Increase
Personal allowance			
age under 65	4,615	4,615	0
age 65-74	6,100	6,610	510
age 75 and over	6,370	6,720	350
Married couple's allowance[1]			
age 65 before 6 April 2000	5,465	5,565	100
age 75 and over	5,535	5,635	100
minimum amount[2]	2,110	2,150	40
Income limit for age-related allowances	17,900	18,300	400
Blind person's allowance	1,480	1,510	30

[1] Tax relief for this allowance is restricted to 10 per cent.

[2] This is also the maximum relief for maintenance payments where at least one of the parties is born before 6 April 1935.

Table A.5: Child and Working Tax Credits rates and thresholds

	2003-04 £ a year
Working Tax Credit	
Basic element	1,525
Couples' and lone parent elements	1,500
30 hour element	620
Disabled worker element	2,040
Enhanced disabled worker element	865
50plus return to work payment, 16–30 hours	1,045
50plus return to work payment, 30+ hours	1,565
Childcare element	
– maximum eligible cost for one child	£135 a week
– maximum eligible cost for two or more children	£200 a week
– per cent of eligible costs covered	70
Child Tax Credit	
Family element	545
Family element, baby addition	545
Child element	1,445
Disabled child additional element	2,155
Enhanced disabled child additional element	865
Common features	
First income threshold	5,060
First withdrawal rate (per cent)	37
Second income threshold	50,000
Second withdrawal rate	1 in 15
First threshold for those entitled to Child Tax Credit only	13,230

Effects on the Scottish Parliament's tax varying powers – statement regarding Section 76 of the Scotland Act 1998

A one penny change in the Scottish variable rate in 2003-04 could be worth approximately plus or minus £260 million in a full year, broadly unaffected by these changes. In the Treasury's view, an amendment of the Scottish Parliament's tax-varying powers is not required as a result of these changes.

National insurance contributions

As announced in the 2002 Pre-Budget Report, the rate of Class 2 national insurance contributions (NICs) for the self-employed is frozen at £2.00 per week, and the rate of Class 3 voluntary contributions is increased in line with inflation to £6.95 per week. The special Class 2 rate for volunteer development workers is increased in line with inflation to £3.85 per week, and for share fishermen is frozen at £2.65 per week. The other NIC rates, thresholds and limits for 2003-04 were announced in Budget 2002. (e, *)

Table A.6: Class 1 national insurance contribution rates 2003-04

Weekly earnings[1]	Employee (primary) NIC rate[2] (per cent)	Employer (secondary) NIC rate[3] (per cent)
Below £77 (LEL)	0	0
£77 to £89 (PT/ST)	0[4]	0
£89 to £595 (UEL)	11	12.8
Above £595	1	12.8

[1] The limits are defined as LEL – lower earnings limit; PT – primary threshold; ST – secondary threshold; and UEL – upper earnings limit.

[2] The contracted-out rebate for primary contributions in 2003–04 is 1.6 per cent of earnings between the LEL and UEL for contracted-out salary-related schemes (COSRS) and contracted out money purchase schemes (COMPS).

[3] The contracted-out rebate for secondary contributions is 3.5 per cent of earnings between the LEL and UEL for COSRS and 1.0 per cent for COMPS. For COMPS, an additional age-related rebate is paid direct to the scheme following the end of the tax year. For appropriate personal pensions, the employee and employer pay NICs at the standard, not contracted-out, rate. An age and earnings-related rebate is paid direct to the personal pension provider following the end of the tax year.

[4] No NICs are actually payable but a notional primary Class 1 NIC will be deemed to have been paid in respect of earnings between LEL and PT to Protect benefit entitlement.

Table A.7: Self-employed national insurance contribution rates 2003–04

Annual Profits[1]	Self employed NICs Class 2	Class 4
Below £4,095 (SEE)	0[2]	0
£4,095 and above	£2 a week	
£4,095 to £4,615 (LPL)		0
£4,615 to £30,940 (UPL)		8 per cent
Above £30,940		1 per cent

[1] The limits are defined as LPL – lower profits limit and UPL – upper profits limit.

[2] The self-employed may apply for exception from paying Class 2 contributions if their earnings are less than, or expected to be less than, the level of the small earnings exception (SEE).

Inheritance tax

Threshold The threshold is increased in line with inflation, to £255,000, for new tax charges arising on or after 6 April 2003. (29)

Charities and giving

Payroll Giving supplement As announced in the 2002 Pre-Budget Report, the 10 per cent government supplement on donations to charities made through Payroll Giving schemes will be extended for a further year, until 5 April 2004. (f)

BENEFITS

Child Trust Fund Budget 2003 introduces a new Child Trust Fund, with entitlement backdated to include children born from September 2002. The Child Trust Fund will provide a Government endowment of £250 for every child at birth, rising to £500 for children from low-income families who also qualify for the full Child Tax Credit. Parents, family and friends will be able to add additional contributions up to an annual limit of £1,000. The fund will mature when the child reaches the age of eighteen. Child Trust Fund accounts are expected to be available from 2005. (13)

Housing Benefit From April 2004 the calculation of Housing Benefit will disregard £11.90 of earnings for all tenants who are claiming, or are entitled to claim, the Working Tax Credit, replacing the current 30 hour premium disregard. (12)

From October 2003, a flat rate Housing Benefit system will be rolled out in Pathfinder areas, under which claims from private rented sector tenants will be paid at the local reference rent for their circumstances, regardless of the accommodation they choose to live in. (b)

As announced in the 2002 Pre-Budget Report, from April 2004 claimants of Incapacity Benefit or Severe Disablement Allowance will be treated in the same way as Jobseeker's Allowance and Income Support claimants when they return to work and will benefit from the Housing Benefit run-on. (*)

Job Grant As announced in the 2002 Pre-Budget Report, from October 2004, the Job Grant will be available to those who move into work following six months on Jobseeker's Allowance, Incapacity Benefit or Income Support, including lone parents, and a new rate of £250 for households with children will be introduced. Partners of benefit claimants will also be eligible. These arrangements will replace the Back to Work Bonus and the lone parent Income Support run-on. (c)

Hospital downrating of benefits From May 2003, the period during which all inpatients continue to receive their full state pension and most of their full benefits will be extended to 52 weeks. Attendance Allowance, Disability Living Allowance and Invalid Care Allowance will cease after four weeks, as now. (16)

Payment to older pensioners From 2003-04 and for the lifetime of this Parliament, households with a pensioner aged 80 or over will receive an extra £100 in addition to the £200 winter fuel payment. (18)

The Social Fund As announced in the 2002 Pre-Budget Report, from April 2003, the maximum payment for the fixed element of the funeral grant rises from £600 to £700, and £90 million will be added to the budget of the Discretionary Social Fund over the three years to 2005-06. (i)

TAX ON CHARGEABLE GAINS AND STAMP TAXES

Tax on chargeable gains

Annual exempt amount The capital gains tax (CGT) annual exempt amount is increased in line with statutory indexation to £7,900. (-)

Taper relief For periods of ownership from 6 April 2004, an asset used in a trade carried on by individuals, trustees of settlements, personal representatives or certain partnerships will qualify as a business asset for CGT purposes, regardless of whether its owner is involved in carrying on the trade. (*)

Options and capital gains A measure will be introduced to restore the basis of calculating gains where assets are acquired by exercising options to the generally understood position before the Court of Appeal judgement in Mansworth v Jelley. It will apply where options are exercised on or after 10 April 2003. (28)

Offshore trusts A measure will be introduced to counter an avoidance device where the trustees of an offshore trust have made capital gains and put in place a structure aimed at distributing capital to beneficiaries without triggering a CGT charge on those beneficiaries. The measure applies to payments made to beneficiaries on or after 9 April 2003. (21)

Simplification A package of measures will be introduced to simplify CGT with effect from 10 April 2003 or for the tax year 2003-04 onwards. They will reduce compliance burdens and allow some capital losses to be carried back and set off against gains of earlier tax years. (*)

Life insurance A measure will be introduced with effect from 9 April 2003 to close two loopholes in the chargeable gains rules for disposals of second-hand life insurance policies. (20)

Stamp duty

Modernising stamp duty Budget 2002 announced immediate measures to counter stamp duty avoidance, and a wide-ranging reform to apply stamp duty fairly to transactions in UK land and buildings from late 2003. Table A.1 in Budget 2002 set out figures for the expected revenue yield. Following consultation, this Budget announces the details of those measures to be introduced in December 2003, and, in Appendix A2, publishes a breakdown of the effect on government revenue.

From December 2003:

- more effective enforcement and compliance powers will take effect, commensurate with those already in place for other taxes;

- anti-avoidance rules will help enforce the charge on all transfers of UK land and buildings;

- a proposed reform of lease duty, which will levy 1 per cent on the net present value of rental payments in new leases, where that value exceeds the relevant zero rate threshold;

- the upper threshold of the zero rate band for non-residential property will be increased from £60,000 to £150,000, for both transfers and new leases. (It will remain at £60,000 for residential transfers and leases);

- VAT will be excluded from chargeable consideration for stamp duty on new leases where the landlord has not opted to charge VAT by the time the lease is granted; and

- the stamp duty treatment of property purchases by individuals funded using certain types of alternative mortgage products will be put on a level footing with those funded using conventional mortgage arrangements.

Shares A measure will be introduced to allow stamp duty to continue applying in respect of stock and marketable securities following the implementation of modernising stamp duty. (*)

Registered Social Landlords Homeless families may be housed by Registered Social Landlords (RSLs) under agreements with the Housing Authorities. The tenancy agreements between the family and the RSL will be exempt from stamp duty. This measure is being backdated to transactions completed on or after 1 January 2000. (*)

BUSINESS TAXES AND SPENDING MEASURES

Tax on business profits

Corporation tax rates
The main rate of corporation tax will be set at 30 per cent for financial year 2004. The small companies rate and the starting rate are unchanged at 19 per cent and zero per cent respectively for financial year 2003. (-)

Deductibility of interest against tax
A measure will be introduced for accounting periods ending on or after 9 April 2003 to formalise the current practice of disallowing interest on certain items – NICs and student loan repayments paid by all employers and tax paid by employers in the construction industry – against tax. (*)

Company liquidations and administrations
There will be a package of measures required to enable implementation of the insolvency provisions of the Enterprise Act 2002. One provision takes effect on 9 April 2003 and the remainder will commence at the same time as the new corporate insolvency rules. (*)

Treasury shares
Department of Trade and Industry (DTI) regulations will allow listed companies to purchase their own shares and hold them in treasury. New tax rules will be introduced to treat shares purchased into treasury as if they had been cancelled, and shares sold out of treasury as new issues. The tax changes and the DTI regulations will be effective from the same date. (*)

Court Common Investment Funds
The provision which deems Court Common Investment Funds to be authorised unit trusts will be amended to extend the category of investors to hold units in such funds with effect from 6 April 2003. (-)

Controlled foreign companies
In line with the announcement on 23 July 2002, controlled foreign companies operating in Ireland can no longer benefit from automatic exemption under the Excluded Country Regulations by virtue of changes to the regulations which were laid before Parliament on 20 September 2002 and took effect for accounting periods commencing on or after 11 October 2002. (q)

As announced in November 2002, the rules for controlled foreign companies in the Hong Kong and Macao Special Administrative Regions of China are being changed to ensure such companies continue to be able to benefit from exemption in cases where it was always intended that they should. The necessary legislation will apply retrospectively with effect from 1 July 1997 (Hong Kong subsidiaries) and 20 December 1999 (Macao subsidiaries). (-)

Life insurance
Two measures will be introduced to simplify and rationalise the taxation of life insurance companies. They affect the rate of tax charged on the policyholders' share of capital gains and rental income, and the way profits are apportioned between policyholders and shareholders. These measures apply for the financial year 2003 onwards and periods beginning on or after 1 January 2003 respectively. (10)

Royalties and other direct taxes

North Sea Taxation
As announced in the 2002 Pre-Budget Report, North Sea Royalty was abolished with effect from 1 January 2003. (h)

From 1 January 2004, petroleum revenue tax will be removed for all new third party tariffing business under contracts completed on or after 9 April 2003 relating to use of pipelines and other infrastructure in the UK and on its continental shelf. (9)

Incentives for businesses and employees

Capital allowances Expenditure from 1 April 2003 on designated water-efficient technologies will qualify for 100 per cent first year allowances. The Government will publish the Water Technology list which will identify the eligible technologies. Claims for the enhanced capital allowances may be made when both the publication of this list and Royal Assent have taken place. (39)

The designated energy-efficient technologies qualifying for 100 per cent first year allowances will be expanded later in 2003, subject to agreement with the European Commission. (40)

The 100 per cent first year allowances for investment by small enterprises in information and communications technology (ICT) will be extended for one further year, until 31 March 2004. (1)

Research and development tax credits The Government will reduce the minimum expenditure to £10,000, simplify the rules for apportioning staff costs and allow companies to claim for the costs of agency workers. These changes will take effect from 9 April 2003 for large companies and from a date to be announced for SMEs. The circumstances in which SMEs can claim under 'large company' rules will also be widened with effect from 9 April 2003. (7)

Urban Regeneration Companies As announced in the 2002 Pre-Budget Report, contributions made by businesses on or after 1 April 2003 towards the running costs of Urban Regeneration Companies will be deductible when computing taxable profits. (*)

Employee share schemes As announced in the 2002 Pre-Budget Report, a statutory corporation tax deduction for the cost of providing shares for employee share schemes will be available for accounting periods commencing on or after 1 January 2003. (a)

Some of the tax-incentivised share schemes rules will be simplified to make them easier for employers to administer with effect from Royal Assent. Other improvements to the schemes will come into effect from 9 April 2003. (19)

Securing the tax base

Leasing and tonnage tax As announced on 19 December 2002, the restrictions on capital allowances that can be claimed by lessors of ships to tonnage tax companies will be extended to all types of leasing arrangements except for ordinary ship charters. The measure will apply to leases entered into from that date. (-)

Life insurance As announced on 23 December 2002, a package of measures will be introduced to prevent a small number of companies from exploiting particular circumstances to pay much less tax than other companies writing similar business and to remove other anomalies. Most of the changes will take effect for accounting periods commencing on or after 1 January 2003. They apply to capital gains and losses, the measure of profits for certain types of business and transfers of business. (m)

Measures will be introduced, with effect from 9 April 2003, to close two loopholes in connection with the taxation of non-charitable trusts; and to prevent tax avoidance on maturity of certain life policies. (*)

Controlled foreign companies As announced in the 2002 Pre-Budget Report, a loophole in one of the exemptions from the controlled foreign company rules that allowed profits from extended warranties, credit protection and other UK source business to escape taxation will be closed with effect for accounting periods commencing on or after 27 November 2002. (o)

Loan relationships and derivative contracts As announced on 30 September 2002, legislation will be introduced to counter an avoidance scheme involving off-market currency contracts and to ensure that surplus non-trading loan relationship deficits are carried forward correctly. The measures will apply from that date. (n)

Measures will be introduced with effect from 9 April 2003 to counter an avoidance scheme involving the connected party rules and to ensure that intra-group transactions are taxed in line with accounts. (22)

Employee Benefit Trusts   As announced in the 2002 Pre-Budget Report, a package of measures will be introduced with effect from November 2002 to prevent employers using Employee Benefit Trusts (EBTs) to avoid tax and NICs. The employer's tax deduction for EBT contributions will be deferred until the EBT makes a payment to the employee that is liable to tax and NICs. It will also be made clear who is responsible for paying NICs on payments made to employees by an EBT. (k)

Service companies   The rules that apply to workers that supply services through an intermediary, such as a service company, will be extended to cover those that are engaged in a domestic capacity, from 10 April 2003 for income tax, with NICs rules coming into force soon after Royal Assent. (25)

Employee share schemes   Some loopholes in the rules relating to share-based remuneration will be closed with effect from 9 and 16 April 2003. In addition, the treatment of restricted shares will be made simpler and fairer, taking effect soon after Royal Assent. (19)

Sale and repurchase agreements   Measures will be introduced, with effect from 9 April 2003, to prevent avoidance involving sale and repurchase agreements (repo) by ensuring that different parts of the repo legislation work together coherently. The changes will also clarify the workings of the repo rules. (23)

Relevant discounted securities   As announced on 27 March 2003, legislation will be introduced with effect from that date to prevent exploitation of the relevant discounted securities (RDS) rules and align the taxation of RDS more closely with that of normal interest bearing securities. (24)

Capital allowances   As announced in the 2002 Pre-Budget Report, businesses will be prevented from claiming artificially accelerated capital allowances with effect from 27 November 2002. (l)

As announced on 26 March 2003, a measure will be introduced to counter an avoidance scheme that exploits the fact that 100 per cent ICT allowances are available for software acquired for licensing, but not for software purchased for leasing. The measure affects expenditure incurred from that date. (-)

Other measures

Withholding tax   As announced in the 2002 Pre-Budget Report, annual interest payments made by recognised clearing houses and recognised investment exchanges while providing central counterparty clearing services, can be paid without deduction of tax at source from 1 April 2003. Payments to the nominees of certain UK tax-exempt bodies can be made without deduction of tax at source from 1 December 2002. (*)

UK-authorised open-ended investment funds   As announced on 16 October 2002, measures will be introduced with effect from that date to make it easier for UK-authorised investment funds to pay interest without deduction of tax to foreign investors and to exempt those investors from the potential charge to inheritance tax on their holdings. (*)

Admissibility of evidence into hearings   The provisions regarding the admissibility of evidence into hearings, when a taxpayer was offered an incentive to provide it, will be updated to make the Inland Revenue's procedures further compliant with human rights legislation. The changes will apply to statements made and documents produced from Royal Assent. (*)

Exchange of information   There will be a minor amendment to the vires for exchange of information under international agreements to bring them into line with international standards. (-)

PAYE regulations   The powers for making PAYE regulations will be modernised to support the Tax Law Rewrite Project's rewrite of the PAYE regulations in line with their original purpose and long-standing practices. (*)

E-payment Mandatory electronic payment will be introduced, from April 2004, for employers with 250 or more employees, to ensure prompt payment of PAYE and other statutory deductions, promote modern communication methods and lower administration costs for Government and business. The cashflow advantage, currently enjoyed by businesses that pay by cheque on the due date, will be built into the system and will not be affected by the change. (30)

VALUE ADDED TAX (VAT)

Simplifying VAT for small businesses The Government will take further steps to help small and newly-registered businesses reduce their VAT compliance costs, improve their cash flow and manage their entry into the VAT system. From 10 April 2003:

- the VAT registration threshold will increase from £55,000 to £56,000 broadly in line with inflation; (3)

- the VAT flat-rate scheme will be extended to businesses with a turnover up to £150,000; (2) and

- the turnover limit for immediate entry to the VAT annual accounting scheme for newly-registered businesses will also rise to £150,000. (*)

Modernising and simplifying VAT From 1 December 2003 a new scheme will allow approved importers to benefit from reductions in the level of bank guarantees they have to provide in order to cover their import VAT liability. (6)

From 1 October 2003 the VAT treatment of a series of business gifts will come into line with that which already applies to single gifts, removing the need for businesses to account for VAT on gifts up to £50 in value. (4)

From 1 July 2003, changes to the VAT place of supply rules, to comply with the E-Commerce Directive, will mean that non-EU businesses providing electronically supplied services to EU consumers will be required to register and account for VAT on their services; a special scheme will allow them to register, account for and pay VAT electronically in the UK. (5)

From Royal Assent, UK legislation concerning mutual assistance between EU tax authorities will be consolidated, and new powers will be introduced to amend references in that legislation to accommodate future changes to EU legislation. (*)

Exemption from VAT was introduced on 31 January 2003 for services provided by state-regulated welfare agencies, consistent with the VAT treatment of similar services provided by charities and public bodies. (g)

From 1 February 2003, privately operated tolls became liable to VAT, complying with a ruling in 2000 by the European Court of Justice. At the time of the ruling the Government stated its intention that there should be no increase in toll charges on account of VAT, and suitable financial arrangements for toll operators were therefore also put in place on 1 February 2003. (j)

Tackling VAT fraud Budget 2003 introduces a package of measures to tackle VAT fraud: (26)

- from midnight on Budget day, businesses that consistently trade in supply chains involving missing traders or those who become insolvent may be required to provide security, as a condition of continuing to trade;

- in order to tackle missing trader fraud, both suppliers and recipients of specified goods and services may become jointly and severally liable for the VAT due from missing traders in the supply chain. This measure takes effect from midnight on Budget day and has built-in safeguards to protect those unwittingly caught; and

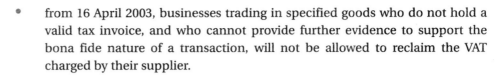

- from 16 April 2003, businesses trading in specified goods who do not hold a valid tax invoice, and who cannot provide further evidence to support the bona fide nature of a transaction, will not be allowed to reclaim the VAT charged by their supplier.

Tackling VAT avoidance   From 1 August 2003 new rules will ensure that businesses making certain ongoing or continuous supplies to connected persons will have to account for VAT on those supplies at least once per year, preventing them from delaying or postponing indefinitely the payment of VAT. (27)

Legislation was introduced at the time of the Pre-Budget Report to prevent avoidance of VAT involving the sale of new freehold commercial buildings. From Budget day, this legislation will be simplified to reduce burdens on non-avoiders, and new rules will strengthen the measure. (p)

From Budget day, new rules will be introduced to prevent VAT avoidance in relation to the private or non-business use of land and buildings. (*)

ENVIRONMENTAL AND TRANSPORT TAXES

Climate change levy   The rates of the climate change levy (CCL) are frozen. (37)

Budget 2003 also introduces a package of technical changes to CCL legislation:

- following Royal Assent, regulations will be laid to confirm the extra-statutory exemption from CCL for products used in secondary recycling processes which compete with exempt primary processes; (-)

- regulations to be laid after Royal Assent will allow qualifying operators of Combined Heat and Power (CHP) stations to claim relief from CCL on input fuel used to produce electricity in accordance with the actual energy-efficiency of their plant; (*) and

- new rules to require electricity suppliers to account for CCL where the amount of levy-free electricity sold exceeds that purchased from renewable or CHP sources. For renewable sources this will take effect for averaging periods ending on or after 31 March 2003. For CHP sources it will apply for averaging periods beginning from 1 April 2003. (*)

Aggregates levy   The rate of aggregates levy is frozen at £1.60 per tonne. (38)

Landfill tax   Following consultation announced in the 2002 Pre-Budget Report, the standard rate of landfill tax will increase by £3 per tonne in 2005-06 to £18 per tonne, and by at least £3 per tonne each year thereafter, on the way to a medium to long-term rate of £35 per tonne. A package of measures will be introduced from 2005-06 to recycle revenue from these increases to business and local government. (36, 48)

Landfill Tax Credit Scheme   From 1 April 2003, the Landfill Tax Credit Scheme is reduced to approximately one-third of its previous level, and refocused on local community environmental projects. The proportion of the remaining funds – £100 million in 2003-04 and £110 million in 2004-05 – to be spent in England has been allocated to public spending on a new sustainable waste delivery programme. (r)

Vehicle Excise Duty   From 1 May 2003 a new car vehicle excise duty (VED) band (AAA) for the least polluting vehicles will be introduced. All other car and van VED rates will increase by £5. The VED rates for Reduced Pollution buses, Reduced Pollution General Haulage vehicles, Trade Licences and Special Trailer duty will all increase by £5. Trailer supplements for rigids over 12 tonnes, that haul drawbars in excess of 4 tonnes, will increase by £7. Motorcycle, lorry and all other VED rates are frozen. (46)

A measure, taking effect from Budget day, will be introduced to put beyond any doubt that articulated goods vehicles are excepted from a higher rate of VED when used with reduced axle numbers in specified circumstances. (-)

Table A.8a: VED bands and rates for cars registered after 1 March 2001 (graduated VED)

VED band	CO_2 emissions (g/km)	VED rate (£)		
		Cars using alternative fuels	Petrol car	Diesel car
AAA	100 and below	55	65	75
AA	101 to 120	65	75	85
A	121 to 150	95	105	115
B	151 to 165	115	125	135
C	166 to 185	135	145	155
D	186 and above	155	160	165

Table A.8b: VED bands and rates for cars and vans registered before 1 March 2001 (pre-graduated VED)

Engine size	VED rate (£)
1549cc and below	110
Above 1549cc	165

Company car tax   The level of CO_2 emissions qualifying for the minimum company car tax charge will be reduced by 5g/km to 140g/km from 6 April 2005. The percentage charge rises in 1 per cent steps to a maximum charge of 35 per cent and the level of CO_2 emissions relating to each percentage charge will also be reduced by 5g/km. (41)

Car fuel scale charges   From 1 May 2003 the VAT car fuel scale charge, which provides a simplified method for taxing the private use of road fuel bought by VAT registered businesses, will be adjusted to reflect changes in pump prices since Budget 2002. (47)

Fuel duties   Duty on road fuel oils will rise in line with inflation from 1 October 2003. This will increase the duty on ultra-low sulphur petrol and diesel by 1.28 pence per litre. (42)

From 1 September 2004, sulphur-free fuels will benefit from a duty differential of half a penny per litre relative to the rate for ultra-low sulphur fuels.

Biodiesel   From 1 October 2003, duty on biodiesel will increase by 1.28 pence per litre. (42)

Bioethanol   As announced in the 2002 Pre-Budget Report, a reduced rate of duty will be introduced for bioethanol, of 20 pence per litre less than the prevailing rate for sulphur-free petrol. This new rate will become effective from 1 January 2005. (43)

Red diesel fuel oil and light oil   The duty rates on rebated gas oil ('red diesel'), fuel oil and light oil used as a furnace fuel increase by 1 penny per litre above revalorisation from Budget day 2003. (44)

Controlled oils scheme As announced at Budget 2002, since January 2003 HM Customs and Excise have approved distributors of rebated gas oil to deal in such fuels under the Registered Distributors of Controlled Oils Scheme. The scheme came into effect on 1 April 2003, and the Government has agreed a light-touch application of the scheme for its first three months, to allow distributors time to align their IT systems with their new record keeping obligations. (s)

Air passenger duty Air passenger duty rates are frozen. (45)

OTHER INDIRECT TAXES AND DUTIES

Tobacco duties From 6pm on Budget day 2003 tobacco duty rates will rise in line with inflation by 2.8 per cent, to maintain the real price of tobacco. (34)

Table A.9: Changes to tobacco duties

	Effect of tax[1] on typical item (increase in pence)	Unit
Cigarettes	8.4	packet of 20
Cigars	3.0	packet of 5
Hand-rolling tobacco	8.1	25g
Pipe tobacco	5.0	25g

[1] Tax refers to duty plus VAT.

Alcohol duties Excise duty rates on spirits, sparkling wine and cider will be frozen, while the rates on beer and wine will rise in line with inflation by 2.8 per cent, from midnight on 13 April 2003. (35)

Table A.10: Changes to alcohol duties

	Effect of tax[1] on typical item (increase in pence)	Unit
Beer	0.9	pint of lager
Wine	3.8	75cl bottle
Fortified wine	5.1	75cl bottle
Lower strength sparkling wine	0.0	75cl bottle
Higher strength sparkling wine	0.0	75cl bottle
Spirits	0.0	70cl bottle
Spirits-based RTDs	0.0	275ml bottle
Still cider	0.0	litre
Strong cider	0.0	litre
Sparkling cider	0.0	75cl bottle

[1] Tax refers to duty plus VAT.

Betting and gaming duties Bingo duty will be abolished from 4 August 2003 and replaced by a 15 per cent tax on the gross profits of bingo companies. (31)

The duty rates for General Betting Duty, pool betting duty and the lottery duty are all frozen at current levels. (-)

From 1 September 2003, bets made on course, except for those at horserace and dog tracks, will be subject to General Betting Duty, and all licensed bookmakers and pool betting operators will be allowed to carry forward losses from one accounting period to the next when calculating the tax due on their gross profits. From 1 June 2003, betting exchanges will be taxed at 15 per cent of the commission they charge their customers for facilitating betting through the exchange. (33)

Gaming duty bandings will rise in line with inflation for accounting periods starting on or after 1 April 2003. (-)

Amusement machine licence fees are frozen at their current levels in Budget 2003, and the Betting and Gaming Duties act 1984 will be updated from Royal Assent, to ensure that machines taking bank notes, debit, credit and smart cards are liable to these fees. (32)

Insurance premium tax From Royal Assent, the definition of 'connected persons' contained within insurance premium tax (IPT) legislation will be extended to bring divided companies (for example 'protected cell companies') within its scope. This will prevent an avoidance scheme, and ensure that insurance provided with certain other products by such companies is liable to the higher rate of IPT. (*)

Enforcing customs duties Following Royal Assent, legislation will be laid to introduce a new system of civil penalties (fines) for breaches of customs laws by importers and exporters, complementing the existing criminal sanctions for more serious offences. (*)

ADDITIONAL SPENDING AND DEBT MANAGEMENT DECISIONS

Managing government debt The Finance Bill will make technical changes to National Loans Fund (NLF) legislation that will enable the accounts for the NLF to be compiled on an accruals basis and make a number of other minor changes. It will also reduce unnecessary administration of the Debt Management Account (DMA) by abolishing the statutory requirement that caps the DMA's borrowing.

Contingency provisions The Government has increased its contingency provision to £3 billion to ensure that resources are available to cover the full cost of the UK's military obligations in Iraq.

Departmental Expenditure Limits This Budget transfers over half a billion pounds over the next three years from within total Departmental Expenditure Limits to the budgets of individual departments. These allocations are:

- £332 million to fund a package of counter-terrorism measures that will enhance the security of the UK and the ability of the police and other security services to counter the terrorist threat;

- £174 million for correctional services in England and Wales; and

- £66 million to the Inland Revenue to support implementation of the new compliance and enforcement package for direct tax and NICs, launched in this Budget.

Annually Managed Expenditure margin As described in Chapter 6, to protect committed investment while responding prudently to heightened global risks, the Government has decided to make no further allocations from the Capital Modernisation Fund (CMF). Instead, unallocated CMF funding will be transferred to Annually Managed Expenditure (AME) to contribute to the rebuilding of the AME margin to ensure that the public spending projections include a prudent and cautious safety margin against unexpected events. Resetting the AME margin to £1 billion, £2 billion and £3 billion for the years 2003-04, 2004-05 and 2005-06, in accordance with usual practice, increases projections for Totally Managed Expenditure (TME) by £1 billion in 2004-05 and by £1.8 billion in 2005-06, compared with those made in the 2002 Pre-Budget Report.

APPENDICES

APPENDIX A1: MEASURES ANNOUNCED IN BUDGET 2002 OR EARLIER

This appendix sets out a number of tax, national insurance contribution (NIC), social security benefit and other changes which were announced in Budget 2002 or earlier and which take effect from April 2003 or later. The revenue effects of these measures have been taken into account in previous economic and fiscal projections.

Table A1.1: Measures announced in Budget 2002 or earlier which take effect from April 2003 or later

		(+ve is an Exchequer yield)			£ million
		2003-04 indexed	2004-05 indexed	2005-06 indexed	2003-04 non-indexed
a	Freeze of income tax personal allowance and national insurance thresholds	+650	+1,050	+1,050	0
b	Additional class 1 primary NICs for employees	+3,500	+3,650	+3,900	+3,500
c	Additional class 1 secondary NICs for employers	+3,900	+4,100	+4,350	+3,900
d	Additional class 4 NICs for the self-employed	+400	+450	+500	+400
e	NICs: Indexation of the Upper Earnings Limit and Upper Profits Limit	0	0	0	–150
f	Working Tax Credit (WTC) for families without children	–200	–300	–300	–300
g	Child Tax Credit and WTC for families with children and associated measures	–2,400	–2,400	–2,400	–2,300
h	Income tax: over-indexation of age-related allowances for ages 65 or over	–230	–400	–570	–310
i	Eligibility of home childcare for the childcare element of WTC	–10	–15	–20	–10
j	Measures to encourage charitable giving	–40	–30	–20	–40
k	E-filing incentives for payroll	0	0	–40	0
l	Stamp duty: removal of £150,000 cap for commercial properties in disadvantaged communities	–90	–50	–50	–90
m	VAT anti-avoidance: face value vouchers	+110	+105	+95	+110
n	£1 per tonne increase in landfill tax each year from 2000 until 2004	+115	+140	+145	+115
o	Extend Statutory Maternity Pay and Maternity Allowance from 18 to 26 weeks from April 2003	–175	–225	–225	–175
p	Introduce two weeks paid paternity leave from April 2003	–65	–65	–65	–65
q	Introduce paid adoption leave for one parent from April 2003	–10	–10	–10	–10
r	Guaranteed increase in basic state pension	–230	–240	–250	–230
s	Introduction of Pension Credit	–985	–2,060	–2,245	–985
TOTAL		**+4,240**	**+3,700**	**+3,845**	**+3,360**

*Negligible

The 2003-04 income tax personal allowance for those aged under 65, the NIC primary and secondary thresholds and the lower profits limits are all frozen at 2002-03 levels. (a)

For 2003-04, there is an additional class 1 primary NIC for employees of 1 per cent on all earnings above the primary threshold. This means that NICs are charged at a rate of 11 per cent on earnings between the primary threshold and the upper earnings limit, and at a rate of 1 per cent on earnings above the upper earnings limit. (b)

For 2003-04, there is an additional class 1 secondary NIC for employers of 1 per cent on all earnings above the secondary threshold. This means that NICs are charged at a rate of 12.8 per cent on earnings above the secondary threshold. (c)

For 2003-04, there is an additional class 4 NIC for the self-employed of 1 per cent on all earnings above the lower profits limit. This means that NICs are charged at a rate of 8 per cent on profits between the lower and the upper profits limits, and at a rate of 1 per cent on profits above the upper profits limit. (d)

For 2003-04, the NICs upper earnings and profits limits are increased in line with inflation. (e)

From April 2003, the Working Tax Credit replaces the previous elements of support for adults, including childcare costs, in the Working Families' Tax Credit, Disabled Person's Tax Credit and the New Deal Employment Credit for those aged 50 and over. The Working Tax Credit also provides support for working households without children or a disabled adult where at least one adult is aged 25 or over and working at least 30 hours a week. The Child Tax Credit replaces the previous, income-related elements of support for children in the Working Families' Tax Credit, Disabled Person's Tax Credit and Children's Tax Credit. From 2004, it will also replace support for children in Income Support and income-based Jobseeker's Allowance. (f, g)

The 2003-04 personal allowance for those aged 65 – 74 is increased to £6,610, and for those aged 75 or over it is increased by £240 above statutory indexation. (h)

From April 2003, eligibility for the childcare element of the Working Tax Credit includes those who use approved childcare in their own home. (i)

Since 6 April 2003, higher rate taxpayers are able to carry back to the previous year their relief on Gift Aid donations and, from April 2004, taxpayers will be able to nominate a charity to receive a tax repayment that is due to them. (j)

Following the recommendations of the Carter Review of Payroll Services, and regulation making powers introduced in Finance Act 2002, regulations will be made to require employers to file their end of year returns electronically. These requirements will be phased in over a number of years beginning for the year 2004-05 for businesses with 250 or more employees. Incentives for small employers to switch to electronic filing will be introduced beginning for the year 2004-05. (k)

All non-residential property transactions completed on or after 10 April 2003 in the 2,000 most disadvantaged areas in the UK will be exempt from stamp duty. (l)

Following consultation, legislation will be introduced from Budget day to ensure that intermediaries who sell face value vouchers account for VAT on the sale. (m)

In line with the Government's commitment in Budget 1999 to increase the standard rate of landfill tax by £1 per tonne each year until 2004, the rate increased from £13 per tonne to £14 per tonne on 1 April 2003. (n)

In Northern Ireland the aggregates levy is being phased in for aggregates used in processed products, as a result of which the rate for aggregate in these products is 20 per cent of the full rate from 1 April 2003.

The Government announced in Budget 2002 that it would – on receipt of EU state aids approval – exempt from the climate change levy two further sources of energy generation sold via licensed electricity suppliers:

- electricity from combined heat and power (CHP) plants; and

- electricity from coal mine methane.

The exemption for electricity from CHP plants was introduced on 1 April 2003.

From April 2003 the duration of Statutory Maternity Pay (SMP) and Maternity Allowance increase from 18 to 26 weeks. The first 6 weeks continue to be paid at 90 per cent of earnings, followed by the flat rate period, which increases from 12 to 20 weeks. (o)

From April 2003 the first ever paid paternity leave is introduced at the same flat rate as SMP for 2 weeks. Low-paid fathers on paternity leave get access to Income Support. (p)

From April 2003 the first ever paid adoption leave is introduced at the same flat rate and duration as SMP. (q)

The full basic state pension has risen to £77.45 a week for single pensioners and £123.80 a week for couples from 7 April 2003. Subsequently, the basic state pension will rise each year by 2.5 per cent or the increase in the September Retail Prices Index, whichever is higher. (r)

From 6 October 2003, the Pension Credit will bring pensioners' income up to a guaranteed minimum entitlement of £102.10 a week for single pensioners and £155.80 for couples. Those aged 65 and over whose savings, second pensions or earnings give them incomes of up to around £139 a week for single pensioners and nearly £204 a week for couples will also be entitled to a reward. (s)

APPENDIX A2: EXPLAINING THE COSTINGS

This appendix explains how the Exchequer effects of the Budget measures are calculated. In the context of these calculations, the net Exchequer effects for measures may include amounts for taxes, national insurance contributions, social security benefits and other charges to the Exchequer and, for HM Customs and Excise, penalties.

Calculating the costings

The net Exchequer effect of a Budget measure is generally calculated as the difference between applying the pre-Budget and post-Budget tax and benefit regimes to the levels of total income and spending at factor cost expected after the Budget. The estimates do not therefore include any effect the tax changes themselves have on overall levels of income and spending. They do, however, take account of other effects on behaviour, where they are likely to have a significant and quantifiable effect on the yield and any consequential changes in revenue from related taxes and benefits. These include estimated changes in the composition or timing of income, spending or other tax determinants. For example, the estimated yield from increasing the excise duty on petrol includes the change in the yield of VAT and other excise duties resulting from the new pattern of spending. The calculation of the expected effect of changes in duty rates on consumer demand for excise goods, assumes that any change in duty is passed on in full to consumers. Where the effect of one tax change is affected by implementation of others, the measures are generally costed in the order in which they appear in tables A.1, A.2 and A1.1.

The non-indexed base columns in Tables A.1, A.2 and A1.1, show the revenue effect of changes in allowances, thresholds and rates of duty (including the effect of any measures previously announced but not yet implemented) from their pre-Budget level. The indexed base columns strip out the effects of inflation by increasing the allowances, thresholds and rates of duty in line with prices in this and future Budgets.

Where the Government has a policy which has been previously announced but not yet implemented, this is also stripped out of the indexed numbers. Such measures are included in tables A.2 or A1.1. Measures announced in this Budget, in table A.1, are assumed to be indexed in the same way for future Budgets.

The indexed base has been calculated on the assumption that, each year:

- income tax and national insurance contribution allowances and thresholds, and the single person, couple, lone parent and disabled worker elements of the Working Tax Credit increase in line with the annual increase in the Retail Prices Index (RPI) to the September prior to the Budget;

- the child elements of the Child Tax Credit will rise in line with the annual increase in average earnings for the lifetime of this Parliament;

- VAT thresholds and gaming duty bands rise in line with the increase in the RPI to the December prior to the Budget; and

- air passenger duty, climate change levy, vehicle excise duty and fuel, tobacco and alcohol duties all rise in line with the projected annual increase in the RPI to the September following the Budget.

Implementation dates are assumed to be: Budget day for fuel and tobacco duties; 4 days after Budget day for alcohol duties; May for amusement machine licence duty; July for insurance premium tax; November for air passenger duty; and April for all other taxes, duties and tax credits.

The yields of anti-avoidance measures represent the estimated direct effect of the measures with the existing level of activity.

These costings are shown on a National Accounts basis. The National Accounts basis aims to recognise tax when the tax liability accrues irrespective of when the tax is received by the Exchequer. However, some taxes are scored on a receipt basis, principally due to the difficulty in assessing the period to which the tax liability relates. Examples of such taxes are corporation tax, self assessment income tax, inheritance tax and capital gains tax. This approach is consistent with other government publications.

Notes on individual Budget issues

The following notes provide further information on the costings for a small number of issues, to help explain the basis for costing the particular measure, or give details of effects on government revenue in the longer term.

Capital gains tax taper relief   The cost is expected to increase to £15 million by 2008-09.

Stamp duty modernisation   The expected yield from measures to reform stamp duty on land and buildings in the UK was published in Budget 2002, when a firm announcement to introduce the reform was made. Following consultation on modernising stamp duty, this Budget confirms the details of and changes to the measures which will be implemented as part of this reform. The estimated yield, set out in table A2.1, has been revised (downwards by £10 million in 2003-04, and £100 million in 2004-05) to reflect these details and more recent data on property transactions.

Table A2.1: Effect on government revenue of stamp duty modernisation

	Indexed cost or yield (£ million) (+ve is an exchequer yield)			
	2002-03	2003-04	2004-05	2005-06
Measures enacted in Finance Act 2002	110	110	130	160
Further anti-avoidance measures	0	*	80	130
Proposed reform of lease duty	0	50	190	210
Increase of zero rate threshold to £150,000 for non-residential transfers	0	–10	–20	–20
Changes to stamp duty consideration (VAT)	0	–10	–30	–30
Alternative property finance arrangements	0	*	*	*
Total	**110**	**140**	**350**	**450**

Negligible

Capital allowances   The revenue effect of extending 100 per cent first year allowances for information and communication technology equipment for small enterprises covers both companies and unincorporated businesses. The yield is expected to decline to £20 million in 2006-07 and then slowly thereafter.

The revenue effect of the 100 per cent first year allowances for water technologies covers both companies and unincorporated businesses. The cost declines slowly after 2005-06.

Tackling VAT fraud   The estimated yield reflects the direct effects expected from these measures with the existing level of activity but excludes additional indirect revenue gains from deterrent effects. Such indirect effects cannot be separated from other indirect effects delivered within the VAT strategy.

Fuel duties The public finances currently assume that the half a penny per litre differential for sulphur-free fuels relative to ultra-low sulphur fuels will be introduced on a revenue-neutral basis. If a decision is made in the future to introduce the differential on a basis that is not revenue-neutral, the revenue impact of this decision would be set out accordingly at the time the decision is made.

APPENDIX A3: TAX ALLOWANCES AND RELIEFS

This appendix provides estimates of the revenue cost of some of the main tax allowances and reliefs.

Tax reliefs can serve a number of purposes. In some cases they may be used to assist or encourage particular individuals, activities or products. They may thus be an alternative to public expenditure. In this case they are often termed "tax expenditures". There may, for instance, be a choice between giving tax relief as an allowance or deduction against tax, or by an offsetting cash payment.

Many allowances and reliefs can reasonably be regarded (or partly regarded) as an integral part of the tax structure – called "structural reliefs". Some do no more than recognise the expense incurred in obtaining income. Others reflect a more general concept of "taxable capacity". The personal allowances are a good example: to the extent that income tax is based on ability to pay, it does not seek to collect tax from those with the smallest incomes. But even with structural reliefs of the latter kind, the Government has some discretion about the level at which they are set.

Many other reliefs combine both structural and discretionary components. Capital allowances, for example, provide relief for depreciation at a commercial rate as well as an element of accelerated relief. It is the latter element which represents additional help provided to business by the Government and is a "tax expenditure".

The loss of revenue associated with tax reliefs and allowances cannot be directly observed, and estimates have to be made. This involves calculating the amount of tax that individuals or firms would have had to pay if there were no exemptions or deductions for certain categories of income or expenditure, and comparing it with the actual amount of tax due. The Government regularly publishes estimates of tax expenditures and reliefs for both HM Customs and Excise and Inland Revenue taxes. Largely because of the difficulties of estimation, the published tables are not comprehensive but do cover the major reliefs and allowances.

The estimates in Table A3.1 below show the total cost of each relief. The classification of reliefs as tax expenditures, structural reliefs and those elements combining both is broad brush and the distinction between the expenditures and structural reliefs is not always straightforward. In many cases, the estimated costs are extremely tentative and based on simplifying assumptions. The figures make no allowance for the fact that changes in tax reliefs may cause people to change their behaviour. This means that figures in Table A3.1 are not directly comparable with those of the main Budget measures.

Estimation of behavioural effects is notoriously difficult. The sizes of behavioural changes will obviously depend on the measure examined and possible alternative behaviours. For example, removing the tax privileges of one form of saving may just lead people to switch to another form of tax privileged saving.

Table A3.1 also gives details relating to VAT, which is collected by HM Customs and Excise. It shows the estimated yield forgone by not applying the standard rate of VAT – 17.5 per cent – to goods and services which are currently zero rated, reduced rated, exempt or outside the scope of VAT. Estimates of the scale of structural reliefs for local authorities and equivalent bodies are also shown. Again, the figures are estimates and must be treated with caution. In line with the treatment of Inland Revenue taxes, they make no allowance for changes in behaviour.

The estimated costs of reliefs and allowances given in Table A3.1 cannot be added up to give a meaningful total. The combined yield of withdrawing two related allowances could differ significantly from the sum of individual costs. Similarly the sum of the costs of component parts of reliefs may differ from the total shown.

Further details on individual tax allowances and reliefs can be found in *Tax ready reckoner and tax reliefs*, published alongside the 2002 Pre-Budget Report.

Table A3.1: Estimated costs of principal tax expenditure and structural reliefs

	£ million	
	2001-02	**2002-03**
TAX EXPENDITURES		
Income tax		
Relief for:		
Approved pension schemes	13,000	13,700
Approved profit-sharing schemes	190	100
Share Incentive Plan	40	150
Approved savings-related share option schemes	240	160
Personal Equity Plans	700	575
Individual Savings Accounts	725	825
Venture Capital Trusts	60	35
Enterprise Investment Scheme	260	240
Professional subscriptions	50	50
Rent-a-room	100	100
Exemption of:		
First £30,000 of payments on termination of employment	850	850
Interest of National Savings Certificates including index-linked certificates	170	160
Tax Exempt Special Savings Account interest	150	100
Premium Bond prizes	110	90
Income of charities	850	900
Foreign service allowance paid to Crown servants abroad	70	80
First £8,000 of reimbursed relocation packages provided by employers	300	300
Tax credits:		
Life assurance premiums (for contracts made prior to 14 March 1984)	95	85
Children's Tax Credit	2,100	2,300
Working Families' Tax Credit	5,500	6,300
Disabled Person's Tax Credit	130	160
Income tax and Corporation tax		
Film tax relief	240	300
Corporation tax		
R&D Tax Credits	150	600
National insurance contributions		
Relief for:		
Approved profit-sharing schemes	130	70
Share Incentive Plan	20	90
Approved savings-related share option schemes	160	110
Employer contributions to approved pension schemes	4,800	4,900
Capital gains tax		
Exemption of gains arising on disposal of only or main residence	6,000	11,000
Retirement relief	70	30

Table A3.1: Estimated costs of principal tax expenditure and structural reliefs

	£ million	
	2001-02	2002-03
Inheritance tax		
Relief for:		
Agricultural property	110	120
Business property	110	90
Exemption of transfers to charities on death	340	330
Value added tax		
Zero-rating of:		
Food	9,150	9,350
Construction of new dwellings (includes refunds to DIY builders)	3,050	3,400
Domestic passenger transport	1,650	1,750
International passenger transport (UK portion)	200	250
Books, newspapers and magazines	1,400	1,450
Children's clothing	800	800
Water and sewerage services	950	950
Drugs and supplies on prescription	750	800
Supplies to charities	150	200
Ships and aircraft above a certain size	450	500
Vehicles and other supplies to disabled people	350	400
Lower rate on domestic fuel and power	1,750	1,850
Lower rate for certain residential conversions	100	100
STRUCTURAL RELIEFS		
Income tax		
Personal allowance	34,800	35,900
Income tax and corporation tax		
Double taxation relief	7,000	7,000
Corporation tax		
Reduced rate of corporation tax on policy holders' fraction of profit	350	150
National insurance contributions		
Contracted-out rebate occupational schemes:		
Rebates deducted at source by employers	6,600	7,470
Rebates paid by the Contributions Agency direct to the scheme	270	310
Personal pensions	2,830	3,770
Value added tax		
Refunds to:		
Northern Ireland Government bodies of VAT incurred on non-business purchases under the Section 99 refund scheme	250	250
Local Authority-type bodies of VAT incurred on non-business purchases under the Section 33 refund scheme	4,850	5,050
Central government, health authorities and NHS Trusts of VAT incurred on contracted-out services under the Section 41 (3) refund scheme	2,650	2,750

Table A3.1: Estimated costs of principal tax expenditure and structural reliefs

	£ million	
	2001-02	2002-03
RELIEFS WITH TAX EXPENDITURE AND STRUCTURAL COMPONENTS		
Income tax		
Age-related allowances	1,400	1,500
Exemption of:		
British Government securities where owner not ordinarily resident in the United Kingdom	750	750
Child Benefit (including one parent benefit)	880	920
Long-term incapacity benefit	140	170
Industrial disablement benefits	90	80
Attendance allowance	250	260
Disability living allowance	460	460
War disablement benefits	90	90
War widow's pensions	50	60
Corporation tax		
Small companies' reduced rate corporation rate	1,900	2,000
Starting rate of corporation tax	160	350
Exemption of gains on substantial shareholdings	0	170
Income tax and corporation tax		
Capital allowances, of which:	16,900	17,700
First year allowances for SMEs	230	400
First year allowances for small enterprises for information and communication technology	70	130
Enhanced capital allowances for energy saving technology	90	90
Accelerated capital allowances for Enterprise Zones	100	100
Capital gains tax		
Indexation allowance and rebasing to March 1982	300	230
Taper relief	530	600
Exemption of:		
Annual exempt amount (half of the individual's exemption for trustees)	1,050	750
Gains accrued but unrealised at death	800	550
Petroleum revenue tax		
Uplift of qualifying expenditure	180	150
Oil allowance	550	450
Safeguard: a protection for return on capital cost	275	180
Tariff receipts allowance	50	45
Exemption for gas sold to British Gas under pre-July 1975 contracts	210	120
Inheritance tax		
Nil rate band for chargeable transfers not exceeding the threshold	7,400	8,300
Exemption of transfers on death to surviving spouses	1,400	1,400
Stamp duties		
Exemption of transfers of land and property where the consideration does not exceed the £60,000 threshold	160	150
Exemption of transfers in designated disadvantaged wards where the consideration does not exceed £150,000	10	70
National insurance contributions		
Reduced contributions for self-employed not attributable to reduced benefit eligibility (constant cost basis)	2,100	1,700

Table A3.1: Estimated costs of principal tax expenditure and structural reliefs

	£ million	
	2001-02	2002-03
Value added tax		
Exemption of:		
Rent on domestic dwellings	2,600	2,750
Rent on commercial property	450	450
Private education	150	150
Health services	600	650
Postal services	400	400
Burial and cremation	100	100
Finance and insurance	2,250	2,350
Betting, gaming and lottery duties	900	900
Small traders	400	400

B THE ECONOMY

Global economic conditions have remained challenging since the 2002 Pre-Budget Report. Last year, concern over accounting scandals and tensions in the Middle East brought uncertainty and volatility to equity and oil prices. In recent months, geo-political risks, particularly surrounding hostilities in Iraq, have compounded global uncertainties. Although oil prices have now fallen back, they have recently been at their highest level for around two and a half years, and global equity and exchange rate markets have witnessed further turbulence since the time of the Pre-Budget Report. Protracted uncertainty has prompted falls in business and consumer confidence and the further deferral of business investment plans, further delaying the global recovery. Consequently, G7 growth this year is forecast to be weaker than expected in the Pre-Budget Report, with prospects for the Euro-area particularly badly affected by a combination of cyclical and structural factors.

International developments continue to be a key influence on UK economic prospects, and subdued external demand has exerted both a direct and indirect drag on GDP growth. Nonetheless, low inflation and sound public finances have allowed macroeconomic policy to support the economy during this period of global weakness and the UK has been better placed than on previous occasions to maintain growth and stability. Last year, the economy grew by 1.8 per cent, above the Pre-Budget Report forecast and behind only North America among the G7 economies. The labour market also performed strongly, with further gains in employment, and unemployment remaining at its lowest level for a generation.

Looking ahead, stronger UK growth prospects are forecast as global uncertainties diminish and the global recovery gathers pace. In the Budget:

- UK GDP is expected to grow by between 2 and 2½ per cent this year, as ongoing global uncertainty continues to subdue demand in key UK export markets and hold back business investment in the first half of the year. Subsequently, reduced uncertainty and a stronger global recovery should allow GDP to grow by 3 to 3½ per cent in both 2004 and 2005 as the economy returns to trend; and

- RPIX inflation is expected to remain a little above target in the coming months, temporarily boosted partly by housing cost effects. Thereafter, RPIX inflation is forecast to ease back as temporary factors unwind, slack in the economy puts downward pressure on domestic prices, and import prices rise. Inflation is expected to settle at target from early 2004.

As in the 2002 Pre-Budget Report, a rebalancing of growth is expected over the forecast horizon. Strengthening world conditions are expected to boost growth in manufacturing output and business investment, while consumption growth gradually reverts to more sustainable rates in response to weaker real income growth and falls in equity prices.

INTRODUCTION[1,2]

B1   This chapter discusses economic developments since the 2002 Pre-Budget Report and provides updated forecasts for the UK and world economies in the period to 2005. It begins with an overview of developments and prospects in the world economy. In the light of this, it then outlines the Government's latest assessment of the UK economy, followed by a more detailed discussion of sectoral issues and risks.

B2   The forecast assumes that geo-political uncertainties will diminish in the second half of this year, prompting a steady recovery in business and consumer confidence.

THE WORLD ECONOMY

Table B1: The world economy

	Percentage changes on a year earlier unless otherwise stated			
			Forecast	
	2002	**2003**	**2004**	**2005**
Major 7 countries[1]				
Real GDP	1½	1¾	2¾	3
Consumer price inflation[2]	1¾	1¼	1½	1½
Euro-area				
Real GDP	¾	1	2¼	2¾
World trade in goods and services	2½	4¾	8½	7¾
UK export markets[3]	1¾	4¼	7½	7

[1] G7: US, Japan, Germany, France, UK, Italy and Canada.
[2] Per cent, Q4. For UK, RPIX.
[3] Other countries' imports of goods and services weighted according to their importance in UK exports.

Overview

B3   During 2002 a number of factors compounded existing uncertainty surrounding the strength of the global recovery. A series of accounting scandals, the ongoing threat of terrorist activity and developments in the Middle East depressed business and consumer confidence across the major economies and prompted volatility in financial markets. As a result, the global recovery had less momentum during the second half of last year than had been anticipated at the time of the last Budget. Since the 2002 Pre-Budget Report, heightened concerns surrounding the conflict in Iraq have triggered a further round of volatility in financial markets. Equity prices have fallen further, oil prices reached two and a half year highs, before falling back once the conflict in Iraq began, and there have been significant movements in the major bilateral exchange rates.

B4   As expected, growth slowed across the G7 economies in the final months of 2002. However, since the turn of the year uncertainty surrounding equity markets has prompted further sharp falls in consumer confidence and weaker than expected household consumption in most of the major economies. With business confidence also remaining at low levels, and further evidence that firms are continuing to defer investment decisions, global economic activity in the first few months of 2003 is now forecast to be weaker than was anticipated at the time of the Pre-Budget Report.

---

[1] The UK forecast is consistent with national accounts and balance of payments statistics to the fourth quarter of 2002, released by the Office for National Statistics on 27 March 2003. A detailed set of charts and tables relating to the economic forecast is available on the Treasury's internet site (http://www.hm-treasury.gov.uk), and copies can be obtained on request from the Treasury's Public Enquiry Unit (020 7270 4558).
[2] The forecast is based on the assumption that the exchange rate moves in line with an uncovered interest parity condition, consistent with the interest rates underlying the economic forecast.

B5   Policy-makers around the world have responded to heightened uncertainty and the weaker near-term outlook for the global economy. Monetary policy has been loosened further in both the US and the Euro-area in recent months, while fiscal policy is continuing to support monetary policy in the US. In Europe, the automatic stabilisers have generally been allowed to work, although in 2003 a tightening of the fiscal stance is planned in some countries.

B6   Despite the weaker short-term outlook, global economic activity is expected to strengthen from the middle of 2003 as uncertainty dissipates and the recovery in the US gathers pace. However, growth in the Euro-area is now expected to be weaker than was anticipated a few months ago. The latest Consensus Forecasts[3] indicate that Euro-area GDP, which was expected to grow by 1.7 per cent in 2003 at the time of the Pre-Budget Report, is now expected to grow by around 1 per cent. The downward revision reflects the impact of a number of cyclical and structural factors, including the recent appreciation of the euro, planned fiscal consolidation in some Euro-area countries, and depressed business and consumer confidence. These ongoing downward revisions to the prospects for the Euro-area further emphasise the need for structural reform. A reduction in uncertainty remains crucial to the global economic outlook. While a stronger recovery could yet materialise should uncertainties dissipate more quickly than currently anticipated, a period of prolonged uncertainty poses the clearest downside risk to the outlook (Box B1).

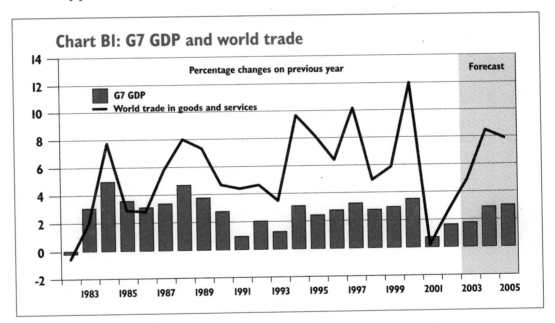

Chart B1: G7 GDP and world trade

G7 activity

B7   G7 GDP is now expected to grow by $1^3/_4$ per cent in 2003 and $2^3/_4$ per cent in 2004. In part this reflects the impact, in the first half of 2003, that heightened uncertainty surrounding events in Iraq is having on activity in the major economies. It also reflects the expectation that growth in most Euro-area economies will now be weaker throughout 2003 than was anticipated at the time of the 2002 Pre-Budget Report. Euro-area GDP is forecast to grow by 1 per cent in 2003 and by $2^1/_4$ per cent in 2004.

---

[3] *Consensus Forecasts*, Consensus Economics Inc.

B8   US GDP growth slowed in the final quarter of last year, but the first quarterly rise in business investment since early 2001 provided further evidence that a recovery is underway. In recent months, heightened concerns about the situation in Iraq have prompted a renewed bout of volatility in financial markets, and these concerns have triggered falls in consumer and business confidence. The latest retail sales and industrial activity data suggest that growth in the early months of 2003 will be slightly weaker than was anticipated at the time of the 2002 Pre-Budget Report. Nonetheless, household consumption, while weaker than previously expected, should continue to support growth, underpinned by low interest rates, tax cuts and a strong housing market. Investment growth is expected to strengthen in the second half of the year as uncertainties dissipate.

B9   Euro-area GDP growth was lower than in the US and Canada last year, and is expected to be lower again in 2003. In part this is due to lower rates of potential growth in the major Euro-area economies, especially Germany, but it is also the result of weak domestic demand. Deteriorating labour markets and increased geo-political uncertainty have already reduced consumer confidence and will continue to weigh on consumer demand in early 2003. Investment remains weak, but is expected to recover as uncertainties recede. Even some of the previously higher growth Euro-area economies, such as Portugal and the Netherlands, are expecting another year of slower growth.

B10   Stronger growth in the US remains key to an improvement in the short-term outlook for the Euro-area. However, net trade, which played an important role in supporting growth in the Euro-area last year, is likely to be adversely affected by the appreciation of the euro. While monetary policy has eased recently, national authorities plan to tighten fiscal policy in some parts of the Euro-area during 2003, particularly in Germany. More generally, Euro-area economies need further structural reform to raise potential growth rates and establish greater resilience to shocks.

B11   Last year saw a strong export-led recovery in Japan, on the back of demand from Asia and the US, but momentum slowed towards the end of the year reflecting the impact of heightened uncertainty on global economic activity. Domestic demand, which surprised on the upside in 2002, now looks set to slow, compounded by the effect of unemployment at near historical highs. Gradual implementation of the Takenaka financial and corporate sector restructuring plan, while providing a boost to medium-term prospects, will also hold back growth this year. With limited scope for further policy easing the economy remains reliant on external demand, and growth is only expected to pick up as the global recovery gathers pace during the second half of this year.

Box B1: Global uncertainty and G7 activity

A series of accounting and corporate governance scandals in the US, the threat of terrorist activity and broader geo-political risks led to sharp falls in equity prices and rises in the price of oil during 2002, depressing business and consumer confidence across the major economies. In recent months heightened concerns about the situation in Iraq have compounded the existing uncertainty. Business confidence has remained at low levels, while consumer confidence has experienced further sharp falls, with sentiment in the US and the Euro-area now at its lowest levels since the early 1990s.

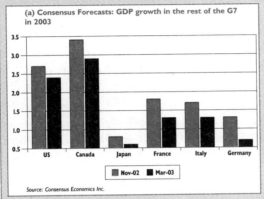

(a) Consensus Forecasts: GDP growth in the rest of the G7 in 2003

Nov-02   Mar-03

Source: Consensus Economics Inc.

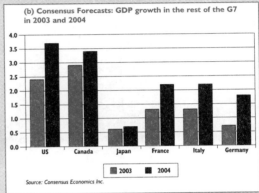

(b) Consensus Forecasts: GDP growth in the rest of the G7 in 2003 and 2004

2003   2004

Source: Consensus Economics Inc.

While forecasters expected developments in Iraq to affect the global outlook in the first few months of this year, retail sales and industrial activity data suggest the impact on activity has been greater than anticipated. As a result, independent forecasters have revised down their projections for growth during 2003 in all G7 economies, and particularly in the Euro-area, in the relatively short space of time since the Pre-Budget Report (see chart a). However, the latest Consensus Forecasts indicate that growth is still expected to recover in the second half of this year and during 2004 as the uncertainties currently affecting the outlook ease (see chart b).

In the current, highly uncertain global environment there is a wider than usual range of possible outcomes for G7 GDP growth. The scale of the recent fall in confidence raises the possibility of a period of more prolonged uncertainty and continued volatility in global financial markets. This risk is particularly pronounced in the US, where prolonged uncertainty could encourage firms to continue deferring investment decisions. Moreover, any further falls in equity prices or deterioration in the labour market could lead to slower than anticipated household consumption growth. A weaker than expected US recovery during 2003 would impact strongly on growth in the Euro-area and Japan, where domestic demand remains weak. However, there are also upside risks to the outlook. In particular, current uncertainties could recede more quickly than generally expected, with a sharper recovery in confidence and growth.

The response of policy-makers in a number of the major economies has played an important role in preventing a more severe slowdown in activity over recent years. The current uncertain environment highlights the need for policy-makers to remain vigilant to the risks facing the global economy, and stand ready to respond should the economic outlook deteriorate further over the coming months.

Emerging markets and developing countries

B12 The disappointing growth performance of emerging economies in Latin America and the Middle East during 2002 contrasted with the robust performance of Central and Eastern Europe and the relatively strong performance of Asia, particularly China. In East Asia growth was underpinned by a combination of strong domestic demand and exports, both within the region and to the US. In Sub-Saharan Africa growth during 2002 was affected by conflict, political instability and poor weather, and the challenge remains to put in place the conditions necessary to meet the Millennium Development Goals.

Box B2: Global confidence measures and growth

Measures of business and consumer confidence are often regarded as forward-looking indicators of economic activity. In the UK, consumer confidence has proven more robust than business confidence during the course of the global slowdown, as a strong labour market and continued house price gains have helped to cushion household wealth from the impact of declines on equity markets. More recently, however, UK consumer confidence has shown signs of easing. This pattern is repeated elsewhere, with sentiment in the US and the Euro-area declining to its lowest since the early to mid-1990s.

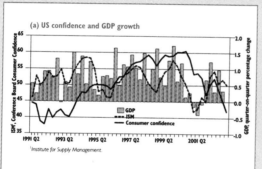

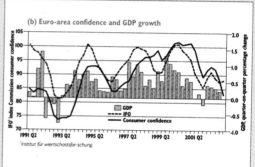

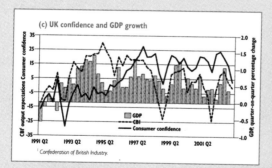

These trends have been driven by a number of factors, including ongoing uncertainty surrounding events in Iraq, and further sharp falls on equity markets. In the UK, these factors have led to a reduction in households' confidence about general economic prospects, but have had a more modest impact on households' perceptions of their own financial position.

There are some signs that activity has weakened in the past couple of months. However, despite recent uncertainties, both consumer and business confidence measures remain above the levels seen in the early 1990s. Moreover, as the charts illustrate, while the correlation between confidence and growth over the medium to long term is reasonably close, in the short term confidence can often prove more sensitive than GDP to temporary factors. For example, although business confidence fell sharply in the UK, the US and the Euro-area at the peak of Asian financial crisis in late 1998, this had little impact on growth in each of these areas. Similarly, US GDP growth picked up sharply in the early 1990s despite consumer confidence taking much longer to recover.

B13   In general, those emerging economies with robust macroeconomic frameworks and sustainable exchange rate regimes appear to have coped better with increased volatility in global financial markets. The possibility of a further deterioration in global activity and an increase in risk aversion among investors pose a clear risk to the outlook. The conflict in Iraq poses a further threat to those economies with trade links in the region, as well as to those with high oil import requirements, heavy reliance on tourism receipts or significant external financing needs. Any significant increase in the incidence of Severe Acute Respiratory Syndrome (SARS) currently concentrated within Asia, could pose a further risk to the economic outlook in the region.

World trade

B14   As anticipated at the time of the Pre-Budget Report, world trade growth slowed during the second half of 2002. In line with the forecast pick-up in global activity, world trade is now expected to grow by 4³/₄ per cent in 2003 and 8¹/₂ per cent in 2004, somewhat slower than expected at the time of the Pre-Budget Report. UK export market growth is also now expected to be slightly weaker, reflecting the impact of weaker growth in the Euro-area.

Oil and commodity prices

B15   The price of oil rose sharply during the final months of 2002, reflecting heightened concerns surrounding the situation in the Middle East and the impact of the strike in Venezuela. While the oil price has fallen back in recent weeks, developments in the Middle East could result in higher and more volatile oil prices over the forecast period. As at the time of the 2002 Pre-Budget Report, non-oil commodity prices are expected to strengthen in line with the global recovery.

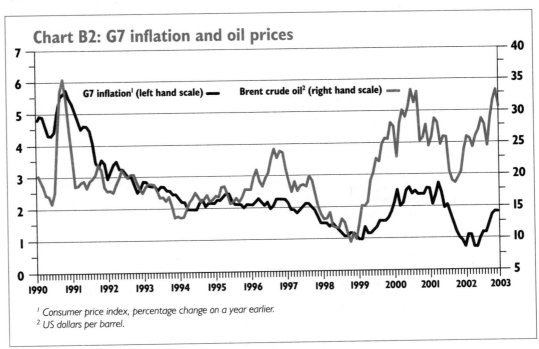

Chart B2: G7 inflation and oil prices

G7 inflation[1] (left hand scale) ▬   Brent crude oil[2] (right hand scale) ▬

[1] Consumer price index, percentage change on a year earlier.
[2] US dollars per barrel.

G7 inflation

B16   Underlying inflationary pressures remain weak in most G7 economies, reflecting the existence of small negative output gaps in most cases. G7 inflation rose around the turn of the year as a result of movements in energy prices, but is expected to fall back during 2003 before settling at $1\frac{1}{2}$ per cent in 2004 as the recovery gathers pace.

Forecast issues and risks

B17   In recent months, heightened concerns about the situation in Iraq have clearly added to the uncertainties already surrounding the global economic outlook. These uncertainties are expected to ease during 2003, but a period of prolonged uncertainty, accompanied by continued volatility in financial markets, weaker equity prices and higher oil prices, poses the clearest downside risk to G7 activity.

B18   The persistent US current account deficit, and the emergence of projected fiscal deficits over the coming years, pose the additional risk of a sudden, sharp fall in the value of the dollar. In Germany, persistent high levels of unemployment and fears about job security continue to pose a downside risk to household consumption growth and raise concerns about more significant structural weaknesses. In Japan, rigorous implementation of the Takenaka plan, while providing a much-needed boost to Japan's medium-term prospects, would further depress activity in the short term.

B19   On the upside, the various uncertainties currently affecting the outlook could dissipate more quickly, and confidence could recover more sharply, than anticipated. Moreover, the recently announced fiscal stimulus package in the US, combined with low interest rates and a strong housing market, could lead to stronger than expected household consumption growth, with knock-on effects to other major economies. Further evidence of strong productivity growth in the US also raises the possibility that other economies might emulate recent information and communication technology (ICT) related improvements. Decisive structural reform in Europe and financial restructuring in Japan could provide a further boost to world growth prospects in the medium term.

UK ECONOMY OVERVIEW

Summary

B20   International developments continue to be a key influence on UK economic prospects, and recently ongoing global uncertainty and subdued external demand have continued to depress UK business confidence and hold back investment and exports. Nonetheless, low inflation and sound public finances have allowed macroeconomic policy to support the economy during this period of global weakness, so that the UK has been better placed than on previous occasions to maintain growth and stability. Interest rates are now at their lowest level for almost fifty years while fiscal policy has supported monetary policy in sustaining domestic demand. A robust labour market and sound economic fundamentals have also helped to support private consumption and offset the drag on growth from global weakness.

B21   Whereas UK GDP growth over the past year has been stronger than in late 2001 and early 2002, in the immediate wake of the events of 11 September 2001, prospects for the UK economy will continue to depend heavily on global developments. UK GDP is expected to accelerate in the second half of 2003 as international uncertainty recedes and the pace of the world recovery strengthens. Growth is also expected to become more balanced over the forecast horizon as deferred business investment comes back on stream, exports pick up in response to stronger global demand, and private consumption growth moderates. Inflation is expected to remain low and close to the Government's target throughout the forecast period.

Table B2: Summary of forecast

| | 2002 | Forecast | | |
		2003	2004	2005
GDP growth (per cent)	1¾	2 to 2½	3 to 3½	3 to 3½
RPIX inflation (per cent, Q4)	2½	2¾	2½	2½

Recent developments

B22   The uncertain global environment that influenced UK economic prospects throughout last year has continued into 2003. Heightened geo-political risks – particularly surrounding events in Iraq – a renewal of turbulence on equity markets, and concerns about the need for further structural reform in the Euro-area, have affected perceptions of the world economic outlook over recent months. This uncertainty, combined with an already sluggish global recovery, has kept business confidence subdued and discouraged firms from bringing deferred investment projects back on stream.

B23   Nevertheless, the UK economy continues to sustain its longest unbroken economic expansion since quarterly GDP records began almost 50 years ago. For the second year running, the UK economy has continued to grow in circumstances of weak global demand and faltering investment, in contrast to the experience of many other industrialised countries and of past world slowdowns (Box B3). With inflation remaining close to target, the Monetary Policy Committee (MPC) of the Bank of England has cut short-term interest rates to their lowest level for almost 50 years. Government spending has also supported domestic demand, with government consumption rising by 3¾ per cent in 2002, its strongest growth since the mid-1970s; and government investment rising by over 9 per cent, its strongest since the early 1990s. These factors helped offset the impact on GDP of declining business investment – experienced in the UK as in most other major economies. This contrasts markedly with previous occasions when falls in corporate capital expenditure have translated into an absolute decline in GDP.

Box B3: Recent growth performance of the major economies

World economic growth slowed sharply in 2001 as the global boom in ICT investment underwent an abrupt correction and equity prices came off their historic peaks. Although a recovery began in 2002, economic and geo-political uncertainties reduced its momentum over the second half of the year.

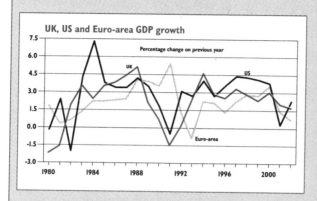

While the highly open UK economy was bound to be affected during this period of global weakness, growth in the UK has proved to be among the most resilient of all major industrialised economies. The UK grew faster than any other G7 country during 2001 and faster than all but North America during 2002. Most forecasters expect the UK and North America to lead the G7 again in 2003.

This experience contrasts favourably with that of previous world slowdowns, during which the UK often fared worse than other industrialised economies. Between the late 1980s and the early 1990s G7 growth fell sharply, from 3.7 per cent in 1989 to just 0.9 per cent in 1991. In the US, GDP contracted by 0.5 per cent during 1991, significantly less than in the UK, where output fell by 1.4 per cent – the largest annual fall in output of any G7 economy bar Canada throughout the whole of the 1990s. This clear distinction between past and present performance provides further evidence that the Government's reforms have greatly enhanced the UK's ability to weather difficult global conditions.

B24 GDP grew by 0.4 per cent in the final quarter of 2002, broadly as expected at the time of the 2002 Pre-Budget Report, to stand 2.2 per cent higher than a year earlier. While this compares with quarterly growth of 1.1 per cent in the third quarter, and 0.6 per cent in the second, the Golden Jubilee celebrations last year affected the quarterly pattern of growth, reducing activity in June. Underlying GDP growth in the second quarter was therefore probably stronger than headline estimates suggest, at between $3/4$ and $1^1/4$ per cent, with underlying growth in the third quarter correspondingly weaker. Nonetheless, even allowing for Jubilee effects, GDP growth since last spring has been stronger than in late 2001 and early 2002, when uncertainty in the wake of the events of 11 September 2001 is likely to have had its most direct impact on economic activity. In 2002 as a whole, UK GDP increased by 1.8 per cent, above the 2002 Pre-Budget Report forecast and behind only North America among the G7 economies.

B25 Private consumption growth more than accounted for the increase in GDP last year, and government consumption also made a positive contribution to growth, together outweighing the negative contributions from investment and trade. With employment continuing to grow and interest rates low, consumers retained a high degree of confidence in the outlook for their own finances, though this has eased back since the turn of the year. Strong house price inflation also helped sustain growth in consumer spending, offsetting the negative impact of declining equity values on total household wealth, while mortgage equity withdrawal added a further stimulus to consumption.

B26 Nonetheless, growth in private consumption has progressively eased back from its peak in 2000, to below 4 per cent last year, and there have been signs of a further moderation in recent months. Retail sales, for example, were broadly unchanged between October 2002 and February 2003. Slower consumption growth, as consumers adjust expenditure patterns to reductions in financial wealth and real income growth, is consistent with previous forecasts, and desirable to the extent that it reflects an orderly adjustment of the household sector's balance sheet. Consumption growth in excess of the economy's trend growth rate, as for the past seven years, cannot be sustained indefinitely.

B27 The UK labour market has continued to go from strength to strength, providing further evidence of the success of the Government's labour market polices. Continued strong growth in employment alongside a substantial rise in the population of working age – characteristic of a strong labour market – has been in stark contrast to the 1980s, when a rising population led to high unemployment before employment adjusted. Over the past year employment has increased by over $1/4$ million, to stand over $1\frac{1}{2}$ million up since early 1997. The employment rate has also risen, particularly since the middle of last year, and over this period earlier small rises in unemployment have reversed leaving the unemployment rate at its lowest for a generation.

B28 RPIX inflation averaged 2.2 per cent in 2002, though it has risen steadily since last summer and in recent months has been slightly above the Government's symmetric $2\frac{1}{2}$ per cent target. Strong growth in house prices – which affect the housing depreciation component of the index – has been the largest single contributor to this rise. By contrast, the Harmonised Index of Consumer Prices (HICP) – which excludes components of housing costs included in RPIX, most notably housing depreciation – has remained a good deal more stable over the past year. UK HICP inflation stood at just 1.6 per cent in February, a fraction above its level a year earlier and significantly below both the EU and Euro-area averages.

B29 While higher oil prices have led to increased petrol and fuel costs, goods inflation remains muted and prices in February were practically unchanged on those a year earlier. Excluding petrol and oil prices, the divergence between goods and services inflation remains historically high, with services inflation standing at 4.5 per cent in February.

B30 As elsewhere in the world, heightened global uncertainty and faltering external demand have continued to undermine private investment intentions, providing strong incentive to defer. With growth in the economy temporarily below trend, businesses have been able to meet demand from within existing capacity, further reducing the need to undertake new capital spending. Business investment declined by 8 per cent in 2002, a smaller fall than that projected in the 2002 Pre-Budget Report forecast. Nevertheless it has shown signs of bottoming out, with a broadly flat quarterly profile since early last year.

B31 While net trade made a significant positive contribution to GDP growth in the second quarter of last year – its largest for three years – latest trade data suggest that a loss of momentum in the global recovery from the middle of 2002 exerted a significant drag on UK exports. In 2002 as a whole, goods and services export volumes were 1 per cent lower than in 2001. With imports picking up slightly through the year, the overall trade deficit widened by over £3 billion between the first and second halves of 2002 as an increased deficit on merchandise trade more than offset a higher surplus on trade in services. Nonetheless, at £18.9 billion, the trade in goods and services deficit in 2002 was around £$3\frac{1}{4}$ billion lower than that in 2001.

The labour market

B32 Despite continued global economic weakness, the UK labour market appears to have strengthened since last summer, providing further evidence of significant supply-side improvements brought about by the Government's policies to deliver employment opportunity for all. Recent labour market performance also differentiates the UK from many other industrialised countries.

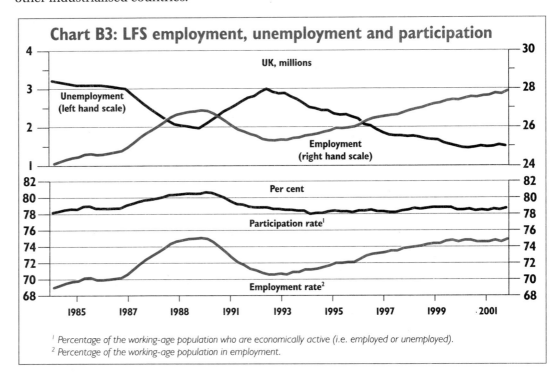

Chart B3: LFS employment, unemployment and participation

[1] *Percentage of the working-age population who are economically active (i.e. employed or unemployed).*
[2] *Percentage of the working-age population in employment.*

B33 Recent months have seen the level of unemployment fall back sharply. On the International Labour Organisation (ILO) definition, unemployment fell by 73,000 in the three months to January to stand 28,000 lower than a year earlier, more than reversing the temporary increase witnessed in the early part of 2002. At 5.0 per cent, ILO unemployment is now the lowest among the G7 economies. Claimant count unemployment has also fallen steadily since last summer, to levels last seen a generation ago, and since early 2001 it has remained below one million for the first time since 1975.

B34 Over the first nine months of last year, a sharp increase in the population of working age was mainly absorbed in higher part-time employment, with the numbers of those in full-time work declining slightly between the fourth quarter of 2001 and the third quarter of 2002. Since then, full-time employment has also expanded, rising by 121,000 in the three months to January compared with the previous three months and more than reversing the decline seen over much of last year. While part-time employment has continued to rise, the proportion of these workers who would prefer to occupy full-time positions remains at record lows, suggesting that the labour market has become more responsive to individuals' needs and circumstances.

B35 Total employment rose by 150,000 between the third and fourth quarters of last year – the largest quarterly rise for almost six years and the second largest since publication of quarterly employment estimates commenced in 1992. The employment rate has also begun to rise again: at 74.6 per cent in recent months it is around $\frac{1}{4}$ percentage points up on a year earlier.

B36   Growth in public sector employment has been a key influence on the labour market, with employment growth in public administration, education and health averaging almost 40,000 a quarter over the past year (on the workforce jobs measure, which has indicated weaker employment growth than the Labour Force Survey measure over this period). Sectors that have seen falls in employment over the past year or so correspond closely with those most affected by international uncertainty, including financial services and manufacturing. The reduction in hours worked over the course of the global slowdown has yet to reverse, with total hours worked broadly flat over the past year and significantly down on the peaks seen between the end of 2000 and mid-2001. This supports the view that the labour market has become significantly more flexible in recent years, and that companies, in choosing to reduce hours rather than staffing levels, have continued confidence in the medium-term prospects for the UK economy.

B37   With GDP expanding and the number of hours worked depressed by the effects of global economic fragility, output per hour worked has picked up since 2001, rising by 1.7 per cent in the year to the final quarter of last year.

B38   Average earnings growth remains below the $4^{1}/_{2}$ per cent level deemed by the MPC to be consistent with the Government's inflation target in the medium term, with the rate excluding bonuses averaging just under 4 per cent since last summer. Private sector earnings growth has recently fallen to around 3 per cent under the influence of lower bonus payments than a year earlier, though excluding bonuses the rate has also been subdued, within the range of $3^{1}/_{2}$ to 4 per cent since last summer. Public sector earnings growth has tended to be stronger, after adjusting for the effects of the delayed settlement for local authority workers which depressed the figures through the middle of last year, and has been running at around 5 per cent in latest months. However, it remains significantly lower than throughout most of 2001 and appears to pose very little near-term risk to overall earnings or inflation prospects. Public sector earnings are discussed further in Box B4.

B39   Despite growth in manufacturing output lagging that in the service sector, average earnings growth in private sector services has recently fallen to about $2^{1}/_{2}$ per cent, well below that in manufacturing where the rate has been around 4 per cent. The fall back in private services is largely accounted for by bonuses, but the relatively strong growth in manufacturing earnings may at least partly reflect a strong pick-up in manufacturing productivity during 2002, with annual growth in output per worker recently at its strongest for over a year and a half. As a result, steady growth in manufacturing earnings has not put any significant upward pressure on unit wage costs, which remain virtually unchanged on a year earlier.

Box B4: Public sector employment and earnings

In order to deliver the Government's aim of improving the quality of public services, the public sector needs to be able to recruit and retain skilled and motivated staff. At the same time, the expansion of the public sector needs to be accommodated within the Government's broader economic objectives.

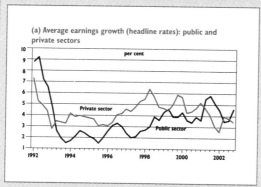

(a) Average earnings growth (headline rates): public and private sectors

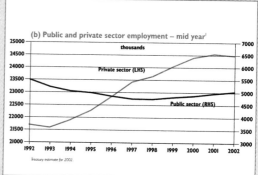

(b) Public and private sector employment – mid year[1]

From the early 1990s until 2001, public sector earnings growth consistently lagged behind that in the private sector by a considerable margin. Private sector annual earnings growth between 1993 and 2000 averaged 4¼ per cent, compared with less than 3 per cent in the public sector. This tended to lower the level of public relative to private sector earnings, increasing the more recent challenge of attracting and retaining the skilled staff necessary to deliver the Government's priorities for improving public services.

Over the past two years, however, earnings growth in the public sector has run ahead of that in the private sector, coinciding with rising public sector employment as the Government's spending plans have come on stream. Indeed public sector employment has been rising since 1999, at about 1½ per cent a year on average, following years of decline. Nonetheless, the differential of public over private sector pay growth, while facilitating a substantial expansion in public services, remains modest, at approximately 1 percentage point in recent months. Moreover, overall growth in whole economy headline average earnings, at around 3½ per cent, has encouraged rather than posed a threat to employment.

Looking ahead, government departments have estimated that an increase in public sector employment of over 200,000 between 2003 and 2006 will be needed to deliver 2002 Spending Review commitments on public services. Departments are preparing pay and workforce strategies, which will help firm up these estimates. This implies an average increase of about 70,000, or just under 1½ per cent, a year. Against the background of recent favourable labour market developments, in particular for average earnings, and trend employment projections, such increases in public sector employment are realistic and achievable within cash spending plans.

Trend output growth

B40 Since the 2002 Pre-Budget Report, revisions have been made by the ONS to GDP from the start of 2001. Table B3 updates historical and forward-looking estimates of the composition of trend output growth in the light of these revised data. However, the revisions have not affected the estimate of trend output growth over the recent past (the first half of 1997 to the third quarter of 2001).

Table B3: Contributions to trend output growth[1]

	Estimated trend rates of growth, per cent per annum					
	Trend output per hour worked[2,3]		Trend average hours worked[3]	Trend employment rate[3]	Population of working age[4]	**Trend output**
	Underlying (1)	Actual (2)	(3)	(4)	(5)	(6)
1986 Q2 to 1997 H1	2.21	2.01	−0.14	0.41	0.22	**2.51**
Over the recent past						
1997 H1 to 2001 Q3						
Budget 2002	2.14	1.96	−0.37	0.36	0.66	**2.63**
PBR 2002	2.35	2.14	−0.47	0.43	0.50	**2.61**
Budget 2003	2.35	2.14	−0.47	0.43	0.50	**2.61**
Projection[5]						
2001 Q4 to 2006 Q4						
Budget 2002	2.1	2.0	−0.1	0.2	0.6	**2¾**
PBR 2002	2.35	2.25	−0.1	0.2	0.5	**2¾**
Budget 2003	2.35	2.25	−0.1	0.2	0.5	**2¾**

[1] *Treasury analysis based on the judgement that 1986 Q2, 1997 H1, and 2001 Q3 were on-trend points of the output cycle. Figures independently rounded. Trend output growth is estimated as growth of non-oil gross value added between on-trend points for the past, and by projecting components going forward. Columns (2)+(3)+(4)+(5)=(6). Full data definitions and sources are set out in Annex A of 'Trend Growth: Recent Developments and Prospects', HM Treasury, April 2002.*

[2] *The underlying trend rate is the actual trend rate adjusted for changes in the employment rate, i.e. assuming the employment rate had remained constant. Column (1)=column (2) + (1-a) column (4), where a is the ratio of new to average worker productivity levels. The figuring is consistent with this ratio being of the order of 50 per cent, informed by econometric evidence and LFS data on relative entry wages.*

[3] *The decomposition makes allowance for the employment rate and average hours worked lagging output. Employment is assumed to lag output by around three quarters, so that on-trend points for employment come three quarters after on-trend points for output, an assumption which can be supported by econometric evidence. Hours are easier to adjust than employment, and the decomposition assumes that hours lag output by just one quarter, though this lag is hard to support by econometric evidence, not least because quarterly LFS data only extend as far back as 1992 Q2. Hours worked and the employment rate are measured on a working-age basis.*

[4] *UK household basis.*

[5] *Neutral case assumptions for trend from 2001Q3 and underlying the mid-points of the GDP forecast growth ranges from 2002 Q4.*

Output and demand

B41 No change in the assessment of the economy's on-trend points since the 2002 Pre-Budget Report means that the start of the current cycle is still provisionally judged to have been in mid-1999. GDP growth was below its neutral trend rate of 2¾ per cent in 2002 implying a widening negative output gap since the economy was last estimated to have been on trend, in the third quarter of 2001. However, the gap at the end of last year is now a little smaller than estimated at the time of the Pre-Budget Report, reflecting the recent revisions to GDP data. The output gap is likely to widen a little further in the short term. From the second half of 2003 the output gap is expected to narrow, as the economy grows at above trend rates.

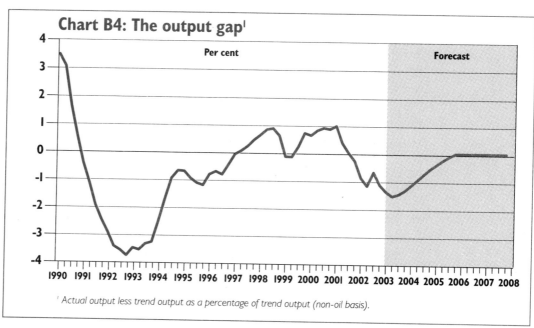

Chart B4: The output gap¹

Per cent

Forecast

¹ Actual output less trend output as a percentage of trend output (non-oil basis).

B42   The combination of sluggish external demand and global uncertainties that strongly shaped developments in 2002 has continued to dominate UK prospects into this year. With hostilities in Iraq ongoing, uncertainty over the geo-political situation, and its potential economic implications, has continued to affect the confidence of the UK corporate sector, and in recent months there has been some emerging evidence that the uncertain global outlook may also be adversely affecting consumer sentiment.

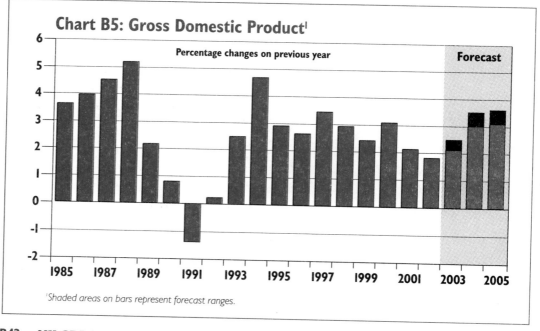

Chart B5: Gross Domestic Product¹

Percentage changes on previous year

Forecast

¹Shaded areas on bars represent forecast ranges.

B43   UK GDP is now expected to rise by 2 to 2½ per cent this year, below its trend rate of growth of 2¾ per cent and the 2002 Pre-Budget Report forecast. This reflects the weaker near-term outlook for the world economy, and especially the UK's key export markets, combined with a continued short-term drag on investment arising from ongoing global uncertainty. However, GDP is expected to accelerate in the second half of 2003 and into 2004, as international uncertainty gradually abates and the expected gathering in the pace of the global economic recovery feeds through. GDP is therefore forecast to increase by 3 to 3½ per cent both next year and the year after, as the economy returns to trend by the end of 2005.

B44   The rebound in confidence as geo-political uncertainties are resolved might be stronger and faster than assumed, leading the output gap to diminish more quickly, with growth faster than projected. Alternatively, the effects of geo-political uncertainty and financial market volatility might, however, be less transitory than assumed. Firms and households could take a more cautious approach to spending decisions both in the UK and other economies, especially if hostilities in Iraq prove more protracted than generally assumed or in the event of terrorist reprisals. This would tend to prolong the economy's return to trend, though to the extent that this would put downward pressure on inflation, there would be some offset from lower interest rates to keep inflation on target.

B45   From this year onwards household consumption is forecast to grow at close to sustainable rates, ending seven years of unsustainable growth and completing the slowdown that began in 2001. Consumers are expected to adjust their expenditure with a lag to weaker real disposable income gains, and reductions in financial wealth following falls in equity prices over recent years. With the ratio of their debt to income at a historically high level, the current economic climate is likely to deter households from wanting to take on further debt.

B46   Ongoing global uncertainty has further affected the short-term outlook for business investment into 2003. With equity and other financial market prices undergoing a further bout of turbulence, and companies still uncertain about near-term global prospects and the duration and impact of hostilities in Iraq, the international environment has continued to make firms extremely hesitant about committing to new capital outlays.

B47   In 2003 as a whole, business investment is forecast to show a small fall on 2002, with some further weakening in the first half, despite its broadly flat path in previous quarters. However, with firms having largely tackled the significant levels of borrowing built up following the late 1990s' ICT boom, the marked improvement in the health of corporate balance sheets suggests that the foundations are largely in place for business investment to make a convincing recovery as global uncertainty lifts and a stronger world environment takes hold. Thus business investment is expected to pick-up from mid-2003 and accelerate into next year as diminished uncertainty in the global outlook encourages firms to continue bringing deferred expenditure back on stream. With government investment continuing to rise strongly, particularly this year, as a result of the Government's spending plans, whole economy fixed capital formation is expected to grow significantly faster than GDP in all forecast years.

B48   Manufacturing activity has remained weak. Despite rebounding in the third quarter, following a sharp fall in output in June as factories closed down for the Jubilee holidays, manufacturing output registered a further modest decline in the final quarter of 2002. Faced with fragile external demand and significant ongoing risks to the global outlook, manufacturers have continued to meet demand partly from existing inventories, rather than by stepping up production. In the final quarter of 2002, manufacturing output was 1.6 per cent lower than a year earlier; the larger fall of 4 per cent between 2001 and 2002 as a whole largely reflects the steep fall during 2001 rather than declines in the course of 2002.

B49   Abstracting from Jubilee effects, the recent trend in overall manufacturing output appears to have been broadly flat, with output in the three months to February this year only fractionally lower than a year earlier. The aggregate figures also continue to mask divergences within the sector. Output of chemicals-related industries remains higher than when the world slowdown began in 2001 while transport equipment has also made solid gains over the past year. Indeed, almost a half of the manufacturing sector registered higher output in the three months to February than a year earlier.

B50 Business survey results have pointed to further subdued manufacturing activity in recent months. Overall, however, business survey indicators have only given a very rough approximation of near-term manufacturing trends over the past year or so.

B51 Strengthening external demand from around the second half of 2003 is expected to underpin a recovery in the manufacturing sector through this year and into 2004, with the recent weakening of sterling against the euro likely to give a further fillip to the recovery in the sector. At the same time, the pick up in business investment, and an associated upswing in demand for ICT equipment, should provide additional impetus to manufacturing production going forward. Manufacturing output is expected to grow by $^1/_4$ to $^3/_4$ per cent this year, rising to $2^1/_4$ to $2^3/_4$ per cent in 2004 before easing back to growth of $1^3/_4$ to $2^1/_4$ per cent in 2005, below the trend rate of growth of the economy reflecting the long-established shift in industrial composition towards services.

Box B5: Developments in the construction sector

The UK construction industry accounts for around five per cent of UK GDP and employs 1.9 million people. UK designers, civil engineers, contractors and component and product manufacturers have first class reputations worldwide and are heavily engaged in both overseas, as well as domestic, construction projects.

In 2002, construction output saw its sharpest increase since 1988 with growth of 7½ per cent, significantly above that of the service sector and other areas of production. Construction output last year accounted for around a third of total output growth – its largest contribution to overall growth for fourteen years. This followed robust growth through 2001, when the level of construction output surpassed its previous peak in 1990 for the first time.

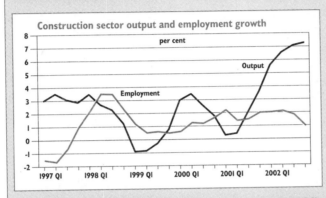

Construction sector output and employment growth

Progress towards realising the Government's commitments on public sector investment has been a key factor underpinning growth in construction output over the past two years. In 2002, total infrastructure output in current prices rose by over 13 per cent, with four fifths of the growth coming from public sector works, largely reflecting a 27 per cent increase in road construction. At the same time, public sector construction output, outside of infrastructure and housing, also rose strongly, increasing by almost 30 per cent compared with 2001. Schools and colleges made the strongest contribution, as investment in higher education continued to come on stream, while construction contracts signed under the Private Finance Initiative have also boosted activity. The construction of health facilities meanwhile rose by almost a quarter last year.

Nonetheless, there have also been areas of strong private sector demand for construction. Railway infrastructure output rose by 26 per cent in 2002, and has more than doubled in the past two years reflecting the upgrading and maintenance of the national network. Construction of entertainment facilities and shops rose by 16 and 27 per cent respectively.

Strong growth in construction sector output, together with continued robust growth in employment, which has risen by around 8¼ per cent since 1997, have begun to be reflected in emerging capacity pressures. For example, the Construction Trends Survey for the fourth quarter of 2002 reported that 59 per cent of building companies and 54 per cent of civil engineering contractors were working at, or close to, full capacity. Moreover, the Chartered Institute of Purchasing and Supply Managers (CIPS) Report on Construction for March indicated that supplier delivery times in the sector were continuing to lengthen. Capacity constraints also appear to be spilling over into prices: producer input prices for construction materials rose by 4½ per cent in the year to February, with the CIPS survey also showing input prices rising at a faster rate in recent months.

B52 A sustained turnaround in UK export volumes is dependent on a gathering in the strength of external demand growth. Goods and service export volumes are forecast to rise by $1^{1}/_{4}$ to $1^{1}/_{2}$ per cent this year, slightly below 2002 Pre-Budget Report projections as a result of a less pronounced pick-up in UK export market growth in the first half of the year. Exports are then expected to accelerate strongly through 2004 as the expansion in world trade gathers further momentum and the gain in competitiveness from the recent weakening of sterling against the euro begins to feed through. The UK's market share is expected to flatten out as the forecast period extends.

B53 Import growth beyond 2003 is forecast to be somewhat less than that of exports. The pick-up in UK business investment and manufacturing output are expected to stimulate a strengthening of import growth from around the middle of this year, on the back of higher demand for capital equipment and manufactured components. However, the rate of import growth is expected to stay below the sharp rates registered during most of the late 1990s, as the increasing share of government spending in GDP, which tends to have a lower import content than private sector expenditure, reduces import growth relative to that of GDP. Net trade is therefore forecast to make a relatively modest negative contribution to growth over the forecast horizon.

B53 The forecast contributions to GDP growth for the various components of demand are shown in Table B4.

Table B4: Contributions to GDP[1] growth[2,3]

| | Percentage points unless otherwise stated | | | |
| | | Forecast | | |
	2002	2003	2004	2005
Private consumption	$2^{3}/_{4}$	2	$1^{3}/_{4}$	2
Business investment	-1	$-^{1}/_{4}$	$^{1}/_{2}$	$^{3}/_{4}$
Government	$^{3}/_{4}$	$1^{1}/_{2}$	1	$^{3}/_{4}$
Change in inventories	0	0	0	0
Net trade (goods and services)	-1	$-1^{1}/_{4}$	$-^{1}/_{4}$	$-^{1}/_{4}$
GDP growth, per cent	$1^{3}/_{4}$	$2^{1}/_{4}$	$3^{1}/_{4}$	$3^{1}/_{4}$

[1] At constant market prices.

[2] Components may not sum due to rounding and omission of private residential investment, the transfer costs of land and existing buildings and the statistical discrepancy.

[3] Based on central case. For the purpose of public finance projections, forecasts are based on the bottom of the forecast GDP range.

Box B6: Chain-linking the UK national accounts

From September 2003, the Office for National Statistics (ONS) will introduce a new method, called annual chain-linking, for calculating the volume measure of real GDP and its components. This method will be used to revise past data as well as to provide latest estimates, and may possibly change measured GDP growth rates to an extent that could affect the interpretation of recent economic history.

Chain-linking uses annually updated 'current' price weights to value the contribution of individual products to total real GDP growth, in contrast to the existing practice of measuring real GDP using the relative prices of a single base year, currently 1995. In the past this base year has been periodically, but not annually, updated.

A key problem with the existing measure of real GDP is that it is prone to bias. The current base year of 1995 is now eight years ago. Relative prices have changed for a number of reasons, for example because some goods, such as electronic consumer goods, can now be produced much more cheaply, or because new products have entered the market. So the 1995 relative price weights no longer reflect the relative value of goods today.

Thus the move to chain-linking will represent a marked methodological improvement in measuring real GDP growth. It is recognised as international best practice, and is a requirement of the European System of Accounts 1995 national accounting standard. Some non-European countries, such as the USA, have also adopted chain-linked volume measures.

Guidance on the possible impact of the introduction of annual chain-linking on measured real GDP growth has been published by the ONS[1]. Chain-linking will not, of course, affect nominal aggregates, including estimates of the public finances.

[1] For example, "The effects of annual chain linking on the output measure of GDP", A. Tuke and G. Reed, Economic Trends, No.575, October 2001.

Inflation

B54 Underlying inflation in the UK remains firmly in check. RPIX inflation, the Government's target measure, averaged 2.2 per cent last year. The average rate of UK HICP inflation over the past three years, at just 1.1 per cent, has been lower than in any other European Union country.

B55 RPIX inflation in February was slightly above target, at 3.0 per cent, whereas HICP inflation stood at 1.6 per cent. Strong house price gains in the second half of last year have temporarily lifted the contribution of housing costs to the 12-month RPIX inflation rate. Petrol prices have also contributed significantly to the recent uplift in inflation as the effects of sharply higher oil prices on a year earlier have fed through.

B56 Other temporary factors appear to have given an additional lift to inflation in February. In particular anecdotal evidence suggests that the New Year sales, especially for clothing and footwear, got underway earlier and ended sooner this season than last, when sales lingered into February, boosting the February inflation rate.

B57 Increases in oil prices have also been the main factor underpinning a pick-up in manufacturers' input costs in recent months, with material and fuel costs rising almost 6 per cent in the year to February, their fastest rate for over a year and a half. However, excluding erratic food, beverages, tobacco and petroleum prices, a still uncertain world outlook has kept underlying producer price inflation subdued, with input prices just 0.4 per cent higher in the year to February.

B58 House price inflation has moderated from its recent peaks in the second half of 2002, when annual price rises reached between 25 and 30 per cent. Monthly rates of growth have eased back, suggesting that the peak in the housing market has now passed. In the three months to March, the Nationwide House Price Index stood 4.4 per cent higher than in the previous three months, a significant moderation compared with its latest three month on three month peak of 7.7 per cent in August.

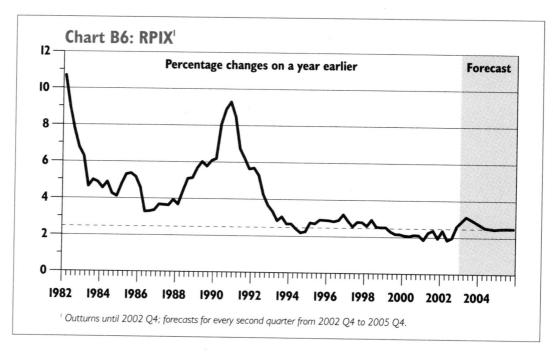

Chart B6: RPIX[1]

Percentage changes on a year earlier

Forecast

[1] *Outturns until 2002 Q4; forecasts for every second quarter from 2002 Q4 to 2005 Q4.*

Box B7: Measuring inflation

The inflation rate targeted by the Bank of England is the Retail Prices Index excluding mortgage interest payments (RPIX). RPIX inflation averaged 2.2 per cent last year. Although it has risen to 3.0 per cent in February of this year, reflecting strong house price gains and higher oil prices feeding through to increases in petrol prices, RPIX inflation is forecast to fall back to its 2.5 per cent target by the first half of next year.

An alternative measure of inflation, used for comparisons within the European Union, is the Harmonised Index of Consumer Prices (HICP)[1]. In 2002, HICP inflation averaged 1.3 per cent. The current rate of UK HICP inflation is 1.6 per cent.

The differences between HICP inflation and RPIX inflation can be primarily explained by:

- a **formula effect**, from individual prices in the HICP being aggregated by a geometric mean rather than the arithmetic mean used in the RPIX; and

- a **coverage effect**, primarily arising from the inclusion in RPIX of some components of housing costs that are excluded from the HICP. There are also some less significant differences in coverage arising from expenditure patterns used to weight the indices. For example, RPIX excludes expenditure by the richest 4 per cent of households, most pensioners and overseas visitors.

While the current differential between HICP and RPIX is 1.4 percentage points, this gap is expected to narrow as house price inflation moderates. The Treasury forecasts the differential to narrow to around half a percentage point from the end of 2004.

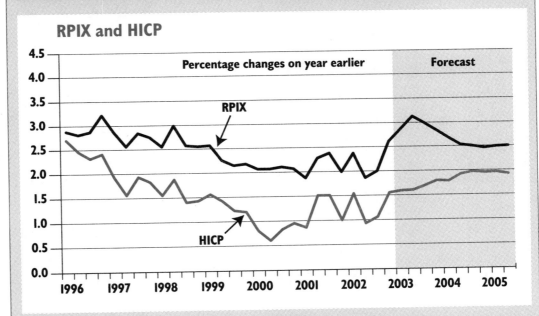

RPIX and HICP

Percentage changes on year earlier   Forecast

RPIX

HICP

[1] HICP is discussed further in "The Harmonised Index of Consumer Prices (HICP) – some factual information", HM Treasury, November 1998.

B59   Although house prices themselves are not a direct element of the RPI, they influence it because they are used in the calculation of housing depreciation. This is expected to remain a significant factor in keeping RPIX inflation slightly above target over coming months. But with house price increases expected progressively to moderate this year, and as last year's gains fall out of the 12-month comparison, the positive influence of housing depreciation on RPIX inflation should wane as the year goes on. Likewise, oil prices are expected soon to contribute to some easing of RPIX inflation, although there is the risk of further volatility.

B60   Other key influences on inflation over the next two years are expected to be: upward pressure from rising import prices, as a result of the recent fall in the exchange rate and the forecast pick-up in the global economy; and the continuing negative, albeit narrowing, output gap, exerting downward pressure on domestically generated inflation.

B61   The combined effect of these factors is that over the next 12 months RPIX inflation is forecast to fall back to its $2^1/_2$ per cent target, as the temporary housing depreciation and oil price effects unwind, and the upward import price effect slightly outweighs the downward output gap effect. Thereafter inflation is expected to remain at target.

Independent forecasts

B62   Independent forecasts for UK GDP growth have been reduced since the 2002 Pre-Budget Report. The latest independent average for growth in 2003 is 2.0 per cent, down from 2.4 per cent at the time of the 2002 Pre-Budget Report but consistent with the lower end of the Budget forecast range. For 2004, the average of independent forecasts for GDP growth is 2.4 per cent, down from 2.9 per cent at the time of the 2002 Pre-Budget Report. Independent forecasters continue to expect inflation to remain close to target this year and next.

Table B5: Budget and independent[1] forecasts

	Percentage changes on a year earlier unless otherwise stated					
	2003			2004		
		Independent			Independent	
	April Budget	Average	Range	April Budget	Average	Range
Gross domestic product	2 to 2½	2.0	−0.4 to 2.7	3 to 3½	2.4	−0.3 to 3.3
RPIX (Q4)	2¾	2.5	1.8 to 3.7	2½	2.4	1.5 to 3.3
Current account (£ billion)	−23¼	−21.1	−30.4 to −9.8	−23¼	−21.3	−41.1 to −8.0

[1] 'Forecasts for the UK Economy: A Comparison of Independent Forecasts', HM Treasury, March 2003.

UK FORECAST IN DETAIL

The household sector

B63   Underlying growth in household consumption – supported by high employment and low interest rates – has remained robust and continued to support UK GDP growth in the face of subdued global demand. Strong house price gains have contributed by shielding household total net wealth from the impact of declining equity prices. Although real income growth has moderated, homeowners' borrowing capacity has been enhanced by significant appreciation in housing wealth, and mortgage equity withdrawal in the fourth quarter of 2002, at 7.2 per cent of post-tax income, was at its highest level since its 1988 peak (see Box B8 for a fuller discussion). In 2002 as a whole, private consumption rose by $3^3/_4$ per cent.

Table B6: Household sector[1] expenditure and income

| | Percentage changes on previous year unless otherwise stated | | | |
| | | Forecast | | |
	2002	2003	2004	2005
Household consumption[2]	3¾	2¾ to 3	2½ to 2¾	2½ to 3
Real household disposable income	2¼	2 to 2½	2½ to 3	2½ to 3
Saving ratio (level, per cent)	5	4¾	5	5

[1] Including non-profit institutions serving households.
[2] At constant prices.

B64 Nonetheless, growth in private consumption has continued to moderate gradually from its most recent peak in 2000, when growth reached over 5 per cent. Retail sales growth fell back in the latter stages of 2002, with growth between the first and second halves at its slowest rate for over two years. While monthly sales growth picked up strongly in December, rising 1 per cent on November, this reflected the particularly late Christmas trading period in 2002. Thus, as widely anticipated, January saw a corresponding fallback in sales volumes; and another, albeit fractional, easing in February provided further confirmation that retail sales growth has slackened. In the year to February retail sales were 3.3 per cent up, around half the rate of growth seen in the year to February 2002. Moreover, excluding December, retail sales have remained virtually flat since October.

B65 Although retail sales account for only 35 per cent of household consumption, other evidence suggests that the slowdown in household expenditure is proving broad based. New car registrations have fallen back from record highs. Consumer confidence has also eased back in recent months; although consumers remain more positive over the outlook for their own finances, sentiment regarding prospects for the general economy has weakened considerably. The composite European Commission/GfK measure of consumer confidence has trended downwards since last summer and in March was at its lowest level since December 1995, albeit only just below its past long-run average. This possibly reflects a partially delayed reaction to last year's stock market turbulence, and renewed equity price weakness this year risks a further unravelling of confidence. However, shifts in confidence also suggest that volatility on financial markets in recent months have begun to have some adverse bearing on households' perceptions of economic prospects, while the recent moderation of underlying house price inflation may have further dampened consumer sentiment. Ongoing concerns over potential terrorist attacks in both the UK and US may also have played a role in reducing confidence.

B66 Lower income growth in 2002 is likely to prompt a continued moderation of private consumption growth through this year. Further recent declines on world equity markets, compounding already sharply reduced valuations in 2000 and 2001, are also expected to feed through to consumption as households adjust spending patterns to reductions in net financial wealth. Moreover, with house price inflation showing signs of having peaked, more moderate growth in valuations can be expected to reduce some of the recent momentum in household consumption too. With household debt having risen rapidly in recent years, increasing by over 40 per cent since 1998, consumers' appetite for further borrowing is likely to wane.

B67 Nonetheless, the strong fundamentals that have militated against any abrupt reversal in the strength of private consumption growth remain in place. Household consumption is therefore expected to continue slowing gradually through this year, growing by 2¾ to 3 per cent in 2003 as a whole. Thereafter growth is forecast to remain at sustainable rates, and significantly below the average of 4¼ per cent a year seen between 1996 and 2002.

Box B8: Mortgage equity withdrawal

Mortgage equity withdrawal (MEW) is that part of borrowing secured against housing that is not invested in property. It expanded rapidly in 2002, supporting further strong growth in consumption as owner occupiers took advantage of significant gains in the value of their houses accrued over the course of the past four to five years. Thus, despite a sharp fall in income growth from its recent peaks in 2001, together with sharply reduced household financial wealth as a result of equity price falls, consumption growth remained robust in 2002.

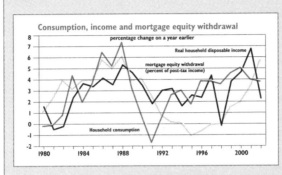

Consumption, income and mortgage equity withdrawal

However, it is unlikely that all of the rise in MEW in 2002 seeped into additional consumption. MEW may simply act as a substitute for other types of borrowing, such as consumer credit, thus not necessarily adding to the sum of consumer demand. Moreover, it may be used to pay off other debt or to fund additions to financial assets rather than consumption. Households could be holding funds generated by MEW to boost housing investment at some future date. Nevertheless, despite these alternative channels, a survey by the Council for Mortgage Lenders provides confirming evidence that MEW has partly boosted recent consumption growth, including spending on some housing related goods.

The recent rise in MEW has no doubt been driven by increases in house prices, which have more than doubled since their trough at the start of 1995, but it has been underpinned by a number of other related factors too. A fall in real interest rates has been one major influence, reducing the cost of borrowing to fund current spending. Furthermore, the fall in nominal interest rates has reduced the up-front cost of borrowing, although low inflation means real costs erode less quickly over time; and the macroeconomic framework is likely to have given households confidence that interest rates will be less volatile going forward. Falling interest rates have boosted housing transactions and remortgaging, facilitating access to housing wealth; and lenders appear to have reduced credit constraints, through the increased use of products such as flexible mortgages, thereby giving a one-off boost to borrowing and consumption.

Looking ahead, further expansion in MEW is likely to be restrained by moderating house price inflation and the already high level of debt relative to income. However, MEW is likely to continue to have a supportive, albeit diminishing, effect on consumption as recent borrowing gradually works through to expenditure.

Investment

B68 Estimates of business investment from the beginning of 2001 have recently been revised up. As a result, business investment expenditure for last year as a whole is now estimated to have fallen by less, and to have been around 3¹/₂ per cent higher, than expected in the Pre-Budget Report.

B69 Nonetheless, these revisions have not significantly changed the recent pattern of business investment expenditure. Although there have been signs of business investment bottoming out, the subdued nature of the global recovery in 2002, together with ongoing international uncertainties, have continued to discourage firms from undertaking new investment. The CBI Industrial Trends Survey for the first quarter of 2003 showed that the importance of political and economic uncertainty as a constraint on investment intentions was at its highest since in the immediate aftermath of 11 September 2001, and similar to the levels witnessed at the height of the late 1990s' Asian crisis.

B70 The sharpest quarterly falls in business investment were concentrated over the second half of 2001 and into the first quarter of 2002, amidst significantly heightened uncertainty in the wake of 11 September. Business investment remained broadly flat between the first and second halves of last year, although it ended the year 5¹/₂ per cent lower than in late 2001. Ongoing international uncertainty and sharp falls on global equity markets through last year and into early 2003 have continued to blunt the incentive to invest.

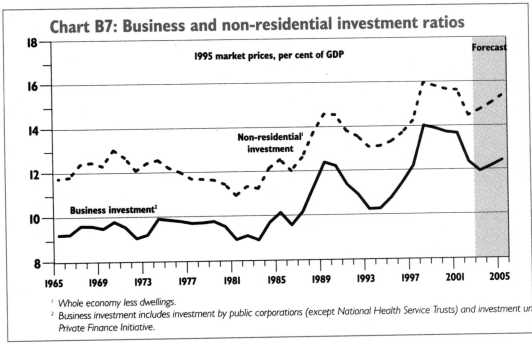

Chart B7: Business and non-residential investment ratios

1995 market prices, per cent of GDP

¹ Whole economy less dwellings.
² Business investment includes investment by public corporations (except National Health Service Trusts) and investment un Private Finance Initiative.

B71 After the sharp downturn in ICT spending in 2001, high-technology investment declined further throughout 2002, accounting for over a quarter of the overall decline in current price business investment for the year as a whole. One factor that may have compounded the global investment downturn in keeping ICT spending subdued in recent years is an extension in the effective lives of many high-technology assets. While ICT equipment is subject to rapid obsolescence as new technologies come onto the market, machines bought around the end of the 1990s and in 2000 were massively more powerful than ones acquired a decade earlier, reflecting the marked increase in computer processor speed. As a result, firms may have been able to continue deriving service streams from ICT equipment for longer, diminishing the need for regular replacement and upgrading of computing systems and other high-technology assets.

B72 Nonetheless, there have been some early encouraging signs that the foundations necessary for a turnaround in business investment are beginning to emerge. Investment expenditure on software and hardware rose by almost 15 per cent in the third quarter and by a further $5^3/_4$ per cent in the final quarter of 2002. Moreover, both imports and production of capital equipment have shown some signs of having flattened out in recent months.

B73 Company profitability has shown encouraging signs of having stabilised. Rates of return in manufacturing have picked up from lows seen in 2001, while service sector rates remained broadly flat over last year as a whole. Moreover, private non-financial corporations have aggressively tackled debts accumulated during the investment boom of the late 1990s, and ran significant financial surpluses throughout last year.

Table B7: Gross fixed capital formation

| | Percentage changes on previous year | | |
| | | Forecast | |
	2002	2003	2004	2005
Whole economy[1]	$-3^1/_4$	$4^1/_4$ to $4^3/_4$	$4^3/_4$ to $5^1/_4$	5 to $5^1/_2$
of which:				
Business[2,3]	-8	$-1^1/_2$ to -1	$4^3/_4$ to $5^1/_2$	$5^1/_4$ to 6
Private dwellings[3]	$13^3/_4$	$4^1/_4$ to $4^1/_2$	2 to $2^1/_2$	2 to $2^1/_2$
General government[3,4]	$9^1/_4$	47	8	$7^3/_4$

[1] *Includes costs associated with the transfer of ownership of land and existing buildings.*

[2] *Private sector and public corporations' (except National Health Service Trusts) non-residential investment. Includes investment under the Private Finance Initiative.*

[3] *Excludes purchases less sales of land and existing buildings.*

[4] *Includes National Health Service Trusts*

B74 Overall, these tentatively encouraging signs are consistent with private sector capital expenditure being at or close to its trough. Nonetheless, the main catalyst for a rebound in business investment in the second half of 2003 is still expected to be a strengthening of the global recovery.

B75 Mirroring the outlook for world growth, the Budget forecast shows business investment remaining subdued in early 2003, as the international environment continues to encourage a cautious approach to capital spending, but picking up from around the middle of the year and growing in the second half. In 2003 as a whole, business investment is forecast to decline by 1 to $1^1/_2$ per cent, which masks growth of over $1^1/_4$ per cent between the first and second halves of this year.

B76 As the global recovery gathers further momentum into 2004, and international uncertainties recede, postponed investment projects are expected to come back on stream as the outlook for demand improves. With firms having largely adjusted to the overhang from the investment boom of the late 1990s, a step-up in new ICT expenditure is expected to emerge over the course of the forecast horizon as a stronger world economy gives firms more confidence to upgrade and expand productive potential. Business investment is therefore forecast to grow by $4^3/_4$ to $5^1/_2$ per cent next year and by $5^1/_4$ to 6 per cent in 2005, accounting for a marked increase in its ratio to GDP.

Trade and the balance of payments

B77   A tentative recovery in world trade in the first half of 2002 temporarily boosted UK exports in the second quarter. However, faltering world trade growth in the second half was reflected in a sharp fall back in UK goods export volumes, which contracted by $5^3/_4$ per cent between the third and fourth quarters. So despite the spurt of growth earlier in the year, goods export volumes declined by nearly 2 per cent in 2002 as a whole, standing at their lowest level for three years in the final quarter. Services export volumes meanwhile increased marginally compared with 2001.

B78   The UK has recently seen a bigger decline in goods export volumes to non-EU markets than to the EU. Indeed, by value, a third of the decline in UK exports last year was attributable to the US alone. To some extent, this appears at odds with the pattern of global growth given GDP growth in the US outstripped that in the Euro-area last year. Moreover, although US imports were relatively weak in the third quarter of 2002, latest data show a sharp pick-up in the fourth quarter still coincided with a further weakening in UK exports to the US.

B79   Sterling has fallen by around 7 per cent against the euro since the 2002 Pre-Budget Report, and presently stands some 11 per cent lower than its most recent peak in February 2002. This should offer a spur to UK exports to the Euro-area. Although a corresponding increase of the sterling-dollar exchange rate over the past year is likely partially to offset any increase in UK market share at the global level, the composite Sterling Exchange Rate Index (ERI) has still eased back by around 7 per cent since early 2002, reflecting the far greater weight of the Euro-area in UK trade. Nonetheless, the lags typically judged to exist between exchange rate movements and trade flows mean that it is too early for these developments to have played a significant role in relative export trends in the course of 2002.

Table B8: Trade in goods and services

	Percentage changes on previous year					£ billion
	Volumes		Prices[1]			Goods and services
	Exports	Imports	Exports	Imports	Terms of trade[2]	balance
2002	−1	$1^1/_2$	$1^1/_2$	−2	$3^3/_4$	$-18^3/_4$
Forecast						
2003	$1^1/_4$ to $1^1/_2$	4 to $4^1/_4$	2	$1^3/_4$	$^1/_4$	$-26^3/_4$
2004	$8^1/_4$ to $8^3/_4$	$7^1/_4$ to $7^3/_4$	3	$3^1/_4$	$-^1/_4$	$-27^3/_4$
2005	7 to $7^1/_2$	$6^1/_4$ to $6^3/_4$	$2^3/_4$	$2^3/_4$	0	$-28^1/_4$

[1] Average value indices.
[2] Ratio of export to import prices.

B80   Imports appeared to resume growing in early 2002, having contracted over most of 2001 as weak manufacturing output and declining business investment reduced demand for both intermediate and capital goods. Nonetheless, any underlying turnaround in imports remains sluggish. Growth appears to have been inflated by a surge in imports of consumer goods through much of 2002, reflecting robust demand for new cars as well as the underlying strength of private consumption. However, with imports of non-car consumer goods having fallen back since the second quarter, goods import volumes in 2002 as a whole were less than 1 per cent up on 2001, and the underlying trend in import volumes in recent months now appears approximately flat.

B8I As a result of some recovery in imports and faltering exports, the deficit on trade in goods and services has widened since the first half of 2002. However, in 2002 as a whole it still narrowed as an increased surplus on services trade more than offset a widening in the goods deficit. This partly reflected a recovery in net exports of insurance services, following substantial insurance losses in 2001 arising from the 11 September tragedies. Moreover, in contrast to goods, underlying services export growth appears to have resumed in the second half of last year.

B82 As in the 2002 Pre-Budget Report, exports are expected to recover over the course of 2003 as world trade growth begins to gather increased momentum. Goods and services export volumes are forecast to rise by $1^1/_4$ to $1^1/_2$ per cent this year, slightly below the 2002 Pre-Budget Report projection as a result of a less pronounced pick-up in UK export market growth in the first half of the year, mainly reflecting a subdued near-term outlook for the Euro-area economies. Thereafter, exports are expected to strengthen considerably as the global recovery becomes more firmly entrenched and as the effects of increased UK price competitiveness from the recent weakening of sterling feed through. The volume of exports of goods and services is forecast to increase by $8^1/_4$ to $8^3/_4$ per cent in 2004 and by 7 to $7^1/_2$ per cent in 2005.

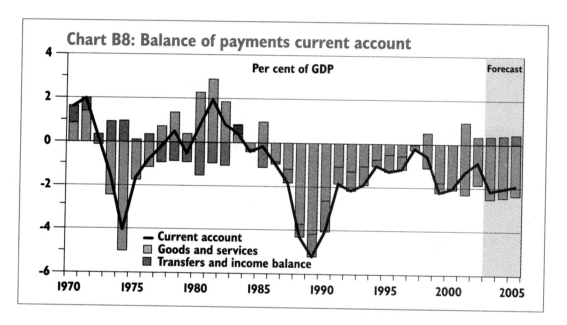

Chart B8: Balance of payments current account

B83 At the same time, a sustained recovery in manufacturing output and renewed growth of UK business investment are expected to feed through to a strengthening of import growth over the forecast horizon. Overall, export and import volumes are expected to grow at broadly comparable rates for the foreseeable future, with the goods and services trade deficit levelling off, at around $2^1/_4$ per cent of GDP, by 2005.

B84 Partly as a result of recent revisions to Balance of Payments data, the current account deficit for 2002, at under £9 billion, was less than half the level forecast in the 2002 Pre-Budget Report. The main reason for this is a stronger position on investment income, with 2002 registering another record surplus. This surplus is expected to moderate over the forecast period as stronger domestic GDP growth raises the relative profitability of overseas businesses operating in the UK and hence investment income debits, especially amongst financial service companies who appear to have been particularly affected by the recent period of weak global growth. Although a strengthening external environment should also give a lift to UK earnings from overseas, the investment income surplus has been unusually high for the past two years or so, and the forecast assumes a return to a position more in line with historical experience. Together with a gradual widening of the deficit on trade in goods and services, this is expected to underpin a higher current account deficit in coming years. However, relative to GDP, the current deficit is expected to remain modest at around 2 per cent.

Table B9: Summary of economic prospects[1]

| | Percentage changes on a year earlier unless otherwise stated | | | | | |
| | | Forecast[2] | | | Average errors from past forecasts[3] | |
	2002	2003	2004	2005	2003	2004
Output at constant market prices						
Gross domestic product (GDP)	1¾	2 to 2½	3 to 3½	3 to 3½	¾	½
Manufacturing output	−4	¼ to ¾	2¼ to 2¾	1¾ to 2¼	1¼	2
Expenditure components of GDP at constant market prices[4]						
Domestic demand	2½	3 to 3½	3 to 3½	3 to 3½	¾	1
Household consumption[5]	3¾	2¾ to 3	2½ to 2¾	2½ to 3	1	1¼
General government consumption	3¾	3¾	4	3	¾	1
Fixed investment	−3¼	4¼ to 4¾	4¾ to 5¼	5 to 5½	2½	2½
Change in inventories[6]	0	0	0	0	¼	¼
Exports of goods and services	−1	1¼ to 1½	8¼ to 8¾	7 to 7½	2½	3
Imports of goods and services	1½	4 to 4¼	7¼ to 7¾	6¼ to 6¾	2¼	3½
Balance of payments current account						
£ billion	−8¾	−23¼	−23¼	−23¼	7¾	9½
per cent of GDP	−¾	−2	−2	−2	¾	¾
Inflation						
RPIX (Q4)	2½	2¾	2½	2½	¼	½
Producer output prices (Q4)[7]	1	1¾	2¼	2	¾	1½
GDP deflator at market prices	3¼	2¾	2½	2½	½	¾
Money GDP at market prices						
£ billion	1043	1094 to 1098	1157 to 1166	1222 to 1238	5	9
percentage change	5	4¾ to 5¼	5¾ to 6¼	5¾ to 6¼	½	¾

[1] The forecast is consistent with the national accounts and balance of payments statistics to the fourth quarter of 2002, released by the Office for National Statistics on 27 March 2003.

[2] The size of the growth ranges for GDP components may differ from those for total GDP growth because of rounding and the assumed invariance of the levels of public spending within the forecast ranges.

[3] Average absolute errors for year-ahead projections made in spring forecasts over the past 10 years. The average errors for the current account are calculated as a per cent of GDP, with £ billion figures calculated by scaling the errors by forecast money GDP in 2003 and 2004.

[4] Further detail on the expenditure components of GDP is given in Table B9.

[5] Includes households and non-profit institutions serving households.

[6] Contribution to GDP growth, percentage points.

[7] Excluding excise duties.

Table B10: Gross domestic product and its components

	Household consumption[1]	General government consumption	Fixed investment	Change in inventories	Domestic demand[2]	Exports of goods and services	Total final expenditure	Less imports of goods and services	Plus statistical discrepancy[3]	GDP at market prices
	£ billion at 1995 prices, seasonally adjusted									
2002	611.0	162.3	148.6	-0.5	921.4	284.8	1206.2	344.2	0.2	862.3
2003	627.0 to 629.2	168.2	155.1 to 155.6	-0.3 to 0.2	949.9 to 953.2	288.1 to 289.1	1238.0 to 1242.3	357.8 to 359.0	0.3	880.6 to 883.6
2004	642.1 to 647.2	174.9	162.4 to 163.7	-0.5 to 0.9	978.8 to 986.6	311.7 to 314.2	1290.5 to 1300.8	383.4 to 386.5	0.3	907.4 to 914.6
2005	658.9 to 667.4	180.0	170.5 to 172.7	-0.3 to 2.0	1009.1 to 1022.1	333.7 to 338.0	1342.7 to 1360.0	407.6 to 412.8	0.3	935.5 to 947.5
2002 1st half	302.7	81.0	74.1	-1.9	455.9	143.1	599.0	171.3	0.1	427.8
2nd half	308.3	81.2	74.5	1.4	465.5	141.7	607.2	172.9	0.2	434.5
2003 1st half	312.1 to 312.7	82.8	77.1 to 77.3	-0.1 to 0.0	471.9 to 472.9	141.7 to 142.0	613.5 to 614.8	176.1 to 176.5	0.2	437.6 to 438.5
2nd half	315.0 to 316.5	85.4	77.9 to 78.3	-0.2 to 0.2	478.1 to 480.3	146.5 to 147.2	624.5 to 627.5	181.7 to 182.6	0.2	443.0 to 445.1
2004 1st half	318.7 to 320.8	87.3	80.0 to 80.5	-0.5 to 0.1	485.4 to 488.7	152.9 to 153.9	638.3 to 642.6	188.3 to 189.6	0.2	450.1 to 453.1
2nd half	323.4 to 326.3	87.6	82.4 to 83.2	0.0 to 0.8	493.4 to 497.9	158.8 to 160.3	652.3 to 658.2	195.1 to 196.9	0.2	457.3 to 461.5
2005 1st half	327.6 to 331.4	88.9	84.3 to 85.3	0.0 to 1.0	500.8 to 506.6	164.3 to 166.2	665.1 to 672.9	201.0 to 203.3	0.2	464.3 to 469.7
2nd half	331.3 to 336.0	91.1	86.2 to 87.4	-0.3 to 0.9	508.3 to 515.4	169.3 to 171.7	677.6 to 687.2	206.6 to 209.5	0.2	471.2 to 477.8
	Percentage changes on previous year[4,5]									
2002	3¾	3¾	-3¼	0	2½	-1	1¾	1½	0	1¾
2003	2¾ to 3	3¾	4¼ to 4¾	0	3 to 3½	1¼ to 1½	2¾ to 3	4 to 4¼	0	2 to 2½
2004	2½ to 2¾	4	4¾ to 5¼	0	3 to 3½	8¼ to 8¾	4¼ to 4¾	7¼ to 7¾	0	3 to 3½
2005	2½ to 3	3	5 to 5½	0	3 to 3½	7 to 7½	4 to 4½	6¼ to 6¾	0	3 to 3½

[1] Includes households and non-profit institutions serving households.
[2] Also includes acquisitions less disposals of valuables.
[3] Expenditure adjustment.
[4] For change in inventories and the statistical discrepancy, changes are expressed as a per cent of GDP.
[5] Growth ranges for GDP components do not necessarily sum to the ½ percentage point ranges for GDP growth because of rounding and the assumed invariance of the levels of public spending within the forecast ranges.

C THE PUBLIC FINANCES

The latest projections for the public finances show that the Government is firmly on track to meet its strict fiscal rules over the economic cycle, using cautious assumptions and in the cautious case, while meeting its international and public spending commitments:

- the average current budget since the start of the present cycle in 1999-2000 is comfortably in surplus, ensuring the Government is on track to meet the golden rule; and

- public sector net debt is projected to be low and stable throughout the next five years, comfortably meeting the sustainable investment rule, and at between 31 and 34 per cent of GDP, the lowest in the G7.

In the short term, the full operation of the automatic stabilisers means that fiscal policy is supporting monetary policy in maintaining economic stability during a period of global uncertainty. In the medium term, the public finances return towards the Budget 2002 profile as economic growth strengthens. The use of cautious assumptions and the 'stress test' against the cautious case help to ensure that the public finances are sound and sustainable, despite the continuing international uncertainty and global economic weakness.

INTRODUCTION

C1   Chapter 2 describes the Government's fiscal policy framework and shows how the projections of the public finances are consistent with meeting the fiscal rules. This chapter explains the latest outturns and the fiscal projections in more detail. It includes:

- five-year projections of the current budget and public sector net debt, the key aggregates for assessing performance against the golden rule and the sustainable investment rule respectively;

- projections of public sector net borrowing, the fiscal aggregate relevant to assessing the impact of fiscal policy on the economy;

- projections of the cyclically-adjusted fiscal balances; and

- detailed analyses of the outlook for government receipts and expenditure.

C2   The fiscal projections continue to be based on deliberately cautious key assumptions audited by the National Audit Office (NAO).

MEETING THE FISCAL RULES

C3   Table C1 shows five-year projections for the current budget and public sector net debt, the key aggregates for assessing performance against the golden rule and the sustainable investment rule respectively. Outturns and projections of other important measures of the public finances, including net borrowing and the cyclically-adjusted fiscal balances, are also shown.

C4   As explained in Chapter 2, the Government's provisional view is that the current economic cycle started in 1999-2000. Based on the assumptions used in these projections, the economy will next return to trend levels, ending the current cycle, in 2005-06.

Table C1: Summary of public sector finances

| | Per cent of GDP | | | | | | | |
| | Outturns | | Estimate | Projections | | | | |
	2000-01	2001-02	2002-03	2003-04	2004-05	2005-06	2006-07	2007-08
Fairness and prudence								
Surplus on current budget	2.2	1.0	−1.1	−0.8	−0.1	0.2	0.4	0.6
Average surplus since 1999-2000	2.2	1.8	1.1	0.7	0.6	0.5	0.5	0.5
Cyclically-adjusted surplus on current budget	1.7	0.9	−0.5	0.2	0.5	0.4	0.4	0.6
Long-term sustainability								
Public sector net debt – end year	31.2	30.2	30.9	32.2	32.7	33.2	33.5	33.8
Core debt	31.3	30.3	30.4	30.9	30.9	31.2	31.6	32.0
Net worth[1]	21.3	26.2	22.9	21.7	20.0	18.5	18.0	17.0
Primary balance	3.8	1.8	−0.6	−0.8	−0.4	−0.3	−0.1	−0.1
Economic impact								
Net investment	0.5	1.0	1.2	1.7	2.0	2.1	2.1	2.2
Public sector net borrowing (PSNB)	−1.7	0.0	2.3	2.5	2.1	1.9	1.7	1.6
Cyclically-adjusted PSNB	−1.2	0.1	1.7	1.5	1.5	1.7	1.7	1.6
Financing								
Central government net cash requirement	−3.7	0.3	2.0	3.2	2.4	2.1	2.2	1.9
Public sector net cash requirement	−3.9	0.3	2.1	2.9	2.3	1.9	2.0	1.7
European commitments								
Treaty deficit[2]	−1.7	0.0	2.3	2.4	2.1	1.9	1.7	1.7
Cyclically-adjusted Treaty deficit[2]	−1.2	0.1	1.7	1.5	1.4	1.7	1.7	1.7
Treaty debt ratio[3]	39.8	37.9	38.0	39.0	39.4	39.6	39.9	40.1
Memo: Output gap	0.9	−0.2	−1.1	−1.4	−0.7	−0.1	0.0	0.0

[1] At end-December; GDP centred on end-December.

[2] General government net borrowing on a Maastricht basis.

[3] General government gross debt.

The golden rule **C5** The projections show that the Government is firmly on track to meet the golden rule. Over the period of this cycle, from 1999-2000 to 2005-06, the current budget is comfortably in surplus. Similarly, the average surplus on the current budget is positive since the start of the cycle and throughout the projection period. The same is true were the current cycle thought to have started in 1997-98. The cyclically-adjusted surplus, which allows underlying or structural trends in the indicators to be seen more clearly by removing the estimated effects of the economic cycle, temporarily shows a deficit in 2002-03, before returning to surplus for the rest of the projection period.

C6 Following a deficit of 3 per cent of GDP in 1996-97, current budget surpluses of more than 2 per cent were recorded in 1999-2000 and 2000-01 and of around 1 per cent of GDP in 2001-02. Largely as a result of cyclical and other temporary factors, the current budget moves into a deficit of 1.1 per cent of GDP in 2002-03, before gradually returning to surplus in 2005-06 and reaching a surplus of 0.6 per cent of GDP by 2007-08.

The sustainable   **C7**   The sustainable investment rule is also comfortably met over this economic cycle. In
investment rule   1996-97, public sector net debt stood at 44 per cent of GDP. The tough decisions on taxation
and expenditure taken by the Government, including the decision to use the proceeds from
the auction of spectrum licences to repay debt, reduced net debt to around 30 per cent of
GDP by the end of 2001-02. It is now projected to grow slowly, but to remain below 34 per cent
of GDP, as the Government borrows modestly to fund increased investment in public services.
The projections for core debt, which exclude the estimated impact of the economic cycle,
increase more slowly to 32 per cent of GDP.

Net worth   **C8**   Net worth is the approximate stock counterpart of the current budget balance.
Current budget surpluses of over 2 per cent of GDP in recent years increased net worth to 26.2
per cent of GDP in 2001-02. Modest declines are projected for later years. At present, net
worth is not used as a key indicator of the public finances, mainly as a result of the difficulties
involved in measuring accurately many government assets and liabilities.

C9   Chart C1 shows public sector net debt and net worth as a per cent of GDP from
1989-90 to 2007-08.

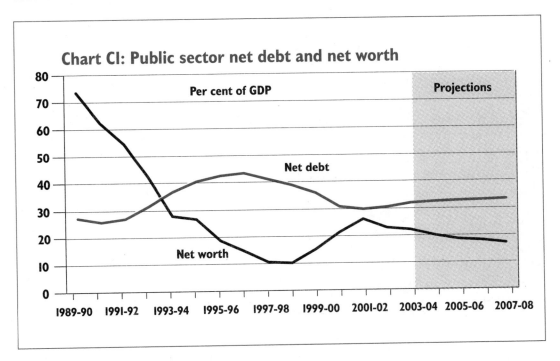

Chart CI: Public sector net debt and net worth

Net investment   **C10**   As a result of decisions taken in the 2002 Spending Review, public sector net
investment is projected to rise steadily to 2¼ per cent of GDP in 2007-08. These increases are
sustainable and fully consistent with the Government's long-term approach and the fiscal
rules, since net debt is being held at a stable and prudent level, well below 40 per cent of GDP.

Net borrowing   **C11**   This increase in net investment, together with the new projections for the current
budget, mean that public sector net borrowing is expected to increase to a maximum of
2½ per cent of GDP in 2003-04, helping monetary policy maintain economic stability while
the economy is below trend, before decreasing to around 1½ per cent of GDP in later years as
the economy moves back to trend. Cyclically-adjusted public sector net borrowing is around
1¾ per cent of GDP or lower in every year from 2003-04.

Financing **C12** The central government net cash requirement was 0.3 per cent of GDP in 2001-02. It is projected to increase in 2002-03 and subsequent years, mirroring the profile of net borrowing.

European **C13** Table C1 also shows the Treaty measures of deficit and debt used for the purposes of **commitments** the Excessive Deficit Procedure – Article 104 of the Treaty. Both the reference levels of 3 per cent of GDP for the deficit and 60 per cent of GDP for gross debt are achieved throughout the projection period.

CHANGES TO THE FISCAL BALANCES

C14 Table C2 compares the latest estimates for the main fiscal balances with those in the Pre-Budget Report and in Budget 2002.

Table C2: Fiscal balances compared with Budget 2002 and the 2002 Pre-Budget Report

	Outturn 2001-02	Estimate[1] 2002-03	Projections 2003-04	2004-05	2005-06	2006-07	2007-08
Surplus on current budget (£ billion)							
Budget 2002	10.6	3.2	7	9	7	9	–
Effect of revisions and forecasting changes	–3.0	–7.9	–12	–7	–3	–1	–
Effect of discretionary changes	–	–1.0	1	0	1	1	–
PBR 2002	7.7	–5.7	–5	3	5	8	10
Effect of revisions and forecasting changes	2.3	–4.1	–4	–3	–1	–1	0
Effect of discretionary changes	–	–1.9	0	–1	–1	–1	–1
Budget 2003	**9.9**	**–11.7**	**–8**	**–1**	**2**	**6**	**9**
Net borrowing (£ billion)							
Budget 2002	1.3	11.2	13	13	17	18	–
Effect of changes in current surplus	3.0	8.9	12	6	2	1	–
Effect of changes in net investment	–3.1	–0.1	0	0	0	0	–
PBR 2002	1.2	20.1	24	19	19	19	20
Effect of changes in current surplus	–2.3	6.0	4	4	3	2	1
Effect of changes in net investment	0.7	–2.1	–1	1	1	0	0
Budget 2003	**–0.4**	**24.0**	**27**	**24**	**23**	**22**	**22**
Cyclically-adjusted surplus on current budget (per cent of GDP)							
Budget 2002[2]	1.0	0.5	0.6	0.7	0.6	0.7	–
PBR 2002	0.7	0.2	0.3	0.6	0.5	0.6	0.7
Budget 2003	**0.9**	**–0.5**	**0.2**	**0.5**	**0.4**	**0.4**	**0.6**
Cyclically-adjusted net borrowing (per cent of GDP)							
Budget 2002[2]	0.2	0.9	1.2	1.2	1.4	1.4	–
PBR 2002	0.2	1.2	1.5	1.3	1.5	1.5	1.5
Budget 2003	**0.1**	**1.7**	**1.5**	**1.5**	**1.7**	**1.7**	**1.6**

[1] The 2002-03 figures were projections in Budget 2002 and PBR 2002.
[2] The 2001-02 figures were estimates in Budget 2002.

C15 In the Pre-Budget Report, receipts for 2002-03 were revised down significantly – mainly as a result of the effects of the global economic downturn. An explanation of the impact of the slowdown on different taxes was included in the Pre-Budget Report.

C16   As explained in Chapter B, the short-term outlook for the world economy has weakened further since the Pre-Budget Report. This has had important implications for the fiscal projections. Table C2 shows that, since the Pre-Budget Report, the current budget has been revised down from a deficit of £5.7 billion to a deficit of £11.7 billion in 2002-03, including provision of £3 billion to meet the cost of the war in Iraq, and from a deficit of £5 billion to a deficit of £8 billion in 2003-04. It also shows that net borrowing has been revised up since the Pre-Budget Report, from £20.1 billion to £24 billion in 2002-03 and from £24 billion to £27 billion in 2003-04. However, the tough decisions on taxation and spending taken by the Government over the course of the last Parliament to reduce debt to low and stable levels, means that even after these revisions, the Government remains on track to meet its strict fiscal rules.

C17   The underlying strength of the fiscal position means that the changes in the fiscal balances in 2003-04 are consistent with the Government's aim of allowing the automatic stabilisers to support monetary policy in maintaining economic stability while the economy is below trend. This interaction between the economic cycle and the public sector finances also explains why there is little difference between the cyclically-adjusted balances in 2003-04 from the Pre-Budget Report projections.

FORECAST DIFFERENCES AND RISKS

C18   The fiscal balances represent the difference between two large aggregates of expenditure and receipts, and forecasts are inevitably subject to wide margins of uncertainty. Over the past ten years, the average absolute difference between year-ahead forecasts of net borrowing and subsequent outturns has been around 1 per cent of GDP. This difference tends to grow as the forecast horizon lengthens. A full account of differences between the projections made in Budget 2000 and Budget 2001 and the subsequent outturns is provided in the *End of year fiscal report*, which was published alongside the Pre-Budget Report.

C19   There are both upside and downside risks to the economic outlook. On the upside, the various uncertainties currently affecting the global economy could dissipate more quickly, and confidence recover more sharply, than anticipated. This would, in turn, help support a stronger than expected improvement in UK economic prospects.

C20   A period of prolonged uncertainty, accompanied by continued volatility in financial markets, weaker equity prices and higher oil prices poses the clearest downside risk to G7 activity. The Government will remain vigilant in the face of these risks. The public finance projections will continue to be based on cautious assumptions, including those for equity prices and the trend rate of growth, and to be 'stress tested' against the cautious case, described in paragraph C23, which builds in a margin for safety in the public finances. The Government remains on track to meet its strict fiscal rules over the economic cycle, including in the cautious case.

C21   Short-term forecasts of the public finances are critically dependent on the path of the economy, as most tax revenues and some public expenditure – notably social security – vary directly with the economic cycle. Earlier work[1] suggested that if GDP growth were one percentage point higher or lower than assumed over the coming year, net borrowing might be lower or higher by 0.4 per cent of GDP in the first year and by a further 0.3 per cent of GDP the following year. These figures are now closer to 0.5 and 0.2 per cent respectively, as the introduction of the corporation tax instalment system has reduced the lag between profits and tax receipts. However, not all cycles will conform exactly to these parameters, notably

---

[1] *Fiscal policy: public finances and the cycle*, HM Treasury, March 1999.

because the estimates are based on historical data (since which time both the state of the economy and the tax regime have changed) and because cycles differ in respects other than magnitude.

C22 Projected differences in short-term growth forecasts may have only a temporary effect on the public finances. For a given path of trend output, higher or lower growth in the short term will be followed by lower or higher growth later on, and the public finances may be little affected on average over the cycle.

C23 However, changes in the estimated cyclical position of the economy in relation to its trend – the output gap – will have a permanent effect on prospects. For this reason, the public finances projections are 'stress tested' against an alternative cautious case, in which the level of trend output is assumed to be 1 percentage point lower than the Government's central view. This scenario would imply that a greater proportion of any projected surplus on the current budget was due to the cyclical strength of the economy – a 1 per cent larger positive output gap reduces the structural surplus on the current budget by about 0.7 per cent of GDP per year. This is illustrated in Chart C2. Even in this cautious case, the cyclically-adjusted current budget is estimated to have been comfortably in surplus over the past four years. The impact of the temporary fall in receipts means that it is projected to move into a modest deficit over the short term, before returning towards balance by the end of the projection period. The average cyclically-adjusted current budget is in surplus in the cautious case over the economic cycle, meeting the 'stress test' of the golden rule.

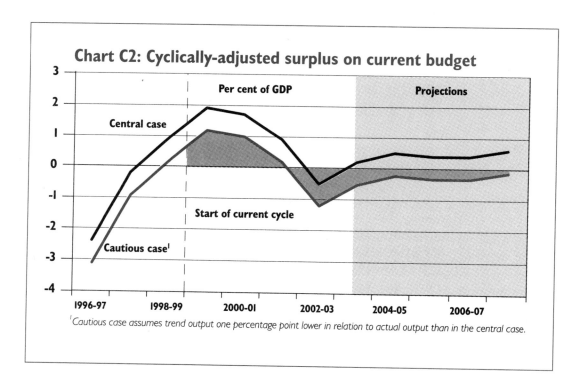

Chart C2: Cyclically-adjusted surplus on current budget

[1]Cautious case assumes trend output one percentage point lower in relation to actual output than in the central case.

ASSUMPTIONS

C24   The fiscal projections are based on the following assumptions:

- the economy follows the path described in Chapter B. In the interests of caution, the fiscal projections continue to be based on the deliberately prudent and cautious assumption of trend output growth of $2\frac{1}{2}$ per cent a year up to 2006-07, $\frac{1}{4}$ percentage point lower than the Government's neutral view. Beyond 2006-07, projections by the Government Actuary imply a slowdown in the growth in the population of working age, due to demographic effects. The Government's neutral view of trend output growth is reduced to $2\frac{1}{2}$ per cent in 2007-08, and so, to maintain a cautious approach, an assumption of $2\frac{1}{4}$ per cent is used in the public finance projections in that year, still $\frac{1}{4}$ percentage point lower than the Government's neutral view;

- there are no tax changes beyond those announced in or before this Budget and the indexation of rates and allowances. Consistent with the *Code for fiscal stability*, the forecast does not take account of measures that cannot be costed accurately, including the Graduate Contributions scheme, described further in Chapter 3;

- firm Departmental Expenditure Limits (DEL) as set out in the 2002 Spending Review up to 2005-06, but adjusted for the impact of policy decisions and DEL/AME reclassifications;

- Annually Managed Expenditure (AME) programmes through to 2005-06 have been reviewed and further additions made for new spending measures announced in this Budget. Following usual practice, the Government has decided to reset the AME margin to £1 billion in 2003-04, £2 billion in 2004-05 and £3 billion in 2005-06;

- prior to spending plans being set in the next Spending Review, assumed real growth in DEL after 2005-06 is in line with the economic growth assumption used for the public finances, supplemented by an addition to allow for the five-year health settlement of the difference between planned health growth and health's long-term average growth of 3.6 per cent. Other current spending in AME is forecast to grow from 2005-06 onwards at $1\frac{3}{4}$ per cent in real terms in line with its recent trend; and

- within these aggregates, net investment is forecast to increase from 2 per cent of GDP in 2005-06 towards an assumption of $2\frac{1}{4}$ per cent in 2007-08, while remaining consistent with the sustainable investment rule.

Table C3: Economic assumptions for the public finance projections

| | Percentage changes on previous year | | | | | | |
| | Outturn | Estimate | Projections | | | | |
	2001-02	2002-03	2003-04	2004-05	2005-06	2006-07	2007-08
Output (GDP)	1¾	2	2¼	3¼	3	2½	2¼
Prices							
RPIX	2¼	2¼	3	2½	2½	2½	2½
GDP deflator	2½	3	2¾	2½	2½	2½	2½
RPI[1] (September)	1¾	1½	2¾	2¾	3	2½	2½
Rossi[2] (September)	1¾	1¼	2	2¼	2	2	2
Money GDP[3] (£ billion)	1005	1056	1108	1173	1239	1301	1363

[1] Used for revalorising excise duties in current year and uprating income tax allowances and bands and certain social security benefits in the following year.

[2] RPI excluding housing costs, used for uprating certain social security benefits.

[3] Not seasonally adjusted.

C25   The key assumptions underlying the fiscal projections are audited by the National Audit Office (NAO) under the three-year rolling review process. Details of the audited assumptions are given in Box C1. The rolling review for Budget 2003[2] covers the assumptions relating to privatisation proceeds, interest rates and tobacco anti-smuggling measures. In addition, the Comptroller and Auditor General was asked to examine a change to the assumption dealing with tobacco revenues, and the revenue impact of a new direct taxation and national insurance contributions compliance and enforcement package.

C26   The Comptroller and Auditor General concluded that the privatisation proceeds assumption was reasonable and not incautious in operation, and that it remains a reasonable and cautious one to use for the purposes of projecting the public finances. Similarly, he concluded that the convention for interest rates was reasonable and cautious over the rolling review period. For the tobacco assumption, he concluded that the fiscal projections over the rolling review period were cautious as tobacco revenues have been greater than forecast.

The new tobacco assumption   **C27**   The tobacco assumption used in previous forecasts was developed at a time when cigarette smuggling was increasing and all the indications were that, with no action, this trend would continue. At the time it was not clear what the impact of the tobacco strategy would be in mitigating the trend because many of the elements were untried in a UK context. For this reason, a cautious assumption was adopted which involved for forecasting purposes:

- taking as a base a hypothetical assumed rise in smuggling in the absence of a strategy; and

- subtracting from this only the more certain of the expected impacts of the strategy.

[2] Audit of Assumptions for Budget 2003, 9 April 2003.

C28   The situation in 2003 is different. The strategy has now been in place for three years. After a long period of decline, UK duty paid consumption has recently stablised. The growth in smuggling has been halted and recent data suggests it is now in decline. In light of this evidence, the NAO audited a revised tobacco assumption for the Pre-Budget Report[3]. However, the Government considers that continued application of this assumption would still result in unduly pessimistic projections of revenue from tobacco duties. In particular, it would result in significant increases in the projected smuggled share of the cigarette market, from 21 per cent in 2001-02 to 28 per cent by 2005-06, despite HM Customs and Excise's target to reduce the share to 17 per cent.

C29   In addition, continuing with the existing assumption would mean that the future change in the smuggling share would continue to be driven by the assumed change in the share in the absence of an anti-smuggling strategy at all. As time passes it becomes much more difficult and less relevant to assess what would have happened without the strategy, making this approach increasingly unsatisfactory.

C30   As a result of these recent trends in smuggling and the success of HM Customs and Excise's strategy, a new assumption has been adopted for Budget 2003, under which the underlying market share of smuggled cigarettes will be set at least equal to the latest published outturn, which currently stands at 21 per cent. The new assumption is intended to be more closely aligned with observed trends in the smuggled market share and HM Customs and Excise's targets to reduce it. The Comptroller and Auditor General has audited the new assumption and concluded that it currently represents a reasonable approach and is cautious to the extent that no account is taken of expected further reductions in the smuggled market share. The impact of applying this new assumption on the projections of tobacco receipts is an extra £3/4 billion a year by 2005-06 and £1 1/4 billion a year by 2007-08.

Inland Revenue **C31**   As described in Chapter 5, Budget 2003 launches a new compliance and enforcement
compliance and package for direct tax and national insurance contributions. An additional £66 million is
enforcement being provided to the Inland Revenue over the next three years to support implementation of
package the package. The package is expected to produce £1.6 billion in total additional revenue over the next 3 years, but in line with the Government's cautious approach to the public finances a lower figure of under £1.4 billion over three years with the annual figure rising to just over £0.6 billion in 2005-06 has been included in the forecast. The Comptroller and Auditor General has audited the projections and concluded that they are based on a reasonable approach and incorporate caution.

---

[3] *Audit of Assumptions for the 2002 Pre-Budget Report*, National Audit Office, 27 November 2002.

Box C1: Key assumptions audited by the NAO

- **Privatisation proceeds**[1,6,11]

  Credit is taken only for proceeds from sales that have been announced.

- **Trend GDP growth**[1,6,9]

  2½ per cent a year to 2006-07 and 2¼ per cent in 2007-08.

- **UK claimant unemployment**[1,4,7,9]

  Rising slowly to 1.03 million in 2005-06, from recent levels of 0.93 million, consistent with the average of independent forecasts.

- **Interest rates**[1,6,7,11]

  3-month market rates change in line with market expectations (as of 28 March).

- **Equity prices**[2,7]

  FTSE All-Share index rises from 1778 (close 28 March) in line with money GDP.

- **VAT**[2,7,10]

  Ratio of underlying VAT to consumption falls by 0.05 percentage points a year.

- **GDP deflator and RPI**[2,7]

  Projections of price indices used to plan public expenditure are consistent with RPIX.

- **Composition of GDP**[3,8]

  Shares of labour income and profits in national income are broadly constant in the medium term.

- **Funding**[3,8]

  Funding assumptions used to project debt interest are consistent with the forecast level of government borrowing and with financing policy.

- **Oil prices**[5,10]

  $26.6 a barrel in 2003, the average of independent forecasts, and then constant in real terms.

- **Tobacco**[6,10,11]

  The underlying market share of smuggled cigarettes will be set at least at the latest published outturn. For Budget 2003, a share of 21 per cent has been used in all forecast years. This is in line with the most recently published outturn figure for 2001-02 and takes account of the indications from duty receipts for 2002-03 that the smuggled share in this year is likely to be lower than 21 per cent.

- **Inland Revenue compliance and enforcement package**[11]

  Only direct and some preventive effects are allowed for.

---

[1] Audit of Assumptions for the July 1997 Budget Projections, 19 June 1997 (HC3693).
[2] Audit of Assumptions for the Pre-Budget Report, 25 November 1997 (HC361).
[3] Audit of Assumptions for the Budget, 19 March 1998 (HC616).
[4] Audit of the Unemployment Assumption for the March 1999 Budget Projections, 9 March 1999 (HC294).
[5] Audit of the Oil Price Assumption for the Pre-Budget Report, November 1999 (HC873).
[6] Audit of Assumptions for the March 2000 Budget, 21 March 2000 (HC348).
[7] Audit of Assumptions for the Pre-Budget 2000 Report, 8 November 2000 (HC959).
[8] Audit of Assumptions for the March 2001 Budget, 7 March 2001 (HC304).
[9] Audit of Assumptions for the April 2002 Budget, 17 April 2002 (HC760).
[10] Audit of Assumptions for the 2002 Pre-Budget Report, 27 November 2002 (HC109).
[11] Audit of Assumptions for Budget 2003, 9 April 2003 (HC627).

FISCAL AGGREGATES

C32 Tables C4 and C5 provide more detail on the projections for the current and capital budgets.

Table C4: Current and capital budgets

	£ billion						
	Outturn	Estimate	Projections				
	2001-02	2002-03	2003-04	2004-05	2005-06	2006-07	2007-08
Current budget							
Current receipts	389.9	397.1	428	460	493	522	550
Current expenditure	366.6	395.0	422	447	475	500	524
Depreciation	13.4	13.8	14	15	16	17	18
Surplus on current budget	**9.9**	**−11.7**	**−8**	**−1**	**2**	**6**	**9**
Capital budget							
Gross investment	27.3	30.5	37	42	45	48	52
Less asset sales	−4.3	−4.5	−4	−4	−4	−4	−4
Less depreciation	−13.4	−13.8	−14	−15	−16	−17	−18
Net investment	9.6	12.2	19	23	25	27	31
Net borrowing	**−0.4**	**24.0**	**27**	**24**	**23**	**22**	**22**
Public sector net debt – end year	**311.4**	**333.8**	**367**	**394**	**421**	**446**	**472**
Memos:							
Treaty deficit[1]	−0.4	24.0	27	24	24	23	24
Treaty debt[2]	381.1	401.1	433	462	491	519	547

[1] *General government net borrowing on a Maastricht basis.*
[2] *General government gross debt.*

C33 The current budget surplus is equal to public sector receipts minus public sector current expenditure and depreciation. The current budget is expected to show deficits from 2002-03 before returning to surplus in 2005-06 and remaining in surplus throughout the rest of the projection period. These temporary deficits are consistent with allowing the automatic stabilisers to operate fully over the economic cycle, while continuing to meet the golden rule.

C34 Underlying the projections of the current budget are steady increases in the ratios of public sector receipts and current expenditure to GDP, shown in Table C5, largely reflecting measures announced in Budget 2002 and the 2002 Spending Review. By 2005-06, when the current cycle ends under the assumptions used in these projections, the accumulated total surplus over this economic cycle will be £32 billion.

C35 Table C4 also shows that net investment is projected to more than double, from £12.2 billion in 2002-03 to £31 billion in 2007-08, as the Government seeks to rectify historical under-investment in public infrastructure. These increases are sustainable and fully consistent with the Government's long-term approach and the fiscal rules, as debt is being held at less than 34 per cent of GDP throughout the projection period, well within the 40 per cent limit set by the sustainable investment rule, as shown in Table C5.

Table C5: Current and capital budgets

	Outturn 2001-02	Estimate 2002-03	Projections 2003-04	2004-05	2005-06	2006-07	2007-08
Current budget							
Current receipts	38.8	37.6	38.6	39.2	39.8	40.1	40.4
Current expenditure	36.5	37.4	38.1	38.1	38.4	38.4	38.5
Depreciation	1.3	1.3	1.3	1.3	1.3	1.3	1.3
Surplus on current budget	**1.0**	**−1.1**	**−0.8**	**−0.1**	**0.2**	**0.4**	**0.6**
Capital budget							
Gross investment	2.7	2.9	3.3	3.6	3.6	3.7	3.8
Less asset sales	−0.4	−0.4	−0.3	−0.3	−0.3	−0.3	−0.3
Less depreciation	−1.3	−1.3	−1.3	−1.3	−1.3	−1.3	−1.3
Net investment	1.0	1.2	1.7	2.0	2.1	2.1	2.2
Net borrowing	**0.0**	**2.3**	**2.5**	**2.1**	**1.9**	**1.7**	**1.6**
Public sector net debt – end year	**30.2**	**30.9**	**32.2**	**32.7**	**33.2**	**33.5**	**33.8**
Memos:							
Treaty deficit[1]	0.0	2.3	2.4	2.1	1.9	1.7	1.7
Treaty debt ratio[2]	37.9	38.0	39.0	39.4	39.6	39.9	40.1

Per cent of GDP

[1] General government net borrowing on a Maastricht basis.
[2] General government gross debt.

RECEIPTS

C36   This section looks in detail at the projections for public sector tax receipts. It begins by looking at the main determinants of changes in the overall projections since the Pre-Budget Report, before looking in detail at changes in the projections of individual tax receipts. Finally, it provides updated forecasts for the tax-GDP ratios.

Changes in total receipts since the Pre-Budget Report

C37   Table C6 provides a detailed breakdown of the main factors that have led to changes in the overall projections since the Pre-Budget Report.

Table C6: Changes in current receipts since the 2002 Pre-Budget Report

| | £ billion | | | | | |
| | Estimate | Projections | | | | |
	2002-03	2003-04	2004-05	2005-06	2006-07	2007-08
Effect on receipts of changes in:						
Assumptions audited by the NAO	–0.1	1	1	1	2	2
of which:						
Equity price assumption	0.0	0	–1	–1	–1	–1
Tobacco assumption	0.0	0	1	1	1	1
Inland Revenue compliance and enforcement package	0.0	0	1	1	1	1
Financial company profits	0.0	–1	–1	0	0	0
Other economic determinants	–0.8	–1	–2	–1	–1	0
Other	–1.8	–1	–1	–1	0	0
Total before policy changes	**–2.7**	**–2**	**–3**	**0**	**0**	**1**
Discretionary changes since PBR 2002	0.0	0	0	1	1	1
Total change	**–2.7**	**–2**	**–2**	**1**	**1**	**2**

C38   Changes to tax determinants that are projected using assumptions audited by the NAO add around £2 billion per year to current receipts by the end of the projection period, compared with the Pre-Budget Report. As described in paragraphs C27 to C31, this is mainly the result of the new assumption regarding the level of tobacco smuggling, and the Inland Revenue compliance and enforcement package.

C39   The revenue impacts of these new assumptions are partly offset by changes in equity prices since the Pre-Budget Report, which reduce receipts by around £½ billion from 2003-04 onwards. Under the audited assumption, equity prices increase in line with money GDP from the existing level of the FTSE All-Share Index, 1778 in these projections compared with the Pre-Budget Report starting point of 1963, a fall of 9 per cent. The impact on receipts of the recent stock market increases over the past week have therefore not been incorporated into the forecast published today.

C40   Also included in the audited assumptions line is the impact of changes in the oil price forecast. The audited oil price assumption is based on the average of independent forecasts for 2003 ($26.6), as this is lower than the high average levels seen over the last three months, which partially reflected uncertainty over events in the Middle East. This is $1½ a barrel higher than assumed in the Pre-Budget Report and leads to slightly higher tax revenues.

C41   As set out in Chapter B, growth in real GDP is expected to be lower in 2003 and this, coupled with recent changes in the composition of GDP in particular lower wages and salaries, has adverse effects on tax receipts in 2003-04 and 2004-05. In later years, the impacts are much smaller as the economy moves back to trend.

C42   The remaining change to current receipts in 2002-03 is explained by other factors. In particular, lower than expected taxes on income and wealth, and stamp duties. From 2003-04 onwards, these impacts are partly offset by higher forecasts of business rates receipts, and lower income tax tax credits, although the latter has little impact on the overall fiscal balances as they are largely matched by increases in the public expenditure element of the tax credits, and by higher council tax receipts, which reflect the convention of forward projections based on the average of recent years' council tax increases.

Tax-by-tax analysis

C43   Table C7 shows the changes to the projections of individual taxes since Budget 2002 and the Pre-Budget Report for 2002-03 and 2003-04. Table C8 contains updated projections for the main components of public sector receipts for 2001-02, 2002-03 and 2003-04.

Table C7: Changes in current receipts by tax since Budget 2002 and the 2002 Pre-Budget Report

| | £ billion | | | |
| | Budget 2002 | | PBR 2002 | |
	2002-03	2003-04	2002-03	2003-04
Income tax (gross of tax credits)	−4.2	−3.9	−0.8	−0.9
Non-North Sea corporation tax[1]	−3.7	−5.8	0.1	0.0
Less tax credits[2]	0.6	−1.7	0.1	0.4
North Sea revenues	−0.4	−1.0	0.1	0.2
Capital taxes[3]	−0.1	−0.6	−0.3	−0.4
Stamp duty	−0.6	−0.8	−0.6	−0.7
Value added tax	−0.3	0.0	−0.9	−0.7
Excise duties[4]	−0.6	−0.8	−0.3	0.1
Social security contributions	−0.6	−0.3	−1.2	−1.0
Other taxes and royalties[5]	0.9	1.7	0.8	0.8
Net taxes and social security contributions	**−9.1**	**−13.2**	**−3.1**	**−2.2**
Other receipts and accounting adjustments	−1.0	0.0	0.4	0.2
Current receipts	**−10.1**	**−13.3**	**−2.7**	**−2.0**

[1] National Accounts measure: gross of enhanced and payable tax credits.
[2] Includes enhanced company tax credits.
[3] Capital gains tax and inheritance tax.
[4] Fuel, alcohol and tobacco duties.
[5] Includes council tax and money paid into the National Lottery Distribution Fund, as well as other central government taxes.

Table C8: Current receipts

	£ billion		
	Outturn 2001-02	Estimate 2002-03	Projection 2003-04
Inland Revenue			
Income tax (gross of tax credits)	110.2	113.3	122.1
Corporation tax[1]	32.1	29.6	30.8
Tax credits[2]	−2.3	−3.4	−4.5
Petroleum revenue tax	1.3	1.0	1.5
Capital gains tax	3.0	1.7	1.2
Inheritance tax	2.4	2.4	2.4
Stamp duties	7.0	7.6	7.9
Social security contributions	63.2	64.3	74.5
Total Inland Revenue (net of tax credits)	**216.9**	**216.5**	**235.8**
Customs and Excise			
Value added tax	61.0	63.6	66.6
Fuel duties	21.9	22.1	23.0
Tobacco duties	7.8	8.1	8.0
Spirits duties	1.9	2.3	2.4
Wine duties	2.0	1.9	1.9
Beer and cider duties	3.1	3.1	3.1
Betting and gaming duties	1.4	1.3	1.3
Air passenger duty	0.8	0.8	0.8
Insurance premium tax	1.9	2.1	2.2
Landfill tax	0.5	0.5	0.7
Climate change levy	0.6	0.8	0.9
Aggregates levy	0.0	0.2	0.3
Customs duties and levies	2.0	1.9	1.9
Total Customs and Excise	**104.9**	**108.8**	**113.1**
Vehicle excise duties	4.2	4.6	4.8
Oil royalties	0.5	0.5	0.0
Business rates[3]	18.0	18.7	18.6
Council tax	15.3	16.6	18.6
Other taxes and royalties[4]	9.9	10.8	11.9
Net taxes and social security contributions[5]	**369.7**	**376.5**	**402.9**
Accruals adjustments on taxes	0.6	−0.3	3.6
Less own resources contribution to European Communities (EC) budget	−3.6	−2.5	−2.5
Less PC corporation tax payments	−0.1	−0.1	−0.1
Tax credits[6]	0.9	1.1	0.6
Interest and dividends	4.5	4.1	4.0
Other receipts[7]	17.9	18.2	19.8
Current receipts	**389.9**	**397.1**	**428.3**
Memo:			
North Sea revenues[8]	5.2	5.0	4.7

[1] *National Accounts measure: gross of enhanced and payable tax credits.*

[2] *Includes enhanced company tax credits.*

[3] *Includes district council rates in Northern Ireland paid by business.*

[4] *Includes money paid into the National Lottery Distribution Fund.*

[5] *Includes VAT and 'traditional own resources' contributions to EC budget. Cash basis.*

[6] *Excludes Children's Tax Credit and other tax credits that score as a tax repayment in the National Accounts.*

[7] *Includes gross operating surplus and rent; net of oil royalties.*

[8] *Consists of North Sea corporation tax, petroleum revenue tax and royalties.*

Income tax C44 Income tax receipts in 2002-03 are expected to be around £0.8 billion lower than forecast in the Pre-Budget Report. Much of this is the result of downward revisions to wages and salaries in the current financial year reflecting lower growth in private sector average earnings. In addition, self assessment tax receipts due at the end of January, which relate to tax liabilities in 2001-02, were also lower than expected. Full details on the shortfall will not be available until later in the year, however, early indications are that it may partly reflect lower than expected income from dividend payments.

C45 Income tax receipts in 2003-04 have been revised down by similar amounts, although this revision is also due to lower tax revenues from interest receipts as a result of the lower interest rate forecast that is audited by the NAO. As a result of these developments, income tax as a per cent of GDP is slightly lower than in the Pre-Budget Report projection in every year.

Non-North Sea corporation tax C46 Non-North Sea corporation tax receipts in 2002-03 are estimated to be around £26 billion, slightly higher than the Pre-Budget Report projection. After 2002-03 there have been a number of changes to the determinants of Non-North Sea corporation tax. Profits of non-financial companies have been revised downwards slightly in 2003-04 and 2004-05, but then recover. The lower equity price assumption has a negative impact on projected corporation tax on gains. Financial companies' profits are assumed to recover more slowly than was the case in the Pre-Budget Report, reflecting the ongoing uncertainty in financial markets, but to rise to similar levels by 2005. The overall forecast for corporation tax as a per cent of GDP is broadly as published in the Pre-Budget Report.

Tax credits C47 The tables in this section show the amounts of tax credits classified as negative tax in line with OECD Revenue Statistics guidelines. The public expenditure amounts are included in Table C11. In the Pre-Budget Report, the estimated split of total tax credits between that scored as tax and that scored as public expenditure was revised, with the negative tax element about £2 billion a year higher from 2003-04 onwards. These revisions were balanced by changes in the public expenditure element of tax credits, such that there was no overall impact on the fiscal balances. Further revisions to this split account for much of the changes in Budget 2003.

North Sea revenues C48 North Sea revenues in 2002-03 are estimated to be £5 billion, broadly in line with the Pre-Budget Report projection. In 2003-04, the Budget projection is £0.2 billion higher than was anticipated at the time of the Pre-Budget Report and there are slightly larger increases in subsequent years. Higher oil prices explain most of these increases. The oil price assumed in these projections is based on the average of independent forecasts for 2003, which is $26.6 per barrel, compared with $25.1 per barrel in the Pre-Budget Report.

Capital taxes C49 Receipts from capital taxes in 2002-03 are expected to be around £0.3 billion lower than projected in the Pre-Budget Report, largely as a result of lower capital gains taxes. These receipts relate to gains realised in 2001-02, and are therefore not a result of recent movements in asset prices. Information on the tax liability underlying the gains realised in 2002-03 will become available in 2004.

C50 The reduction in the capital taxes forecast from 2003-04 onwards is largely explained by the reduction in the equity price forecast, along with new information on the composition of assets liable for inheritance tax.

Stamp duty   **C51**   Stamp duty receipts in 2002-03 are estimated to be around £0.6 billion lower than forecast in the Pre-Budget Report, as a result of lower revenues from land and property transactions. This partly reflects lower than expected volumes of residential transactions and prices. Downward revisions to the projected levels of these tax determinants, along with lower forecasts for commercial prices explain most of the downward revisions to revenues in future years.

C52   Although equity prices were lower than expected at the time of the Pre-Budget Report in 2002-03, higher trading volumes have meant that revenues from stamp duty on shares are broadly in line with expectations. This pattern is expected to continue throughout the projection period.

Social security   **C53**   Receipts from social security contributions in 2002-03 are expected to be around £1.2
contributions   billion lower than projected in the Pre-Budget Report. This is partly a result of lower wages and salaries, but also because personal pension rebates have been higher than expected. These two factors also explain much of the revision in 2003-04. Measured as a per cent of GDP, receipts remain slightly below their Pre-Budget Report levels in later years.

VAT receipts   **C54**   VAT receipts in 2002-03 are estimated to have been £63.6 billion, around £0.9 billion lower than projected in the Pre-Budget Report. This is largely because of lower than expected receipts in recent months. The forecast of VAT revenues from 2003-04 onwards continues to be governed by an assumption that is audited by the NAO, which stipulates that the ratio of VAT to consumers' expenditure should decline gradually, by 0.05 percentage points a year, after the effects of VAT policy decisions are taken into account. Therefore, the shortfall in 2002-03 automatically depresses receipts in future years. However, this is partly offset by the Budget forecast of higher consumers' expenditure growth from 2003-04 onwards and the VAT measures described in Chapter A. Therefore, VAT receipts are expected to be around £0.7 billion a year lower than their Pre-Budget Report levels from 2003-04 onwards.

Excise duties   **C55**   Excise duties in 2002-03 are estimated to be around £0.3 billion lower than forecast in the Pre-Budget Report, and around £0.1 billion higher in 2003-04. Fuel duty receipts were around £0.2 billion lower than forecast in the Pre-Budget Report in 2002-03. This is mainly because the later than usual date of the Budget means that the additional receipts associated with the forestalling of road fuel duties will now be received in the early part of 2003-04. This timing issue decreases receipts in 2002-03 by around £0.2 billion with an offsetting increase in 2003-04. This increase in 2003-04 is offset by the fuel duty measure described in Chapter A, and higher oil prices that are assumed to increase pump prices and decrease demand. Alcohol duty receipts are broadly as forecast in the Pre-Budget Report.

C56   Tobacco duty receipts in 2002-03 are slightly lower than projected in the Pre-Budget Report as a result of downward revisions to the level of overall consumption. However, from 2003-04 onwards, receipts are expected to be higher than in the Pre-Budget Report. This is the result of the revised assumption regarding the levels of tobacco smuggling discussed in paragraphs C27 to C30, which has been audited by the NAO to ensure that it remains reasonable and cautious.

Other receipts   **C57**   Receipts from business rates in 2002-03 are estimated to be £0.7 billion higher than forecast in the Pre-Budget Report. This reflects new information on in year receipts. Other receipts in 2003-04 have also been revised up by similar amounts, largely as a result of higher council tax receipts, which reflect the convention of forward projections based on the average of recent years' council tax increases.

Tax-GDP ratio

C58   Table C9 shows projections of receipts from major taxes as a per cent of GDP, and Table C10 sets out current and previous projections of the overall tax-GDP ratio.

Table C9: Current receipts as a proportion of GDP

	Per cent of GDP						
	Outturn 2001-02	Estimate 2002-03	2003-04	2004-05	Projections 2005-06	2006-07	2007-08
Income tax (gross of tax credits)	11.0	10.7	11.0	11.2	11.4	11.6	11.7
Non-North Sea corporation tax[1]	2.9	2.5	2.5	2.9	3.2	3.3	3.4
Tax credits[2]	–0.2	–0.3	–0.4	–0.4	–0.4	–0.4	–0.3
North Sea revenues[3]	0.5	0.5	0.4	0.4	0.4	0.4	0.4
Value added tax	6.1	6.0	6.0	6.0	6.0	5.9	5.9
Excise duties[4]	3.6	3.5	3.5	3.4	3.3	3.2	3.2
Social security contributions	6.3	6.1	6.7	6.9	6.8	6.9	6.9
Other taxes and royalties[5]	6.7	6.6	6.6	6.7	6.8	6.9	7.0
Net taxes and social security contributions[6]	**36.8**	**35.6**	**36.3**	**37.1**	**37.6**	**37.9**	**38.2**
Accruals adjustments on taxes	0.1	0.0	0.3	0.2	0.2	0.1	0.2
Less EC transfers	–0.4	–0.2	–0.2	–0.2	–0.2	–0.1	–0.1
Tax credits[7]	0.1	0.1	0.0	0.0	0.0	0.0	0.0
Other receipts[8]	2.2	2.1	2.1	2.1	2.1	2.1	2.1
Current receipts	**38.8**	**37.6**	**38.6**	**39.2**	**39.8**	**40.1**	**40.4**
Memo:							
Current receipts (£ billion)	389.9	397.1	428	460	493	522	550

[1] National Accounts measure: gross of enhanced and payable tax credits.
[2] Tax credits scored as negative taxation in net taxes and social security contributions.
[3] Includes oil royalties, petroleum revenue tax and North Sea corporation tax.
[4] Fuel, alcohol and tobacco duties.
[5] Includes council tax and money paid into the National Lottery Distribution Fund, as well as other central government taxes.
[6] Includes VAT and 'own resources' contributions to EC budget. Cash basis.
[7] Tax credits scored as negative taxation in net taxes and social security contributions but as expenditure in the National Accounts.
[8] Mainly gross operating surplus and rent, excluding oil royalties.

Table C10: Net taxes and social security contributions[1]

	Per cent of GDP						
	Outturn[2] 2001-02	Estimate[3] 2002-03	2003-04	2004-05	Projections 2005-06	2006-07	2007-08
Budget 2002	37.0	36.7	37.6	38.1	38.3	38.3	–
PBR 2002	37.1	36.3	37.0	37.7	38.2	38.3	–
Budget 2003	**36.8**	**35.6**	**36.3**	**37.1**	**37.6**	**37.9**	**38.2**

[1] Cash basis. Uses OECD definition of negative tax personal tax credits. Net of enhanced company tax credits.
[2] The 2001-02 figures were estimates in Budget 2002.
[3] The 2002-03 figures were projections in Budget 2002 and PBR 2002.

C59   Table C10 shows that the tax-GDP ratio is now expected to fall to 35.6 per cent of GDP in 2002-03, compared with the Pre-Budget Report projection of 36.3 per cent and the Budget 2002 projection of 36.7 per cent. Similarly, the tax-GDP ratio is expected to be well below the Pre-Budget Report and Budget 2002 projections throughout the projection period.

C60   Chart C3 shows the tax-GDP ratio from 1978-79 to 2007-08.

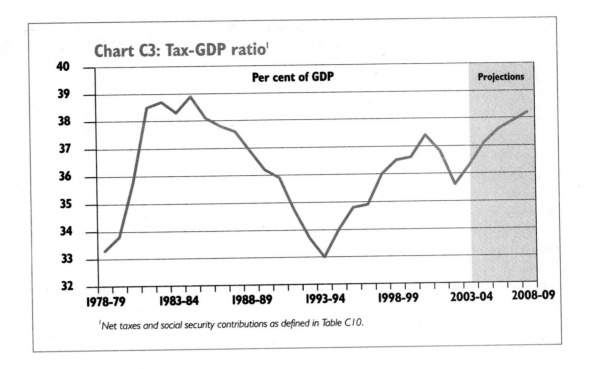

Chart C3: Tax-GDP ratio[1]

[1] Net taxes and social security contributions as defined in Table C10.

PUBLIC EXPENDITURE

C61   Table C11 shows projections for public expenditure up to 2005-06, the last year covered by the 2002 Spending Review. The projections cover the whole of the public sector, using the National Accounts aggregate Total Managed Expenditure (TME). TME is split into Departmental Expenditure Limits (DEL) – firm three year limits for departments' programme expenditure – and Annually Managed Expenditure (AME) – expenditure that is not easily subject to firm multi-year limits.

Table C11: Total Managed Expenditure 2001-02 to 2005-06

	£ billion				
	Outturn 2001-02	Estimate 2002-03	Projections 2003-04	Projections 2004-05	2005-06
Departmental Expenditure Limits					
Resource Budget	215.8	241.6	249.1	263.8	283.5
Capital Budget	18.0	20.7	25.1	26.8	29.1
Less depreciation	−9.6	−18.3	−10.4	−11.1	−11.8
Total Departmental Expenditure Limits	**224.1**	**244.0**	**263.8**	**279.5**	**300.7**
Annually Managed Expenditure					
Social security benefits[1]	101.1	105.5	111.0	116.7	121.9
Tax credits[1]	8.7	9.8	11.7	12.1	12.5
Housing Revenue Account subsidies	4.5	4.3	4.3	4.0	4.1
Common Agricultural Policy	3.7	2.6	2.3	2.3	2.3
Net public service pensions[2]	10.1	3.5	0.2	0.1	−0.1
National Lottery	1.7	1.9	2.2	1.9	1.5
Non-cash items in AME	23.4	27.9	25.2	26.4	27.5
Other departmental expenditure	0.2	2.3	2.2	1.8	1.9
Net payments to EC institutions[3]	0.8	2.3	2.3	3.0	3.4
Locally financed expenditure	19.8	20.7	23.0	24.6	26.1
Central government gross debt interest	22.1	20.8	21.8	23.2	24.3
Public corporations' own-financed capital expenditure	1.5	2.2	2.6	2.7	2.7
Total AME before margin and accounting adjustments	**197.7**	**203.8**	**208.9**	**218.9**	**228.2**
AME margin	0.0	0.0	1.0	2.0	3.0
Accounting adjustments[4]	−32.2	−26.7	−18.0	−15.7	−15.4
Annually Managed Expenditure	**165.5**	**177.0**	**191.9**	**205.2**	**215.8**
Total Managed Expenditure	**389.6**	**421.0**	**455.7**	**484.7**	**516.5**
of which:					
Public sector current expenditure	366.6	395.0	422.3	446.5	475.2
Public sector net investment	9.6	12.2	18.9	23.0	25.4
Public sector depreciation	13.4	13.8	14.4	15.2	15.9

[1] For 2001-02 to 2004-05, child allowances in Income Support and Jobseekers' Allowance, which, from 2003-04, are paid as part of the Child Tax Credit, have been included in the tax credits line and excluded from the social security benefits line. This is in order to give figures on a consistent definition over the forecast period.

[2] Net public service pensions expenditure is reported under FRS17 accounting requirements.

[3] Net payments to EC institutions exclude the UK's contribution to the cost of EC aid to non-Member States (which is attributed to the aid programme).

Net payments therefore differ from the UK's net contribution to the EC Budget, latest estimates for which are (in £ billion):

2001-02	2002-03	2003-04	2004-05	2005-06
1.5	3.1	3.2	3.7	4.0

The trended forecast for 2002-03 is £3.0 billion.

[4] Excludes depreciation.

C62   Chart C4 shows TME as a per cent of GDP from 1970-71 to 2005-06.

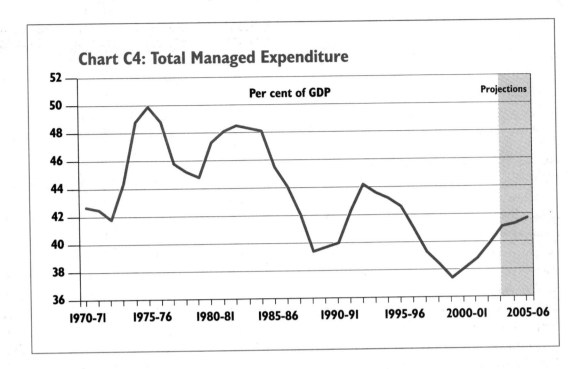

Chart C4: Total Managed Expenditure

C63   The 2002 Spending Review was the first to be conducted on a full resource basis. Resource accounting and budgeting (RAB) replaces the previous approach of planning and controlling public expenditure on a cash basis and applies the best financial and disclosure practices of commercial accounting to central government finances. Resource budgeting was introduced in two stages, and prior to the 2002 Spending Review budgets were set on a 'near cash' basis – a hybrid of resource budgeting and the previous cash management system.

C64   From 2003-04 onwards, departmental budgets will be controlled on a full resource budgeting basis, which means that the full economic cost of departmental activity will be recognised in budgets. Table C12 shows DEL in terms of resource and capital budgets. These figures have been adjusted to reflect classification changes since the Pre-Budget Report. These include: the reduction in the cost of capital charge that, under RAB, reflects the opportunity and financing costs of capital; and changes to the discount rate applied to future liabilities, as agreed with the independent Financial Reporting Advisory Board (FRAB). Both of these changes are TME neutral.

C65   Defence estimated outturn in 2002-03 has increased by £9.5 billion since the Pre-Budget Report. The majority of this increase is a result of changes arising from the quinquennial revaluation of its asset base in line with Generally Accepted Accounting Practice, the continued implementation of the asset management plan following on from the Strategic Defence Review and recognition of future liabilities. These items are all non-cash and TME neutral. An additional allocation of £1 billion was also made from the special reserve.

Table C12: Departmental Expenditure Limits – resource and capital budgets

£ billion

	Outturn 2001-02	Estimate 2002-03	2003-04	Plans 2004-05	2005-06
Resource Budget					
Education and Skills[1]	17.0	20.6	22.0	23.7	25.6
Health[1]	52.1	57.4	63.0	68.7	74.9
of which: NHS	*50.9*	*55.1*	*60.8*	*66.5*	*72.7*
Transport	4.4	6.0	7.3	7.5	8.4
Office of the Deputy Prime Minister	2.7	4.1	4.8	5.2	5.4
Local government	36.9	37.4	41.0	44.1	48.0
Home Office	10.3	11.3	11.7	11.6	12.4
Lord Chancellor's departments	3.1	3.3	3.1	3.4	3.5
Attorney General's departments	0.4	0.5	0.5	0.5	0.5
Defence[2]	32.3	41.4[3]	30.8	31.5	32.3
Foreign and Commonwealth Office	1.4	1.6	1.7	1.5	1.6
International Development	3.2	3.6	3.6	3.8	4.5
Trade and Industry	5.4	4.6	4.7	4.9	5.4
Environment, Food and Rural Affairs	2.7	2.7	2.7	2.7	2.8
Culture, Media and Sport	1.2	1.3	1.4	1.5	1.5
Work and Pensions	6.2	7.5	8.0	8.0	8.2
Scotland[4]	16.0	17.3	18.4	19.4	20.6
Wales[4]	8.2	9.1	9.8	10.4	11.1
Northern Ireland Executive[4]	5.7	6.2	6.4	6.7	7.1
Northern Ireland Office	1.0	1.2	1.1	1.1	1.1
Chancellor's departments	4.1	4.6	4.6	4.7	4.9
Cabinet Office	1.5	1.7	1.8	1.8	1.9
Invest to Save Budget	0.0	0.0	0.0	0.0	0.0
Capital Modernisation Fund	0.0	0.0	0.0	0.0	0.0
Reserve	0.0	0.0	0.0	0.0	0.0
Unallocated special reserve[5]	0.0	0.0	0.7	1.2	1.7
Allowance for shortfall[6]	0.0	2.0	0.0	0.0	0.0
		−3.8			
Total Resource Budget DEL	**215.8**	**241.6**	**249.1**	**263.8**	**283.5**
Capital Budget					
Education and Skills	2.1	2.6	3.3	3.8	4.3
Health	1.8	2.1	3.0	3.5	4.5
of which: NHS	*1.7*	*2.0*	*2.9*	*3.4*	*4.4*
Transport	2.4	3.0	3.3	3.6	3.3
Office of the Deputy Prime Minister	1.8	1.5	1.9	2.0	2.1
Local government	0.1	0.2	0.3	0.3	0.3
Home Office	0.6	0.9	1.1	1.1	1.1
Lord Chancellor's departments	0.1	0.1	0.1	0.1	0.1
Attorney General's departments	0.0	0.0	0.0	0.0	0.0
Defence	5.8	6.3	6.1	6.4	7.0
Foreign and Commonwealth Office	0.1	0.1	0.1	0.1	0.1
International Development	0.0	0.0	0.0	0.0	0.0
Trade and Industry	0.1	0.4	0.5	0.2	0.2
Environment, Food and Rural Affairs	0.3	0.4	0.3	0.3	0.3
Culture, Media and Sport	0.0	0.1	0.1	0.1	0.1
Work and Pensions	0.1	0.2	0.0	0.2	0.1
Scotland[4]	1.4	2.0	2.0	2.2	2.3
Wales[4]	0.5	0.8	0.8	0.9	1.0
Northern Ireland Executive[4]	0.4	0.6	0.4	0.5	0.5
Northern Ireland Office	0.0	0.1	0.1	0.1	0.1
Chancellor's departments	0.2	0.4	0.3	0.3	0.3
Cabinet Office	0.2	0.2	0.6	0.2	0.2
Invest to Save Budget	0.0	0.0	0.0	0.0	0.0
Capital Modernisation Fund	0.0	0.0	0.0	0.0	0.0
Reserve	0.0	0.0	0.8	0.8	1.1
Allowance for shortfall[6]	0.0	−1.2	0.0	0.0	0.0
Total Capital Budget DEL	**18.0**	**20.7**	**25.1**	**26.8**	**29.1**
Depreciation	**−9.6**	**−18.3**	**−10.4**	**−11.1**	**−11.8**
Total Departmental Expenditure Limits	**224.1**	**244.0**	**263.8**	**279.5**	**300.7**
Total education spending	49.4	53.6	58.6	62.9	68.5

[1] From 2003-04 onwards this includes employer contributions for cost of pension increases.
[2] Cost of capital charge and provisions discount rate classification changes have only been applied to the Ministry of Defence figures from 2003-04 onwards.
[3] One-off increase in defence non-cash expenditure in line with agreed asset management policy.
[4] For Scotland and Wales and Northern Ireland, the split between current and capital budgets is decided by the respective executives.
[5] This is the remaining contingency provision for costs of military operations in Iraq after an allocation of a preliminary £1 billion to Ministry of Defence from the £3 billion total.
[6] In 2001-02 and 2002-03, DEL is controlled on a near-cash basis (see Table C13). The numbers have been translated onto a Stage 2 basis, for comparison purposes. They have been adjusted since PBR 2002 to take account of changes to non-cash, classification changes and other items that have no impact on total public spending. From 2003-04, DEL will be controlled fully on a Stage 2 basis.

C66   In 2001-02 and 2002-03, departmental expenditure was controlled on a 'near cash' basis. Table C13 shows outturns and plans on this basis. Both tables have been updated since the Pre-Budget Report to reflect transfers between departments and programmes, additions and allocations from central funds and reclassifications.

C67   At the Pre-Budget Report planned DEL for 2002-03 on a 'near cash' basis was £231.4 billion. Since then £2.3 billion has been added to total planned DEL reflecting the addition to the special reserve and classification changes, giving a total planned DEL of £233.7 billion. As Table C13 shows, in 2002-03 total DEL spending remains within plans. In line with previous practice, an allowance for shortfall of £4.0 billion, representing estimates of the likely underspend beneath departmental estimates, is made.

Table C13: Departmental Expenditure Limits on a 2000 Spending Review basis – resource and capital budgets

	£ billion	
	Outturn 2001-02	**Estimate 2002-03**
Resource Budget		
Education and Skills	16.5	20.0
Health	48.7	54.5
of which: NHS	*47.5*	*52.3*
Transport	2.7	3.1
Office of the Deputy Prime Minister	1.3	1.8
Local government	36.9	37.4
Home Office	9.7	10.4
Lord Chancellor's departments	2.9	3.1
Attorney General's departments	0.4	0.5
Defence	18.5	20.2
Foreign and Commonwealth Office	1.3	1.4
International Development	3.2	3.4
Trade and Industry	3.5	3.8
Environment, Food and Rural Affairs	2.7	2.2
Culture, Media and Sport	1.0	1.2
Work and Pensions	6.2	7.4
Scotland[1]	14.2	16.1
Wales[1]	7.5	8.5
Northern Ireland Executive[1]	4.7	5.7
Northern Ireland Office	1.0	1.1
Chancellor's departments	3.8	4.2
Cabinet Office	1.3	1.4
Invest to Save Budget	0.0	0.0
Capital Modernisation Fund	0.0	0.0
Reserve	0.0	0.0
Unallocated special reserve[2]	0.0	2.0
Allowance for shortfall	0.0	−3.1
Total Resource Budget DEL	**188.1**	**206.3**
Capital Budget		
Education and Skills	2.5	3.2
Health	1.9	2.2
of which: NHS	*1.8*	*2.1*
Transport	4.3	5.6
Office of the Deputy Prime Minister	2.6	3.2
Local government	0.1	0.2
Home Office	0.8	1.1
Lord Chancellor's departments	0.1	0.1
Attorney General's departments	0.0	0.0
Defence	5.9	6.3
Foreign and Commonwealth Office	0.1	0.1
International Development	0.0	0.0
Trade and Industry	0.5	1.0
Environment, Food and Rural Affairs	0.5	0.6
Culture, Media and Sport	0.1	0.1
Work and Pensions	0.2	0.2
Scotland[1]	2.2	2.0
Wales[1]	0.9	1.1
Northern Ireland Executive[1]	0.5	0.5
Northern Ireland Office	0.0	0.1
Chancellor's departments	0.2	0.4
Cabinet Office	0.2	0.2
Invest to Save Budget	0.0	0.0
Capital Modernisation Fund	0.0	0.0
Reserve	0.0	0.0
Allowance for shortfall	0.0	−0.9
Total Capital Budget DEL	**23.7**	**27.3**
Total Departmental Expenditure Limits	**211.8**	**233.7**
Total education spending	49.4	53.6

[1] For Scotland and Wales and Northern Ireland, the split between current and capital budgets is decided by the respective executives.

[2] This is the remaining contingency provision for costs of military operations in Iraq after an allocation of a preliminary £1 billion to the Ministry of Defence from the £3 billion total.

C68   Table C14 shows changes in DEL and AME components since the Pre-Budget Report. It has also been updated to incorporate reclassifications including between DEL and AME as well as between current and capital DEL, and the reduction in DEL brought about by the reallocation of the Capital Modernisation Fund (CMF) and measures announced in this Budget. Net public service pensions figures are now reported on a Financial Reporting Standard 17 (FRS17) basis. This means that the measure of expenditure for this component has changed from being a cash record of flows in and out of the schemes to one that records the movements in the liability of the various pension schemes, including the accruing costs as members serve additional years. Additional non-cash costs are also now included in the non-cash items in AME line. This change is neutral on TME but does mean that meaningful comparisons between the net public service pensions, non-cash items in AME and the accounting adjustments lines shown in Table C11 and in the Pre-Budget Report cannot be made and these lines have therefore been excluded from this table.

C69   As described in Chapter 6, the Government has made a special reserve allocation of £3 billion to ensure that resources are available to cover the full cost of the UK's military obligations in Iraq, of which £1 billion has already been allocated to the Ministry of Defence budget. The full amount of the provision has been allocated to 2002-03, although it is not yet clear when these costs will fall. In the light of continuing uncertainty, and in order to protect committed investment while responding prudently to heightened global risks, the Government has decided to make no further allocations from the CMF. Instead, the unallocated CMF funding will contribute towards the rebuilding of the AME margin to ensure that the public spending projections include a prudent and cautious safety margin against unexpected events.

C70   Total DEL spending in 2002-03, net of depreciation, is now estimated to be around £2.7 billion higher than in the Pre-Budget Report. £2.2 billion of this is due to the further allocations to the special reserve of £2 billion and a £0.2 billion increase in capital DEL from reclassified PFI projects. The remainder reflects changes in non-cash items, other than depreciation, which are then removed in the AME accounting adjustments and are therefore TME neutral. DEL changes in later years are due to reclassifications and other switches between DEL and AME and between resource and capital DEL.

Table C14: Changes to Total Managed Expenditure since the 2002 Pre-Budget Report

	£ billion				
	Outturn 2001-02	Estimate 2002-03	2003-04	Projections 2004-05	2005-06
Departmental Expenditure Limits					
Resource Budget	2.7	11.4	–3.3	–3.2	–3.2
Capital Budget	–0.1	–0.6	–0.1	–0.8	–1.0
Less depreciation	0.0	–8.1	0.7	0.4	0.4
Total Departmental Expenditure Limits[1]	**2.6**	**2.7**	**–2.7**	**–3.7**	**–3.9**
Annually Managed Expenditure					
Social security benefits	-0.2	0.6	0.9	1.0	0.9
Tax credits	0.1	–0.2	0.0	–0.2	–0.2
Housing Revenue Account subsidies	0.0	0.0	0.1	–0.2	–0.1
Common Agricultural Policy	–0.1	0.2	0.0	–0.1	–0.2
National Lottery	0.0	–0.1	0.0	0.0	0.0
Other departmental expenditure	–0.5	0.8	1.6	0.7	1.1
Net payments to EC institutions	0.0	0.7	0.1	0.0	0.0
Locally financed expenditure	–0.4	–0.2	0.7	1.2	1.4
Central government gross debt interest	–0.1	0.1	0.3	–0.6	0.4
Public corporations' own-financed capital expenditure	–0.4	–0.4	–0.2	0.1	0.1
AME margin	0.0	–0.1	–0.8	1.5	2.5
Annually Managed Expenditure	**–4.9**	**–1.5**	**3.6**	**6.7**	**8.8**
Total Managed Expenditure	**–2.3**	**1.2**	**0.9**	**3.0**	**4.9**
of which:					
Public sector current expenditure	–3.0	3.7	1.8	2.2	3.9
Public sector net investment	0.7	–2.1	–0.7	1.1	1.3
Public sector depreciation	0.0	–0.3	–0.3	–0.3	–0.3

[1] DEL in 2001-02 and 2002-03 is controlled on a 'near cash' basis as set out in paragraph C67.

C71 Forecasts of individual AME programmes were reviewed in the Pre-Budget Report and have been reviewed again for this Budget. In addition, and following usual practice, the Government has decided to reset the AME margin to £1 billion in 2003-04, £2 billion in 2004-05 and £3 billion in 2005-06.

C72 The main economic assumptions underpinning AME projections are set out in Box C1 and Table C3. In particular, it is assumed that UK claimant unemployment will increase slightly, in line with the average of independent forecasts, from its recent level of 0.93 million (the average of the three months ending in March 2003) to 1.03 million in 2005-06.

C73   Higher forecasts for inflation – which affects the uprating of benefits – and claimant unemployment have increased the social security expenditure forecast since the Pre-Budget Report by around £½ billion from 2004-05. New interim population projections based on the 2001 Census have also had an upward effect of around £0.2 billion from 2004-05, largely because of an increase in the forecast growth of the pensioner population. In addition, the additional funding for pensioners and other social security payments announced in this Budget add a further £0.2 billion in the last two years.

C74   Locally financed expenditure is also higher at the end of the projection period, and reflects the convention of forward projections based on the average of recent years' council tax increases. However, this has a broadly neutral impact on the fiscal balances as it is matched by additional resources raised at the local level.

C75   With the exception of 2004-05, central government gross debt interest payments are higher than at the Pre-Budget Report. This reflects higher borrowing and higher forecasts for inflation, affecting the accrued uplift on index-linked gilts, offset by lower market expectations for interest rates. In 2004-05 the forecast for inflation is lower than at the Pre-Budget Report and this, in combination with lower interest rates, more than offsets the effects of higher borrowing.

C76   The main accounting adjustments, which consist of those items within TME but outside DEL and AME main programmes, are shown in Table C15. Accounting adjustments also reflect the impact on DEL of a fall in the cost of capital charge made to departments. This change is TME neutral and constitutes a reduction in non-cash spending in DEL and a corresponding reduction in AME of the accounting adjustment that removes non-cash spending.

Table C15: Accounting adjustments

	£ billion				
	Outturn	Estimate		Projections	
	2001-02	2002-03	2003-04	2004-05	2005-06
Removal of non-cash spending in DEL[1]	−11.2	−10.0	−6.6	−6.9	−7.3
Financial transactions in DEL	−1.6	−1.5	−1.9	−1.4	−1.4
Removal of non-cash spending in AME	−29.4	−27.1	−23.6	−24.7	−25.6
Financial transactions in AME	0.1	−0.4	−0.1	0.7	0.6
Adjustments for public corporations	3.3	3.1	3.6	3.6	3.8
Central government non-trading capital consumption	8.3	8.5	9.0	9.4	9.9
VAT refunded on general government expenditure	7.6	8.8	9.8	10.6	11.6
EC contributions	−6.1	−4.2	−4.5	−4.2	−4.1
Tax credits	0.9	1.3	0.8	0.8	0.9
Intra-general government debt interest	−3.0	−3.6	−2.5	−2.8	−2.8
Other accounting adjustments	−1.1	−1.7	−2.0	−0.7	−0.9
Total accounting adjustments	**−32.2**	**−26.7**	**−18.0**	**−15.7**	**−15.4**

[1] Excluding depreciation in resource DEL.

C77   Table C16 shows public sector capital expenditure from 2001-02 to 2005-06.

Table C16: Public sector capital expenditure

	£ billion				
	Outturn	Estimate		Projections	
	2001-02	2002-03	2003-04	2004-05	2005-06
Capital Budget DEL	18.0	20.7	25.1	26.8	29.1
Locally financed expenditure	1.2	1.3	1.5	1.8	1.7
National Lottery	0.9	0.9	1.2	1.1	0.8
Public corporations' own-financed capital expenditure	1.5	2.2	2.6	2.7	2.7
Other capital spending in AME	1.3	0.9	2.9	5.1	5.9
AME margin	0.0	0.0	0.1	0.8	1.1
Public sector gross investment[1]	**23.0**	**26.0**	**33.4**	**38.2**	**41.3**
Less depreciation	13.4	13.8	14.4	15.2	15.9
Public sector net investment	**9.6**	**12.2**	**18.9**	**23.0**	**25.4**
Proceeds from the sale of fixed assets[2]	4.3	4.5	3.8	3.8	3.8

[1] This and previous lines are all net of sales of fixed assets.

[2] Projections of total receipts from the sale of fixed assets by public sector.

C78   Table C17 shows estimated receipts from loans and sales of assets from 2001-02 to 2005-06. The figures for sales of financial assets include proceeds of £0.1 billion for the sale of a stake in QinetiQ (formerly the Defence Evaluation and Research Agency) in the first quarter of 2003. The total proceeds of the Public Private Partnership (PPP) will be £0.2 billion, including receipts in 2001-02 and those due in future years.

Table C17: Loans and sales of assets

	Outturn	Estimate		Projections	
	2001-02	**2002-03**	**2003-04**	**2004-05**	**2005-06**
£ billion					
Sales of fixed assets					
Central government	0.9	1.0	1.0	1.0	1.0
Local authorities	3.4	3.5	2.8	2.8	2.8
Total sales of fixed assets	**4.3**	**4.5**	**3.8**	**3.8**	**3.8**
Total loans and sales of financial assets	**−1.8**	**−2.6**	**−2.1**	**−1.4**	**−1.5**
Total loans and sales of assets	**2.5**	**1.9**	**1.6**	**2.4**	**2.2**

PRIVATE FINANCE INITIATIVE

C79   Under the Private Finance Initiative (PFI) the public sector purchases services from a private sector partner. In addition to requiring capital investment to be undertaken by the private sector, the ability of the private sector partner to be innovative and manage risks appropriately allocated to it can result in a specified level of service at a price that represents value for money.

C80   The PFI has now become one of the established methods of delivering many public services that require significant investment in capital asssets. Projects have been approved in such diverse areas as schools, colleges, hospitals, local authorities, defence and property management since May 1997. Approval of a PFI scheme depends on value-for-money based on an assessment of the lifetime costs of both providing and maintaining the underlying asset and the running costs of delivering the required service.

C81   The Government is committed to developing PFI and other partnership arrangements with the private sector to further enhance the delivery of public services, ensure value for money for the public sector and to ensure the delivery of a higher sustainable level of public sector investment. The Government wants to exploit all commercial potential and spare capacity in public sector assets through a sensible balance of risk and reward.

C82   Table C18 shows a breakdown by department of the estimated public sector investment resulting from signed contracts and Table C19 shows those expected to reach preferred bidder stage within the next three years.

C83   Under PFI, the public sector contracts for services facilities availability and management not assets. Capital investment is only one of the activities undertaken by the private sector in order to supply these services. The figures in Tables C18 and C19, therefore, do not reflect the total value of the contracts.

Table C18: Departmental estimate of capital spending by the private sector (signed deals)

	£ million		
		Projections	
	2003-04	2004-05	2005-06
Education and Skills[1]	0	0	0
Health	338	210	89
Transport[2]	6 624	552	370
Local government[3,4]	1 940	2 330	2 700
Home Office	186	150	46
Lord Chancellor's department	52	6	11
Defence	175	0	0
Foreign and Commonwealth Office	5	5	5
Trade and Industry	6	2	0
Environment, Food and Rural Affairs	3	0	0
Work and Pensions	14	22	0
Scotland	381	330	1
Wales	43	34	0
Northern Ireland Executive	13	3	0
Chancellor's departments	49	24	11
Cabinet Office	12	4	0
Total	**9 841**	**3 672**	**3 233**

[1] Excludes private finance activity in education institutions classified to the private sector. Schools projects funded through Revenue Support Grant are included in the local government figures.
[2] Includes the capital expenditure for Tubelines (part of the London Underground Limited Public Private Partnerships (LUL PPP) contracts) in 2003-04. Such investments that are found to be on balance sheet also score as public sector net investment.
[3] Figures represent spending on projects supported by central government through Revenue Support Grant.
[4] PFI activity in local authority schools is included in the local government line.
Source: Office of Government Commerce.

Table C19: Estimated aggregated capital value of projects at preferred bidder stage

	£ million		
		Projections	
	2003-04	2004-05	2005-06
Health	145	197	193
Transport[1]	10 759	32	11
Home Office	26	17	0
Lord Chancellor's department	19	19	0
Defence	1 364	1 393	0
Scotland	9	48	16
Wales	96	0	0
Northern Ireland Executive	31	33	0
Total	**12 449**	**1 739**	**220**

[1] The 2003-04 figure includes the estimated capital value of the LUL PPP contracts not yet signed over the next 15 years.
Source: Office of Government Commerce.

C84   Table C20 shows a forecast of the estimated payments for services flowing from new private investment in signed projects over the next 25 years. Actual expenditure will depend on the details of the payment mechanism for each contract. Payments may be lower than estimated due to deductions from the service payments caused by the supplier's failure to meet the required performance standards. In addition, variances may occur due to changes in the service requirements agreed during the course of the contracts. Payments may also vary as a result of the early termination of a contract triggering contractual arrangements for compensation on termination.

Table C20: Estimated payments under PFI contracts – April 2003 (signed deals)[1]

	£ billion		
	Projections		
2003-04	5.4	2016-17	4.8
2004-05	5.7	2017-18	4.1
2005-06	5.8	2018-19	3.6
2006-07	6.0	2019-20	3.4
2007-08	6.0	2020-21	3.6
2008-09	5.8	2021-22	3.2
2009-10	5.8	2022-23	3.1
2010-11	5.6	2023-24	3.1
2011-12	5.3	2024-25	3.1
2012-13	5.1	2025-26	3.0
2013-14	5.0	2026-27	1.6
2014-15	4.9	2027-28	1.3
2015-16	4.8	2028-29	1.2

[1] The figures between 2003-04 and 2016-17 include estimated payments for the Tubelines LUL PPP contracts. These contracts contain periodic reviews every 7.5 years and therefore the service payments are not fixed after 2009-10.
Source: Office of Government Commerce.

Box C2: Transparency in reporting liabilities and contingent liabilities

The United Kingdom is one of the few countries in the world in which the Government has a statutory requirement to report its liabilities, assets and all other key financial information in the same way as private sector companies. Since 1997, the Government has introduced a series of reforms to ensure greater transparency and increased availability of information about national and departmental finances.

The *Code for fiscal stability* commits the Government to apply best-practice accounting methods in the production of its accounts. In 2000, the Government introduced new legislation that requires departmental accounts to follow Generally Accepted Accounting Practices (UK GAAP), adapted as necessary for the public sector context. In line with these statutory requirements, departments now produce full resource accounts.

The UK has an extremely transparent system for reporting liabilities, including contingent liabilities:

- departmental resource accounts include full disclosure of all actual and contingent liabilities. These accounts are independently audited and laid before Parliament; and

- departmental contingent liabilities that are reportable to Parliament, either under statute or because they are above £100,000 and outside the course of normal business, are drawn together in the Supplementary Statements to the Consolidated Fund and National Loan Funds accounts.

The Government is committed to further improvements. In particular, it is working towards the production of Central Government Accounts (CGA) as part of the staged approach to preparing Whole of Government Accounts (WGA). Both CGA and WGA represent a significant step forward by making available, for the first time, consolidated accounts information about central government and, subsequently, the public sector as a whole. One of the benefits of CGA and WGA will be consolidated information on contingent liabilities.

FINANCING REQUIREMENT

C85 Table C21 presents projections of the net cash requirement by sector, giving details of financial transactions that do not affect net borrowing (the change in the sector's net financial indebtedness) but do affect its financing requirement. The large difference in accounts receivable/payable between 2002-03 and 2003-04 is due to a combination of factors affecting differences between cash and accrued receipts and spending. This is partly a result of the cash and accrual implications of the national insurance contribution measures announced in Budget 2002. These increase accrued receipts by more than cash receipts – reducing public sector net borrowing by more than the public sector net cash requirement.

Table C21: Public sector net cash requirement

£ billion

	2002-03				2003-04			
	General government		**Public corporations**	**Public sector**	General government		**Public corporations**	**Public sector**
	Central government	**Local authorities**			**Central government**	**Local authorities**		
Net borrowing	**24.5**	**–0.7**	**0.1**	**24.0**	**27.2**	**–0.1**	**0.2**	**27.3**
Financial transactions								
Net lending to private sector and abroad	2.7	–0.1	0.0	2.6	2.2	–0.1	0.0	2.1
Cash expenditure on company securities	0.0	0.0	0.0	0.0	0.0	0.0	0.0	0.0
Accounts receivable/payable	–1.0	0.0	0.0	–1.0	4.7	–0.1	0.0	4.7
Adjustment for interest on gilts	–1.5	0.0	0.0	–1.5	–1.0	0.0	0.0	–1.0
Miscellaneous financial transactions	–1.7	0.0	0.1	–1.6	0.0	0.0	–0.7	–0.7
Own account net cash requirement	23.0	–0.8	0.2	22.5	33.2	–0.3	–0.5	32.4
Net lending within the public sector	–1.6	1.5	0.1	0.0	2.1	–0.3	–1.9	0.0
Net cash requirement[1]	**21.4**	**0.7**	**0.3**	**22.5**	**35.3**	**–0.5**	**–2.3**	**32.4**

[1] *Market and overseas borrowing for local government and public corporation sectors.*

C86 In order to comply with the *Code for fiscal stability,* the *Provisional Debt Management Report 2003-04* (PDMR) was published on 20 March 2003 in advance of Budget 2003. As well as updating the financing arithmetic for 2002-03, it also outlined provisional financing plans for 2003-04. The forecasts for both years' financing arithmetic were based on the public finance forecasts published in the Pre-Budget Report. For 2003-04, the provisional net financing requirement was £51.3 billion. This was to be met by gross gilts issuance of £40 billion and a £9.8 billion adjustment in the net short-term debt position.

C87 Table C22 updates the financing arithmetic for both 2002-03 and 2003-04 in line with the new forecasts for the public finances. The forecast for the central government net cash requirement for 2002-03 is £21.4 billion, an increase of £2.7 billion from the Pre-Budget Report forecast. Additionally, there have been changes to the level of the Debt Management Office's (DMO's) buy-backs of near maturity stock, their cash deposit at the Bank of England (BoE) and National Savings and Investments' (NS&I's) net contribution. Overall, this means that the net financing requirement for 2002-03 has been revised to £38.3 billion. This was met by gross gilts sales in 2002-03 of £26.3 billion and a net short-term debt adjustment of £12 billion. These changes have resulted in an end-March 2003 level for the DMO's net cash position of £4.5 billion, £2.3 billion lower than forecast in the PDMR.

C88 The forecast for the central government net cash requirement for 2003-04 is £35.3 billion, an increase of £5.1 billion from the forecast published in the PDMR. The net financing requirement is forecast to be £54.8 billion, an increase of £5 billion from the forecast published in the PDMR .

C89 In order to meet this financing requirement, the DMO's remit has been revised such that:

- gross gilt sales have been increased by £7.4 billion to £47.4 billion; and

- net-short term debt sales have decreased by £2.4 billion to £7.4 billion.

C90 Full details of these measures and complete financing tables for 2002-03 and 2003-04 can be found in the *Debt and Reserves Management Report 2003-04*, which is being published alongside this Budget.

Table C22: Financing requirement forecast

| | £ billion | | | | | | |
| | | 2002-03 | | | | 2003-04 | |
	Mar-2002 Original remit[1]	Apr-2002 Budget remit	Nov-2002 Pre-Budget Report	Mar-2003 PDMR[2]	Apr-2003 Budget	Mar-2003 PDMR[2]	Apr-2003 Budget
Central government net cash requirement	13.6	13.5	18.7	18.7	21.4	30.2	35.3
Gilt redemptions	17.2	17.0	17.0	17.0	17.0	21.1	21.1
Debt buy-backs	0.0	0.0	0.3	0.3	0.4	0.0	0.0
Gross financing requirement	30.8	30.5	36.0	36.0	38.8	51.3	56.4
Less assumed net NS&I's contribution	−1.5	−1.5	−1.0	0.2	0.7	1.5	1.5
Less change in DMO's cash balance at BoE	0.0	−0.1	−0.1	−0.1	−0.2	0.0	0.1
Net financing requirement	32.3	32.1	37.1	35.9	38.3	49.8	54.8
Financed by							
Gross gilt sales	23.0	22.4	26.2	26.4	26.3	40.0	47.4
Changes in short term debt	9.3	9.7	10.9	9.5	12.0	9.8	7.4

Note: Figures may not sum due to rounding.
[1] The Debt and Reserves Management Report 2002-03 was published on 14 March 2002 in advance of Budget 2002 to comply with the Code for fiscal stability.
[2] The Provisional Debt Management Report 2003-04 was published on 20 March 2003 in advance of Budget 2003 to comply with the Code for fiscal stability.

ANALYSIS BY SUBSECTOR AND ECONOMIC CATEGORY

C91   Table C23 shows a breakdown of general government transactions by economic category for 2001-02 to 2005-06. Table C24 shows a more detailed breakdown for public sector transactions by sub-sector and economic category for 2002-03 and 2003-04.

Table C23: General government transactions by sub-sector

	Outturn	Projections			
£ billion	2001-02	2002-03	2003-04	2004-05	2005-06
Current receipts					
Taxes on income and wealth	145.1	143.5	152.9	168.8	184.8
Taxes on production and imports	136.1	143.3	149.1	157.3	166.3
Other current taxes	18.3	19.8	22.0	23.7	25.7
Taxes on capital	2.4	2.4	2.4	2.7	2.8
Social contributions	63.1	63.6	76.2	80.8	85.1
Gross operating surplus	8.3	8.5	9.0	9.4	9.9
Rent and other current transfers	2.2	2.0	1.6	1.7	1.7
Interest and dividends from private sector and abroad	4.0	3.5	3.4	3.9	4.1
Interest and dividends from public sector	7.2	7.0	7.6	7.8	8.0
Total current receipts	**386.6**	**393.7**	**424.1**	**456.0**	**488.5**
Current expenditure					
Current expenditure on goods and services	196.4	212.7	232.0	247.3	264.2
Subsidies	6.0	7.7	7.6	8.6	9.9
Net social benefits	124.1	129.6	136.3	142.9	149.2
Net current grants abroad	−1.9	0.5	−0.2	−0.9	−1.6
Other current grants	19.4	23.2	23.4	23.7	26.9
Interest and dividends paid	22.4	21.2	22.2	23.5	24.6
AME margin	0.0	0.0	0.9	1.2	1.9
Total current expenditure	**366.5**	**395.0**	**422.2**	**446.3**	**475.0**
Depreciation	8.3	8.5	9.0	9.4	9.9
Surplus on current budget	**11.8**	**−9.8**	**−7.0**	**0.3**	**3.6**
Capital expenditure					
Gross domestic fixed capital formation	12.4	14.5	19.7	22.6	24.6
Less depreciation	−8.3	−8.5	−9.0	−9.4	−9.9
Increase in inventories	0.0	0.5	0.1	0.3	0.3
Capital grants (net) within public sector	1.3	1.4	0.6	0.6	0.6
Capital grants to private sector	6.9	7.0	9.8	10.6	11.4
Capital grants from private sector	−0.9	−0.9	−1.1	−1.0	−1.0
AME margin	0.0	0.0	0.1	0.8	1.1
Net investment	**11.4**	**14.0**	**20.1**	**24.5**	**27.1**
Net borrowing[1]	**−0.4**	**23.8**	**27.1**	**24.2**	**23.5**
of which:					
Central government net borrowing	−0.5	24.5	27.2	23.0	23.0
Local authority net borrowing	0.1	−0.7	−0.1	1.3	0.5

[1] Although this is based on the ESA95 definition of general government net borrowing (GGNB), the forecasts are identical to GGNB calculated on a Maastricht definition.

Table C24: Public sector transactions by sub-sector and economic category

	£ billion			
	2002-03			
	General government			
	Central government	Local authorities	Public corporations	Public sector
Current receipts				
Taxes on income and wealth	143.5	0.0	−0.1	143.5
Taxes on production and imports	143.1	0.1	0.0	143.3
Other current taxes	3.2	16.6	0.0	19.8
Taxes on capital	2.4	0.0	0.0	2.4
Social contributions	63.6	0.0	0.0	63.6
Gross operating surplus	4.7	3.8	9.2	17.7
Rent and other current transfers	2.0	0.0	0.6	2.6
Interest and dividends from private sector and abroad	2.8	0.7	0.6	4.1
Interest and dividends from public sector	6.2	0.8	−7.0	0.0
Total current receipts	**371.6**	**22.1**	**3.4**	**397.1**
Current expenditure				
Current expenditure on goods and services	130.3	82.5	0.0	212.7
Subsidies	6.6	1.1	0.0	7.7
Net social benefits	117.0	12.6	0.0	129.6
Net current grants abroad	0.5	0.0	0.0	0.5
Current grants (net) within public sector	78.4	−78.4	0.0	0.0
Other current grants	23.2	0.0	0.0	23.2
Interest and dividends paid	20.8	0.3	0.1	21.3
AME margin	0.0	0.0	0.0	0.0
Total current expenditure	**376.9**	**18.0**	**0.1**	**395.0**
Depreciation	4.7	3.8	5.2	13.8
Surplus on current budget	**−10.0**	**0.2**	**−1.9**	**−11.7**
Capital expenditure				
Gross domestic fixed capital formation	5.9	8.7	4.6	19.1
Less depreciation	−4.7	−3.8	−5.2	−13.8
Increase in inventories	0.5	0.0	0.0	0.5
Capital grants (net) within public sector	7.3	−5.9	−1.4	0.0
Capital grants to private sector	5.9	1.1	0.3	7.3
Capital grants from private sector	−0.4	−0.5	0.0	−0.9
AME margin	0.0	0.0	0.0	0.0
Net investment	**14.5**	**−0.5**	**−1.8**	**12.2**
Net borrowing	**24.5**	**−0.7**	**0.1**	**24.0**

Table C24: Public sector transactions by sub-sector and economic category

| | £ billion 2003-04 | | | |
| | General government | | | |
	Central government	Local authorities	Public corporations	Public sector
Current receipts				
Taxes on income and wealth	152.9	0.0	–0.1	152.8
Taxes on production and imports	148.9	0.1	0.0	149.1
Other current taxes	3.4	18.6	0.0	22.0
Taxes on capital	2.4	0.0	0.0	2.4
Social contributions	76.2	0.0	0.0	76.2
Gross operating surplus	4.9	4.0	10.5	19.5
Rent and other current transfers	1.6	0.0	0.7	2.3
Interest and dividends from private sector and abroad	2.7	0.7	0.6	4.0
Interest and dividends from public sector	5.1	2.5	–7.6	0.0
Total current receipts	**398.2**	**26.0**	**4.2**	**428.3**
Current expenditure				
Current expenditure on goods and services	139.7	92.3	0.0	232.0
Subsidies	6.4	1.1	0.0	7.6
Net social benefits	123.4	12.9	0.0	136.3
Net current grants abroad	–0.2	0.0	0.0	–0.2
Current grants (net) within public sector	85.3	–85.3	0.0	0.0
Other current grants	23.4	0.0	0.0	23.4
Interest and dividends paid	21.8	0.3	0.1	22.3
AME margin	0.9	0.0	0.0	0.9
Total current expenditure	**400.7**	**21.4**	**0.1**	**422.3**
Depreciation	4.9	4.0	5.5	14.4
Surplus on current budget	**–7.5**	**0.5**	**–1.4**	**–8.4**
Capital expenditure				
Gross domestic fixed capital formation	9.0	10.7	4.5	24.2
Less depreciation	–4.9	–4.0	–5.5	–14.4
Increase in inventories	0.1	0.0	0.0	0.1
Capital grants (net) within public sector	7.3	–6.7	–0.6	0.0
Capital grants to private sector	8.6	1.2	0.3	10.1
Capital grants from private sector	–0.4	–0.7	0.0	–1.1
AME margin	0.1	0.0	0.0	0.1
Net investment	**19.7**	**0.4**	**–1.2**	**18.9**
Net borrowing	**27.2**	**–0.1**	**0.2**	**27.3**

HISTORICAL SERIES

Table C25: Historical series of public sector balances, receipts and debt

Per cent of GDP

	Public sector current budget	Public sector net borrowing	Cyclically adjusted public sector net borrowing	Public sector net cash requirement	General government net borrowing[1]	Net taxes and social security contributions	Public sector current receipts	Public sector net debt[2]	General government gross debt[3]	Public sector net worth[4]
1970-71	6.7	−0.6	−0.8	1.2	−2.1		43.3			
1971-72	4.2	1.1	0.5	1.4	−0.7		41.4			
1972-73	2.0	2.8	2.7	3.6	2.2		39.0			
1973-74	0.3	4.9	5.7	5.9	4.4		39.5			
1974-75	−1.1	6.6	7.2	9.0	4.1		42.3	52.1		60.4
1975-76	−1.6	7.0	6.5	9.3	4.8		42.9	53.9		58.7
1976-77	−1.2	5.5	4.8	6.4	4.1		43.3	52.4		59.1
1977-78	−1.4	4.3	3.8	3.7	3.6		41.5	49.0		57.1
1978-79	−2.6	5.0	4.8	5.2	4.3	33.3	40.2	47.1		56.2
1979-80	−1.9	4.1	4.0	4.7	3.0	33.8	40.7	43.9		51.8
1980-81	−3.0	4.9	2.9	5.2	3.8	35.8	42.4	46.1		52.9
1981-82	−1.4	2.3	−1.7	3.3	3.3	38.5	45.8	46.1		51.7
1982-83	−1.5	3.0	−1.1	3.2	3.1	38.7	45.5	44.8		50.4
1983-84	−2.0	3.8	0.6	3.2	3.8	38.3	44.5	45.3		50.4
1984-85	−2.2	3.7	1.0	3.1	3.3	38.9	44.4	45.2		50.3
1985-86	−1.2	2.4	0.9	1.6	2.6	38.1	43.1	43.4		49.5
1986-87	−1.4	2.1	1.9	0.9	2.3	37.8	42.0	41.1		48.9
1987-88	−0.3	1.0	2.1	−0.7	1.3	37.6	41.1	36.8	46.5	75.8
1988-89	1.7	−1.3	1.2	−3.0	−0.9	36.9	40.7	30.6	40.6	81.8
1989-90	1.4	−0.2	2.5	−1.3	0.3	36.2	39.9	27.7	35.5	73.5
1990-91	0.4	1.0	2.6	−0.1	1.4	35.9	39.0	26.2	33.3	62.3
1991-92	−1.9	3.8	3.2	2.3	3.7	34.7	38.6	27.4	34.4	54.5
1992-93	−5.6	7.6	5.5	5.9	7.4	33.7	36.6	32.0	40.6	42.1
1993-94	−6.2	7.8	5.4	7.1	7.8	33.0	35.8	37.1	45.9	27.9
1994-95	−4.8	6.3	4.9	5.3	6.5	34.0	36.9	40.8	49.4	26.7
1995-96	−3.4	4.8	4.1	4.3	5.0	34.8	37.8	42.8	51.9	18.6
1996-97	−3.0	3.7	3.1	2.9	3.9	34.9	37.4	43.7	52.1	14.7
1997-98	−0.2	0.8	0.8	0.1	0.9	36.0	38.5	41.4	49.1	10.6
1998-99	1.2	−0.5	−0.2	−0.8	−0.5	36.5	38.8	39.2	46.3	10.2
1999-00	2.2	−1.7	−1.4	−0.9	−1.7	36.6	39.1	36.3	43.2	15.1
2000-01	2.2	−1.7	−1.2	−3.9	−1.7	37.4	39.8	31.2	39.8	21.3
2001-02	1.0	0.0	0.1	0.3	0.0	36.8	38.8	30.2	37.9	26.2

[1] UK National Accounts definition.
[2] At end-March; GDP centred on end-March.
[3] Maastricht measure from 1993.
[4] At end-December; GDP centred on end-December.

Table C26: Historical series of government expenditure

	£ billion (2001-02 prices)				Per cent of GDP			
	Public sector current expenditure	Public sector net investment	Public sector gross investment[1]	Total Managed Expenditure	Public sector current expenditure	Public sector net investment	Public sector gross investment[1]	Total Managed Expenditure
1970-71	161.9	30.4	49.7	211.6	32.6	6.1	10.0	42.7
1971-72	169.3	26.8	46.6	215.9	33.3	5.3	9.2	42.5
1972-73	177.0	25.8	46.6	223.6	33.1	4.8	8.7	41.8
1973-74	194.5	29.0	52.3	246.8	35.0	5.2	9.4	44.4
1974-75	215.1	30.6	55.6	270.7	38.8	5.5	10.0	48.8
1975-76	219.8	30.0	55.3	275.1	39.9	5.5	10.0	49.9
1976-77	225.9	24.5	50.6	276.5	39.9	4.3	8.9	48.8
1977-78	222.5	16.6	42.7	265.2	38.4	2.9	7.4	45.8
1978-79	229.2	14.5	41.1	270.3	38.4	2.4	6.9	45.2
1979-80	234.9	13.4	40.5	275.3	38.2	2.2	6.6	44.8
1980-81	241.7	10.8	38.1	279.9	40.8	1.8	6.4	47.3
1981-82	252.7	5.5	32.7	285.4	42.6	0.9	5.5	48.1
1982-83	258.5	9.1	35.5	293.9	42.7	1.5	5.9	48.5
1983-84	266.7	11.2	37.5	304.2	42.3	1.8	5.9	48.3
1984-85	274.2	9.9	34.8	309.0	42.6	1.5	5.4	48.1
1985-86	274.1	8.3	30.6	304.7	41.0	1.2	4.6	45.5
1986-87	278.1	5.0	27.5	305.6	40.1	0.7	4.0	44.1
1987-88	281.8	4.8	25.6	307.4	38.6	0.7	3.5	42.1
1988-89	275.4	2.7	24.3	299.7	36.2	0.4	3.2	39.4
1989-90	277.2	9.3	31.0	308.2	35.7	1.2	4.0	39.7
1990-91	279.0	11.2	30.1	309.1	36.1	1.4	3.9	40.0
1991-92	295.8	14.2	30.2	325.9	38.4	1.8	3.9	42.3
1992-93	310.5	15.5	30.4	340.9	40.3	2.0	3.9	44.2
1993-94	320.8	12.7	27.3	348.1	40.1	1.6	3.4	43.6
1994-95	332.0	12.5	27.6	359.6	39.9	1.5	3.3	43.2
1995-96	337.1	12.0	27.3	364.4	39.4	1.4	3.2	42.6
1996-97	340.5	6.0	20.2	360.7	38.7	0.7	2.3	41.0
1997-98	337.9	5.4	19.1	356.9	37.2	0.6	2.1	39.3
1998-99	337.7	6.5	20.0	357.7	36.2	0.7	2.1	38.4
1999-00	342.3	4.6	17.9	360.2	35.6	0.5	1.9	37.4
2000-01	357.3	5.3	18.7	376.0	36.2	0.5	1.9	38.1
2001-02	366.6	9.6	23.0	389.6	36.5	1.0	2.3	38.8

[1] Net of sales of fixed assets.

CONVENTIONS USED IN PRESENTING THE PUBLIC FINANCES

> ## FORMAT FOR THE PUBLIC FINANCES
>
> The June 1998 Economic and Fiscal Strategy Report (EFSR), set out a new format for presenting the public finances that corresponded more closely to the two fiscal rules. The three principle measures are:
>
> - the surplus on current budget (relevant to the golden rule);
> - public sector net borrowing; and
> - the public sector net debt ratio (relevant to the sustainable investment rule).
>
> These measures are based on the National Accounts and are consistent with the European System of Accounts 1995 (ESA95). Estimates and forecasts of the public sector net cash requirement (formerly called the public sector borrowing requirement) are still shown in the FSBR, but they are given less prominence.
>
> The fiscal rules are similar to the criteria for deficits and debt laid down in the Treaty but there are important definitional differences:
>
> - UK fiscal rules cover the whole public sector, whereas the Treaty deficit and debt only includes general (i.e. central and local) government;
> - the fiscal rules apply over the whole economic cycle, not year to year;
> - the current budget excludes capital spending, which is included in the Treaty deficit measure; and
> - the UK debt measure is net of liquid assets, whereas the Treaty measure uses gross debt.
>
> From February 2000 the Treaty deficit moved to being reported on an ESA95 basis.

NATIONAL ACCOUNTS

The National Accounts record most transactions, including most taxes (although not corporation tax), on an accruals basis, and impute the value of some transactions where no money changes hands (for example, non-trading capital consumption). The principle measures drawn from the National Accounts are described below.

The current budget (formerly known as the current balance) measures the balance of current account revenue over current expenditure. The definition of the current budget presented in this chapter is very similar to the National Accounts concept of net saving. It differs only in that it includes taxes on capital (mainly inheritance tax) in current rather than capital receipts.

Public sector net borrowing (formerly known as the financial deficit in the UK National Accounts) is the balance between expenditure and income in the consolidated current and capital accounts. It differs from the public sector net cash requirement in that it is measured on an accruals basis and because certain financial transactions (notably net lending and net acquisition of other financial assets, which affect the level of borrowing but not the public sector's net financial indebtedness) are excluded from public sector net borrowing but included in the public sector net cash requirement.

General government net borrowing, which excludes net borrowing of public corporations, is the most internationally comparable measure of the budget deficit. It was established as the European Commission's reported measure under the Maastricht Treaty, although its definition has since been slightly modified to depart from that in ESA95.

PUBLIC SECTOR CURRENT RECEIPTS

Net taxes and social security contributions (NTSSC) is a measure of net cash payments made to UK government and differs in several respects from the National Accounts measure of total public sector current receipts (PSCR). A reconciliation between the two aggregates is given in the lower half of Table C8. The main adjustments are:

- accruals adjustments, mainly on income tax, national insurance contributions and VAT, are added to change the basis of figures from cash to National Accounts accruals;

- some tax payments that are collected by the government, but then paid to the EC, are subtracted as they do not score as government receipts in the National Accounts;

- tax paid by public corporations is also subtracted, as it has no impact on overall public sector receipts;

- an adjustment is made for tax credits. In NTSSC, all tax credits are scored as negative tax to the extent that they are less than or equal to the tax liability of the household, and as public expenditure where they exceed the liability, in line with OECD Revenue Statistics guidelines. Although the Office for National Statistics (ONS) have adopted this treatment for the Working Tax Credit and Child Tax Credit, due to be introduced in April 2003, they have continued to treat the Working Families' Tax Credit (WFTC), the Disabled Person's Tax Credit (DPTC) and enhanced and payable company tax credits entirely as public expenditure in the National Accounts. Those parts of WFTC, DPTC and company tax credits that offset tax liability in NTSSC are added back into current receipts in Table C8; and

- interest and other non-tax receipts, which are excluded from NTSSC, are added. This excludes oil royalties, as they are already included in NTSSC, even though the National Accounts treat them as non-tax receipts.

TOTAL MANAGED EXPENDITURE

Public expenditure is measured across the whole of the public sector using the aggregate Total Managed Expenditure (TME). TME is the sum of public sector current expenditure, public sector net investment and public sector depreciation. These aggregates are based on National Accounts definitions defined under ESA95.

Public sector current expenditure is the sum of expenditure on pay, and related costs, plus spending on goods and services, and current grants made to the private sector. Current expenditure is net of receipts from sales of goods and services.

Public sector capital expenditure is shown in Table C16. It includes:

- gross domestic fixed capital formation (i.e. expenditure on fixed assets such as schools and hospitals, roads, computers, plant and machinery and intangible assets) net of receipts from sales of fixed assets (e.g. council houses and surplus land);

- grants in support of capital expenditure in the private sector; and

- the value of the physical increase in stocks (for central government, primarily agricultural commodity stocks).

Public sector net investment: in Table C1 nets off depreciation of the public sector's stock of fixed assets.

Public sector depreciation: is the annual charge that is made in relation to the reduction in value of the public sector's capital assets over a particular financial year.

For budgeting purposes, TME is further split into:

Departmental Expenditure Limits (DEL) are firm three-year spending limits for departments. In general DEL will cover all running costs and all programme expenditure except that spending that is included in departmental Annually Managed Expenditure due to it not being reasonably subject to close control over the three year period. DEL has distinct resource and capital budgets, as shown in Table C13.

Annually Managed Expenditure (AME) is spending that cannot be reasonably subject to firm multi-year limits. AME components are shown in Table C11 and are defined as follows:

Social security benefits in AME expenditure covers contributory, non-contributory and income-related benefits for children, people of working age and pensioners. Broadly, benefits are paid in respect of retirement, unemployment, incapacity or disability, caring responsibilities and bereavement, as well as housing costs for all groups. Some expenditure on housing-related benefits is, however, covered by the Housing Revenue Account subsidies and locally financed expenditure categories.

Tax credits scored as expenditure includes spending on the Working Families' Tax Credit and Disabled Person's Tax Credit and that element of the Working Tax Credit and the Child Tax Credit that is classified as public expenditure under National Accounts definitions. For 2001-02 to 2004-05, expenditure related to the child allowances in Income Support and Jobseekers' Allowance, which, from 2003-04, are paid as part of the Child Tax Credit, have been included in the tax credit line rather than in the social security benefits line in order to present figures on a consistent definition over the period shown.

Housing Revenue Account subsidies relates to two main areas of public expenditure: Housing Benefit paid to tenants of local authority-owned social housing; and subsidy to meet deficits on local authority Housing Revenue Accounts as part of a national redistributive system.

Common Agriculture Policy expenditure comprises direct payments to farmers and market price supports (intervention purchases and export refunds).

Net public service pensions. The main unfunded public service pension schemes, following FRS17, report any increase in liabilities accrued in the period less contributions received from employers, employees and inward transfers. This line does not include an amount for the unwinding of the discount rate on the liability (which scores elsewhere in AME). For some small unfunded schemes, information is not available on an FRS17 basis, and these schemes report the difference between the cash paid out during the year and any contributions received.

National Lottery expenditures relate to the distribution of the money received from the National Lottery for good causes. Funds are drawn down by Distributor Bodies and directed towards Lottery funded projects.

Non-cash items in AME. Under the 2002 Spending Review resource budgeting regime, a department's spending budget includes certain items that do not have a cash component at the time when the expense is recorded. Examples include depreciation, cost of capital charges and provisions.

Other departmental expenditure aggregates all other expenditure made by departments that is not seperately identified in the AME table.

Net Payments to EC (European Communities) institutions is the balance between the UK's gross contribution to the EC Budget minus the UK abatement and public sector receipts from the EC Budget (net contribution to EC budget). For domestic public expenditure planning purposes part of the UK's contribution to the EC budget is attributed to the overseas aid programme and excluded from the net payments to EC institutions figures.

Locally financed expenditure consists of local authority self-financed expenditure (LASFE) and Scottish spending financed by local taxation (non-domestic rates and, if and when levied, the Scottish variable rate of income tax). LASFE is the difference between total local authority expenditure, including most gross debt interest but net of capital receipts, and central government support to local authorities (i.e. Aggregate External Finance (AEF), specific grants and credit approvals).

Central government debt interest is shown gross – only interest paid within the public sector is netted off. All other receipts of interest and dividends are included in current receipts. The capital uplift on index-linked gilts is also scored here as interest at the time it accrues as is the amortisation of discounts on gilts at issue.

Public corporations' own-financed capital expenditure. This is the amount of capital expenditure by public corporations that is not financed by general government.

AME margin is an unallocated margin on total AME spending and is included as a measure of caution against AME expenditure exceeding its forecast levels.

The accounting adjustments include various items within TME but outside DEL, which are not shown separately in Table C11. The definition of each line is as follows:

Removal of non-cash spending in DEL[4] and AME pertain to a number of non-cash expenditure items recorded as DEL and AME expenditure that are not consistent with TME defined under a National Accounts basis.

Financial transactions in DEL and in AME are deducted. This is because TME measures the current and capital expenditure of the public sector, as defined in the National Accounts. This excludes expenditure on the acquisition of financial assets since in the National Accounts these are classified as financial transactions, not capital expenditure. Departmental budgets include the net acquisition of certain types of financial assets. These are assets acquired for policy purposes rather than cash flow management and typically refer to transactions in shares and lending to businesses and individuals.

---

[4] Excluding depreciation in resource DEL.

Adjustments for public corporations. Under the 2002 Spending Review, departments' budgets score transactions with their public corporations. These adjustments remove those transactions and move the scoring of public corporations' spending onto a National Accounts basis.

Central government non-trading capital consumption (i.e. depreciation) as measured by ONS for National Accounts is added.

VAT refunded on general government expenditure is added back and covers refunds obtained by central government departments, local authorities and certain public corporations. DEL and AME programme expenditure are measured net of these refunds, while TME is recorded with VAT paid.

EC contribution deducts traditional own resources (i.e. payments of Customs duties and agricultural and sugar levies) and VAT contributions to European Community, which are included in the net payments to EC institutions line in AME but excluded from TME.

Tax credits are only added back if they score as public expenditure under National Accounts conventions but are not included as expenditure in AME. This includes Mortgage Interest Relief, Life Assurance Premium Relief, Private Medical Insurance Premium Relief, Vocational Training Relief (part up to 1998-99; all from 1999-2000), Working Families' Tax Credit and Disabled Person's Tax Credit (from 1999-2000) and the Research and Development Tax Credit (from 2001-02).

Intra-general government debt interest is deducted as it removes intra-public sector debt interest and dividend payments and receipts, which are included elsewhere in DEL and AME. The reason for this is that TME is consolidated public sector expenditure; so it records only those distributive transactions that are paid outside the public sector. Payments of grants and interest that are within the public sector do not score in TME. So it is necessary to deduct any interest payments to the public sector included in DEL or the debt interest figures in AME in other AME.

Other accounting adjustments shows other adjustments and includes, among others, the deduction of grants paid to local authorities by non-departmental public bodies classified to the central government sector, loan and debt write-offs and loan guarantees.

DEBT AND WEALTH

Public sector net debt is approximately the stock analogue of the public sector net cash requirement. It measures the public sector's financial liabilities to the private sector and abroad, net of short-term financial assets such as bank deposits and foreign exchange reserves.

General government gross debt, the Treaty debt ratio, is the measure of debt used in the European Union's Excessive Deficit Procedure. As a general government measure, it excludes the debt of public corporations. It measures general government's total financial liabilities before netting off short-term financial assets.

Public sector net worth represents the public sector's overall net balance sheet position. It is equal to the sum of the public sector's financial and non-financial assets less its total financial liabilitites. The estimates of tangible assets are subject to wide margins of error, because they depend on broad assumptions, for example about asset lives, which may not be appropriate in all cases. The introduction of resource accounting for central government departments will lead in time to an improvement in data quality, as audited information compiled from detailed asset registers becomes available.

LIST OF ABBREVIATIONS

ALSF	Aggregates Levy Sustainability Fund
AME	Annually Managed Expenditure
AMLD	Amusement Machine Licence Duty
APD	Air passenger duty
CBI	Confederation of British Industry
CCL	Climate change levy
CDFI	Community Development Finance Institutions
CEO	Chief Executive Officer
CGA	Central Government Accounts
CGNCR	Central government net cash requirement
CGT	Capital gains tax
CHP	Combined heat and power
CIPS	Chartered Institute of Purchasing and Supply Managers
CMF	Capital Modernisation Fund
CPA	Comprehensive Performance Assessment
CTF	Child Trust Fund
DDA	Disability Discrimination Act
DEFRA	Department for Environment, Food and Rural Affairs
DEL	Departmental Expenditure Limit
DfES	Department for Education and Skills
DfID	Department for International Development
DMA	Debt Management Account
DMO	Debt Management Office
DMR	Debt Management Report
DPTC	Disabled Person's Tax Credit
DTI	Department of Trade and Industry
DVLA	Driver and Vehicle Licensing Agency
DWP	Department for Work and Pensions
EBT	Employee Benefit Trust
ECA	Enhanced capital allowance
EEF	Engineering Employers' Federation
EES	European Employment Strategy
EFSR	Economic and Fiscal Strategy Report
EIS	Enterprise Investment Scheme
EMA	Education Maintenance Allowance
EMU	Economic and Monetary Union
ERI	Exchange Rate Index
ERM	Exchange Rate Mechanism
ESA	European System of Accounts
ESRC	Economic and Social Research Council
ETP	Employer Training Pilot
ETS	Emissions Trading Scheme
EU	European Union
EYF	End-year flexibility

FRC	Financial Reporting Council
FRS	Financial Reporting Standard
FSA	Financial Services Authority
FSBR	Financial Statement and Budget Report
G7	Group of Seven. A group of seven major industrial countries (comprising: Canada, France, Germany, Italy, Japan, UK and US).
GAAP	Generally Accepted Accounting Practices
GAD	Government Actuary's Department
GCSE	General Certificate of Secondary Education
GDP	Gross Domestic Product
GGNB	General government net borrowing
HEIF	Higher Education Innovation Fund
HICP	Harmonised Index of Consumer Prices
HIPC	Heavily Indebted Poor Countries
HIV/AIDS	Human Immunodeficiency Virus/Acquired Immunodeficiency Syndrome
HRG	Health Resource Group
HSMP	Highly Skilled Migrant Programme
ICT	Information and communication technologies
IFF	International Finance Facility
ILO	International Labour Organisation
IMF	International Monetary Fund
IPT	Insurance premium tax
ISA	Individual Savings Account
JSA	Job Seeker's Allowance
LDO	Local Development Order
LEA	Local Education Authority
LFS	Labour Force Survey
LPC	Low Pay Commission
LSC	Learning and Skills Council
MA	Modern Apprenticeship
MDGs	Millennium Development Goals
MEW	Mortgage equity withdrawal
MIG	Minimum Income Guarantee
MoD	Ministry of Defence
MPC	Monetary Policy Committee
MtC	Million tonnes of carbon
NAO	National Audit Office
NDDP	New Deal for disabled people
NDLP	New Deal for lone parents
NDYP	New Deal for young people
ND25+	New Deal for the over 25s
NHS	National Health Service
NICE	National Institute for Clinical Excellence
NICs	National insurance contributions

NLF	National Loans Fund
NSF	National Service Framework
NTSSC	Net taxes and social security contributions
NVQ	National Vocational Qualification
OECD	Organisation for Economic Cooperation and Development
OFSTED	Office for Standards in Education
OFT	Office of Fair Trading
OGC	Office of Government Commerce
ONS	Office for National Statistics
PAYE	Pay as You Earn
PBR	Pre-Budget Report
PCT	Primary Care Trust
PDMR	Provisional Debt Management Report
PFI	Private Finance Initiative
PPG	Planning Policy Guidance
PPP	Public Private Partnership
PSA	Public Service Agreement
PSCR	Public sector current receipts
PSNB	Public sector net borrowing
PSNI	Public sector net investment
R&D	Research and development
RAB	Resource accounting and budgeting
RDA	Regional Development Agency
RDS	Relevant discounted securities
RPI	Retail Price Index
RPIX	Retail Price Index excluding mortgage interest payments
RRS	Rapid Response Service
RSL	Registered Social Landlords
SBIC	Small Business Investment Companies
SBS	Small Business Service
SCI	Street Crime Initiative
SFLG	Small Firms Loan Guarantee
SMEs	Small and medium-sized enterprises
SMP	Statutory Maternity Pay
SRO	Scientific research organisation
TME	Total Managed Expenditure
TUC	Trades Union Congress
ULF	Union Learning Fund
ULSD	Ultra-low sulphur diesel
ULSP	Ultra-low sulphur petrol
URC	Urban Regeneration Company
VAT	Value Added Tax
VCT	Venture Capital Trust
VED	Vehicle excise duty

WFTC	Working Families' Tax Credit
WGA	Whole of Government Accounts
WPUK	Work Permits UK
WTC	Working Tax Credit
WTO	World Trade Organisation

LIST OF CHARTS

Economic and Fiscal Strategy Report

Financial Statement and Budget Report

LIST OF TABLES

Economic and Fiscal Strategy Report

Financial Statement and Budget Report

Cover photography:
011464 Ecoscene / Anthony Cooper
015951 Ecoscene / Angela Hampton
Alvey and Towers Picture Library
John Harris (Report Digital)
Julia Martin / Photofusion
www.digitalvisiononline.co.uk
www.educationphotos.co.uk
www.JohnBirdsall.co.uk

Printed in the UK by The Stationery Office Limited
on behalf of the Controller of Her Majesty's Stationery Office
19585   04/03   840208